The Discipleship Series
Leader's Guide

Campus Crusade for Christ

DISCIPLESHIP SERIES LEADER'S GUIDE

Copyright © 1980 by Campus Crusade for Christ, Inc.
All rights reserved
Published by Here's Life Publishers, Inc.
P.O. Box 1576, San Bernardino, CA 92402
ISBN 0-918956-75-7
HLP Product No. 60-166-6

Printed in the United States of America

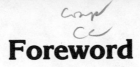

Foreword

The greatest spiritual advance in the history of man is now taking place throughout the world. More people are hearing the gospel, receiving Christ and training to serve Him than at any time since the Great Commission was given 2000 years ago.

We have the manpower, the technology and the finances to fulfill the Great Commission now—in this generation. But if we are to learn from history, we must realize that this unprecedented opportunity for spiritual awakening like other great awakenings—Pentecost, the Reformation, the Wesleyan revivals— will come to an end. We dare not miss this opportunity! If ever we plan to do anything for the Lord Jesus Christ and His kingdom we must do it now!

Jesus spoke, lived and died as has no other man of history. He was both perfect God and perfect man, and to Him all authority in heaven and earth is given. He commissioned us to go into all the world and make disciples of the people of all nations (Matthew 28:19,20).

We the Christians of the 20th century, have the privilege of participating with our living Lord in the fulfillment of His Great Commission in our generation. From the time we awaken each day until our last conscious thought or act at night, all Christians should be involved in the fulfillment of His Commission. We should do so as an expression of our love and gratitude to our Lord for all the benefits and blessings that are ours by His grace, and as an act of obedience to His command.

You can help to change the world by introducing men to Jesus Christ, the only one who can produce a changed campus, a changed community—city, state, nation—even a changed world.

Many lessons learned through personal contacts with thousands of individuals and in hundreds of meetings, large and small, are included in this training manual. Small discipleship groups represent one of the most effective ways to help believers grow to maturity in Christ. The praying, caring, loving attitude of each member of a discipleship group contributes to a dynamic spiritual growth which is difficult to achieve through any other means. However, a word of caution. The inspiration, challenge, faith and vision-building importance of larger group meetings, especially through local church fellowship and worship, deserves equal emphasis.

This material is placed in your hands with the prayer that it will greatly enrich your life and that it will multiply in many ways the effectiveness of your personal witness for Christ.

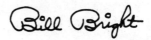

Introduction

Today, as never before in human history, our world needs disciples and disciplers—people who are willing to follow the Master in order to bring spiritual life and biblical values to a dying generation. Many Christians face the national and world situation with a sense of hopelessness and fear. Such attitudes often lead to a paralysis of involvement and willingness to reach into a non-Christian world with the love and the justice of Christ. However, an unprecedented challenge awaits men and women of faith and vision. The harvest is ripe, the opportunities are countless. Christians by the millions must move into action.

This Discipleship Series will assist you in capturing these opportunities.

The Discipleship Series is arranged in the following divisions:

Leading Your Group

This division of your Leader's Guide is separated into two parts. **Part I, Methods For Teaching the Discipleship Series**, communicates the "behind the scenes" information you need to know to lead and teach your group effectively.

Part II, Biblical Philosophy of Teaching the Discipleship Series, contains five Articles which explain the biblical philosophy of small group discipleship and gives some practical how-to's for developing a ministry of spiritual multiplication. With each Article is a group Leader's Guide in the Leadership Group Division which is a lesson plan the leader can use to lead a discussion of the corresponding Leadership Article. This discussion will help the members practically apply the concept they have read.

Discovery Group Lesson Plans

The Discovery Group will help you give your potential disciples "the basics" needed to live a victorious Christian life and begin to share their faith with others.

Discipleship Group Lesson Plans

The Discipleship Group will help your disciples grow to a deeper level of spiritual maturity and learn not only more effective means of winning others to Christ, but how to disciple those who become Christians.

Leadership Group Lesson Plans

The Leadership Group Leader's Guides are tools which are unique on the Christian market today. This series of articles and discussion questions will enable you to train your group members to lead groups of their own. This is the multiplication tool of the Discipleship Series. If one or more of your group members learns to lead a group of his own, and one or more of his group members learns to do the same, the potential of your influence will expand to many generations of your disciples.

NOTE: Each group of lesson plans (Discovery, Discipleship, Leadership) has its own corresponding Study Guide. It is not intended or even possible to use the Study Guides apart from these Leader's Guides.

Appendices

These sections are designed to assist you in "customizing" your group meeting to your own objectives for the group and the needs of your group members. Starting with Leadership Group Lesson 1 you will need to use the Practical Ministry Appendices (Vision, Strategy and Training) to develop the Practical Ministry sections of each lesson plan. *Step-by-step instructions explaining how to prepare this section of your lessons are also given in Lesson 11 and Lesson 13 of the Discipleship Group Division.*

In a series of essays edited by the Russian Nobel prize winning novelist, Alexander Solzhenitsyn, a prominent historian wrote these prophetic words, ". . . A Christian initiative is needed to counter the Godless humanism which is destroying mankind. Christian activism must lead not to a reformation but to a transformation of Christian consciousness and life, and through it to a transformation of the world."*

This is our challenge and the reason for this Discipleship Series. Let us make disciples and thus help to transform our world for Christ.

J. Kent Hutcheson

J. Kent Hutcheson
Director of Training
Campus Crusade for Christ

*Evgeny Barabanov, "A Schism Between the Church and The World" in *From Under the Rubble*, ed. Alexander Solzhenitsyn, Copyright © 1975, pp. 192,193: Little, Brown & Company, Boston, Massachusetts.

Benefits

The Leader's Guide you are holding is the product of more than a decade of experimentation, development, testing and revision. Literally tens of thousands of hours of small group leading experience throughout the country and around the world have been brought together in the design of this approach to small group discipleship. As with any other highly developed tool, some knowledge of the design and methodology will greatly multiply your effectiveness in getting the most out of this Leader's Guide.

There are a number of unique aspects to this Discipleship Series. A few of these have been reflected in other Bible study materials, but undoubtedly these distinctives have never all been brought together in one small-group material before. They include:

Bible Passages in Context. Generally, one or two longer passages are used to develop a particular topic or Christian teaching. This helps group members to ground their convictions in Scripture and models for them the important practice of reading Bible verses in context. It also helps them identify each teaching with a central passage or two which they may more readily locate again in the future.

Stimulating Questions. Most questions in the material are the "open" type which tends to stimulate maximum group involvement and participation.

Transferability. In Lessons 1-12, complete and detailed instructions are given to the leader so that even an inexperienced leader can lead a successful, stimulating discussion.

"Decreasing Props." Beginning with Lesson 13 less and less detail is given, and the leader is having to develop more and more of the lesson so that by Lessons 19 and 20 the leader is developing the entire lesson from a brief outline. In this way he learns by modeling how to develop his own effective Discipleship Group studies in the future.

Flexibility. Each lesson plan includes a brief outline and a list of resources which will help more creative and experienced leaders to adapt and customize the lessons to the needs of their groups. An experienced leader could teach the entire lesson simply using the outline.

Specific Application. Each Bible study ends with questions that lead group members to make specific personal applications of the truths they are studying.

Practical Ministry. Time is given in each meeting for Practical Ministry so that group members will gradually be drawn into a ministry of evangelism and discipleship.

Table of Contents
The Discipleship Series

Foreword iii

Introduction v

Benefits vii

Division: Leading Your Group 1

    Part I—Methods for Teaching the Discipleship Series

        1. Using the Materials Effectively 3

        2. How to Conduct a Discipleship Group Meeting 6

        3. Understanding the Lesson Plan Format 7

        4. How to Teach Each "Section" in Your Lesson Plan 15

        5. Checklist for Leading the Discipleship Series 19

        6. How to Ask Good Questions 21

        7. What If 24

    Part II—Biblical Philosophy of Teaching the Discipleship Series

        Article 1—"The Biblical Basis for Discipleship Groups" 29

        Article 2—"Discipleship Principles of the Master" 39

        Article 3—"Characteristics of a Discipleship Group" 49

        Article 4—"Discipling Your Group Members" 59

        Article 5—"Being Involved in a Spiritual Movement" 67

Division: Discovery Group Lesson Plans 1-6 77

Lesson 1—"Jesus, Worthy of Our Trust" 79

Lesson 2—"Our New Relationship With God" 119

Lesson 3—"Living in the Power of the Spirit" 135

Lesson 4—"Walking With Christ" 155

Lesson 5—"Becoming People of Action" 173

Lesson 6—"Sharing Christ With Others" 189

Division: Discipleship Group Lesson Plans 7-20 225

Lesson 7—"Developing My Relationship With My Heavenly Father" 227

Lesson 8—"Our New Life in Christ" 247

Lesson 9—"The Christian's Walk and Warfare" 265

Lesson 10—"Ministry of Reconciliation" 283

Lesson 11—"Expanding Your Circle of Confidence" 301

Lesson 12—"Witnessing Experience" 315

Lesson 13—"The Biblical Strategy for Spiritual Multiplication" 327

Lesson 14—"Our Identification With Christ".......................... 345

Lesson 15—"Effective Prayer"....................................... 359

Lesson 16—"Dealing With Temptation" 371

Lesson 17—"Discovering God's Will" 383

Lesson 18—"Becoming a World Christian" 409

Lesson 19—"Making My Life Count".................................. 421

Lesson 20—"Learning to Study God's Word" 433

Division: Leadership Group Lesson Plans 1-5 449

The Leadership Group Lesson Plans 1-5 are five lessons which help prepare your group members to begin and lead groups of their own. These lessons would generally come after Lesson 20. By that time most members should have been involved in personal evangelism and follow-up to the point where they are ready to begin leading a Discovery Group. (Some members may have already begun their groups.)

Lesson 1—"The Biblical Basis for Discipleship" 453

Lesson 2—"Discipleship Principles of the Master" 465

Lesson 3—"Characteristics of a Discipleship Group" 475

Lesson 4—"Discipling Your Group Members" 487

Lesson 5—"Being Involved in a Spiritual Movement".................. 501

Division: Appendices I—V

I. Sharing Appendix

  A. Purpose of Group Sharing 515

  B. Conducting a Sharing Time 516

II. Practical Ministry—Vision Appendix

  A. Purpose... 519

  B. Resource Ideas 519

  C. Vision Passages 522

III. Practical Ministry—Strategy Appendix

  A. Purpose... 527

  B. Strategy Chart for STUDENT and ADULT Ministries 528

  C. Strategy Explanations 531

IV. Practical Ministry—Training Appendix

   A. Purpose 533

   B. Training Units 534

   C. Sample Surveys 565

V. Prayer Appendix

   A. Purpose 567

   B. Conversational Prayer 567

   C. Samples of Leading Conversational Prayer 568

   D. Motivating Your Group to Pray 572

   E. Scripture References for Specific Prayer 575

   F. Portions of Praise 577

   G. Portions of Promise 580

Discipleship Series Bibliography 585

Division:
Leading Your Group
Part I and Part II

Part I
Methods for Teaching
the Discipleship Series

1. Using the Materials Effectively

Generally, the lessons are organized to move a person from lower levels of spiritual growth and commitment to increasingly higher levels. Lessons 1 through 6, for use in a Discovery Group, teach a person the basics of the Christian life and encourage him to develop a personal ministry of his own. Lessons 7 through 20 are designed for people with a higher level of spiritual maturity who have a commitment to building their own ministries.

After a group has completed Lessons 1 through 6, the leader will usually challenge the members to a Discipleship Group. However, the material is designed to allow for flexibility in meeting the needs of people in varying ministry situations. For instance, if group members are not ready to move on to a higher commitment level after Lesson 6, the leader can continue using Lessons 7-20 and challenge them when they *are* ready (often by Lesson 12). In other words, the lessons and the time of challenge can be modified to meet the needs of the group.

In most church ministries, formal challenges to higher levels of commitment are not used. Many pastors simply begin with Lesson 1 and continue through Lesson 20 and following. Often, people simply drop out of the group because of a lack of commitment or interest. Therefore, the group helps to filter out the least committed people in a natural way.

In the Campus Ministry, sometimes there is also a need for an intermediate group for those who have completed the Discovery Group (1-6) but are not yet ready for a Discipleship Group commitment. For example, if the standards for being in a Discipleship Group at State University include already having your own Discovery Group, then many students would not qualify after Lessons 1-6 and should not be challenged to a Discipleship Group. However, the Bible Study content in Lessons 7-20 may still be taught and members may be challenged to a Discipleship Group commitment at a later date when they meet the standards. In such groups, weekly evangelism by the members with the leader should be the rule, not the exception.

3

Names for such groups can vary by campuses, but two names sometimes used are "witnessing discovery group" and "alpha group."

Lesson Plan Considerations

The lesson plans are divided into the following sections: Sharing, Bible Study, Practical Ministry and Prayer. Study guides for each Discipleship Series lesson are provided for use by group members in a bound booklet form.

THREE TEACHING METHODS

Educational studies have defined three basic methods of teaching—lecture, discussion and example. Most teachers use all three, since creativity and variety are important in teaching. If we are always predictable, people get bored. Think of Jesus' teaching ministry. He lectured to the great multitudes that followed Him, He led discussions with His disciples and, as He lived with them every day, His life was their moment-by-moment example.

An effective teacher will vary his methods, and all three methods produce results, depending on the objective. Lecture can be a valuable teaching method when a lot of information must be given in a short amount of time. But in the lecture method the teacher also monopolizes the meeting; so be careful not to over-use this method. Discussion encourages disciples to express different viewpoints and thus enables a teacher to influence their attitudes. But the most effective method for changing behavior is example. Consider how a child learns from his parents. If his parents tell him the right way to do something and discuss it with him, but they themselves set a poor example, the child will more than likely follow their example.

A combination of example and discussion is extremely powerful. Example alone can be too limited—a disciple can learn to relate very well to his teacher without learning to relate to other Christians. By working with a small group, the teacher can set an example and also help group members learn to live together in Christian love.

Jesus Himself said that when a disciple completes his learning, he will be like his teacher. Ultimately, Jesus is our Teacher and someday we will all be like Him. But in the same way, we also take on the characteristics of our human teachers. Notice how young evangelists often sound like Billy Graham. And seminary students sometimes remind you of their hometown pastors. After you have trained your disciples, they will spiritually resemble you. They will reflect your spiritual strengths, but they will also reflect your weaknesses. If you don't pray often or share your faith much or read the Word of God consistently, your disciples probably will not do those things either. Thus, the *character* of the teacher is much more important in teaching by example than in the other two methods.

4

Being an example is an awesome responsibility. We must examine our lives and ask God to make us examples worthy to be followed. If you want to disciple others for Jesus Christ, you must intimately involve your life with those whom you are teaching. Show them how to live.

Jesus got dramatic, long-lasting results from His disciples because He committed His life to them for three years. He shared with them the victories and the struggles of His life. He welcomed them to the glory of the Mount of Transfiguration and also to the agony of Gethsemane. He was a living example to them. He taught them about servanthood and discussed the concept with them, but the lesson took hold in an unforgettable way when He knelt and washed their dirty feet.

Jesus did not ask His disciples to do anything which He had not demonstrated Himself. After they watched Him preach, He sent them on a preaching mission. After they watched Him cast out demons, He gave them authority over evil spirits. After they watched Him heal the sick, He gave them power to heal. After they watched Him suffer torture and persecution, forgive His enemies and die an agonizing death without crying out against God, He required a martyr's death of most of them. They did not follow Him perfectly every time, but without His living example they would never have become men who "turned the world upside down."

These Discipleship Series lessons are constructed to meet all three educational objectives. In order to do this, a significant emphasis on personal example is required along with sound biblical knowledge. The Bible Study section is the foundation for increasing knowledge. The inductive method of Bible study is used to enhance discovery and retention of material while using a sound scholastic approach. The discussions during this time, particularly in the Application section, will do much to influence attitudes. The Practical Ministry section will provide a framework for practicing basic truths. It is here that your example will be most crucial and effective. A Sharing time is provided for mutual encouragement. This will help disciples to recognize that they, too, must be examples to each other and it will help you to see growth in them. Finally, a Prayer time is indicated in each lesson so that you may have fellowship with the Lord and bring before Him all the needs and issues that were identified during the meeting. These four sections—Sharing, Bible Study, Practical Ministry and Prayer—have been designed to give you and your disciples an optimum environment for spiritual growth and multiplication.

2. How to Conduct a Discipleship Series Meeting

The group is assembled. The appointed time has arrived. You can hardly believe it, but you're leading the group! As you open your leader's guide, however, you suddenly realize that you've thought through everything except how to lead the meeting! The leader's guide is assembled to make your preparation simple, not unnecessary. Each Discipleship Series lesson will require some preparation on your part to make it a success.

NOTE: When you use the Discipleship Series lesson plans, observe the following guidelines:

1. Meet in an informal atmosphere and be enthusiastic (but not phony).

2. You don't have to carry your entire leader's guide into the meeting. You may carry your study guide and remove the appropriate leader's guide pages.

3. Experienced leaders often transfer information beforehand from their leader's guide into the study guide. Then, they take only the study guide into the group session. This creates a more informal atmosphere.

4. Have the Bible open at all times. Extensive use of the Scriptures will be required. If your group members are new Christians or are unfamiliar with the Bible, they may need help in finding Scripture passages.

5. Don't *read* the leader's guide mechanically. Familiarize yourself beforehand with its content so that the material can be covered informally.

6. Maintain eye contact with the members.

7. Allow enough time for sharing and building rapport at the beginning of each meeting. Don't be afraid to laugh and joke.

8. Listen for the group members' needs and seek to meet them, either in the group or later. It is not wrong to stop in the middle of the content to pray for a specific need if you sense it would be appropriate.

9. Be sure to prepare the group for witnessing during Lesson 6. They should be paired up with an experienced person. You can go with only one of them, so you may need to recruit several people who are experienced in sharing their faith to go with the others.

10. Above all, be yourself. Nobody expects you to be "super spiritual," so don't try to be. Just walk in the Spirit and relax.

Remember, as you lead the group members, you are seeking to build their commitment to the point that they will want to learn how to develop their own ministry of discipleship and evangelism.

7
Developing My Relationship
═══With My Heavenly Father═══

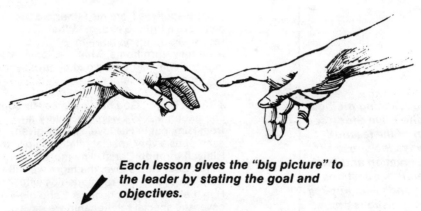

> *Each lesson gives the "big picture" to the leader by stating the goal and objectives.*

OVERVIEW GOAL

The goal of this lesson is to motivate group members to make their relationships with God a priority through having daily quiet times.

LEARNING OBJECTIVES

1. Explain why they should want to develop their relationships with God.

2. Identify five elements of a profitable quiet time as demonstrated in Psalm 143.

Time/Section	Outline/Questions and Learning Activities

10-15

Watch the time break-downs for each section.

30-40

Motivation

The teaching method of the Bible Study section of the lesson always includes observation and interpretation questions and ends with application questions and suggestions.

Observ./Interp.

Ephesians 1:3-8a

Application

Sharing

Have the group members share any opportunities they had to tell others about Christ during the past week.

A general outline of each lesson is provided along with transitions to the next major point.

Bible Study

A. STORY OF A YOUNG MAN

   1. What responses from his father did the son have a right to expect? What responses might he hope for?
   2. After his return home, what are some feelings the son might have had about spending time with his father?

   TRANSITION: "God has made us His sons and daughters. We were once very far from Him; but in His love, He has given each of us a very special relationship with Himself through Christ. The more we learn about God's love, the more we will want to develop our relationships with Him. Let's look at Ephesians 1 and discover the special relationship we have with Him."

B. DISCOVERING THE LOVE OF MY HEAVENLY FATHER

   1. According to this passage, what are some things that God has done for us?
   2. Since God has chosen us to know Him (vs. 4) and has adopted us as His children (vs. 5), what are some conclusions we can draw about His love for us?
   3. What are some things that our heavenly Father desires us to have as His adopted children?
   4. Although we don't deserve it, our heavenly Father has adopted us and has forgiven us all our sins. In response, what

Time/Section	Outline/Questions and Learning Activities
	should be some of our desires concerning our relationships with Him?
	TRANSITION: "Since we should want to spend time with God and develop our relationships with Him, let's look at some ways we can spend time with God through quiet times or devotional times. In Psalm 143, we can identify some characteristics of the psalmist's devotional time."
Observ./Interp.	C. SPENDING TIME WITH MY HEAVENLY FATHER
Psalm 143	1. What are some things that David might have felt as he wrote this prayer to God?
	2. Why do you think David was able to communicate his attitudes so openly to God?
Application	3. What do you see in David's relationship with God that you would like to see present in your relationship with your heavenly Father?
	4. What are some elements in this prayer that we could use in our time with God each day?
	5. What are some ways that we can consider what God has said and done in the past?
	6. What are some ways we can make our relationships with our heavenly Father a priority this week?
	7. Five things to remember in our quiet times
	Action Point Develop a plan for beginning a regular quiet time with your heavenly Father.
15-25	# Practical Ministry
	A. HOW TO DEAL WITH THE RESPONSES TO THE TWO QUESTIONS FOLLOWING THE CIRCLES
	1. The questions
	2. Responses to the circles

Preparation

PERSONAL PERSPECTIVE

Never forget to read this carefully. Often the lesson requires you to bring special materials.

Set aside at least one-half hour when you will not be disturbed. Take your Bible and Discipleship Group study guide and be especially aware of the presence of God during this time. As you study Ephesians 1:3-8, ask your heavenly Father to communicate to you how much He loves you. Use the study questions on Psalm 143 to help you consider how David spent time with God. Ask God to show you how you can use David's psalm as a model for your daily quiet times.

There is potential in this lesson to get off on a tangent concerning predestination versus the free will of men. Although that is an interesting and important issue, the concern of this lesson is how to develop our relationship with our heavenly Father. If the group does begin to discuss an issue not pertaining directly to the lesson, it would be good to say something like this: "This is an issue which has fascinated men for centuries. Actually there are many Scriptures which talk about God choosing us and many others which talk about us choosing God. I think that there are some things about the Christian life that we just won't understand until we get to heaven! Predestination emphasizes God's perspective on our salvation, while our discussion today is more concerned with man's response as he develops his relationship with his heavenly Father." Then continue with the lesson.

INTRODUCTION TO EPHESIANS

Background information is provided for the passages to be studied.

This letter was written to the church at Ephesus about 61 or 62 A. D. The theme of the book is right living in light of our new position in Christ. Chapter 1 focuses on the blessings of God in Christ.

INTRODUCTION TO PSALM 143

Apparently this psalm was written as part of David's quiet time one day when he had a specific need. The Psalms as we have them today fall into two basic categories. Some were written for use in corporate worship. These generally are a call to worship God for His faithfulness. The second category, of which Psalm 143 is a part, is much like a quiet time journal we might have today. Psalm 143 was David's written prayer to God after he had spent time with Him and had considered His past faithfulness (vs. 5).

This is where you begin to teach.

Leader's Guide

The lefthand column gives instructions to the leader. Don't read them to the group.

Developing a relationship with God is the greatest adventure in life.

Sharing
(10-15 Minutes)

Have the group members share any opportunities they had to tell others about Christ during the past week. Be sure to keep it positive.

This motivational quote or statement appears on page 1 of your group members' study guides. It is designed as a "teaser," and you do not need to read or discuss it during the meeting unless you particularly desire to do so.

Bible Study
(30-40 Minutes)

Open the Bible study in a brief prayer, asking God to teach the group.

If the material is "boxed in," that means it appears in the study guide.

Motivation   (2)

Have a group member read the story.

The number in parenthesis refers to the page number in the study guide.

A. STORY OF A YOUNG MAN

The story is told of a young man who wanted to leave home and seek his fortune. Although his parents felt that he was too immature to leave home, the son insisted that he should be able to go. The son was aware of the contents of his father's will; and not wanting to wait around for his father's death, he asked for his part of the inheritance in advance. Although the parents didn't think this was wise, they decided to let the son go and gave him his share of the estate.

As soon as the son moved to another city, he spent all his money and became involved with a rough crowd. Eventually, he ended up in jail. The judge was willing to release him if he would pay a $500 fine. Since he didn't have any money, the son realized that his only hope was to write to his folks and ask for help, even though he had not written or communicated with them for an entire year. The son was particularly concerned about his father's reaction, since he had strongly warned the son that something like this might happen. "Will my father send the money?" he wondered. The young man wrote a letter asking for understanding and help.

DISCUSSION:

Direct the group in a discussion of the questions. Share the suggested answers only if necessary. Summarize the group's answers after discussing each question, and encourage group members to write the conclusions in their study guides.

Answers are not always complete but suggest the thoughts which ought to be captured before moving on.

1. What responses from his father did the son have a right to expect? What responses might he hope for?

   He had no right to expect anything positive—maybe a letter lecturing him that his time in jail would teach him a lesson! He might hope for a check to bail him out and for his father's forgiveness.

Underlined sentences mean that this is a suggested answer to the questions. Suggested answers do not appear in the study guides. The essence of the suggested answer needs to be given before you continue the lesson. Help guide the discussion so group members reach the suggested answers on their own.

READ:

Much to the son's surprise, his father showed up at the jail a few days later. He paid the fine and hugged his son. With tears in his eyes, the father told the son how much he had missed him and that he had prayed each day for his safe return. A large party was planned to welcome the son home and to celebrate his becoming a partner in his father's business.

2. After his return home, what are some feelings the son might have had about spending time with his father?

He would have felt privileged to spend
time with him because he would have realized that his father loved him unconditionally. He would have a greater
respect for his father's wisdom and values
and would realize that his father had
much to teach him. Therefore, he would
greatly appreciate each hour spent with
him.

Clarifying Questions:

Use these questions if you need to rephrase the main question to stimulate discussion or to draw out a more concise answer.

2a. What are some other feelings the son might have experienced?
2b. What are some things the son probably learned about his father through this situation?
2c. Do you think the son would want to spend time with someone who loved him as much as his father did?

SAY:

"The story we have just looked at is a modern day version of the parable of the prodigal son in Luke 15."

If your group members are relatively young Christians, you may want to take time to read the parable.

TRANSITION:

"God has made us His sons and daughters. We were once very far from Him; but in His love, He has given us a very special relationship with Himself through Christ. The more we learn about God's love, the more we will want to develop our relationships with Him. Let's look at Ephesians 1 and discover the special relationships we have with Him."

> 3. Begin by setting a reasonable goal such as:
>
> _____ minutes in Bible study to learn what God is like and what He promises.
>
> _____ minutes in praise/thanksgiving and expressing your trust in God.
>
> _____ minutes making requests of God to meet your needs, to guide you for the day and to express yieldedness to His will.

Unboxed materials are not found in the study guide. When the word "relate" occurs, do not try to read the material word for word. Put it into your own words.

RELATE:

"In our next lesson we'll be discussing 'Our New Life in Christ.' The main passage we'll be looking at is Colossians 3:1-17. To get the most out of our discussion, I'd encourage you to read over this passage beforehand and even spend some time studying it.

Practical Ministry
(15-25 Minutes)

Vision
Share a witnessing experience that you had when you were first learning to share your faith. Seek to encourage your group members by making the point that God can use us in spite of our lack of experience.

Lessons 7-10 have the Practical Ministry sections written into the lesson plan itself. Starting with Lesson 11 you will need to use the Practical Ministry Appendices (Vision, Strategy and Training) to develop this section of each lesson. Step-by-step instructions explaining how to prepare this section are given in Lesson 11 and repeated in Lesson 13.

Strategy

RELATE:

"For the next few weeks we will concentrate on learning techniques that will make us more effective in sharing Christ with our friends and acquaintances.

4. How to Teach Each "Section" In Your Lesson Plan

Each lesson contains four sections: A. Sharing, B. Bible Study, C. Practical Ministry, D. Prayer.

A. Sharing section (10-15 minutes): The Sharing section is designed to open the lesson with an opportunity for the group members to share what God is doing in their lives.

   1. Read or review the I. Sharing Appendix when you prepare for the meeting.

   2. Make this as informal and challenging as possible.

   3. Seek to create an atmosphere in which everyone wants to share.

   4. Don't prolong the sharing time. When it "dries up," move on to the next section.

   5. Your sharing times will be a thermometer for the evangelistic activity in your group. If the members rarely share about their evangelism ministries, then you will need to provide more ministry leadership for the group.

B. Bible Study section (30-40 minutes): The observation, interpretation, application method of Bible study is used. This section normally centers around two main passages of Scripture. Other passages are also noted, but usually only as back-up references. After Lesson 12, the amount of structured content gradually decreases, allowing the leader more flexibility, but also requiring more preparation. This change in format will help the leader develop more skill as a student and teacher.

   1. Keep an open Bible before you. Emphasize what is in the Bible, not what is written in the leader's guide.

   2. If you are an experienced teacher, you can prepare for each lesson by making notes on the outline in your leader's guide or in a copy of the study guide. Then simply carry the notes to the group and leave the rest of your leader's guide at home. However, don't forget to take along any necessary Practical Ministry materials.

   3. If you feel less experienced in teaching, make notes in your leader's guide as you prepare, and then teach the lesson from it. If you are unfamiliar with the passage, work through the study guide on your own.

   4. Don't be mechanical. Strive for informality and a relaxed atmosphere. Have fun.

5. Be available as you teach to meet changing needs as they arise. (Example: one of your group members has just failed an exam or lost his job and needs help in dealing with the problem) You are not obligated to finish all the content every week, though you should not get sloppy about it and forget your objectives.

6. Use your own personal illustrations. This is the greatest thing you can do to build rapport in the group.

7. Do not skip the Application portion. Allow at least one-third of your Bible Study time for the Application questions.

8. Seek to make direct applications to the group members' present situations. The more specific you can be, the better.

9. Allow plenty of discussion. This is not a lecture.

10. To pace yourself, estimate the time you want to spend on each question and write it in the margin.

11. Remember: "The content you present is less important than the atmosphere you create!" (Howard Hendricks)

C. Practical Ministry section (15-25 minutes):

1. Vision (2-5 minutes): See the II. Practical Ministry-Vision Appendix (p. 519).

This section is designed to challenge and increase your group members' vision in areas of personal ministry and faith. For Lessons 7,8,9 and 10, the content for the Vision portion is already written in your lesson plans. Refer to Discipleship Group Lessons 11 and 13 or Leadership Group Lesson 1 for step-by-step instructions to develop this section from the Appendix.

Except for the witnessing time in Lesson 12, after Lesson 10 you should choose a sample passage and outline from the Vision section of the Appendix to meet the particular needs of your group. Or you may choose to share a personal experience or passage of your own. Remember, the purpose of this section is not solely to communicate information, but to raise the sights of group members so that they will believe God for more. If possible, relate this passage to the Strategy and Training segments which follow.

2. Strategy (3-5 minutes): See the III. Practical Ministry-Strategy Appendix (p. 527).

This section is closely tied to the training you will give in every group meeting. When leading the Discipleship Series, discipleship denotes ministry. Ministry assumes both strategy and training. During your meeting, you can meet the specific training needs of individual members. This training would be supplementary to strategy and training, which they might receive at a Leadership Training Institute or Class, and should be closely related to the various outreach and ministry strategies your group is involved in. These strategies might range from evangelism and follow-up to planning and promoting large outreaches, such as a city or campus-wide Josh McDowell series. So the strategy discussion in your group meeting should allow you to discuss upcoming events in your plan to capture your community or campus for Christ. A chart relating strategies to corresponding training units appears in the Strategy Appendix. Samples of how to lead the group through this section are given in Lessons 7,8,9 and 10, and in the II. Practical Ministry-Strategy Appendix. You may use the instructions in Discipleship Group Lessons 11 and 13 or Leadership Group Lesson 1 to develop the Strategy portions of the lessons.

3. Training (10-15 minutes): See the IV. Practical Ministry-Training Appendix (p. 533).

Again, as you train your group members, it makes sense to tie your present ministry strategy to that training. For example, it would be foolish to train your group to reach athletes if you were presently involved in surveying a dorm or apartment complex. Thus, we have listed various kinds of training appropriate for a number of different strategies. Once the strategy has been identified from the chart in the above Strategy Appendix, the training unit can be selected. Detailed instructions for each unit are outlined in the Training Appendix.

You do not have a great deal of time in any of the group lessons to do training, so you will probably have to present and review each training unit over a period of several weeks.

Samples of how to use the Training section are given in Lessons 7,8,9 and 10. Discipleship Group Lessons 11 and 13 or Leadership Group Lesson 1 give step-by-step instructions on how to use the Appendices. After these lessons, feel free to choose your own training and strategy segments with the help and counsel of your Discipleship Group leader, pastor or a Campus Crusade staff member.

D. Prayer Section (5-10 minutes): See the V. Prayer Appendix (p. 567).

1. This should be one of the richest times of the group meeting. If prayer goes longer than the allotted time, don't worry.

2. Pray about group members' needs as well as ministry strategy. Seek to build faith through prayer.

3. Show them how to pray for those people whom they are or will be discipling.

NOTE: Because of the special design of some lessons, the four sections noted above may take different forms. For example, Lessons 1-6 are only 60 minutes in length and are designed for new Christians or a less committed group. For this reason, the Practical Ministry section has been deleted from Lessons 1-6 (except for Training times in Lessons 5 and 6). Lessons 7-20 are 60 to 90 minutes in length. As noted under point C above, the leader is directed to the Appendices to develop his own Practical Ministry time for Discipleship Group Lessons 11, 13-20 and for the Leadership Group lessons. Step-by-step instructions are given for using the Appendices in Lessons 11 and 13.

5. Checklist for Leading the Discipleship Series

The following principles are helpful reminders of the things that you should be seeking to do as you disciple your group members.

Review these principles each week as you prepare for your group meeting, and ask the Lord to give you sensitivity in how and when to apply them. Some principles should be applied regularly as a way of life; others can be applied less frequently.

Check the boxes if they apply.

( ) Do you have the actions and attitudes of an "adoptive parent" (I Thessalonians 2:7)?

( ) Are you building meaningful personal relationships with your disciples through:

    ( ) Being available and sensitive to meet personal needs by pointing your disciples to the sufficiency of Christ?

    ( ) Doing things of common interest together like shopping, sports or other activities?

( ) Are you creating an atmosphere of prayer with your disciples not only in your regular meetings but also in special times of intercession before God? Are you praying regularly for your disciples?

( ) Are you discipling your members in an atmosphere of evangelism?

    ( ) Have you formulated a ministry outreach objective and plan for your group?

    ( ) Have you held an open house or informal gathering for your neighbors in order to help establish friendships with non-Christians?

    ( ) Are you sharing Christ as a way of life and taking your group members with you as you minister?

    ( ) Are you building friendships with non-believers through social events of common interest, having lunch or dinner together, attending sports events together or other activities?

( ) Are you helping your group members to form their own groups through:

    ( ) Encouraging them to pray regularly for 10 people who will become part of their Discovery Group?

    ( ) Teaching and modeling the importance of consistent evangelism?

    ( ) Teaching them how to pray for their future group members?

( ) Teaching them how to teach the Discipleship Series lesson plans? (Allow your members occasional opportunities to teach a portion from one of the lessons of the Discipleship Series.)

( ) Teaching them how to win and build their friends for Christ?

( ) Visiting occasional meetings which your group members are leading? (This will allow you to offer helpful suggestions to your members as they begin to teach others.)

( ) Are you taking your group members with you on follow-up appointments in order to teach them how to build relationships with new Christians and disciple them?

( ) Are you arranging overnights or mini-retreats with your group members and their friends? These overnights will provide time for relaxed and meaningful fellowship. You can use overnights to:

1. Have a relaxed time of fellowship, sharing, fun, singing and prayer.
2. Answer miscellaneous questions regarding the Christian life.
3. Study God's Word inductively and seek to relate the study to questions and "need areas" that you have sensed during your regular group meetings.
4. Give a message which relates to growth needs in the lives of your disciples.
5. Cover, in depth, a lesson plan from the Discipleship Series.
6. Spend unhurried time worshiping the Father and praising Him. Pray also for:

   a. Your own needs.
   b. The needs of your family.
   c. The needs of your group members.
   d. The needs of your church.
   e. The needs of your city.
   f. The needs of your country.
   g. The needs of the world.

6. How to Ask Good Questions

Have you wondered what makes one question provoke seemingly unlimited discussion, while another "perfectly good" question falls deaf on the ears of a group? There are a number of factors that cause this, but one of the most important is the quality of the questions. Good questions are phrased to provoke and further stimulate discussion. Questions raised by your group members during the discussion can also be used to increase learning.

A. Types of Questions

There are four basic types of questions. Each has important and valuable uses in various situations, but not all are useful in a group discussion. They are:

1. Leading—A leading question implies the answer that the leader expects.

   Example: "Paul says we are to rejoice always, doesn't he?"

   Value for a discussion: *None.* It's great for a lecture, but it can kill a discussion because a response is not even required. These questions should be used only as a last resort to bring out a critical point that the group has failed to discover through more open questions. Try to get along without these.

2. Limiting—A limiting question limits the answer to specific details desired by the leader.

   Example: "What are three great truths in this passage?"

   Value for a discussion: *None.* It begins a mind-reading competition with the leader because it is clear that you have an exact answer in mind.

   Exception: The type of limiting question that requires a "Yes" or "No" answer may be valuable to use in finding out the attitudes of other members of the group. Example: "Would the rest of you agree?"

3. Open—An open question allows the group to explore the passage. It clearly indicates that there may be a variety of acceptable responses.

   Example: "What are some truths you see in this passage?"

   Value for a discussion: *Much.* It allows complete freedom to discover one, two, three or more "truths." The emphasis is on discovery, not on finding "the answer."

4. Wide-open—A wide-open question draws the group into continued discussion after someone has expressed an opinion, or has answered or asked a question.

   Example: "Any other ideas?"

   Value for a discussion: *Very much*. It keeps the topic of discussion on the floor.

Of these four types of questions, your discussion should contain about 90% open and wide-open questions. A limiting or leading question should be used only as a last resort, when the group cannot see a point crucial to understanding the content under discussion. In this case, it is better to ask a limiting question than to tell them the answer. One caution about writing open questions: they must clearly indicate that a variety of responses is possible. Otherwise, they may be interpreted as limiting questions. For example, you may ask, "What did Paul say to Timothy?" thinking that there are at least six things in your passage. However, your group may hear, "What one important thing did Paul say to Timothy?" The question would be better worded, "What are some things Paul said to Timothy?" You will see this characteristic wording, "What are some . . ." frequently in your leader's guide.

B. How to Use Questions:

In a real discussion, when you have five or six people talking and asking questions and the rest of the group is silent, what are you going to do? Here is a brief guideline on how to use good questions to control and draw out discussion:

1. Leader-initiated questions

   a. Direct—A direct question is aimed at one individual. Use these to either draw out silent members of the group or to direct the discussion away from someone who may be dominating the group.
   b. General—A general question is one directed to the whole group, which anyone may answer.

2. Leader's response to member-initiated questions:

   a. Reverse—A reverse question is returned to the one who raised it. It is particularly useful when you are asked a leading question.
   b. Relay—A relay question is returned to the whole group. It enhances the discussion because it keeps the leader from being the final authority on questions raised by the group.

You should use the "clarifying questions" that are provided in your leader's guide only if the members do not give the suggested answers in response to the main question.

CAUTION: Use clarifying questions *only* if necessary. Your objective is to help the group members to discover spontaneously the right answers for themselves from God's Word.

This sense of discovery happens most often when members are responding to open or wide-open questions from the leader. In many cases, members will state the essence of the suggested answers in response to the main (numbered) question. If the members do not come up with something close to the suggested answers or the leader feels the point needs to be amplified further, then (and only then) the leader can use one or more of the clarifying questions.

Generally, the first clarifying question is either wide-open ("Any other ideas?") or open (a re-phrasing of the original question). In the second or third clarifying question you will often find a limiting or even leading question. These are given as a "last resort" and should be used sparingly and only if you feel the point is critical to continuing the discussion. The more experience you gain as a leader, the less you will need to resort to using these limiting and leading questions:

Beginning with Lesson 13, you will need to develop many of the clarifying questions yourself. Basically, these questions should follow the same pattern as above and be used in leading the discussion only when necessary. In some of the later lessons you will also need to develop main questions from general ideas or statements. In this way, you will be developing your skill as a leader so that asking effective questions can become a natural part of your skills in leading discussions.

7. WHAT IF . . .

There are some things that you can almost plan on as you begin leading a small group. Following are a few of these "what ifs" and a suggested way to handle each one.

What if only one shows up? Consider it a special time from the Lord to get to know that person better. Be sure not to speak negatively of those who didn't make it. If you know the others will be there next week, take the time with that person to review the lesson and plan for next week's meeting.

What if three people forget their study guides? Have them share study guides. (It's always good to have an extra study guide on hand.)

What if nobody can buy the study guide? In some cases, "I can't afford it" means it really isn't a priority in that person's mind. Take this as a check-point to be sure that everyone in the group really wants to grow in their walk with the Lord. When you challenge them to be in your group, allow them to look over the book thoroughly before you tell them the cost. If they can't afford it, work out a plan that allows them to pay for it over a period of time.

What if two people are 45 minutes late? Quickly brief them on what you have been doing and then allow them to join in if possible.

What if they want to talk about something irrelevant to the lesson? In other words, what if they get off the subject? Make a statement like, "I think we're on another subject. Why don't we, for the sake of time, get back on the topic of . . ." and name the central truth. (Example: ". . . the Holy Spirit and how He fits into our relationship with Christ.")

If the subject they want to discuss is important for all of them to know about, or is something they are all interested in, make a note of the subject and agree on a time when you can study it later.

What if they all have to leave early? If there definitely isn't time for the lesson, quickly overview the lesson you were to cover, and have a time of prayer with them.

What if you don't get through your lesson plan? At the next week's meeting, review what you covered the week before and start on your lesson plan at that point. You might evaluate here if you have been planning a lesson that is too long or covers too much material for the time available.Upsets will occur even with the best of planning and most fervent prayer. The main thing to remember in each of these situations is to keep a positive attitude and always be excited about those who are there! Allow yourself the opportunity of learning to flex and deal with upsets patiently. Paul probably experienced the same feelings you do, but he learned simply to trust God with the lives of his disciples and to express thanks for the qualities God was building into his own life through the experience.

In Romans 5:3-5 he says, "We can rejoice, too, when we run into problems and trials for we know that they are good for us—they help us learn to be patient. And patience develops strength of character in us and helps us trust God more each time we use it until finally our hope and faith are strong and steady. Then, when that happens, we are able to hold our heads high no matter what happens and know that all is well, for we know how dearly God loves us, and we feel this warm love everywhere within us because God has given us the Holy Spirit to fill our hearts with His love "(Living Bible).

Many great men have apparently fallen many times before they finally succeeded—for example, Abraham Lincoln or Alexander Graham Bell. It even appeared that Jesus Christ Himself had been defeated on the cross, but that event was really only the beginning of a great victory.

So don't worry about the inevitable upsets. Simply take them as a challenge to become more successful. Your disciples will learn as much from your response as they will from the lesson itself!

Part II
Biblical Philosophy of Teaching the Discipleship Series
—a series of five articles

The Biblical Basis for ━━ Discipleship Groups ━━

A spark is in the air. You can almost hear its crackle, and feel its tingle. It is happening in our generation. The power of Pentecost and the intimacy of the upper room are becoming part of the contemporary experience of thousands of Christians in today's world.

In homes, business offices, churches and universities, Christians are finding new strength and outreach opportunities through "conversational prayer cells," "home Bible studies," "group sharing" and "discipleship groups." In our fragmented, frantic, depersonalized age, we are returning to the methods of the carpenter from Nazareth and are rediscovering the dynamic of first century Christianity.

The Incendiary Fellowship

The current explosion of small groups in the Christian community raises some interesting questions. How have these groups of interacting Christians been able to find a new vitality in their fellowship and witness?

More important, why have we overlooked for so long the potential of such groups in our strategy of Christian ministry? Certainly, the early Church knew the value of small groups. The book of Acts records the struggle of small groups who prayed, shared, studied and suffered together. Through their "incendiary fellowship," the first century Christians set the whole world aflame.

The central figure in the history of the church is a man who spent the entire three years of His active ministry with a small band of 12 men. Jesus Christ was not known as a rebel or as a creative genius, but rather as a teacher. During His lifetime, two elements of His teaching ministry became evident. The first element was that of proclamation. Jesus proclaimed the coming of the Kingdom of God (the same message that John the Baptist had preached). The Jewish nation was unresponsive and confused. As the nation's rejection became apparent, Christ's ministry turned to teaching. It was this kind of people-centered instruction, the second element, that was to characterize the rest of His life and ministry.

As Christ turned from proclamation to teaching, the 12 who followed Him became known as disciples, which simply means "learners." And although Christ often taught large groups, the heart of His approach was His involvement with the 12 disciples. These men were, in a sense, His own discipleship group, and Jesus expected them to use the same pattern of discipleship to begin the Church.

Christ was very explicit about this in His final instructions to the disciples in Matthew 28:18-20:

> "And Jesus came up and spoke to them, saying, 'All authority has been given to Me in heaven and on earth. Go therefore and make disciples of all the nations, baptizing them in the name of the Father and the Son and the Holy Spirit, teaching them to observe all that I commanded you; and lo, I am with you always, even to the end of the age.'"

The meaning of the Great Commission comes into clearer focus when it is studied in the original Greek text. In order to convey the true emphasis of the command, it should be translated in this way:

> "Make disciples of all nations by going, baptizing . . . and teaching . . . ."

Only one concrete verb is part of this command: "*Make* disciples." The participles explain that the process will include going, baptizing and teaching. Christ commissioned the disciples to do exactly what He had done—make disciples.

The pattern that Christ chose to begin the Church was *discipleship*, with special emphasis on His own disciples. And this same pattern became the method of ministry for the early New Testament Church. Within this basic method of small group discipleship, at least four significant principles can be seen.

The Methods of the Master

The first principle that our Lord used in discipleship was to build qualitatively into the lives of a few while He was evangelizing and ministering to the masses. After carefully seeking guidance from His Father, Jesus selected His disciples and then spent the majority of His time with them. Part of this qualitative building process involved teaching His men in the context of *real life experiences*.

Consider Luke 14:25-35:

"Now great multitudes were going along with Him; and He turned and said to them, '. . . Whoever does not carry his own cross and come after Me cannot be My disciple. For which one of you, when he wants to build a tower, does not first sit down and calculate the cost, to see if he has enough to complete it? Otherwise, when he has laid a foundation, and is not able to finish, all who observe it begin to ridicule him, saying, "This man began to build and was not able to finish." Or what king, when he sets out to meet another king in battle, will not first sit down and take counsel whether he is strong enough with ten thousand men to encounter the one coming against him with twenty thousand? Or else, while the other is still far away, he sends a delegation and asks terms of peace. So therefore, no one of you can be My disciple who does not give up all his own possessions. Therefore, salt is good; but if even salt has become tasteless, with what will it be seasoned? It is useless either for the soil or for the manure pile; it is thrown out. He who has ears to hear, let him hear.'"

Although it is not mentioned specifically, the disciples of Jesus were undoubtedly with Him when He spoke these words. But did they learn only from hearing the words of Jesus? In what context did they learn the lessons of discipleship? In a theoretical vacuum? No. The lessons were taught in the context of reality; and as we read through the New Testament, this principle becomes vividly clear. The disciples were with Jesus during confrontations with the Pharisees; they were with Him when He healed the sick; and they were with Him when He taught the masses.

This does not mean that He did not spend special time alone with the disciples; but it does mean that His time alone with them had as a backdrop all that had happened during the days, weeks, months and years of His ministry.

Too often, however, we do not allow our disciples to see us in real life ministry situations. We may think that discipling others means praying and studying God's Word in a small group, isolated from the needs and distractions of the world. When this happens, we are not building qualitatively into our disciples' lives. Discipleship apart from the context of constant evangelism and ministering to others does not catalyze faith, which is at the root of all spiritual growth. When we are involved in a spiritual battle for the souls of men, we are cast upon the resources of God. This produces in us the life of faith; and when we are dependent upon God, we are right where He wants us to be.

If this first principle is not applied, we will tend to involve ourselves in ministries without ever focusing our time on a few choice people. Although Jesus did minister to the masses, we need to keep in mind that He also was simultaneously using His ministry experiences as a means to teach His key men. Had He neglected this step, His men would have been untrained for the task He left them following His resurrection. The lesson for us should be clear. When we fail to concentrate on a specific small group as we minister to the masses, we fail to expose people to the model of our life. It is impossible to live with the masses; we can live with only a few.

Spiritual Multiplication

The second principle that Jesus emphasized in His ministry was the principle of spiritual multiplication. When we have adopted the principle of building qualitatively into a small group of people, we unlock the secret of spiritual multiplication. Christ viewed each disciple as the center of a reproducing ministry. He understood that when you build your life qualitatively into the lives of a few, you begin a multiplication process that never ends.

Jesus could have spent His life as an itinerant preacher, moving from city to city, without ever involving Himself in the life of any one person or group. If he had taken this approach, He would have blessed the lives of countless thousands. But would His ministry have made an impact on the world?

Jesus was able to visit only a few places in His lifetime. If He had viewed Himself as being solely responsible for spreading the gospel, would the task of world evangelism have been accomplished? Probably not. However, Jesus knew that His disciples and their disciples would spread themselves into multitudes of villages and cities that He Himself would never visit. And so He taught men, by the model of His life, to involve themselves in the lives of a few as they ministered to many others.

The apostle Paul stated the principle of spiritual multiplication in this way:

> "And the things which you have heard from me in the presence of many witnesses, these entrust to faithful men, who will be able to teach others also" (II Timothy 2:2).

Time Enough to Do the Father's Will

The third principle of our Lord involves a willingness to make discipling others a priority. Most of us are busy people, caught in the pace of frantic, modern living. However, in the pressure of daily responsibilities, or even in the rush of a spiritual ministry, we often can neglect *people*. We can, in very subtle ways, become selfish with our time. There is always a message to prepare, an errand to run or an administrative detail to attend to. In the process, we program individuals and their needs right out of our lives.

When Jesus was on earth, He probably had less time than we do, but He had all the time He needed to do the Father's will. Throughout the gospel narrative, we never find an occasion when Jesus was in a hurry or too busy for people. It seems that we are always in a hurry, but seldom have time to do God's will. There is a sharp and bitter "barrenness in busyness." When we are too busy to disciple others, there is something fundamentally wrong with our concept of Christian responsibility.

"Only one life t'will soon be past, only what's done for Christ will last."*

C.T. Studd

Jesus had three and one-half years to do the job God had called Him to do. Was this tremendous task a source of pressure to Jesus? No. He was never under pressure because He operated on the basis of priority. He knew exactly the pattern He would follow and was never bogged down with extraneous matters. He was always with His small group of men. After He was gone, this qualitative ministry would multiply. And the result was so cataclysmic that the pagan world would testify of His discipleship group: "These are they who have turned the world upside down!"

A Focus on Potential

A fourth principle that can be found in Jesus' ministry is the focus on potential, not problems.

When we meet people, we must communicate a fresh, personal vitality and a genuine concern for them. Forming close relationships with one person or ten brings us into a painful awareness of each individual's needs and problems. The basic issue, however, is our perspective. Do we relate to individuals on the basis of their problems or their potential?

*Norman Grubb, *C.T. Studd*, Copyright © 1972, p. 141: Used by permission of Christian Literature Crusade, Fort Washington, Pennsylvania.

Take careful note of the men with whom Jesus chose to work. Quite frankly, they were an unimpressive lot. Jesus was faced with the prospect of launching a worldwide enterprise with men who lacked education and self-control, and who were immature in many ways. Peter Marshall, the former chaplain of the United States, said that if the 12 disciples had been reviewed by a church examining committee in our day, they would have been abruptly turned down for missionary service.

If we were in Jesus' position, would we have picked Peter for a disciple? Here was a man who was constantly making the wrong comments at the wrong time. At one point, Jesus was even forced to say to Peter, "Get behind me, Satan" (Matthew 16:23). Or would we think of adding Thomas to an outreach committee in our church? Thomas would probably have 25 reasons why outreach would not work in the community! Most of the disciples' characteristics could be listed under a column labeled "problems."

But amazingly enough, after prayerful consideration, Jesus chose these particular 12 men. The purpose of forming this small group was that they might be with Him to share His life so that eventually He might send them forth to minister to others (Mark 3:13,14). From all the multitudes that followed Him, Jesus chose only 12 men, and not one of them was perfect!

God never chooses men and women because of what they *are*, but because of what they will *become*. He knows us completely and is aware of our weaknesses. He is, however, in the revolutionary business of transforming our lives from the inside out. And so, despite our awareness of our problems—our rebellion, our separation from God and our hopeless condition—God sees that we have great potential. Jesus operated on the basis of potential, not problems.

Still, there can be frustration involved in leading small, face-to-face groups. We begin to encounter tremendous conflicts, weaknesses and problems in our group members' lives. Sometimes, we attempt to avoid this frustration by running away from deep relationships with people. "You should see the people I have to work with," we say. Another way to avoid the frustration of using Jesus' methods is to work only with programs, or large masses of people. Ceaseless activity or treating individuals as faceless, monolithic masses can keep us insulated from people and their problems. When this happens, the very example of our Lord Himself is being violated, and the rich, people-changing potential of Christianity becomes hidden in depersonalized rituals, programs and mass meetings.

The challenge of discipleship is to see beyond the problems of the individual to what he can become through Christ. This perspective brings a refreshing honesty and a life-changing dynamic into our relationships. The challenge for us is to develop Christ-centered relationships with two or more individuals. In His own ministry, Jesus multiplied Himself through a core of men who were, for the most part, ignorant fishermen with no formal education. The priority of His three-year ministry was to spend time with them and to build positive qualities into their lives. He saw them in terms of their potential.

Summary: Purpose and Power

When we discuss small groups and "the methods of the Master," there is a natural tendency to become lost in the "process" and to lose sight of our overall objective—to help fulfill the Great Commission. Discipling others in the context of small groups is an exciting, rewarding experience. It should not, however, become an end in itself.

Suppose we had the opportunity to ask Jesus the following question: "Jesus, why are you discipling your men?" Would He have answered, "I'm discipling my men so that we can get close to one another and build love relationships in the Spirit"?

It is doubtful Jesus would have answered in this way. Rather, His answer would have been super-charged with spiritual power and a world-changing vision. Jesus always had His eyes on changing the world through a revolutionary movement of disciples who were controlled and empowered by the Holy Spirit. Clearly, He was committed to "building a movement of Spirit-filled Christians who were obedient to His Word and were actively involved in helping to fulfill His Great Commission in every generation." Matthew 28:18-20 is a final confirmation of this perspective.

It is also important to keep in mind that it is the power of the Holy Spirit—and not our small group strategy—that insures success in the discipleship process. The methods we have reviewed *are* the principles that Jesus used in discipling His men and directing them toward His ultimate objective. However, He also realized that His physical presence with the disciples in a small group had its own limitations. Soon, He told them, He would be going to the Father, and He would disciple them through the ministry of the Holy Spirit (John 14,16). The book of Acts is a portrait of Christ's Spirit powerfully etching itself on the canvas of history.

Jesus loved His men (John 17) and chose to disciple them through a small group. But with the outpouring of the Holy Spirit at Pentecost, He is also

37

free to touch the lives of people around the world, and in an instant of time awaken millions of sleeping Christians in powerful currents of spiritual revival.

Thus, small discipleship groups do have a strong basis in biblical history. But we should never lose our perspective on the role of small groups in helping to reach our ultimate objective: the fulfillment of the Great Commission. Furthermore, the Holy Spirit is not limited to working through small groups in the discipleship process. Yet if we understand and experience the power of Christ's Spirit and help our group members to do the same, we will always be on the cutting edge of a worldwide ministry.

Discipleship Principles
═══ of the Master ═══

A young boy had a dream of becoming a great concert pianist. He read the biographies of Van Cliburn and Rubenstein and listened endlessly to records by these men. Finally, his parents bought a piano for him, and he began working to make his dream a reality.

He bought a beginner's book on "How to Play the Piano" and devoted himself to practicing scales and arpeggios for hours each day. Eventually, he was able to play simple pieces; but when he moved to more difficult compositions, his abilities seemed to reach their limit. He kept working, but only became more and more frustrated. His dream appeared to be beyond his capabilities.

Just as he was about to give up completely, he noticed an advertisement for a music class which was going to be taught in his city by a master pianist. The boy enrolled immediately. After only a few weeks of instruction, his playing improved dramatically. Following the guidelines of his expert instructor, he finally gained enough expertise to become a master pianist himself. He saw his dream fulfilled.

Similarly, as believers who want to see our lives maximized in the fulfillment of the Great Commission, we need to become like the Master of discipleship. Just as the inexperienced pianist needed training and advice from an expert in his field, so also we need to look to the expert in discipleship for our example—Jesus Christ. Jesus was a living example of what it means to disciple others. Understanding and applying the principles He used in training His men will give us a framework for our own discipleship ministries. But the framework will collapse if we build it in our own strength. We must depend upon the power of the Holy Spirit, allowing Him to change hearts and cause growth. As we let the Spirit work in our lives and in the lives of others, we not only will use the Master's strategies but we also will become like the Master Himself, and He will work powerfully through us.

Jesus' Strategy

Robert Coleman says in *Master Plan of Evangelism* that Jesus' life was ordered by His objective to reach the world: "Everything He did and said was a part of the whole pattern. It had significance because it contributed to the ultimate purpose of His life in redeeming the world for God. This was the motivating vision governing His behavior. His steps were ordered by it. Mark it well. Not for one moment did Jesus lose sight of His goal."* (See also John 17:4)

Jesus' objective was to reach the world, but men were His means of accomplishing that objective. He knew that the men He chose would be responsible for carrying out the Great Commission after His own ministry on earth had ended. Since His whole plan hinged on these few men, He was very careful when "He appointed twelve, that they might be with Him, and that He might send them out to preach" (Mark 3:14).

*Robert Coleman, *Master Plan of Evangelism*, Copyright © 1964, p. 18: Used by permission of Fleming H. Revell Company, Old Tappan, New Jersey.

Obviously, discipling by small groups is not the *only* way that men and women become Spirit-filled and committed to reaching the world. Jesus did not exclude others from following Him or refuse to meet the masses. In fact, He chose His men from a large number of followers. Since Pentecost, God the Holy Spirit has continued to use a variety of experiences to build into the lives of potential disciples. Although the Holy Spirit is not bound to use only small group discipleship, we will see that this was one of the primary elements of Jesus' discipleship ministry.

Jesus gave high priority to His group of men and expressed this by spending quality time with them. This was the crux of His training program. They ate, slept, fished and sailed together.

The disciples witnessed firsthand Jesus' miracles and teaching. They learned how to pray and worship from His example. Such commitment to them required the Master's constant attention and personal sacrifice, and He gladly gave it.

At the same time, Jesus required commitment from His men. In Matthew 16:24, He told them, "If any one wishes to come after Me, let him deny himself, and take up his cross, and follow Me." Jesus did not scatter His time among those who wanted to make their own terms of discipleship. Being a disciple of Christ involved surrender of one's whole life to the Master. There could be no compromise. Jesus said, "No servant can serve two masters; for either He will hate the one, and love the other, or else he will hold to one, and despise the other . . ." (Luke 16:13). Yet still, He patiently endured their human shortcomings because they were willing to follow Him.

He also patiently corrected their shortcomings. "His disciples came to Him. And opening His mouth He began to teach them" (Matthew 5:1b-2). Jesus was the master teacher, never missing an opportunity to instruct His men. The Sermon on the Mount, recorded in Matthew 5-7, is an example of a lecture situation He used in the teaching process. During these times, He often would use questions and answers, such as, "Who do people say that the Son of Man is? Who do you say that I am?" (Matthew 16:13,15). At other times, He told stories to illustrate His point. (See Matthew 13:3-9, the parable of the sower.)

Jesus' lectures were always accompanied by real life situations that illustrated and applied the principles He taught. For instance, He used the calming of the storm on the Sea of Galilee to teach the disciples a lesson on faith (Mark 4:33-41). He used His miracles to demonstrate that He was the Son of God (Mark 2:5-12). He used their mistakes as an opportunity to teach them the correct way to think and act (Luke 9:46-48). And He turned His encounters with other people into teaching situations which His disciples could observe (Mark 9:25-29).

Teaching by Example

He taught them by example, and He set an example for them in every area of their lives. He told them, "For I gave you an example that you also should do as I did to you" (John 13:15).

Take, for instance, His example in prayer. It was no accident that Jesus often let His disciples see Him conversing with the Father (Luke 11:1-13). He didn't force this lesson on them—He just prayed. His example caused the disciples to hunger to pray, and they asked Him to teach them how. He also demonstrated a proper use and understanding of the Scriptures (Luke 24:32). Most important, they saw His heart to win men and women to Himself (Luke 19:10). Evangelism was lived before them in spirit and technique. Watching Him, they learned how to do it.

As Jesus demonstrated to His disciples how to minister to others, He gave them practical assignments to help them begin following His example. He delegated responsibility to them to witness, baptize, heal and cast out demons: "And He summoned the twelve and began to send them out in pairs; and He was giving them authority over the unclean spirits" (Mark 6:7). He also gave them administrative responsibilities such as getting food, arranging accommodations and handling money. Such delegation was important because the disciples needed to be able to take over when Jesus left. Also, as they carried out tasks that contributed to the cause, their commitment to the cause grew. Just as a mother eagle teaches her young to fly by pushing them out of the nest, so Jesus taught His men the skills they needed for discipleship by pushing them out into the world.

Yet as He pushed, He watched and supervised. After returning from their assigned mission of evangelism and healing, "the apostles gathered together with Jesus; and they reported to Him all that they had done and taught" (Mark 6:30). He heard their reports and shared their joy. But after reports like these, He also would explain the practical applications of their experiences to their lives. For example, in Mark 9:25-29, He responded to their futile efforts in healing an afflicted boy by gently rebuking their lack of prayer and belief in God. Many other illustrations could be cited to show how Jesus checked up on the actions and reactions of His disciples in various situations. His plan of teaching—by example, assignment and constant check-up—was calculated to bring out the best in each of them.

But Jesus did more than simply build character and ministry skills into His men. He also commissioned His disciples to reproduce their lives into the lives of others, just as He had done with them. Therefore, although it would be enough for us to have only Jesus as an example, we also have clear models of the discipleship process in the ministries of the apostles. The book of Acts records how Jesus' disciples spiritually reproduced their lives into the lives of many. Their impact was so great that the non-believers in Thessalonica shouted in rage that these were the men who had upset the world (Acts 17:6).

There was nothing haphazard in Jesus' plan for reaching the world—there was no wasted energy, never an idle word. His objective was clear, and He lived every moment of His life accordingly. We each need to decide if we are going to be obedient to God by having the same objective and plan as Jesus did. If we do have the same objective, but are not committed to carrying out the plan step by step, then at the end of our lives we will have to look back on a dream that was never fulfilled.

At the end of Jesus' life, He was able to say, "I glorified Thee on the earth, having accomplished the work which Thou hast given Me to do" (John 17:4). Jesus was able to say those words because He had discipled a group of men who eventually turned the world upside down.

Crucial Choices

How do we begin implementing Jesus' principles in a discipleship ministry of our own?

Selection of our disciples is obviously the first step we must take, and it can also be the most crucial one. If we do not choose our disciples carefully, then the remaining principles of discipleship may frustrate us and the people we are trying to disciple. Let's examine the Master's method of selection more closely, applying it to our situation today.

Looking again at Jesus' example, we see that the most important part of his selection process was His dependence on God. In John 5:30, He said, "I can do nothing on My own initiative. As I hear, I judge; and My judgment is just, because I do not seek My own will, but the will of Him who sent Me." How much more essential it is for *us* to depend on the Father and the guidance of the Holy Spirit as we choose and disciple others! God is the only one who can give us success or produce fruit through our lives. Christ said, "I am the vine, you are the branches; he who abides in Me, and I in him, he bears much fruit; for apart from Me you can do nothing" (John 15:5).

Another important factor in Jesus' selection of His men was prayer. "And it was at this time that He went off to the mountain to pray, and He spent the whole night in prayer to God. And when day came, He called His disciples to Him; and chose twelve of them, whom He also named as apostles" (Luke 6:12,13). A clear demonstration of our dependence on God is to pray for disciples and expect results. (See also Matthew 9:37,38 and Matthew 21:22.)

After Jesus prayed, He then took the initiative to call His disciples, challenging them to follow Him (Matthew 4:17-19). The Lord's initiative action began in evangelism and continued to the point of challenging people to discipleship. After we have prayed for disciples, we also need to take the initiative. This is sometimes a difficult step, but it is a very necessary one. It is our active response to the Lord's command in Matthew 28:19: "Go therefore and make disciples of all the nations, baptizing them in the name of the Father and the Son and the Holy Spirit."

As Jesus chose His men, He also looked for particular qualities in their lives. Two that were important were a desire to know God and availability. After Jesus called Simon and Andrew, they "immediately" left the nets, and followed Him" (Matthew 4:20). The fact that these men followed Him shows that they had a desire to know Him. The word "immediately" emphasizes their availability to the Lord. Two other qualities Christ looked for in His disciples were teachability and faithfulness. The disciples demonstrated their teachability by taking the initiative to go to Jesus to be taught (Matthew 5:1,2). Jesus often mentioned the value of faithfulness, as in the parable of the faithful slave (Matthew 25:21).

Following Jesus' example, we need to look for these same qualities in our potential disciples: a heart for God, availability, teachability and faithfulness.

Besides these four qualities, we also need to look for people who have the ability to lead others.

The world won't be reached without spiritual multiplication, and spiritual multiplication won't take place without potential multipliers—people who have the ability to lead. II Timothy 2:2 says, "And the things which you have heard from me in the presence of many witnesses, these entrust to faithful men, who will be able to teach others also." Paul didn't say that these faithful men were already dynamic leaders (although some were), but that they were able to teach others. Our disciples need to have a potential for leadership that can be developed, even if it is not already there. To discern if people have leadership abilities, observe their present involvement in leadership as well as their relationships with their peers.

Watch Your Step!

There are several pitfalls along the path of the selection process. Knowing what these pitfalls are can help you avoid them as you choose your key disciples.

The first pitfall is losing sight of our objective. Our objective is not merely to build our own ministries; it is to reach the world for Christ. Having this clear objective before us will keep us from settling for some other objective that may be reached more quickly.

Another common pitfall is choosing people who are not "full of faith." Acts 6:5a says that, "The statement found approval with the whole congregation; and they chose Stephen, a man full of faith and of the Holy Spirit." We are looking for people who demonstrate the kind of faith that moves them into action. The kind of action necessary is that which results in a discipleship ministry. Unfortunately we often try for too long to disciple someone who isn't responding to the leading of the Holy Spirit to become a man or woman "full of faith." This usually results in a frustrated leader, a follower who is unteachable and a breakdown in the spiritual multiplication process.

A third pitfall is to ignore elements of maturity that are crucial for a spiritual multiplier. One element is social maturity, the ability to relate well to others. Another is emotional maturity, the ability to follow through on commitments and responsibilities.

These two elements of maturity will have a lasting effect on the quality of spiritual multiplication we see through our disciples. People with these qualities will multiply faster, will reach more people, and ultimately, will become your major resource in accomplishing your overall objective.

Another pitfall to avoid is ignoring the ability and sphere of influence of a potential disciple.

Everyone has an influence on others, and we should capitalize on that influence. However, we tend to avoid those who have the greatest amounts of influence because we tend to relate to people who are on or below our social-cultural level. For maximum impacts, however, we should be trying to reach and disciple those at the highest possible level of leadership. There are two reasons for this. First, leaders need and want to know God personally just as everyone else does. Also, the Bible says that all leaders are sovereignly placed by God. He may want to use their scopes of influence to reach many others for Himself. In light of this, we need to begin our ministries with people who can relate or can learn to relate to leaders.

A final pitfall to avoid is having an imbalance in group affinity. There may be too much affinity between group members, resulting in the group becoming too in-grown, and exclusive. Or, there may be too little affinity, which could inhibit the development of friendships. Either extreme could seriously harm the relationships that are so crucial to quality discipleship.

Unlimited Potential

Jesus Christ left us a perfect model of discipleship. As we study His life, we can see clearly the principles He used and how we can apply them to our ministries. Just as the boy pianist learned from the expertise of the master pianist, so too we can learn from Jesus' expertise. And because we have the Holy Spirit living in us and empowering us, we can actually become *like* the Master. As we equip ourselves with the knowledge of His methods and yield to His direction in our lives, we will have unlimited potential to be used by God in helping to reach the world for Christ.

Characteristics of a ===Discipleship Group===

Is your discipleship group actively involved in helping to reach the world for Christ? In this article we will examine three vital characteristics of a multiplying discipleship group that will help you determine whether your group is moving toward this objective.

The Fellowship of the Burning Heart

In 1947, several young men signed a pledge which they entitled, "The Fellowship of the Burning Heart." Under the tutorship of Dr. Henrietta Mears, these men enthusiastically committed their lives to be used by God in whatever fashion He should choose to help win a needy world to Christ. Then, they drafted the following four disciplines to underscore the importance of remaining wholeheartedly committed to their objective:

1. One hour each day spent alone with God in prayer, Bible study and devotional reading.
2. A life of personal holiness, maintained by a life of self-denial and self-discipline.
3. A life of obedience and faithfulness in every possible opportunity to witness for Christ.

4. An offering of one's self "in all sobriety to be expendable for Christ."*

Since then, the dedication and love for Christ demonstrated by these men, among them Dr. Richard Halverson, the pastor of the Fourth Presbyterian Church of Washington, D.C.; Louis Evans, Jr., the pastor of the National Presbyterian Church in Washington, D.C.; and Dr. Bill Bright, founder and president of Campus Crusade for Christ International, have been multiplied into the lives of millions of people around the world.

Characteristics of a Discipleship Group

A true discipleship group has three vital characteristics. First, its members exhibit a growing dependence upon and love for Christ. Second, they experience a growing love for each other and for other Christians within the Body of Christ. And third, they have an increasing compassion and concern for a lost world. This compassion is demonstrated by personal involvement in discipleship and evangelism and a desire to help fulfill the Great Commission.

A Growing Dependence Upon and Love for Christ

As demonstrated in the ministry of Dr. Mears, the most important characteristic of a Discipleship Group is a complete love for and dependence upon Christ. It is foundational to the group's objective and supports the other two characteristics.

A good example of this characteristic was the Church at Thessalonica. Paul wrote these words to the believers there:

"Constantly bearing in mind your work of faith and labor of love and steadfastness of hope in our Lord Jesus Christ in the presence of our

*Ethel May Baldwin and David V. Benson, *Henrietta Mears and How She Did It*, Copyright © 1966, pp. 232,240,241: Used by permission of Gospel Light Publications, Glendale, California.

God and Father . . . For the word of the Lord has sounded forth from you, not only in Macedonia and Achaia, but also in every place your faith toward God has gone forth, so that we have no need to say anything. For they themselves report about us what kind of reception we had with you, and how you turned to God from idols to serve a living and true God, and to wait for His Son from heaven, whom He raised from the dead, that is Jesus, who delivers us from the wrath to come" (I Thessalonians 1:3,8-10).

The Thessalonians were having a tremendous impact on the world around them, but the foundation of their activity was their love for and faith in Jesus Christ. This characteristic is evidenced in group members' lives by their desire to be conformed to the image of Christ and to serve God from their hearts. The sufficiency of Christ and His lordship should be the basis for group meetings, personal relationships and involvement in helping to fulfill the Great Commission.

A member's true dependence should be on Christ and His limitless resources, not upon the leader or other group members. To foster dependence on the Lord, the discipleship group leader should reinforce the group member's need to take each problem, trial and heartache to Christ. The leader helps to place his group members in touch with Christ's infinite resources—His love, wisdom, sensitivity, courage, grace, integrity, power and vision for a lost world.

Without this foundational characteristic, the discipleship group will begin to have problems. Without a growing love for and dependence upon Christ the group will become introspective. The word 'introspective' means to focus inward. This is exactly what happens to a group whose members are not focusing on Christ. Personal opinions, rather than the authority of God's Word, begin to dominate the group. The members become *overly* focused on themselves and their own problems. This creates a very unhealthy, self-centered atmosphere (II Corinthians 10:12).

Furthermore, without a proper emphasis on our dependence upon and love for Christ, a group will share no common objective and will lack loyalty. Without Christ as the central focus, the group can lose sight of both the group's purpose and source of unity. Individuals may begin wanting to do their own thing. Any or all of these problems may lead to the ultimate failure of the group.

There are several ways that the discipleship group leader can direct his group members to grow in dependence upon and love for Christ. First, the group leader can illustrate how Christ is sufficient to meet their needs by telling group members about specific problems or circumstances in his life in which he has seen Christ work. Christ's sufficiency can be kept before the group by continually talking about the adequacy of Christ in their personal daily lives. Don't focus on the problems, focus on the solution (Philippians 4:6-8).

Second, it is always good for the leader to point group members to God's Word by showing them examples of biblical characters who faced problems or circumstances similar to theirs. The Old Testament characters are especially good examples: for instance note David and his responses of joy, hurt and cries for help in the Psalms.

The leader should also show the group promises in the Bible that relate to their needs. Group members should be encouraged to personalize these promises. A good illustration of this is found in Romans 4:20,21, where Abraham is described as trusting God's promises against all odds: "Yet, with respect to the promise of God, he did not waver in unbelief, but grew strong in faith, giving glory to God, and being fully assured that what He had promised, He was able also to perform."

Third, an emphasis on prayer, praise and thanksgiving will help the group members to focus on Christ (Philippians 4:6-8). The discipleship group leader can influence his members by demonstrating attitudes of thanksgiving and praise as he deals with various circumstances in his life (see Philippians 4:9). He must also be looking for these qualities in the lives of his group members as a helpful measure of their love for Christ and their dependence upon His power.

As group members grow in their dependence on the Lord, respect for God's Word and its authority will increase (I John 2:3-5). This includes being obedient to God's Word in spite of feelings. There will be times when feelings will go back and forth: "I want to . . . I don't want to . . ." But a person who is growing in his dependence on God will be learning to act according to what the Bible says, regardless of how he feels.

Dependence on Christ is also made evident by a growing prayer life. A group member who is growing in his dependence on the Lord will be initiating prayer and learning how to give praise and thanks in response to his circumstances (Romans 8:28, I Thessalonians 5:18).

Finally, an increasing dependence on the Lord should result in a growing faith. The object of our faith is the Creator God of the universe, who is also our heavenly Father. As we learn more about His love, His power, His grace and His justice, our confidence in Him is built up. Group members indicate that they are growing in their faith when their discussions do not center around personal problems but on solutions in Christ (Hebrews 12:1-3).

A Growing Love and Concern for Each Other

Dr. Mears stressed to her disciples that a love for God would ultimately result in a growing love and concern for other members of the discipleship group, as well as other Christian brothers and sisters (John 13:34,35). Centuries ago, during the Roman persecution, Christians met together in subterranean catacombs and attempted to protect their brothers and sisters at the risk of martyrdom. Under these circumstances, the early Christians not only persevered, but they also grew in number.

This revolutionary growth in the first-century Church was directly related to the love and concern the believers had for one another:

'And they were continually devoting themselves to the apostles' teaching and to fellowship, to the breaking of bread and to prayer. And everyone kept feeling a sense of awe; and many wonders and signs were taking place through the apostles. And all those who had believed were together, and had all things in common; and they began selling their property and possessions, and were sharing them with all, as anyone might have need. And day by day continuing with one mind in the temple, and breaking bread from house to house, they were taking their meals together with gladness and sincerity of heart, praising God, and having favor with all the people. And the Lord was adding to their number day by day those who were being saved" (Acts 2:42-47).

Unfortunately, love and unity among Christians is not always evident in today's world, with the end result that the whole Body of Christ suffers. "And if one member suffers, all the members suffer with it; if one member is honored, all the members rejoice with it" (I Corinthians 12:26). If love is not practiced within a discipleship group, then that group becomes a poor example to both Christians and non-Christians. God wants us to demonstrate in our lives what it means to love others, as did the Thessalonians: "You also became imitators of us and of the Lord, having received the word in much tribulation with the joy of the Holy Spirit, so that you became an example to all the believers in Macedonia and in Achaia" (I Thessalonians 1:6,7).

Members of a discipleship group can show love and concern for each other by spending time together outside the group meetings. Getting together for meals, shopping, sporting events or studies can be practical ways for group members to encourage and minister to each other.

We also demonstrate a genuine interest in others by asking questions and listening closely to their answers. Sharing both the joys and hurts in each others' lives will draw group members closer together. Finally, the group needs to be involved together in areas of personal development.

This would involve the leader spending individual time with each group member, perhaps suggesting a book or article that would help meet a personal need, or encouraging him in setting a goal. Those involved in a discipleship group need to commit themselves to one another and ask God to show them creative ways to demonstrate love and concern.

A third characteristic of a discipleship group will result as group members learn to depend on Christ and grow in their love for others.

A Growing Compassion and Concern for a Lost World

The following story relates how God uses His children to demonstrate love and compassion for those without Christ.

In 1813, Adoniram and Ann Judson, not yet 25 years old, arrived in the stifling heat of Rangoon, Burma, after constant travel for more than a year and a half. They came uninvited, without knowing the language, having no political pull and with no influential friends. But they were driven by the conviction that God was real, man was sinful and Christ had died on the cross to save anyone who would believe in Him. In simple faith they planned to confront the Buddhist religion, which declares that there is no personal God who will save and no sin to be saved from. Their simple prayer was, "God, grant that we may live and die among the Burmans, though we never should do anything else than smooth the way for others."

Nearly 10 years later, a colonial war with Britain erupted in Burma, and Adoniram was imprisoned as a hated foreign spy. Judson spent 21 months in a death prison—a matted floor with rotting animals, nearly 100 degrees each day. Much of his time was spent in stocks. Two iron rings were attached to each ankle and joined by a chain through which the jailer slid a bamboo pole. He then raised the pole with fiendish precision until only Adoniram's shoulders rested on the ground.

Ann Judson, miraculously spared through these torturous months, kept Adoniram alive through her visits to the prison. During that time, Ann bore their third child, a little girl. Two months after Adoniram was released, his wife was dead; six months later he buried little Maria, his third child to die in Burma.

Yet the biographer of this great missionary tells us that in spite of his heartbreak, Judson "placed his feet squarely and began preaching the gospel." After some time he married again, and he and his new wife continued the ministry of the gospel to the Burmese.

Twenty-three years after Judson began his ministry in Burma, he completed his translation of the Bible, so accurate in every sense that it stands as the best Burmese Bible in existence. After this accomplishment, Sarah, his second wife, became gravely ill and died.

After a brief return to the United States, he married a third time and, undaunted, returned to Rangoon to continue his mission to the Burmese people. Plagued by recurring bouts with dysentery and tuberculosis, he began a Bible dictionary which still serves as the basis for study of the Burmese language.

Judson labored for six years before the first person in Burma trusted Christ. In the next seven to eight years, only 18 people became Christians. But before his death in 1850, the Christian Church was planted in Burma with hundreds of converts, and at a considerable price.*

As we review the histories of men like Judson, Hudson Taylor, C.T. Studd and others who gave their own lives and the lives of their families to proclaim the gospel of Christ, can we remain unmoved? The majority of us are living in comfortable homes with relatively secure incomes. But does the same burden for the lost which sent men like Judson to the mission fields of the world fill our hearts and captivate our minds? Will the mission fields of our own homes, schools, communities, cities, states and nations be reached for Christ?

As we grow in our love for Christ and for His people we will also grow in our concern for those who don't know God. Christ's heart burden will become ours.

> "And seeing the multitudes, He felt compassion for them, because they were distressed and downcast like sheep without a shepherd. Then he said to His disciples, 'The harvest is plentiful, but the workers are few. Therefore beseech the Lord of the harvest to send out workers into His harvest'" (Matthew 9:36-38).

What are some problems and consequences that arise when this characteristic is not growing in the lives of the discipleship group members? Tragically, people die without Christ. This is made clear in II Corinthians 2:15,16:

> "For we are a fragrance of Christ to God among those who are being saved and among those who are perishing; to the one an aroma from death to death, to the other an aroma from life to life. And who is adequate for these things?"

Moreover, without spiritual multiplication the purpose of a discipleship group is not fulfilled. Remember that the objective of discipleship is to develop a movement of Spirit-filled Christians who are obedient to God's Word and are actively involved in helping to fulfill the Great Commission. If concern for the world isn't growing in each group member's heart, then he will not be motivated to take an active part in fulfilling that objective.

*Courtney Anderson, *To the Golden Shore*, Copyright © 1972, pp. 157-178: Used by permission of Zondervan Publishing House, Grand Rapids Michigan.

What can a group leader do to encourage group members to grow in this area? First, he should pray that group members will see the need of the lost for Christ. Then, he should continue to take his disciples sharing with him. It is important that he do more than just take group members on evangelistic appointments; he should seek to share his faith as a way of life whenever he is with his disciples. He must continually use the Bible to show them God's desire to see the world reached and saved:

"The Lord is not slow about His promise, as some count slowness, but is patient toward you, not wishing for any to perish but for all to come to repentance" (II Peter 3:9).

Jesus looked over Jerusalem and said, "O Jerusalem, Jerusalem, the city that kills the prophets and stones those sent to her! How often I wanted to gather your children together, just as a hen gathers her brood under her wings, and you would not have it" (Luke 13:34).

Can we identify with Jesus Christ? Through the ages—from the disciples of the first century down to modern day disciples like Adoniram Judson and those influenced by Dr. Mears—a compassion for those who do not know Christ has characterized the men and women who have made a great impact for Jesus. A person who has committed himself to the Lord cannot remain untouched by the fact that a multitude of people are lost without Him. The love of Christ compels him to go to them with the news of God's plan, His forgiveness and His promise of eternal life.

Discipling your === Group Members ===

"Know well the condition of your flocks, and pay attention to your herds" (Proverbs 27:23).

There are five underlying principles of the discipleship process that are essential to discipling your group members. These principles, along with some helpful suggestions for meeting the needs of your disciples, will be discussed in this article.

Defined Objective

The first underlying principle which the group leader should always keep in mind is to have a clearly defined objective. Howard Hendricks once said, "A leader is one who knows where he's going and is able to persuade others to go along with him."* As mentioned previously, the objective of a discipleship group is to develop a movement of Spirit-filled Christians who are obedient to God's Word and are actively involved in helping to fulfill the Great Commission in this generation. Keeping this objective in focus is crucial to prevent discipling others as an end in itself.

*Howard Hendricks, "How to Lead I," in *The Ministry of Management*, Steven B. Douglas and Bruce E. Cook, Copyright © 1972: Used by permission of Campus Crusade for Christ, Inc., Arrowhead Springs, California.

Biblical Content

The need for biblical content is the second valuable underlying principle. Reliance upon the authority of Scripture is the basic ingredient for discipling group members (Hebrews 4:12; II Timothy 2:15; 3:16,17, II Peter 1:21).

We live in a culture that operates on the basis of feelings. We are beseiged by man-made philosophies that are often quite subtle, steering us away from God's truths. There is constant pressure on us to conform to these ways of thinking.

Like the psalmist, we need God's Word to direct our lives: "How can a young man keep his way pure? By keeping it according to Thy Word. With all my heart I have sought Thee; do not let me wander from Thy commandments. Thy Word I have treasured in my heart, that I may not sin against Thee" (Psalm 119:9-11).

Because studying the Word tests our thoughts and helps us draw principles and conclusions for our lives, it is essential to use Scripture in discipling our group members.

"Game Plan" for Discipleship

The third principle is illustrated in the story of Pug Jones, a football coach who wanted his team to win the big game very badly. He met with his team day after day and, being a gifted speaker, he exhorted them to win for the glory of old Pine Needle University. Each time he gave a pep-talk, the team would respond enthusiastically. "Man, when he speaks, he really delivers the goods!" team members would say. "Am I ever charged up!" But the coach never designed a game plan for his team or taught them any plays. Although his team was motivated to win, they didn't have a plan for making touchdowns. There was a lack of unified direction.

On the day of the game, what do you think happened? Probably a slaughter of Pug Jones' team! Unlike Pug Jones, we need to have a "game plan and plays" in the discipleship process. We must be equipped with a strategy and tools in order to reach our objective.

Tragic as it may seem the story of Pug Jones reveals one of the biggest problems in the Christian world today. Many people in churches, Bible studies and discipleship groups have been thoroughly inspired to reach the world for Christ; yet they don't know how to begin to accomplish this goal. After a while, having a vision without a plan to achieve it results in defeat and frustration for many sincere Christians.

Many times, we as discipleship group leaders inspire our disciples with a godly vision for reaching the world, but we don't design a strategy or train them to be more effective. Therefore, although we want victory for the cause of Christ, our team is defeated and demoralized.

The following diagram shows a simple strategy for building a disciple after he becomes a Christian. In this "game plan," biblical content has been arranged in a sequence of ministry tool lesson plans or "plays." These lesson plans insure that we are discipling a person in the basics of the Christian life while we are accomplishing our objective.

In the chart we find that our basic tools for evangelism are the Four Spiritual Laws and the Holy Spirit booklets; our tools in basic individual follow-up are the "Beginning Your New Life" booklets 1-5; our tools in basic small group follow-up are Discovery Group Lessons 1-6, and our ministry tools for discipleship training are the Discipleship Group Lessons 7-20.

We use these "plays" as a part of our "game plan" to build our disciples toward the ultimate goal of helping to fulfill the Great Commission.

Jesus, the master teacher, understood this third principle well. In Luke 10:1a we read, "Now after this the Lord appointed seventy others, and sent them two and two ahead of Him." A careful reading of the next 15 verses reveals that after Jesus commissioned the disciples he trained them. He taught them where to go, what to say and how to react to various circumstances. Structure, therefore, in the form of thorough training, will accelerate our ability to equip millions of workers for the cause of the Great Commission.

Spiritual Environment

The fourth underlying principle in the discipleship process is to provide a proper context or spiritual environment for your group members. This context includes four elements: modeling, building relationships, vision and evangelism.

"Modeling" involves the influence of your personal life and ministry on the lives of your group members.

The apostle Paul said to the Philippian church, "The things you have learned and received and heard and seen in me, practice these things; and the God of peace shall be with you" (Philippians 4:9). Paul also refers to modeling in his letter to the church at Corinth: "Be imitators of me, just as I also am of Christ" (I Corinthians 11:1).

Most of us probably wouldn't want to say that to our disciples! This point shouldn't create guilt, however. None of us are perfect, and the Lord accepts us just as we are. But as group leaders, we are in positions of tremendous responsibility. Our disciples will imitate us—in the things we say, in our attitudes toward life, sometimes in our lifestyle, and occasionally, even in our manner of speech! Much more is "caught" than is formally "taught."

Another element in the context of discipleship is building relationships. Building relationships involves building friendships (I Thessalonians 2:7-20), which consist of encouragement and correction. As we disciple others, we should be constantly encouraging them to live godly lives. Encouragement is discussed in the book of Hebrews: "And let us consider how to stimulate one another to love and good deeds, not forsaking our own assembling together, as is the habit of some, but encouraging one another" (Hebrews 10:24,25a).

As we disciple others, we function as godly parents. Parents desire to build their children to maturity, and building a child involves correction. If we allow a child to go without correction, he will harm himself. Because we love those whom we are discipling, we may need to correct them on occasion. But the Scripture gives us the guidelines for exhorting a brother or sister who is walking in sin.

Correction in relationships is described in Galatians 6:1 as follows: "Brethren, even if a man is caught in any trespass, you who are spiritual, restore such a one in a spirit of gentleness; looking to yourselves, lest you too be tempted."

The final two elements that are found in a healthy spiritual environment are vision and evangelism. The best way for you to impart vision for evangelism to your group members is through your own example.

Also, you can encourage your group members to grow in these areas by planning together a strategy to reach a part of your campus or community. Or, you might go witnessing together, or take them to conferences, or pray with them about their friends and families.

Right Perspective on Circumstances

The last underlying principle of the discipleship process is that our circumstances are used by the Lord to mold us into what *He* wants us to be. He is the "Ultimate Discipler." He has his own discipleship curriculum, uniquely designed for each of our lives. Various circumstances, in the forms of trials, victories, failures or pressures, drive us to the Lord and result in our growth.

The first chapter of James presents God's perspective on trying circumstances: "Consider it all joy, my brethren, when you encounter various trials, knowing that the testing of your faith produces endurance. And let endurance have its perfect result, that you may be perfect and complete, lacking in nothing" (James 1:2-4). Furthermore, God promises to use these circumstances for our best welfare (Romans 8:28,29).

As disciplers, we will want to help our disciples realize that God desires to build our characters through circumstances. "In this you greatly rejoice, even though now for a little while, if necessary, you have been distressed by various trials, that the proof of your faith, being more precious than gold which is perishable, even though tested by fire, may be found to result in praise and glory and honor at the revelation of Jesus Christ" (I Peter 1:6,7).

With these five underlying principles in mind—a clearly defined objective, biblical content, a game plan and plays, context and circumstances—let's briefly discuss some practical hints of discipleship that will be useful inside and outside your group meetings.

Practical Hints for Discipleship

The primary focal points of discipleship outside the group are in the social, ministry and personal areas. Each of these areas lends itself to creative activities and goals that will help to strengthen the discipleship process in your group. Social activities might include eating dinner together, participating with each in sports or amusements, or planning events with Christian brothers and sisters outside your group. Ideas for ministry development could include outreaches to college groups, the community, businesses, or living areas. Personal development would include spending individual time with each group member. Recognizing needs, planning creative solutions and setting goals could be some ways to aid your group members in their personal development.

Inside the group—or during the group meetings—the use of a format that includes a time of sharing, Bible study, practical ministry and prayer has been found to be most helpful.

As we are using this format to lead our groups, we need to be aware of two types of needs that will affect our group members: constant needs and changing needs.

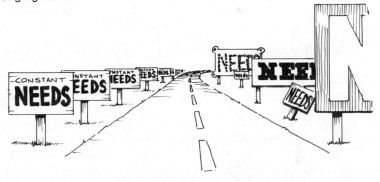

Constant needs are needs that always remain, regardless of positive or negative emotions, or changing circumstances. For instance, the constant need of every person in every culture is salvation. Similarly, there are certain major truths in the Bible which are essential to every Christian. In order to live healthy Christian lives, we must know about the deity and uniqueness of Jesus, how to put our faith in Christ and receive salvation, how to be assured of our salvation, how to live moment-by-moment by trusting Christ, how to share our faith with others and how to experience the power of the Holy Spirit in our lives. No matter what personal problems we may be going through at the moment, we have a constant need to know the central truths of Scripture.

Changing needs, however, come and go depending on circumstances, emotions, current issues and interests. For instance, suppose a group member is puzzled about the question, "How can a loving God allow evil and suffering?" The leader can decide whether to discuss this subject with the group or deal with it at another time. There are many changing needs which can and will arise in the course of your group discussions. If every changing need is addressed, there will be an inevitable loss of direction in the group.

For this reason, the discipleship group lesson plans are primarily designed to meet constant needs. Group leaders are encouraged to meet these constant needs by teaching the suggested topics, but they should also make regular application to changing needs. For example, when you teach submission to authority, you can emphasize application to husband-wife relationships, to parent-child relationships, to government-citizen relationships or to employer-employee relationships, depending on the changing needs of your group members.

In summary, the five underlying principles of the discipleship process are: a clearly defined objective, a solid biblical content, a game plan, a proper context or spiritual environment, and a right perspective on circumstances. Understanding and applying these principles will help us to build a movement of Spirit-filled Christians who are obedient to God's Word and are actively involved in helping to fulfill the Great Commission in this generation.

Being involved in a
═══Spiritual Movement═══

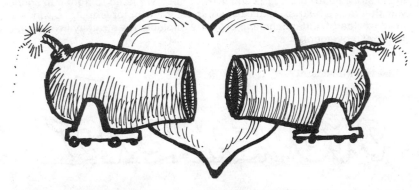

"There is a great battle going on all over the world which, in the final analysis, is a struggle for men's hearts, minds and souls."*

That statement is true. Yet it was not made by a spiritual leader as might be expected. It is a statement made by a committed Communist.

The aim of the members of the Communist Party is very clear; they have never concealed it. They are committed to making this a Communist world. In the past half-century they have achieved one-third of that aim. On any scale, that is a remarkable achievement, probably an unprecedented one.

Communist Party members are a very small minority—36 million—in comparison to some of the other groups contending for men's hearts and minds. There are, for example, 400 million Moslems and more than 500 million Catholics in the world, the majority living outside Communist countries. These other great world movements have immensely larger human resources at their disposal than the Communist Party. Yet no one could claim

*Douglas Hyde, *Dedication and Leadership*, Copyright © 1966, p. 10: Used by permission of University of Notre Dame Press, Notre Dame, Indiana.

that, in the period in which Communism has existed, they have achieved anything near its success. A movement is critical to changing the world. The communists understand this.

How did this nucleus of individuals so drastically alter the course of history? Individual members of the Communist Party are taught to believe that together, they and others like them can change the world in their lifetime. They are convinced that this is not just a dream, for they have techniques and a Marxist science of change-making which provide them with the means to accomplish their goal. When you have instilled in men a dynamic force such as this, it is so powerful that you can motivate them to accomplish what would otherwise be impossible. The dull and humdrum becomes meaningful. Life becomes purposeful and immensely more worth living.

We Christians are fighting in the same battle that the Communists are waging; a struggle for the hearts and lives of men. We need to fight it in such a way that men's hearts, minds and souls will be won for Christ. To win, we need to clearly understand and properly implement a strategy involving a *spiritual* movement.

What Is a Movement?

As you think of any effective movement, whether it be communism, Women's Liberation or Naziism, several characteristics will be pronounced.

The term "movement" itself connotes action. Not just random activity, but very deliberate, *organized action* that powerfully elicits involvement. To have organized action with a high degree of motivation means to *involve many people at all levels of commitment*. Everyone can't be a general or a private; there must be a balance among all levels.

Any effective movement will get its share of opposition. Therefore, its members must not only be motivated, but *highly dedicated* as well. They need to be ready for things to get tough. Often, movements stop because of unexpected opposition—opposition from within the ranks of the movement itself. Division, criticism and antagonism from within eat at a movement's very heart, until people are no longer involved in organized action. So an effective movement must also have a significant degree of *unity* among those involved.

Such unity often centers around a dynamic individual who incites others to action. As long as the leader exerts his influence, action results. But take away that leader, and many movements crumble. Thus, for a movement to be long-lasting and accomplish long-range goals, there must be a *constant development of qualified leaders* so the movement will be self-perpetuating. A movement grows only as fast, or lasts as long, as its leadership is developed.

Probably the most important element of an effective world-changing movement, however, is *purpose*. Those involved must be corporately committed to a common goal. Individual and personal goals of the members must be consistent and embrace the goal of the movement or it will face chaos and internal breakdown.

These basic characteristics of a movement form the backdrop for what is potentially the most dynamic influence in history—a spiritual movement. With the all-powerful Lord in control of a movement of committed, unified members, the highest goals are attainable!

In addition to these basic characteristics every successful movement has three essential elements; momentum, multiplication and management.

These elements form a network of interdependencies and all three are equally vital in keeping a spiritual movement dynamic and on target. A problem develops in many spiritual movements when the interdependencies are not observed or understood. Often, one or two elements are neglected, causing the movement to turn into a program or system of activities. Activities are essential, but when they are done out of the context of a movement, they merely lead group members away from the movement's overall objective.

Before we examine each of these foundational elements, we need to remind ourselves of the immense power and creativity of the Holy Spirit in drawing people to Christ. His presence in a spiritual movement will insure its success. Yet His work is not limited to the structure of an organized movement. Because of the Spirit, people can come to know Christ through books or television and can be grounded in the essentials of their new faith through tapes of messages or occasional talks with Christian friends. Great revivals have occurred merely because the Spirit chose to work creatively in people's lives.

For instance, in 1904, during a great revival in Wales, more than 100,000 people received Christ as their personal Savior and Lord. The impact of that revival was felt throughout society. The liquor trade suffered great financial losses and many taverns went out of business. These closures resulted in a vast improvement of public morals.

Life in the coal mines changed drastically. Managers testified of the change of conduct in their employees. Prayer meetings became common in the mines and so many of the miners stopped using foul language that the pit ponies were confused, not understanding their new commands.

Magistrates in several areas had no cases at all to try. Long standing debts were paid, stolen goods returned and people of all walks of life converted.*

So we must be cautious not to replace our dependence on the Spirit with a dependence on strategy. Rather, we should master our strategy, understanding thoroughly the roles of the three elements of a movement, and allow the Spirit to use it to reach and disciple people in the most effective way possible.

Momentum: A Modern Example

Let's look at a present-day example of how a few Spirit-filled people, committed to and excited about a common goal, combined their enthusiasm and saw tremendous resulting momentum.

On a certain campus in the United States, Campus Crusade for Christ was not a movement but a social club. The atmosphere of the campus along with hostile and a radical philosophy had infiltrated the thinking of students. At the end of the year, a Leadership Training Institute was held. About 30 students came, but half were sent by a radical group to undercut the staff's efforts and to recruit for their own radical movement.

*J. Edwin Orr, *The Flaming Tongue*, Copyright © 1973, pp. 17,18: Moody Press, Chicago, Illinois.

So the Campus Crusade movement had a core of 12 students the next year. They began aggressively addressing students with the claims of Christ. After two or three months, they had a very small number of disciples. One afternoon, a large demonstration was held in the city park. The director got the 12 together, and within an hour they were passing out leaflets and waving signs declaring Jesus was the answer to people's problems. Scores of people flocked around the students. They were mocked and challenged, but the rally caused a marked increase in the new disciples' commitment, and their witness on campus increased.

When more disciples emerged, a Jesus March was held, with 200 participating in a torrential downpour. All of the placards were destroyed and the public address system did not work, but Christians had taken a stand. Through the media coverage of the rally, they saw that they could influence their city for Christ.

After the rally, students began taking on leadership in the movement. A Leadership Training Class was begun, and a retreat drew many students. Later, another LTI attracted close to 200 students. They learned how to disciple others, and prayer efforts were intensified.

The movement on campus continued to mushroom, and it soon spilled into the community. A lay movement began, and outreaches through businesses and local churches became regular occurrences. In this atmosphere, the Here's Life campaign began. A reservoir of disciples from years of discipling was available to train hundreds of laymen for the effort. When the campaign was over, thousands of people indicated a desire to learn more about knowing Christ as their personal Savior, and over 10,000 decisions for Christ were recorded. In one sense, the campaign will never finish, and there is an intense interest in that community toward the message of Christ even to this day.

Let's see how some of the elements of a spiritual movement were operating in this real life situation. The momentum was the result of activities sparked by people who were enthusiastic about a common goal and were willing to become actively involved. The momentum attracted new people who also became involved. These new people needed to be discipled, so rapid multiplication occurred.

Multiplication

However, momentum alone won't create multiplication. Multiplication in a movement is the continued expansion and reproduction of disciples who are producing other disciples. In the case study, multiplication began with only 12 students. More disciples emerged because of their enthusiastic action. A specially-designed curriculum made it possible for even new Christians to begin teaching others within a few weeks. As a result, 400 to 500 students were soon involved in small groups. Discovery groups began among employees in a factory and when Here's Life began, disciples trained hundreds of laymen. Obviously, this demonstrates that a movement expands only as fast as new leadership is developed.

Multiplication is not a new concept. In II Timothy 2:2, Paul tells Timothy to take the things he has heard from Paul and teach them to faithful men who will, in turn, teach others also. This is the familiar geometric progression of numbers. In other words, Paul's method of reaching the world was through the process of multiplying discipleship.

To see the significance of the multiplication method, we can contrast it with another approach. This second approach seems to be the way many Christians think the world will be reached. In it, the individual's actual objective is to reach the world of 4,500,000,000 people for Christ. He believes that the best way he can reach his objective is to speak to as many people as possible about the claims of Christ. He devises a plan by which he will speak to 1,000 different people a day, never taking a day off. At this rate, it will take him only 10,958 years to reach the world for Christ, assuming there is no population growth.

In contrast, this is what would happen with a multiplication process: An individual living in an average community shares Christ with his neighbors and friends until he finds three who want to develop in their faith and become multiplying disciples. After a year's time, these three each find three others into whom they can reproduce their lives. Now there are nine. In another year the number grows to 27 as each of those nine finds and builds three others. In 21 years, there would be 10,460,353,203 disciples.

Through the multiplication method, the world could be totally discipled (not just exposed to the gospel) in 20 years, starting with just one individual.

This example may be idealistic. God works uniquely in each individual's life, making it impossible to program reproduction into neat one-year segments. However, the example does point to a very important fact. If we want our lives to have a significant impact for God, we will want to be involved in multiplication. It is easy to see now why Paul's method of discipleship was multiplication.*

Management

The third and final element of a movement is management—planning, organizing, leading and controlling. It is essential for a movement to have an organized leader who will keep reins on the momentum and multiplication aspects of the movement. Otherwise, the movement will tend to sway in one direction or the other and eventually will dissolve. Also, without good management, the common goal could disappear, resulting in a divided group and a breakdown in unity. Another problem which may arise is the loss of enthusiasm. In a sense, management is the hub of the wheel that keeps a movement rolling.

Why Me?

Some people may ask, "Why should I be involved in a movement? I can build multiplying disciples on my own!" That's true. We can build disciples on our own, but we need to ask ourselves: How can we have the maximum impact on the world—through discipling people on our own, or through discipling in the context of a movement? It is obvious as we look at the effect that momentum has on multiplication that we can have the maximum impact as we disciple in the context of a movement. But there are other advantages of being involved in a movement.

*Doug Hartman and Doug Sutherland, *Guidebook to Discipleship*, Copyright © 1976, pp. 25-27: Harvest House Publishers, Irvine, California.

First, being involved in a movement helps expand our vision (Proverbs 29:18). There is a great deal of isolation among Christians, which often leaves them feeling like they are all alone in their convictions. Being part of a movement allows us to be encouraged by others who are committed to the same goal that we are. Like-minded people help us continue in the right direction even when we don't feel like it. In a movement, we know we are not alone. That helps us to stand firmly in our convictions.

A movement also gives credibility to our ministries, overall and individually. Take, for example, a team meeting—an evangelistic meeting in which the gospel is presented to people with whom we share a common interest. If you or I as an individual went to an organization president and asked to share Christ with his group, he very likely would say no. But if we went to him saying we were with Campus Crusade for Christ, which has presented thousands of programs like this, he would be very likely to say yes!

There are many Christians who want to share their faith in an evangelistic meeting or have a personal ministry, but they simply do not know how. So they either do it in a way that they are ineffective and become frustrated, or they don't try at all. Through a movement, they can receive constant training. If they are new, they learn to share their faith with others. Later, they are trained to lead a group, share their testimonies, speak to larger groups, etc.

Taking part in such things helps us to break faith barriers (Luke 10:3). As long as we're here on earth, our faith needs to grow. If we step out only in situations in which we feel confident, our faith will tend to stagnate. People who are involved in a movement seldom feel ready or qualified to do what they are asked to do. But when they stand up in front of 50 people to share their testimony, or ask a club president if they can speak to his group, or raise financial support, they break faith barriers and are then able to believe God for more.

Another advantage of being involved in a movement is constant exposure to godly leadership. We tend to become like those with whom we spend time and especially like those we admire. If we are not part of a movement, we generally won't be exposed to Christians who are more mature or visionary than ourselves.

Finally, a movement gives us many different kinds of exposure to ministry situations (Matthew 4:19). We can have opportunities to minister to a wide range of people outside our own sphere of influence.

To have the greatest impact on the world, we need to be involved in a spiritual movement that allows us to multiply our time, talents and resources most effectively. Associating with like-minded, highly-committed people will help us generate momentum that multiplies and produces a movement glorifying to God.

Division:
Discovery Group
Lesson Plans 1-6

1
Jesus — Worthy of
═══Our Trust═══

As the leader, you have two options for this first discipleship group, depending on whether you desire the first meeting to be an evangelistic Bible study or not.

USE OPTION ONE IF:

A.   You know that there are one or more non-Christians in the group.

B.   You are uncertain whether some members have received Christ.

C.   All are Christians, but you feel they would benefit from reviewing from Scripture how a person trusts Christ.

Note: A review of these scriptural principles could be of benefit to all Christians at any level of maturity. As you go through the study you may emphasize different sections of this study depending on the group's maturity. Parts of option one are included in option two.

USE OPTION TWO IF:

A.   You are sure that all the members have already received Christ and that they would benefit more from an extended time of getting acquainted with one another.

B.   There is only one non-Christian in the group who has already been through the Four Spiritual Laws booklet and who would benefit from the option two approach.

OPTION ONE

OVERVIEW GOAL

The goal of this lesson is to enable group members to understand the concept of faith, to see why they need to put their faith in Christ and to understand how they can express their faith to receive Him.

LEARNING OBJECTIVES

By the end of this lesson, group members will be able to:

1. Explain why Jesus is a trustworthy object for a person's faith.

2. Explain why a person needs to trust Christ as his Savior and Lord.

3. Pray, trusting Christ as their Savior and Lord, if they desire to do so.

Time/Section	Outline/Questions and Learning Activities
	OPTION ONE
5-10	**Sharing** Have group members briefly share their names, backgrounds, interests or present fields of endeavor. Ask them how they happened to come to the group and what they hope to gain from it. Distribute Discovery Group study guides to group members. Read through the Table of Contents in the study guide.
35-45	**Bible Study**

Motivation	A. STORY OF AN UNTRUSTWORTHY AIRPLANE
	
	   1. Is this a good illustration of sound faith? Why or why not?
	   2. Definition of sound faith
	
	     TRANSITION: "The trustworthy object of the Christian faith is Jesus Christ, but many people today have misconceptions about who He is. Let's begin to search the historical records found in Scripture and see if we can learn more about Jesus Christ, the object of our faith."

Observ./Interp.	B. JESUS, THE OBJECT OF BIBLICAL FAITH
John 10:30-33	1. What do you think Jesus meant by these words? 2. What did the Jews understand Jesus to say?
John 14:6-9	3. According to what Jesus told Thomas, how could men reach God? 4. What did Jesus tell Philip about Himself?
Mark 2:5-12	5. What was unique about what Jesus said? 6. How did He prove He had the authority to do what He said?

Time/Section	Outline/Questions and Learning Activities
	7. Jesus claimed to be God, and others recognized that He was making that claim. He also claimed to be the only way to God the Father, and He claimed to forgive sins as only God can.
Matthew 14:13-34	8. The miracles Jesus performed proved that He was God.

C. IS JESUS TRUSTWORTHY?

1. If His claims were false and He knew it, He was a liar.
2. If they were false and He didn't know it, He was a lunatic.
3. Do the character and teachings of Jesus Christ indicate that He was either a liar or a lunatic? Why or why not?
4. Jesus was who He claimed to be—God, the Savior of mankind, a trustworthy object of our faith.
5. The Trilemma: Jesus claimed to be God.

Observ./Interp.

D. WHY DO WE NEED JESUS?

Romans 3:23; 6:23

1. According to these verses, how would you describe man's dilemma?
2. What are some things that a person separated from God would be experiencing or not experiencing?

Romans 5:6-10

3. How does Paul describe a person before and after he becomes a Christian?
4. According to these verses, what are some things we can say about God's love for us?

I Peter 2:24;
II Corinthians 5:21

5. According to I Peter 2:24 and II Corinthians 5:21, what are some reasons that Christ died on the cross?

Ephesians 2:4-9

6. According to Ephesians 2:4-9, what is the only way we can be saved from the penalty of our sins?
7. Why can't a person be saved by works or self-effort?

Time/Section	Outline/Questions and Learning Activities
Application Ephesians 2:8,9	E. HOW CAN WE TRUST JESUS? 1. These verses say we are saved by grace through faith. What do you think it means to believe in Christ or to have faith in Him? 2. Revelation 3:20 3. Suggested prayer: 4. What do you think would happen if a person sincerely prayed this prayer? 5. How can you know that Christ is in your life, according to Revelation 3:20?
5	**Prayer** Close the session in prayer. Emphasize the trustworthiness of God's Word.
45-60	

Preparation

PERSONAL PERSPECTIVE

Set aside at least one half hour to become completely familiar with the entire Discovery Group leader's guide for this lesson. Answer all the questions in the study guide without referring to your leader's guide.

Note: "See also" references in the leader's guide are provided for additional scriptural resources for the leader.

Because of the probable immaturity of your group members, in Lessons 1-6 you will find some limiting and closed questions. Also, because you may have a less mature or a less committed group, the Practical Ministry times have been deleted in Lessons 1-4 and appear only in Lessons 5 and 6.

SUPPLIES

Study guides for your group members.

RESOURCES

The Four Spiritual Laws booklet
Transferable Concept 1, "How to Be Sure You Are a Christian"
Evidence That Demands a Verdict, by Josh McDowell

> "God is ready to do a great deal for you if you are
> willing to take Him at His Word."*
>   Donald Grey Barnhouse

Sharing
(5-10 Minutes)

Have group
members briefly
share their names,
backgrounds, inter-
ests or present
fields of endeavor.
Ask them how they
happened to come
to the group and
what they hope to
gain from it.

SAY:

Do not let this shar-
ing time run over or
you will not finish
this lesson in the
alloted time.

"Why don't we take a few minutes and share a little
bit about ourselves. Start by sharing your name
and where you are from. Include some information
about your background and personal interests as
well as your present school year or job.

"Why don't we each share how we happened to
come to this group meeting and what we hope to
gain from it."

Distribute Discov-
ery Group study
guides to group
members.

RELATE:

"In our times together, we will be using this study
guide, in which we'll record our own thoughts and
ideas. Let's look at the Table of Contents to get a
brief idea of the topics we will be covering."

Read through the
Table of Contents.

SAY:

"Now turn to the first lesson. You will probably
want to take notes during the meeting on the blank
lines provided after each question."

*Donald Grey Barnhouse, *Let Me Illustrate,* Copyright © 1967, p. 106: Used
by permission of Revell Publishers, Old Tappen, New Jersey.

Bible Study
(35-45 Minutes)

Open the Bible
study in a brief
prayer, asking God
to teach the group.

Motivation   (2)

A. STORY OF AN UNTRUSTWORTHY
AIRPLANE

READ:

Suppose that as you looked at this plane, the
flight attendant smiled and said, "Would you
climb aboard, please?"

When you hesitated, she said, "Oh, don't
worry. Just have faith and we'll get there all
right."

DISCUSSION:

Direct the group in
a discussion of the
questions. Share
the suggested
answers only if
necessary. Sum-
marize the group's
answers after dis-
cussing each ques-
tion, and encour-
age group
members to write
the conclusions in
their study guides.

1. Is this a good illustration of sound faith?
Why or why not?

No. Because it would be foolish to board
the kind of aircraft pictured here. This is
stupidity, not faith.
_____
_____

SAY:

"Let's consider what sound faith is."

READ:

2. Definition of sound faith.

Have the students (3)
fill in the blanks.

Sound faith means putting your trust in a *trustworthy object*. If the object of my faith is not trustworthy, then I would be foolish to commit myself to it or trust in it.

TRANSITION:

"The trustworthy object of the Christian faith is Jesus Christ, but many people today have misconceptions about who He is. Let's begin to search the historical records found in Scripture and see if we can learn more about Jesus Christ, the object of our faith.

Observ./Interp.

Direct group members to look up the Scriptures. You may need to assist them. Ask someone to read the passages as you come to them.

Discuss the following questions. Follow the same procedure as before.

JOHN 10:30-33
B. JESUS, THE OBJECT OF BIBLICAL FAITH
   1. What do you think Jesus meant by these words?

   He said that He was one with the Father— that He was God.

2. What did the Jews understand Jesus to say?

That He was God.

JOHN 14:6-9
3. According to what Jesus told Thomas, how could men reach God?

Jesus claimed to be the only way to the Father.

4. What did Jesus tell Philip about Himself?

That seeing Him was seeing God.

MARK 2:5-12
5. What was unique about what Jesus said?

He said He could forgive sins.

6. How did He prove He had the authority to do what He said?

He healed the paralyzed man.

RELATE:

"The Jews understood that only God could forgive sins. Therefore, they understood Jesus was claiming to be God.

"Before we go any further, let's summarize what we have discovered so far about Jesus."

READ:

7. Jesus claimed to be God, and others recognized that he was making that claim. He also claimed to be the only way to God the Father, and He claimed to forgive sins as only God can.

Have the passage read.

> MATTHEW 14:13-34
> 8. The miracles Jesus performed proved that He was God.

SAY:

"Matthew 14 explains that Jesus fed 5,000 people with a few loaves of bread and two fish. He also walked on the water. His bodily resurrection in Matthew 28 and many other miracles all point to the fact that Jesus was more than a man. He was God Himself."

READ: (4)

C. IS JESUS TRUSTWORTHY?

1. If Jesus Christ said the things we have just read, but His claims were false and He knew it, it would mean that he was a liar.

2. If Jesus Christ said the things we have just read, but His claims were false and He thought they were true, it would mean He really believed that He was God. Therefore, He would be insane or a lunatic.

Discuss study question 3. Share the suggested answers if necessary.

3. Do the character and teachings of Jesus Christ indicate that He was:

a. A liar? (Why or why not?) A liar would not have love and concern for others as his primary motivation in life. The ego of a liar would cause him to use and abuse others, not to help them. Only a fool would die for a lie.

b. A lunatic? (Why or why not?) An insane man would not have demonstrated the same quality of teaching that Jesus did. Could an insane man have delivered the Sermon on the Mount or the parables? Conclusion: Jesus was neither a liar nor a lunatic.

READS:

> 4. On the other hand, if His claims were true, we can conclude that Jesus was who He claimed to be—God, the Savior of mankind, a trustworthy object of our faith.
>
>

SAY: "Point 5 has been provided to help us picture what we have just considered."

READ: (5)

> 5. The Trilemma: Jesus claimed to be God.
>
> Two Alternatives
>
> His claims were FALSE.　　　His claims were TRUE.
>
> Two Alternatives　　　　　　He is Lord.
>
> He knew　　He did　　　　　Two Alternatives
> His claims　not know
> were FALSE. His claims　　You can　You can
> 　　　　　　were FALSE.　ACCEPT. REJECT.
>
> He made a　He was sin-
> deliberate　cerely de-
> misrepre-　luded.
> sentation.
>
> He was a　He was a
> LIAR.　　　LUNATIC.

RELATE:

"Look at the chart you have in your workbooks. Jesus claimed to be God. He did not leave us with any other options concerning His claim."

The following is taken from Josh McDowell's explanation of the trilemma. Thoroughly familiarize yourself with it and explain it to the group in your own words.

"First, consider that His claim was false. If it was false, then we have two, and only two, alternatives. He either knew His claim was false or He did not know it was false. If, when Jesus made His claims He knew that He was not God, then He was lying. But if He was a liar, then He was also a hypocrite, because He told others to be honest whatever the cost, while He Himself was living a lie.

And more than that, He was a demon, because He told others to trust Him for their eternal destinies. If He could not back up His claims and knew it, then He was unspeakably evil.

Finally, He would also be a fool because it was His claim of being God that led to His crucifixion.

Someone who lived as Jesus lived, taught as Jesus taught and died as Jesus died could not have been a liar. What other alternatives are there?

If it is inconceivable that Jesus was a liar, then could He not actually have thought Himself to be God, but been mistaken? After all, it is possible to be both sincere and wrong.

But we must remember that someone who thinks He is God, especially in a culture that is fiercely monotheistic, and then tells others that their eternal destinies depend upon their believing in Him, is indulging in no slight fantasy. These would be the thoughts of a lunatic in the fullest sense."*

RELATE:

"If His claims were true, He is Lord and God and there are only two options available to us. One, we can accept Him as Savior and Lord; or two, we can reject Him and suffer the consequences of our decision.

"From the evidence we have seen, it is reasonable to believe that Jesus is God. If He is God, let's consider why we need Him."

*Josh McDowell, *Evidence That Demands a Verdict*, Copyright © 1972, p. 108: Used by permission of Campus Crusade for Christ, Inc., Arrowhead Springs, California.

Leader's Guide

Observ./Interp.

Ask a member to
read the Scriptures
from his study
guide.

Discuss study
questions. Share
the suggested
answers if
necessary.

(6)

ROMANS 3:23; 6:23
D. WHY DO WE NEED JESUS?

1. "For all have sinned and fall short of the
glory of God" (Romans 3:23).

"For the wages of sin is death, but the free
gift of God is eternal life in Christ Jesus
our Lord" (Romans 6:23).

According to these verses, how would you
describe man's dilemma?

All men have sinned and fall short of
God's perfect standard. The wages or
payment for man's sin is death.

2. "Death" in Romans 6:23 refers not only to
physical death, but also to spiritual death,
which involves separation from God and
from the life He offers.

What are some things that a person
separated from God would be experiencing or not experiencing?

He would experience guilt because of his
sins and loneliness because of his separation from God. He would not be able to
experience God's best in life because he
has no relationship with God. He would
not be able to enjoy life to the fullest.

Clarifying
Questions:
See also John
10:10b

Ask a group
member to read the
Scripture.

2a. What would life be like for the person
who is separated from God?
2b. What kind of life does Christ offer?

ROMANS 5:6-10
3. How does Paul describe a person before
and after he becomes a Christian?

Before: helpless, ungodly, sinful, subject to God's wrath and an enemy of God.

After: Justified, saved from the wrath of God, reconciled to God and saved by Christ's life.

READ THE DEFINITIONS:

Ask the group to fill in the blanks.

Continue to discuss.

Justified means to be declared not guilty for our sins. *Reconciled* means to be made a friend after being an enemy. *Saved* means to be rescued from death and God's wrath, which is the penalty for our sins.

4. According to these verses, what are some things we can say about God's love for us?

He demonstrated His love by having Christ die for us so that we can be justified (declared righteous) and reconciled to Him. He loved us even when we didn't deserve it.

Continue to ask group members to read the Scriptures as you come to them.

5. "And He Himself bore our sins in His body on the cross, that we might die to sin and live to righteousness; for by His wounds you were healed" (I Peter 2:24).

"He made Him who knew no sin to be sin on our behalf, that we might become the righteousness of God in Him" (II Corinthians 5:21).

(7)

What are some reasons that Christ died on the cross, according to these verses?

Christ died in our place as a substitute to pay the penalty for our sins. On the cross He bore the penalty for our sins and He became the object of God's righteous judgment on sin. His death made it possible for God to righteously free us from the penalty of sin when we trust Christ to forgive our sins.

Clarifying
Questions:

5a. What are some other things that you see?

5b. Why do you think it was necessary for Christ to die?

EPHESIANS 2:4-9

6. According to this passage, what is the only way we can be saved from the penalty of our sins?

By grace through faith in Christ, not by works. "Grace" means that God loves us even when we do not deserve it.

Clarifying
Questions:

6a. Can anybody be good enough to save himself? Why or why not?

6b. What does Ephesians 2:8,9 mean in your own words?

---

7. Why can't a person be saved by works or self-effort?

Because a righteous judge must penalize those who break the law. We have all sinned (Romans 3:23). Therefore, we are accountable before God.

SAY:

"Let's now consider how we can place our faith or trust in Christ."

Application

> EPHESIANS 2:8,9
> E.   HOW CAN WE TRUST JESUS?
>
> 1.   These verses say that we are saved by grace through faith. What do you think it means to believe in Christ or to have faith in Him?
>
> To trust and rely on Jesus as the only means for forgiveness of sin; to believe He is all that He claimed to be--that He is God, raised from the grave and alive today, able to come into your life and forgive your sins.

SAY:

"You might ask yourself, could a person truly believe in Christ without trusting in His promises?

"Let's look at a promise that Jesus made to everyone who has not yet trusted Him."

READ: (8)

> 2.   "Behold, I stand at the door and knock; if any one hears my voice and opens the door, I will come into him" (Revelation 3:20).
>
> Our part is to believe Him and open the doors of our lives.
>
> Christ's promise is that He will come in if we invite Him in.
>
> We receive Christ's forgiveness of our sins through faith, as an act of our wills.
>
> We must choose to accept or reject His offer.

SAY:

"We have seen in Ephesians 2:8,9 that we are saved by grace through faith. Prayer is one way of expressing faith. I'd like to share with you a prayer that many people have used to express their faith in Jesus."

READ:

3. Suggested prayer:

    "Lord Jesus, I need you. Thank you for dying on the cross for my sins. I open the door of my life and receive You as my Savior and Lord. Thank You for forgiving my sins and giving me eternal life. Take control of the throne of my life. Make me the kind of person You want me to be."

4. What do you think would happen if a person sincerely prayed this prayer?

    Christ would come into that person's life as He promised and forgive all his sins.

GIVE THE GROUP MEMBERS AN OPPORTUNITY TO RECEIVE CHRIST BY RELATING:

Be positive, this is the greatest thing that could happen to them!

Read suggested prayer slowly, phrase by phrase, allowing them time to pray silently. Refer back to Point 3.

"Some of you may never have had the opportunity to place your faith in Christ by asking Him to come into your life. Some of you may not be certain Christ is in your life. I'd like to pause right now and give you that opportunity to receive Christ as your Savior and Lord. Simply pray silently with me as I read the prayer out loud. Remember prayer is just a way of expressing faith."

RELATE:

"Some of you may have prayed just now and asked Christ into your life. Let's answer the final question to see how you can be sure that Christ is now in your life."

ASK:

> 5.   How can you know that Christ is in your
>   life, according to Revelation 3:20?
>
>   He promised that if I opened my heart He
>   would come in. By the trustworthiness of
>   His Word.
>   _____
>   _____

SAY:

"Next week we will be looking at how God totally
forgives us and accepts us when we receive
Christ."

Prayer
(5 Minutes)

Close the lesson in
prayer. Emphasize
the trustworthiness
of God's Word.

Arrange the time
and place of the
next meeting.

DISCIPLESHIP HINTS FOR THE LEADER

Remember, this is your initial meeting. What you do to cultivate a personal
relationship with each of your group members before your next meeting is
crucial to the success of your group. Here are some suggestions:

1.   Attempt to meet or call each group member individually for informal
     fellowship.

2.   If group members have special needs, give them appropriate books or
     booklets or seek counsel from a mature Christian friend on how to help
     them.

3.   Introduce your group members to Christian fellowship in a good church
     and other places where they can observe and learn from Christians.

In many countries in Asia and Latin America, group leaders invite their
members to spend one night a week with them. During the night they sing,

pray, study the Word and fellowship together. Dr. Joon Gon Kim, the national director of Campus Crusade in Korea, has proven the validity of his statement, "If I can spend 100 hours with new Christians after they have been spiritually born, they will become disciples." The principle behind Dr. Kim's statement is this: attempt to surround new Christians with fellowship and teaching from the Word of God.

In a ministry with students, spending one evening per week with your disciples will pay high dividends.

In a ministry with laymen, a monthly or bimonthly overnight fellowship will accomplish more than many one-hour meetings.

OPTION TWO

OVERVIEW GOAL

The goal of this lesson is to enable the group members to understand the concept of faith, to trust Christ with their daily needs and to motivate them toward continued participation in the discovery group.

LEARNING OBJECTIVES

By the end of this lesson, group members will be able to:

1. Explain why Jesus is worthy of their trust.

2. Express ways in which they desire to trust Christ with their needs.

3. Understand what is included in the overall content of future discovery group lessons.

4. Make a commitment to attend the other five discovery group meetings.

Time/Section	Outline/Questions and Learning Activities
	OPTION TWO
15-20	## Sharing
	Spend a lengthy amount of time getting acquainted by having group members share about themselves in some depth. Ask questions which stimulate open communication. Distribute Discovery Group study guides to group members.
25-30	## Bible Study
Motivation	A. STORY OF AN UNTRUSTWORTHY AIRPLANE
	1. Is this a good illustration of sound faith? Why or why not?
	2. Definition of sound faith.
	TRANSITION: "The trustworthy object of the Christian faith is Jesus Christ, but many people today have misconceptions about who He is. Let's begin to search the historical records found in Scripture and see if we can learn more about Jesus Christ, the object of our faith."
Observ./Interp.	B. JESUS, THE OBJECT OF BIBLICAL FAITH
John 10:30-33	1. What do you think Jesus meant by these words?
	2. What did the Jews understand Jesus to say?
John 14:6-9	3. According to what Jesus told Thomas, how could men reach God?
	4. What did Jesus tell Philip about Himself?
Mark 2:5-12	5. What was unique about what Jesus said?
	6. How did He prove He had the authority to do what He said?
	7. Jesus claimed to be God, and others recognized that He was making that claim.

Time/Section	Outline/Questions and Learning Activities
Matthew 14:13-34	He also claimed to be the only way to God the Father, and He claimed to forgive sins as only God can. 8. The miracles Jesus performed proved that He was God. C. IS JESUS TRUSTWORTHY? 1. If His claims were false and He knew it, He was a liar. 2. If they were false and He didn't know it, He was a lunatic. 3. Do the character and teachings of Jesus Christ indicate that He was either a liar or a lunatic? Why or why not? 4. Jesus was who He claimed to be—God, the Savior of mankind, a trustworthy object of our faith. 5. The Trilemma: Jesus claimed to be God. D. HOW CAN WE TRUST CHRIST WITH OUR DAILY LIVES?
I Peter 5:6,7; Philippians 4:6,7 **Application**	1. What are some characteristics of the person who trusts Christ in his life? 2. According to I Peter 5:6,7 and Philippians 4:6,7, what are some ways a person can trust Christ in his daily life? 3. What are some problems or needs in your life that you would like to entrust to Christ? TRANSITION: "Now that we've begun to see how Jesus can change our lives, we will discover in the next few weeks how He can make our lives significantly different. I would like to overview the next five lessons so that you will know what we will be covering in the coming weeks."

Time/Section	Outline/Questions and Learning Activities
	E. OVERVIEW OF LESSONS 2-6
	1. Lesson 2, "Our New Relationship With God." Why is it important to know that God totally forgives us of all our sins?
Galatians 5:22,23	2. Lesson 3, "Living in the Power of the Spirit." Galatians 5:22,23 describe a person who relies on the power of the Holy Spirit to live the Christian life. Which of these qualities do you feel are most needed among Christians today? Why?
	3. Lesson 4, "Walking With Christ."
Romans 10:13-15	4. Lesson 5, "Becoming People of Action." According to Romans 10:13-15, why is it important that Christians share their faith?
	5. Lesson 6, "Sharing Christ with Others."
	6. Do these topics sound like things you would like to study? Why?
5-10	**Prayer**
	Close the lesson in prayer. Emphasize the trustworthiness of Christ and express anticipation toward the coming weeks.
45-60	

Preparation

PERSONAL PERSPECTIVE

Set aside time to become completely familiar with the leader's guide for option two. Notice that option two uses only the first half of the group member's study guide. That is because the last half of the study guide is evangelistic in nature and will not be used in this option. The first parts of options one and two are the same because both young and mature Christians will benefit from seeing that Jesus Christ is worthy of their trust. Note, however, that the questions for the last half of option two are written in your leader's guide, but are not included in your group members' study guides.

A full explanation of how to lead option two is written into this lesson. The lesson has a special focus on how to trust Christ with our daily needs and includes a motivational overview of the coming weeks. You will need to consult the "Discipleship Hints" at the end of option one and implement these ideas in your contact with your group members.

Note: "See also" references in the leader's guide are provided as additional scriptural resources for the leader.

Because of the probable immaturity of your group members, in Lessons 1-6 you will find some limiting and closed questions. Also, because you may have a less mature or a less committed group, the Practical Ministry times have been deleted in Lessons 1-4 and appear only in Lessons 5 and 6.

SUPPLIES

Study guides for your group members.

RESOURCES

Evidence That Demands a Verdict, by Josh McDowell

> "God is ready to do a great deal for you if you are willing to take Him at His Word."*
>
> Donald Grey Barnhouse

Sharing
(15-20 Minutes)

SAY:

"I imagine that all of you are here for a variety of reasons. Some of you came because I invited you. Some came out of curiosity. Regardless of your reason for coming, I know that you are going to find this time very profitable. We will have the excitement of seeing our lives influenced by Jesus Christ.

"Let's spend a few minutes getting to know each other."

Unless all of your group members already know each other, ask them to give their names and their major fields of study or occupations. Ask them how they happened to come to the group. The following questions will be helpful in finding out the background of each group member. Choose one or more of the following questions to ask the group.

How would you describe your relationship with your parents?

Who was your favorite childhood friend and why?

How would you describe your current attitude toward religion or spiritual things?

When did God become more than just a name to you?

*Donald Grey Barnhouse, *Let Me Illustrate*, Copyright © 1967, p. 106: Used by permission of Revell Publishers, Old Tappan, New Jersey.

RELATE:

"In the course of this study, I'm sure we'll think of and answer many questions about the Christian faith. Yet one of the greatest challenges facing Christians today is that of learning how to communicate their faith to others. Therefore, our purpose in going through these studies is not only to learn many new things ourselves, but also to learn how to communicate these truths to others."

Distribute the study guides.

RELATE:

"In our times together, we will be using this study guide in which we'll record our own thoughts and ideas. Let's look at the Table of Contents to get a brief idea of the topics we will be covering."

Read through the Table of Contents.

SAY:

"Let's begin by looking at the first lesson entitled, 'Jesus—Worthy of Our Trust.'"

Bible Study
(25-30 Minutes)

Open the Bible study in a brief prayer, asking God to teach the group.

Motivation

A. STORY OF AN UNTRUSTWORTHY AIRPLANE

READ:

Suppose that as you look at this plane, the flight attendant smiled and said, "Would you climb aboard, please?"

When you hesitated, she said, "Oh, don't worry. Just have faith, and we'll get there all right."

DISCUSSION:

Direct the group in a discussion of the questions. Share the suggested answers only if necessary. Summarize the group's answers after discussing each question, and encourage group members to write the conclusions in their study guides.

1. Is this a good illustration of sound faith? Why or why not?

   No. Because it would be foolish to board the kind of aircraft pictured here. This is stupidity, not faith.

SAY:

"Let's consider what sound faith is."

READ:

Have the students fill in the blanks.

2. Definition of sound faith

Sound faith means putting your trust in a *trustworthy object*. If the object of my faith is not trustworthy, then I would be foolish to commit myself to it or trust it.

TRANSITION:

"The trustworthy object of the Christian faith is Jesus Christ, but many people today have misconceptions about who He is. Let's begin to search the historical records found in Scripture and see if we can learn more about Jesus Christ, the object of our faith."

Observ./Interp.

Direct group
members to look
up the Scriptures.
Be sensitive if any
individuals need
assistance in locat-
ing the passage.
Ask someone to
read the verses as
you come to them.

Discuss the follow-
ing questions.
Follow the same
procedure as
before.

JOHN 10:30-33
B. JESUS, THE OBJECT OF BIBLICAL FAITH

1. What do you think Jesus meant by these
    words?

    He said that He was one with the Father--
    that He was God.
    _____
    _____

2. What did the Jews understand Jesus to
    say?

    That He was God.
    _____
    _____

JOHN 14:6-9
3. According to what Jesus told Thomas,
    how could men reach God?

    Jesus claimed to be the only way to the
    Father.
    _____
    _____

4. What did Jesus tell Philip about Himself?

    That seeing Him was seeing God.
    _____
    _____

MARK 2:5-12
5. What was unique about what Jesus said?

    He said He could forgive sins.
    _____
    _____

6. How did He prove He had the authority to
    do what He said?

    He healed the paralyzed man.
    _____
    _____

RELATE:

"The Jews understood that only God could forgive
sins. Therefore, they understood Jesus was claiming to be God.

"Before we go any further, let's summarize what we have discovered so far about Jesus."

READ:

> 7. Jesus claimed to be God, and others recognized that He was making that claim. He also claimed to be the only way to God the Father, and He claimed to forgive sins as only God can.
>
> Matthew 14:13-34
> 8. The miracles Jesus performed proved that He was God.

Have the passage read.

RELATE:

"Matthew 14 explains that Jesus fed 5,000 people with a few loaves of bread and two fish. He also walked on the water. His bodily resurrection in Matthew 28 and many other miracles all point to the fact that Jesus was more than a man. He was God Himself."

READ:

> C. IS JESUS TRUSTWORTHY?
>
> 1. If Jesus Christ said the things we have just read, but His claims were false and He knew it, it would mean that He was a liar.
>
> 2. If Jesus Christ said the things we have just read, but His claims were false and He thought they were true, it would mean He really believed that He was God. Therefore, He would be insane or a lunatic.
>
> 3. Do the character and teachings of Jesus Christ indicate that He was:
>
> a. A liar? (Why or why not?) A liar would not have love and concern for others as his primary motivation in life. The ego of a liar would cause him to use and abuse others, not to help them. Only a fool would die for a lie.
>
> b. A lunatic? (Why or why not?) An insane man would not have demonstrated the same quality of teaching that Jesus did. Could an insane man

Discuss study question 3. Share the suggested answers if necessary.

have delivered the Sermon on the
Mount or the parables? Conclusion:
Jesus was neither a liar nor a lunatic.

READ:

4. On the other hand, if His claims were true,
we can conclude that Jesus was who He
claimed to be—God, the Savior of mankind, a trustworthy object of our faith.

SAY:

"Point 5 has been provided to help us picture what
we have just considered."

READ:

5. The Trilemma: Jesus claimed to be God.

Two Alternatives

His claims were FALSE.   His claims were TRUE.

Two Alternatives   He is Lord.

He knew   He did   Two Alternatives
His claims   not know
were FALSE.   His claims   You can   You can
                 were FALSE.   ACCEPT.   REJECT.

He made a   He was sin-
deliberate   cerely de-
misrepre-   luded.
sentation.

He was a   He was a
LIAR.   LUNATIC.

Leader's Guide

RELATE:

"Look at the chart you have in your workbooks. Jesus claimed to be God. He did not leave us with any other options concerning His claim."

The following is taken from Josh McDowell's explanation of the tri-lemma. Thoroughly familiarize yourself with it and explain it to the group in your own words.

"First, consider that His claim was false. If it was false, then we have two, and only two, alternatives. He either knew His claim was false or He did not know it was false. If, when Jesus made His claims He knew that He was not God, then He was lying. But if He was a liar, then He was also a hypocrite, because He told others to be honest whatever the cost, while He Himself was living a lie.

And more than that, He was a demon, because He told others to trust Him for their eternal destinies. If He could not back up His claims and knew it, then He was unspeakably evil.

Finally, He would also be a fool because it was His claim of being God that led to His crucifixion.

Someone who lived as Jesus lived, taught as Jesus taught and died as Jesus died could not have been a liar. What other alternatives are there?

If it is inconceivable that Jesus was a liar, then could He not actually have thought Himself to be God, but been mistaken? After all, it is possible to be both sincere and wrong.

But we must remember that someone who thinks He is God, especially in a culture that is fiercely monotheistic, and then tells others that their eternal destinies depend upon their believing in Him, is indulging in no slight fantasy. These would be the thoughts of a lunatic in the fullest sense."*

RELATE:

"If His claims were true, He is Lord and God and there are only two options available to us. One, we can accept Him as Savior and Lord; or two, we can reject Him and suffer the consequences of our decision.

*Josh McDowell, *Evidence That Demands a Verdict*, Copyright © 1972, p. 108: Used by permission of Campus Crusade for Christ, Inc., Arrowhead Springs, California.

"From the evidence we have seen, it is reasonable to believe that Jesus is a trustworthy object of our faith. The rest of this lesson is designed to help individuals trust Christ as Savior and Lord if they have not done so. Since we have all done so, I would like for us to consider how we can trust Christ with our daily needs."

NOTE TO LEADER: The study guides do not contain the rest of option two as you have it here. Note the absence of boxes on these pages. The outline is provided for the leader's benefit.

SAY:

"We will not need to refer to our study guides during the remainder of our time."

D. HOW CAN WE TRUST CHRIST WITH OUR DAILY LIVES?

Discuss these questions. Follow the same procedure as before.

1. What are some characteristics of the person who trusts Christ in his life?

   Peace, joy, confidence in life, boldness, patience, thankful prayer life.

2. According to I Peter 5:6,7 and Philippians 4:6,7, what are some ways a person can trust Christ in his daily life.

   He can cast all his cares upon God, humble himself before God and trust that God will exalt him at the proper time. He can pray about everything and not be anxious, but thank God in advance for His provision. (For example, he can trust Christ to meet his financial needs and to provide for his family. He can trust God with his

job—that God will promote him in His tim-
ing, etc.)

Application

Group members
may or may not be
willing to share. Be
sensitive. You
might say that it's
alright if they do
not wish to respond
verbally, but they
should answer the
questions within
themselves.

3. What are some problems or needs in your
life that you would like to entrust to
Christ?

School, friends, job, future, girlfriend/boy-
friend, marital problems, finances, etc.

RELATE:

"Before we continue, I would like for us to stop
and spend a few minutes in silent prayer. During
this time, you can tell God that you want to trust
Him with these areas of your life. I'll close our
prayer time in two or three minutes."

TRANSITION:

"Now that we've begun to see how Jesus can
change our lives, we will discover in the next few
weeks how He can make our lives significantly different. I would like to overview the next five lessons so that you will know what we will be covering in the coming weeks."

Instruct group
members to turn to
the Table of Con-
tents in the front of
their study guides.

E. OVERVIEW OF LESSONS 2-6

1. Lesson 2, "Our New Relationship With
God."

Lesson 2 explains how we can know that
God loves us and totally forgives us. Why
is it important to know that God totally
forgives us of all our sin?

If we do not realize that he loves and
accepts us, we will always be feeling
unnecessary guilt and fear.

Ask someone to
read Galatians
5:22,23

See also
Ephesians 5:18

ASK:

2. Lesson 3, "Living in the Power of the Spirit."

   Lesson 3 explains how to experience your new lifestyle as a Christian. Galatians 5:22,23 describe a person who relies on the power of the Holy Spirit to live the Christian life. Which of these qualities do you feel are most needed among Christians today? Why?

   _____

   _____

3. Lesson 4, "Walking With Christ."

   Lesson 4 continues our study of how to walk moment-by-moment with Christ, experiencing His power to live the Christian life.

Ask a group
member to read
Romans 10:13-15

4. Lesson 5, "Becoming People of Action."

   Lesson 5 begins an exciting study of how to share the message of Christ with others. We will spend some time learning how to use the Four Spiritual Laws booklet. According to Romans 10:13-15, why is it important that Christians share their faith?

   Because if people do not hear the gospel
   they will not believe; and if Christians do
   not share their faith, people will not hear.

   _____

   _____

5. Lesson 6, "Sharing Christ With Others."

   Lesson 6 continues our study on becoming people of action.

ASK:

6. Do these topics sound like things you would like to study? Why?

   _____

   _____

   _____

SAY:

"I really look forward to getting to know each of you better during the next few weeks and I'm really excited about what I know God is going to do in each of our lives as we continue to meet together and study these topics."

Prayer
(5-10 Minutes)

Close the lesson in prayer. Emphasize the trustworthiness of Christ and express your anticipation toward the coming weeks.

Arrange the time and place for the next meeting.

DISCIPLESHIP HINTS FOR THE LEADER

Remember, this is your initial meeting. What you do to cultivate a personal relationship with each of your group members before your next meeting is crucial to the success of your group. Here are some suggestions:

1. Attempt to meet or call each group member individually for informal fellowship.

2. If group members have special needs, give them appropriate books or booklets or seek counsel from a mature Christian friend on how to help them.

3. Introduce your group members to Christian fellowship in a good church and other places where they can observe and learn from Christians.

In many countries in Asia and Latin America, group leaders invite their members to spend one night a week with them. During the night they sing, pray, study the Word and fellowship together. Dr. Joon Gon Kim, the national director of Campus Crusade in Korea, has proven the validity of his statement, "If I can spend 100 hours with new Christians after they have been spiritually born, they will become disciples." The principle behind Dr. Kim's statement is this: attempt to surround new Christians with fellowship and teaching from the Word of God.

In a ministry with students, spending one evening per week with your disciples will pay high dividends.

In a ministry with laymen, a monthly or bimonthly overnight fellowship will accomplish more than many one hour meetings.

2
Our New Relationship
══With God══

OVERVIEW GOAL

The goal of this lesson is to enable group members to be secure in their relationships with God, knowing that they have eternal life and that all their sins are forgiven.

LEARNING OBJECTIVES

By the end of this lesson, group members will be able to:

1. Explain how they know Christ is in their lives.

2. Explain how they know all their sins are forgiven.

3. State how they can be sure they have eternal life.

4. Explain how they know God will not deal with them in anger when they sin.

Time/Section	Outline/Questions and Learning Activities
10	## Sharing Have group members reintroduce themselves. Lead the group in sharing about the previous week.
45	## Bible Study
Motivation	A. STORY OF A DOUBTFUL BELIEVER 1. What do you think was the root cause of this man's poor relationship with God? 2. How do you think God was feeling as He saw this man's faith become weaker and weaker? TRANSITION: "Many people are not experiencing the abundant Christian life because they have failed to take God at His Word. Some are not confident in their relationship with God because they do not realize that their relationship with God is founded and built upon the promises of God. First, let's consider how a person can be confident that Christ is in his life."
Observ./Interp. Hebrews 11:6; Jeremiah 29:11-13; Revelation 3:20 **Application**	B. OUR NEW RELATIONSHIP WITH GOD IS BUILT ON FAITH 1. What are some things that you see about faith in Hebrews 11:6? 2. What are some things that the doubtful man in our story failed to understand about these truths in Hebrews 11:6 and Jeremiah 29:11-13? 3. According to Revelation 3:20, how can a person express faith? 4. Suppose we sincerely expressed our faith in Christ and asked Him to forgive our sins and to come into our lives. How can we be confident that Christ did forgive us and that He did come into our lives?

Time/Section	Outline/Questions and Learning Activities
	TRANSITION: "In order for us to fully enjoy and benefit from our relationship with God, we must also understand that we are totally forgiven for our sins. Otherwise, we will continue to experience unnecessary guilt over our past sins. Let's look at some verses that talk about what God has done with our sins."
Observ./Interp.	C. OUR RELATIONSHIP WITH GOD IS ONE OF TOTAL FORGIVENESS
Colossians 2:13,14	1. According to these verses, what are some things God has done with our sins?
Application	2. How many of your sins were future when Christ died on the cross?
	TRANSITION: "Since all our sins are forgiven, we do not have to live in fear of God. Remember our story of the doubtful believer? He ended up living in fear of what God would do to him when he sinned. Let's look at some verses that explain that our new relationship with God is a relationship of peace."
Observ./Interp.	D. OUR RELATIONSHIP WITH GOD IS A RELA-TIONSHIP OF PEACE
Romans 5:1,2,8-11	1. How does the Word of God describe us in these verses? 2. What are some things you see in verses 8-11 that describe our past, present and future relationship with God?
Application	3. Suppose you were talking with a friend who lived in fear of God's wrath and punishment and was constantly feeling guilty about his sins. From what we've discussed thus far in our study, what are some things you would tell your friend? 4. Suppose that after you explained the grace and love of Christ to your friend, he said, "Oh great! That means I can sin whenever I want, since God will forgive me." What are some things you would tell your friend? Read Hebrews 12:5-11 and I John 2:4 to help you answer.

121

Time/Section	Outline/Questions and Learning Activities
	TRANSITION: "Now that we understand that God totally loves us and forgives our sins, let's look at some verses that explain how a person can know that he has eternal life."
Observ./Interp.	E. OUR RELATIONSHIP WITH GOD IS ETERNAL
I John 5:11-13	1. What are some things that these verses say about eternal life?
Application	2. How then do you know that you have eternal life?
5	**Prayer**
_____ 60	Thank God for this new relationship that we have.

Preparation

PERSONAL PERSPECTIVE

This lesson is designed to help any believer understand that God accepts him and has given him eternal life. Justification is explained in a simple manner; however, do not get bogged down with justification. The heart of the matter is that God applies the righteousness of Christ to us when we place our faith in Christ. If you do not understand this concept, be sure to go to a more mature Christian and get him to explain it or refer to the resource books suggested below.

Be sure that you fully understand the answers to each question and know how to use the clarifying questions if necessary.

Note: You will find the directions—"See also: (verse or verses)"—throughout the leader's direction column. These are provided as an extra resource for the leader to aid in study and preparation. They are to be introduced into the actual lesson if you desire.

RESOURCES

Five Steps of Christian Growth
Transferable Concept 1, "How to Be Sure You Are a Christian"
Unger's Bible Handbook

> The most important thing in life is to know that God has forgiven us and accepts us.

Sharing
(10 Minutes)

Have group members reintroduce themselves and meet newcomers.

ASK: "How was your week? Would anyone like to share something that you think would encourage the rest of us?"

Bible Study
(45 Minutes)

Open the Bible study in a brief prayer, asking God to teach the group.

Motivation

RELATE: "Let's consider a story that describes many Christians today."

READ: (10)

A. STORY OF A DOUBTFUL BELIEVER

There once was a man whose life had been characterized by many years of gross sin and rebellion against God. After becoming a Christian, he experienced many "highs," as well as many "lows." He would often feel deep guilt as his mind reflected on his past. Many times, he would wonder if Christ had really come into his life. Doubts would multiply and he would say, "Maybe I'm not forgiven. Do I really have eternal life?" Gradually he stopped all attempts to develop his relationship with God. He became convinced in his own mind that only special people were meant to enjoy the abundant life that Christ offers. This man ended up living in fear of what God would do to him when he sinned.

RELATE:

"This story describes too many Christians today."

DISCUSSION:

Direct the group in a discussion of the questions. Share the suggested answers only if necessary. Summarize the group's answers after discussing each question, and encourage group members to write the conclusions in their study guides.

Clarifying Questions:

1. What do you think was the root cause of this man's poor relationship with God?

   The root of his problem was that he never was confident that Christ had come into his life and forgiven his sins. That doubt undermined his motivation and confidence to build a relationship with God.

1a. What do some of the rest of you think?
1b. What are some things about his relationship with God that he didn't understand?

2. How do you think God was feeling as He saw this man's faith become weaker and weaker?

   He was disappointed that this man did

> not trust Him. He loved the man and
> longed for his fellowship.
> _____
> _____

2a. What do you think God desired in His
relationship with this man?
2b. Do you think God wanted to develop a
meaningful relationship with this man?

TRANSITION:

"Many people are not experiencing the abundant
Christian life because they have failed to take God
at His Word. Some are not confident in their relationship with God because they do not realize that
their relationship with God is founded and built
upon the promises of God. First, let's consider how
a person can be confident that Christ is in his life."

Observ./Interp.

(11)

Direct group
members to look
up the Scriptures.
Be sensitive to
anyone who may
need assistance.
Ask someone to
read the passages
as you come to
them.

Ask a group
member to read
these verses in his
study guide.

HEBREWS 11:6
B. OUR NEW RELATIONSHIP WITH GOD IS
BUILT ON FAITH

1. What are some things that you see about
faith in Hebrews 11:6?

It is impossible to please God without
faith. For a person to know and understand God, he must believe that God
exists and that if he seeks a relationship
with God, God will reward him.
_____
_____

"'For I know the plans that I have for you,'
declares the Lord, 'plans for welfare and not
for calamity to give you a future and a hope.
Then you will call upon Me and come and
pray to Me, and I will listen to you. And you
will seek Me and find Me, when you search
for Me with all your heart'"
(Jeremiah 29:11-13).

EXPLAIN:

"The person who believes in God needs to understand that God will reward him for seeking a relationship with God. Also, the plans God has for him
are good and are for his welfare."

Discuss the study questions. Share the suggested answers if necessary.

2. What are some things that the doubtful man in our story failed to understand about these truths in Hebrews 11:6 and Jeremiah 29:11-13?

   He did not believe God. He did not trust that God would reward him for seeking to develop a relationship with Him.

3. According to Revelation 3:20, how can a person express faith?

Ask a group member to read the verse from his study guide.

(12)

"Behold, I stand at the door and knock; if any one hears My voice and opens the door, I will come in to him, and will dine with him, and he with Me" (Revelation 3:20).

He can open the door of his life and invite Christ into his life to forgive his sins. Then he can trust that Christ kept His promise.

Application

> 4. Suppose we sincerely expressed our faith in Christ and asked Him to forgive our sins and to come into our lives. How can we be confident that Christ did forgive us and that He did come into our lives?
>
> <u>We can be confident because of His prom-</u>
> <u>ise. He and His Word are trustworthy</u>
> <u>objects of our faith. He would not lie.</u>

RELATE:

"When we sincerely invite Christ into our lives, we can be confident that Christ is in our lives just as He promised. When we have that confidence, we can be bold in developing a meaningful relationship with God.

TRANSITION:

"In order for us to fully enjoy and benefit from our relationship with God, we must also understand that we are totally forgiven for our sins. Otherwise, we will continue to experience unnecessary guilt over our past sins. Let's look at some verses that talk about what God has done with our sins."

Observ./Interp.

> COLOSSIANS 2:13,14
> C. OUR RELATIONSHIP WITH GOD IS ONE OF TOTAL FORGIVENESS

Read the verses. Discuss:

> 1. According to these verses, what are some things God has done with our sins?
>
> <u>He has forgiven us for all our sins. He has</u>
> <u>cancelled out the debt of things done</u>
> <u>wrong and has nailed our sins to the</u>
> <u>cross. He paid for all our sins.</u>

Application

> 2. How many of your sins were future when Christ died on the cross?
>
> <u>All our sins were future when Christ died</u>
> <u>nearly 2,000 years ago.</u>

RELATE:

"Hebrews 10 also tells us that when Christ offered Himself on the cross as a payment for our sins, it was a payment for our sins for all time. Therefore, there will never be a sin that we could commit that is not already paid for.

TRANSITION:

"Since all our sins are forgiven, we do not have to live in fear of God. Remember our story of the doubtful believer? He ended up living in fear of what God would do to him when he sinned. Let's look at some verses that explain that our new relationship with God is a relationship of peace."

Observ./Interp.
Ask a group member to read the verses.
ASK: (13)

ROMANS 5:1,2,8-11
D. OUR RELATIONSHIP WITH GOD IS A RELATIONSHIP OF PEACE

1. How does the Word of God describe us in these verses?

   We are justified; we have peace with God; we stand in grace; we exult in the hope of God; we are sinners; we are loved; we are saved from the wrath of God; we are reconciled to God; we are saved by Christ's life.

SAY:

"Since there are some words here that you may not understand, let me explain them for you so you can better understand these verses.

You may want to ask if anyone knows the definition of these words. Do not dwell on these definitions. They are intended to be an introduction to these concepts. If interest is stirred, direct them to the Bible handbook referred to on the Preparation page.

"Justified (vs. 1,9): In simple terms this word means that a person is declared to be innocent of his sins--as a judge would say, 'not guilty.' We are declared not guilty because Jesus paid the penalty for our sins.

"Grace (vs. 2): Grace simply means that we receive favor or goodness from God that we do not deserve.

"Reconciled (vs. 10): You may have heard this term used when two friends are 'reconciled' after years of hard feelings and not speaking to one another. Reconciled means to restore to friendship. As verse 10 tells us, we were God's enemies, but now we are reconciled or made to be His friends."

Discuss:

Note: The suggested answers appear in the following content.

> 2. What are some things you see in verses 8-11 that describe our past, present and future relationship with God?
> _____
> _____
> _____
> _____
> _____
> _____
> _____

After a minute or two have the group share what they found.

SAY:

"As you share something you have found, also tell us its significance in our relationship with God."

Suggested answers: be sure these points are covered in the discussion.

"Demonstrates" (vs. 8) is present tense, describing Christ's death as a continuing demonstration of God's love for us at any point in time.

"Having now been justified" (vs. 9) is present and past tense. It reminds us that our past act of receiving Christ caused us to be justified and that justification is still in effect.

"We shall be saved from the wrath" (vs. 9) is future tense but the sense of the future here is that it affects our past and present as well.

"Were enemies" (vs. 10) indicates that we can never be God's enemies again.

"Were reconciled" (vs. 10) is a past action. Having been reconciled is a past action that has continuing effect in the present and future. God not only changed us from enemies to friends but also insured that the change is permanent.

See also Hebrews 7:25

"We shall be saved by His life" (vs. 10) is used by Paul in reference to Christ being our advocate in heaven. His advocacy in heaven saves us from God's wrath daily as well as for eternity. I John 2:1,2 explains that Christ is like our personal lawyer in heaven, He continually defends us when Satan accuses us before the Father.

"We also exult in God" (vs. 11) is a present action, communicating that what God has done for us causes us to rejoice continually in who God is and what He has done for us.

"We have now received the reconciliation" (vs. 11) is a present idea that tells us we are in a continual state of being loved and accepted by God.

SAY:

"All these principles communicate that we have a secure and unshakable relationship of peace with God."

Application

READ:

3. Suppose you were talking with a friend who lived in fear of God's wrath and punishment and was constantly feeling guilty about his sins.

Continue discussion of the questions.

See also I John 4:17-19

From what we've discussed thus far in our study, what are some things you would tell your friend?

I would tell him that his relationship with God is secure; that it is a love relationship. I'd show him the verses that talk about our standing in grace (Romans 5). I'd explain that we don't get what we deserve (God's wrath) when we sin because Christ paid

131

for that sin. I'd also explain that "justified" means God has declared him "not guilty."

(14) 4. Suppose that after you explained the grace and love of Christ to your friend, he said, "Oh great! That means I can sin whenever I want, since God will forgive me."

What are some things you would tell your friend? Read Hebrews 12:5-11 and I John 2:4 to help you answer.

God corrects us because He loves us. God is like a good parent who disciplines and corrects us when we sin. God does not ignore sin. The Scriptures also suggest that a person who wants to sin may not even be a child of God (I John 2:4).

RELATE:

"I John 1:7-9 suggests that a Christian who sins is walking in darkness and his fellowship with God is hindered.

"Another reason we should not purposefully sin is that we have to live with the consequences of that sin. Although God forgives us, He does not normally remove the consequences. For example, God will forgive a Christian woman who becomes pregnant outside of marriage; but the woman must bear the consequences of that pregnancy.

TRANSITION:

"Now that we understand that God totally loves us and forgives our sins, let's look at some verses that explain how a person can know that he has eternal life."

Observ./Interp.

Read the verses.
Discuss:

Application

Have the group
members answer
this question in
their workbooks.
Then ask if two or
three would like to
share what they
wrote.

See also
Hebrews 13:5

Clarifying
Questions:

RELATE:

I JOHN 5:11-13
E.   OUR RELATIONSHIP WITH GOD IS
     ETERNAL

1.   What are some things that these verses
     say about eternal life?

     God has given it to us. Eternal life exists
     in Christ. If a person has Christ, he also
     has eternal life. If a person doesn't have
     Christ in his life, he doesn't have eternal
     life. He can know he has eternal life when
     he believes Christ.

2.   How then do you know that you have
     eternal life?

     I can know that I have eternal life because
     Christ is in my life, according to His prom-
     ise in Revelation 3:20. Since I have Christ,
     I have eternal life, too.

2a. What do some of the rest of you
     think?
2b. If you are sure Christ is in your life,
     how can you also be sure you have
     eternal life?

"Let's review briefly. First our relationship with
God is built on faith—faith in His promise that He
will come into our lives if we invite Him. Also, God
totally forgives our sins through Christ's death on
the cross. Third, we have a relationship of peace
with God in which He never deals with us in anger.

"Finally, we can know that we have eternal life.
Since it is not possible to have eternal life one day
and not the next, we can be secure in our relationship with God for all eternity.

"In our next lesson we will be discussing how we can live in His power in our relationship with Him."

Prayer
(5 Minutes)

SAY:

If you have a mature group, you may ask two or three to pray short sentence prayers.

Arrange the time and place for the next meeting.

"Let's thank God for this new relationship we have."

DISCIPLESHIP HINTS FOR THE LEADER

Meet with your group members in informal situations. As time allows, help the group members to work through the application from the most recent Bible study.

If one of the members did not attend the first meeting, attempt to visit him and take along one of his friends in the group. Show love and concern. Share the content of Lesson 1 and help him work through the application. Encourage him to come to the next meeting.

Begin to arrange witnessing appointments with your group members. Ask them to introduce you to some of their friends who are not Christians. As you meet their friends, invite them to your discipleship group. Share the Four Spiritual Laws whenever the opportunity arises. When you share the gospel, be certain that a group member is with you to observe. Give the group member an opportunity to share how he became a Christian. Remember that evangelism is one of the best ways to stimulate spiritual growth in the lives of your disciples.

3
Living in the Power
of the Spirit

OVERVIEW GOAL

The goal of this lesson is to enable group members to understand how to be filled with the Holy Spirit and to give them an opportunity to be filled.

LEARNING OBJECTIVES

By the end of this lesson, group members will be able to:

1. State why being filled with the Holy Spirit is essential to living a victorious Christian life.

2. Explain the command and the promise for appropriating the filling of the Holy Spirit.

3. Explain how to pray in faith to be filled with the Holy Spirit.

Time/Section	Outline/Questions and Learning Activities
5-10	## Sharing
	Have the group members share what God has been teaching them that might be an encouragement to others.
35-45	## Bible Study
Motivation	A. THE STORY OF THE CHEESE AND CRACKER CHRISTIAN
	TRANSITION: "As I said, many people today have tried to live the Christian life but are frustrated and defeated. The Bible explains why this is so. Let's look at three kinds of people described by the apostle Paul in I Corinthians 2 and 3."
Observ./Interp.	B. THE THREE KINDS OF PEOPLE
	1. Natural man—one who has not received Christ
	2. Spiritual man—one who is directed and empowered by the Holy Spirit
	3. Carnal man—one who has received Christ but who lives in defeat because he trusts in his own efforts to live the Christian life
	TRANSITION: "Let's look at a passage that describes what it is like to live in our own self-effort. This passage was written by the apostle Paul to describe what it is like when a Christian relies on his own strength to live the Christian life."
	C. THE FRUSTRATING LIFE OF SELF-EFFORT
Romans 7:14-25	1. What are some things that Paul says about his desires to do right in Romans 7:14-25?
	2. What are some reasons Paul gives for having this dilemma?

Time/Section	Outline/Questions and Learning Activities
Galatians 5:17	3. What similarities do you see between Galatians 5:17 and what we found in Romans 7?
Application	4. What are some possible reasons why God does not want you to live a life of self-effort and defeat?
	TRANSITION: "God does love us and has provided for us to experience joy and victory in our lives. Let's look at some verses that describe God's solution to a life of self-effort and defeat."
Observ./Interp.	D. GOD'S SOLUTION TO A LIFE OF SELF-EFFORT AND DEFEAT
Galatians 5:16; Romans 8:1-4;	1. What do you see in these verses that describes God's solution to a life of self-effort?
Ephesians 5:18-20	2. In Ephesians 5:18 we are commanded to be filled with the Holy Spirit. Verses 19 and 20 describe the results of being Spirit-filled. What differences do you see between a Spirit-filled Christian and one who is trying to live in his own efforts (Romans 7)?
	3. Paul contrasts being drunk with wine with being filled with the Holy Spirit. What are some ways this contrast helps us understand what it means to be filled with the Holy Spirit?
	4. What then do you think it means to be filled with the Holy Spirit?
	5. What do you think the relationship is between being "filled with the Holy Spirit" and "walking in the Spirit"?
Application	6. How do you know that it is God's will for you to be filled with the Holy Spirit?
	E. HOW TO BE FILLED WITH THE HOLY SPIRIT
	1. You must *sincerely desire* to be directed and empowered by the Holy Spirit.*
	2. Confess any *unconfessed sin*.
	3. Present *every area* of your life to God. Why do you think it would be necessary to present every area of your life to God before He will fill you with His Spirit?

*Italicized words are blanks in the study guide.

Time/Section	Outline/Questions and Learning Activities
	4. By *faith*, claim the fullness of the Holy Spirit, according to: His command and His promise. 5. Express your faith *through prayer*.
5	**Prayer**
———— 45-60	Close in prayer, thanking the Lord for what He has taught the group from the study.

Preparation

PERSONAL PERSPECTIVE

The truths presented in this lesson are probably the most crucial you could ever present to any Christian. The lesson is designed to produce conviction in the group members. However, there is no substitute for your own personal conviction and enthusiasm. Spend some time alone with the Lord and ask Him if you are really experiencing the truths of this lesson. Then pray that God will mightily and consistently change your group members through this lesson.

Read over the lesson for the following week so that you will know what is covered on the topic of spiritual breathing.

RESOURCES

Transferable Concept 3, "How to Be Filled with the Spirit"
Ten Basic Steps Toward Christian Maturity, Teacher's Manual
Ten Basic Steps Toward Christian Maturity, Step 3, "The Christian and the Holy Spirit"

> "The greatest realization came to me when I saw that there was nothing I had to do to receive His power but submit to Christ, to allow Him to control me. I had been trying to do everything myself; now I let Christ take me completely. I said to Christ that if He wanted anything from me that He would have to do it Himself. My life was changed from that moment on."*
>
> Henrietta Mears

Sharing
(5-10 Minutes)

Introduce any new members.

Have the group members share what God has been teaching them.

SAY: "Has anything happened this week that you would like to share with the group? Maybe God has been teaching you something that would be an encouragement to the rest of us."

Bible Study
(35-45 Minutes)

Open the Bible study in a brief prayer, asking God to teach the group.

Motivation

SAY: "I'd like to begin with a story that is typical of the way many Christians live today. As I read the story aloud, you can follow along in your study guides."

*Ethel May Baldwin and David V. Benson, *Henrietta Mears and How She Did It*, Copyright © 1966, p. 159: Used by permission of Gospel Light Publications, Glendale, California.

READ: (16)

A. THE STORY OF THE CHEESE AND CRACKER CHRISTIAN

A man booked passage on a ship that was crossing the Atlantic. He brought with him just enough money to buy a ticket, a block of cheese and some crackers for the long voyage. The first few days at sea the crackers and cheese tasted good, but eventually they became stale. Each day as he watched the porters carry large steaks, lobsters, chickens and other delicious foods to the ship's guests, he became very hungry. In fact, he became so hungry that he grabbed one of the porters. "I'll do anything to get one of those steaks," he said, "I'll wash dishes, clean rooms, even mop the deck." The porter replied, "You bought a ticket, didn't you? The meals come with the ticket."*

RELATE:

"The reason that this man did not experience the full enjoyment of his trip was because he was uninformed about all that the price of his ticket included. Many people today do not experience the abundant Christian life because they are unaware of the great resources that God has made available to them. As a result, they try to live the Christian life through their own resources. They try to do what is right, but they find that the standards of the Christian life are impossible to fulfill. The Christian life is not hard to live, it's impossible to live. The only way a Christian can live the life is if Christ lives it through him.

*Bill Bright, *How to Experience God's Love and Forgiveness*, Copyright © 1971, pp. 24,25: Used by permission of Campus Crusade for Christ, Inc., Arrowhead Springs, California.

TRANSITION:

"As I said, many people today have tried to live the Christian life but are frustrated and defeated. The Bible explains why this is so. Let's look at three kinds of people described by the apostle Paul in I Corinthians 2 and 3."

Observ./Interp.

Explain Section B.

B.   THE THREE KINDS OF PEOPLE

1.   NATURAL MAN—one who has not received Christ

Ask group members to read the verses from their study guides as you come to them in your explanation.

"But a natural man does not accept the things of the Spirit of God; for they are foolishness to him, and he cannot understand them, because they are spiritually appraised" (I Corinthians 2:14).

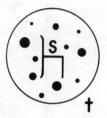

(17)

2.   SPIRITUAL MAN—one who is directed and empowered by the Holy Spirit

"But he who is spiritual appraises all things, yet he himself is appraised by no man" (I Corinthians 2:15).

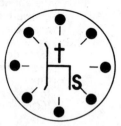

Briefly review with your group the following traits.

Some personal traits which result from trusting God:

Christ centered
Empowered by the Holy Spirit
Introduces others to Christ
Effective prayer life
Understands God's Word
Trusts God
Obeys God
Love
Joy
Peace
Patience
Kindness
Faithfulness
Goodness

3. CARNAL MAN—one who has received Christ, but who lives in defeat because he trusts in his own efforts to live the Christian life

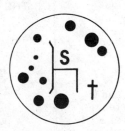

Some or all of the following traits may characterize the Christian who does not fully trust God:

(18)

Ignorance of his spiritual heritage
Unbelief
Disobedience
Loss of love for God and for others
Poor prayer life
No desire for Bible study
Legalistic attitude
Impure thoughts
Jealousy

> Guilt
> Worry
> Discouragement
> Critical spirit
> Frustration
> Aimlessness

EXPLAIN:

"The carnal Christian is defeated because he trusts in his own efforts to live the Christian life. One becomes carnal when he knowingly takes control of his life and continually refuses to confess his sin.

TRANSITION:

"Let's look at a passage that describes what it is like to live in our own self-effort. This passage was written by the apostle Paul to describe what it is like when a Christian relies on his own strength to live the Christian life."

Ask the group members to look up the verses and have someone read them.

DISCUSSION:

Direct the group in a discussion of the questions. Share the suggested answers only if necessary.

Summarize the group's answers after discussing each question and encourage group members to write the conclusions in their study guides.

ROMANS 7:14-25
C.   THE FRUSTRATING LIFE OF SELF-EFFORT

1.   What are some things that Paul says about his desires to do right?

He doesn't understand what he is doing.
He wants to do good, but he doesn't do it.
In fact, he does the very things he doesn't
want to do. He agrees that his actions are
wrong and that he has impulses that are
against God's ways. He feels like a
wretched man.

Clarifying
Questions:

1a. What are some other ways that Paul describes himself?
1b. What does Paul say about his desires?
1c. Is Paul living the kind of life that he desires? Why or why not?

---

2. What are some reasons that Paul gives for having this dilemma?

He is of the flesh, sold into bondage to sin. Nothing good dwells in his flesh. Evil is present within him. He is concerned with the law of God but in his body is a different law which is waging war against the law of his mind. He has become a prisoner of the law of sin in his members.

Clarifying
Questions:

2a. What do some others of you see?
2b. How else does Paul describe the cause of his dilemma?
2c. What does Paul say about his dilemma in verses 22-24?

RELATE:

"One of the things Paul says about himself is that evil is present in him (vs. 21). This presence of the desire to do evil in the believer is described throughout the New Testament. For instance, let's look at Galatians 5:17."

Ask a group
member to read the
verse from his
study guide.

GALATIANS 5:17
3.   What similarities do you see between Galatians 5:17 and what we found in Romans
7?

"For the flesh sets its desire against the
Spirit, and the Spirit against the flesh; for
these are in opposition to one another, so
that you may not do the things that you
please" (Galatians 5:17).

In both cases we, along with Paul, cannot
do what we please; there is a war going
on.

(19)

EXPLAIN:

"The flesh is the part of us that continues to want
to do evil even after we receive Christ. There are
many ways to describe the desire to do evil."

These are some
ways Paul des-
cribes the desire to
do evil. Share them
with the group only
if necessary.

Indwelling sin (vs. 17,20). The principle or law of
evil (vs. 19,21). A different law in the members of
the body (vs. 23). Law of sin (vs. 23,25).

CONTINUE TO
EXPLAIN:

"In Galatians 5:17 and Romans 7, Paul describes the battle that continues to take place in the Christian as long as he lives in the world. That battle is so intense that the Christian is doomed to failure and defeat if he relies on his own strength to overcome the flesh and to live the Christian life."

Application

4. What are some possible reasons why God does not want you to live a life of self-effort and defeat?

He loves me and He wants the best for me. It's impossible for me to obey if I live in my own strength, and He certainly does not want me to live a life of sin and disobedience, etc.

TRANSITION:

"God does love us and has provided for us to experience joy and victory in our lives. Let's look at some verses that describe God's solution to a life of self-effort and defeat."

Observ./Interp.

Ask a group member to read the verses.

Discuss the following questions. Follow the same procedure as before.

GALATIANS 5:16; ROMANS 8:1-4
D. GOD'S SOLUTION TO A LIFE OF SELF-EFFORT AND DEFEAT

1. What do you see in these verses that describes God's solution to a life of self-effort?

By walking in the Spirit, we can fulfill the law rather than the desire of the flesh.

Clarifying
Questions:

1a. What do some of the rest of you see?
1b. What does Romans 8:4 say?

SAY:

"Now let's look at a passage that helps us understand how we can walk in the Spirit."

Ask a group
member to read the
verse.

EPHESIANS 5:18-20
2. In Ephesians 5:18 we are commanded to
be filled with the Holy Spirit. Verses 19 and
20 describe the results of being Spirit-
filled. What differences do you see
between a Spirit-filled Christian and one
who is trying to live in his own efforts
(Romans 7)?

A Christian living by self-effort is defeated
and powerless. The Spirit-filled person is
experiencing joy and thankfulness, and he
makes melody in his heart to the Lord.

(20)
3. Paul contrasts being drunk with wine with
being filled with the Holy Spirit. What are
some ways this contrast helps us understand what it means to be filled with the
Holy Spirit?

When a person is drunk, the alcohol controls him and produces certain results.
When a person is filled with the Holy
Spirit, the Spirit controls and empowers
him to live the kind of life Christ would
want him to. He is not able to live this life
in his own power.

Clarifying
Questions:

3a. Any other ideas?
3b. Why do you think Paul chose to compare being drunk with being filled
with the Holy Spirit? What is similar
about these two conditions?

4. What then do you think it means to be
filled with the Holy Spirit?

It means to be directed and empowered
by the Holy Spirit in such a way that we
can live as He wants us to live.

Итアイ stop

Leader's Guide

EXPLAIN:

"When a person receives Christ, the Holy Spirit comes to indwell or live in him. Although the Holy Spirit lives within every Christian, He only fills those who let Him.

"We are filled with the Holy Spirit by faith as an act of our wills. As we allow the Holy Spirit to direct us and empower our lives, we will overcome the desires of the flesh in our lives. The filling of the Holy Spirit is a moment-by-moment, hour-by-hour, day-by-day experience. The verb, 'be filled,' means in the original language, 'to be continually filled.'"

DISCUSS:

5. What do you think the relationship is between being "filled with the Holy Spirit" and "walking in the Spirit"?

   It is only by being filled moment-by-moment with the Holy Spirit that we can walk day-by-day and week-by-week in the Spirit—that is to rely step-by-step on the Holy Spirit to empower and direct us.

Application

6. How do you know that it is God's will for you to be filled with the Holy Spirit?

   He commanded it in Ephesians 5:18.

SAY:

"Since we know it is God's will, let's consider how we can be filled with the Holy Spirit."

READ:

Instruct group members to fill in the blanks in their study guides. Emphasize the italicized words in points 1-5.

E. HOW TO BE FILLED WITH THE HOLY SPIRIT

1. You must *sincerely desire* to be directed and empowered by the Holy Spirit.

Ask group members to read the Scriptures as you come to them.

"Blessed are those who hunger and thirst for righteousness, for they shall be satisfied" (Matthew 5:6).

2. Confess any *unconfessed sin*.

"If we confess our sins, He is faithful and righteous to forgive us our sins and to cleanse us from all unrighteousness" (I John 1:9).

RELATE: "God will not fill a dirty vessel; through confession we become clean. Confession is agreeing with God concerning our sin and thanking Him for His forgiveness because of Christ's death on the cross. As we discussed last week, God has already forgiven us; but as we confess our sins, we experience anew what He has already done for us."

READ: (21) 3. Present *every area* of your life to God.

"I urge you therefore, brethren, by the mercies of God, to present your bodies a living and holy sacrifice, acceptable to God, which is your spiritual service of worship" (Romans 12:1).

DISCUSS:

> Why do you think it is necessary to present every area of your life to God before He will fill-you with His Spirit?
>
> <u>Because the Holy Spirit desires to take total control of our lives. He cannot fill us if we are consciously holding back an area from Him.</u>

READ:

Make sure group members fill in the correct word.

4. By *faith*, claim the fullness of the Holy Spirit, according to:

   a. His command

   > "And do not get drunk with wine, for that is dissipation, but be filled with the Spirit" (Ephesians 5:18).

   b. His promise

   > "And this is the confidence which we have before Him, that, if we ask anything according to His will, He hears us. And if we know that He hears us in whatever we ask, we know that we have the requests which we have asked from Him" (I John 5:14,15).

      1) What does I John 5:14,15 tell us about prayer?

      > <u>If we pray according to God's will, He will hear us and answer our prayer.</u>

(22)

      2) If we were to pray in faith to be filled with the Holy Spirit, how could we be confident that God would answer our prayer?

> God said if we ask anything according to His will He will answer. We can have confidence in the trustworthiness of God and His Word.
>
> 3) We are filled with the Holy Spirit by faith alone. Prayer is one way of expressing faith.

SAY:

"I would like to share with you a suggested prayer that many people have used to express faith in God's command and promise."

> 5. Express your faith *through prayer*.
>
> "Dear Father, I need you. I acknowledge that I have been directing my own life and that, as a result, I have sinned against You. I thank You that You have forgiven my sins through Christ's death on the cross for me. I now invite Christ to again take His place on the throne of my life. Fill me with the Holy Spirit as You commanded me to be filled, and as You promised in Your Word that You would do if I asked in faith. I pray this in the name of Jesus. As an expression of my faith, I now thank You for directing my life and for filling me with the Holy Spirit."

ASK:

"Does that prayer express the desire of your heart? If it does, I would like to give you an opportunity to pray that prayer in a minute.

"Remember, we said in order to be filled we need to confess any known sin in our lives and present every area of our lives to Christ. Let's have a moment of silent prayer to do that now."

Pause for silent prayer.

After a minute ask them to follow along silently as you pray the suggested prayer, if it expresses the desires of their hearts.

SAY:

"Now that you have asked God to fill you, consider how you can know you are filled."

Ask a group member to read I John 5:14,15.

SAY:

"In these verses God promises that if we ask anything according to His will He will do it. He can't lie. You can know that you are filled, not on the basis of feelings, but on the trustworthiness of God.

"Next week we'll consider how to continue to experience God's love and power in our lives. I would like to recommend that you read Transferable Concept 3, 'How to Be Filled with the Spirit' this week."

Arrange the time and place of the next meeting.

Prayer
(5 Minutes)

Close in prayer, thanking the Lord for what He has taught the group from the study.

DISCIPLESHIP HINTS FOR THE LEADER

Continue to meet with your group members informally in places of common interest. Use the time to meet personal needs.

Continue to meet the friends of your group members. Ask a group member to invite a friend for lunch or a snack. Use this time to share your faith with the friend. Involve the group member in the sharing process by asking him to give a brief testimony.

Invite your group members to go witnessing with you.

Remember that the Discovery Group serves as a filter to find those who genuinely desire to make their lives count for Christ. As some begin to drop out, we should maintain our concern but realize that many left Christ while He was on earth. Continue to encourage those who no longer come to your group, to be involved. Give them literature to read, invite them to Christian meetings and show your love. Visit them occasionally. However, do not be discouraged. Some group leaders have started two or three groups before they find men or women with genuine hearts for the Lord.

4
Walking With
═══ Christ ═══

OVERVIEW GOAL

The goal of this lesson is to enable group members to walk in the Spirit moment-by-moment through applying four key principles.

LEARNING OBJECTIVES

By the end of this lesson, group members will be able to:

1. Explain and apply spiritual breathing.

2. List the three forces that wage war against the believer.

3. Explain the importance of knowing our rights as children of God and the role of faith in our Christian walk.

Time/Section	Outline/Questions and Learning Activities
5-10	## Sharing Have them share how learning about the Spirit-filled life has helped them.
35-45	## Bible Study
Motivation	A. CASE STUDY OF THE NEWLY SPIRIT-FILLED CHRISTIAN TRANSITION: "Let's consider four key principles that will enable us to walk in the Spirit. Note the remaining points of our Bible study state the four principles—to walk in the Spirit we must be filled with the Spirit, we must be prepared for spiritual conflict, we must know our right as children of God and we must live by faith."
Observ./Interp.	B. TO WALK IN THE SPIRIT, WE MUST BE FILLED WITH THE SPIRIT 1. Review of how to be filled with the Spirit 2. How to breathe spiritually—review of page 15 in the Holy Spirit booklet 3. Two examples of spiritual breathing
Psalm 32:1-5	4. What are some things David said about himself when he did not confess his sin?
Application	5. What else do you see in these verses that should motivate us to confess sin when God shows it to us? TRANSITION: "The second key principle of walking in the Spirit is to be prepared for spiritual conflict."
Observ./Interp.	C. TO WALK IN THE SPIRIT, WE MUST BE PREPARED FOR SPIRITUAL CONFLICT 1. Conflict with the flesh 2. Conflict with the world 3. Conflict with Satan

Time/Section	Outline/Questions and Learning Activities
	TRANSITION: "Another principle of walking in the Spirit is to know your rights as children of God."
	D. TO WALK IN THE SPIRIT, WE MUST KNOW OUR RIGHTS AS CHILDREN OF GOD
Romans 8:16,17	1. How does Romans 8:16,17 describe us and what are some reasons this description is significant?
Matthew 7:7-11	2. What do these verses say about our privileges as children of God?
	TRANSITION: "The final principle of walking in the Spirit is to live by faith."
Colossians 2:6	E. TO WALK IN THE SPIRIT, WE MUST LIVE BY FAITH
	1. How does a person receive Christ?
	2. How should a Christian walk with Christ?
	3. Story of a bitter Christian
Application	4. Colossians 2:7 says we should be overflowing with gratitude to God. Considering the preceding story and your own experience, what are some reasons that thankfulness is essential for living the Christian life?
5	## Prayer
	Pray silently about any bitter attitudes toward God and demonstrate faith by thanking Him for any problems.
45-60	

Preparation

PERSONAL PERSPECTIVE

Set aside at least 45 minutes when you will not be disturbed. Take your Bible, the Holy Spirit booklet and your discipleship group study guide. Pray that the Spirit will be at work in the group members' lives, enabling them to understand what it means to be controlled by the Spirit. Become completely familiar with the Holy Spirit booklet and be sure that you are Spirit-filled! Put yourself in the place of a group member and remember how you first discovered the Spirit-filled life.

INTRODUCTION TO PSALM 32

This psalm of repentence is the first of 13 Maskil psalms (psalms of spiritual instruction). It was probably written as a result of David's sin with Bathsheba. One of the themes of this psalm is that suppressed guilt becomes an intolerable burden (vs. 3,4), but joy results when we receive the Lord's forgiveness through confession (vs. 1,2,5).

INTRODUCTION TO I JOHN

This letter was written by the apostle John about 85-90 A.D. Its main theme is fellowship with God the Father and other believers. Chapter 2 deals with obedience, love and maturity as they relate to overcoming sin and continuing in fellowship with God the Father.

SUPPLIES

A Holy Spirit booklet, "Have You Made the Wonderful Discovery of the Spirit-filled Life?" for each group member

RESOURCES

Unger's Bible Handbook
Transferable Concept 4, "How to Walk in the Spirit"

> "The Holy Spirit is the source of power who meets our need to escape from the miserable weakness that grips us."*
>
> Billy Graham

Sharing
(5-10 Minutes)

Have the group members share about their successes and failures in allowing Christ to control them. Create an open, honest and accepting atmosphere so group members feel free to communicate their lack of understanding of the Spirit-filled life. Try to determine their level of understanding and answer any questions they may have.

SAY:

"The Spirit-filled life is not a once-and-for-all experience, but rather a moment-by-moment experience of allowing Jesus Christ to live His life in and through us."

Bible Study
(35-45 Minutes)

Open the Bible study with a brief prayer, asking God to teach the group.

* Billy Graham, *The Holy Spirit*, Copyright © 1978, p. 11: Used by permission of Word Books, Waco, Texas.

Motivation   (24)   A.   CASE STUDY OF THE NEWLY SPIRIT-
                              FILLED CHRISTIAN

READ: John learned about the Spirit-controlled life
                              and prayed to be filled with the Holy Spirit.
                              Things seemed to be going pretty well for him
                              and he had a new sense of joy and inner
                              peace. However, during the week the pressure
                              to meet work deadlines caused him to worry
                              and become frustrated. Then one day Frank, a
                              man he was training at work, asked John for
                              his help on a project. John replied harshly and
                              told Frank that he had no time for him. For the
                              remainder of that week he felt guilty and tried
                              to avoid Frank. When he remembered that he
                              had asked to be filled with the Spirit just a few
                              days earlier, he became disillusioned. He
                              thought that the Christian life was just too dif-
                              ficult and complicated to live.

ASK: "What advice would you give to John?"

Wait for the group
to respond.

RELATE: "John's experience is not uncommon. It is possible
                              though to experience the Spirit-filled life on a con-
                              sistent basis. This is called walking in the Spirit.
                              However, anyone who desires to be filled with the
                              Holy Spirit on a consistent basis will experience
                              difficulty.

TRANSITION: "Let's consider four key principles that will enable
                              us to walk in the Spirit. Note the remaining points
                              of our Bible study state the four principles—to
                              walk in the Spirit we must be filled with the Spirit,
                              we must be prepared for spiritual conflict, we must
                              know our rights as children of God and we must
                              live by faith."

Observ./Interp.

SAY: "The first principle is to be certain we are filled
                              with the Holy Spirit."

B. TO WALK IN THE SPIRIT, WE MUST BE
    FILLED WITH THE SPIRIT

1. Review of how to be filled with the Spirit.

SAY:

"Let's briefly review what we said last week about how to be filled with the Spirit. To help us review, I would like to use this booklet, 'Have You Made the Wonderful Discovery of the Spirit-filled Life?' It contains the essence of what we discussed last week."

Pass out the booklets.

SAY:

"Look on pages 2 and 3. Here is the natural, spiritual and carnal man we discussed last week. Does anyone recall when it is that a Christian becomes carnal?"

Give the following answer if the group members do not do so.

A person becomes carnal when he knowingly takes control of his life and continually refuses to confess sin that God has shown him.

ASK:

"Can anyone explain how a person can become Spirit-filled after he has taken control of his own life?"

Give the following answer if the group members do not suggest it.

A person can become Spirit-filled again by confessing his sin and by again claiming the fullness of the Holy Spirit. This process is called spiritual breathing.

SAY:

"We are going to look at spiritual breathing in more detail, but first, let's review the main points in this booklet.

"On page 4 it says that 'God has provided for us an abundant and fruitful Christian life.' But page 6 explains that 'carnal Christians cannot experience the abundant and fruitful Christian life.' The solution is on page 8, which says, 'Jesus promised the abundant and fruitful life as the result of being filled (directed and empowered) by the Holy Spirit.' Page 10 reminds us that, 'we are filled (directed and empowered) by the Holy Spirit by

161

faith; then we can experience the abundant and fruitful life which Christ promised to each Christian.' On page 11 we read about God's command to be filled and His promise to answer our prayers when we pray according to His will. Page 12 tells us that we are filled with the Holy Spirit by faith and that prayer is one way of expressing true faith.

"Page 13 reminds us that we can know we are filled not on the basis of our feelings, but on the basis of the trustworthiness of God and His Word. Page 14 provides some thoughts on how to walk in the Spirit and page 15 explains spiritual breathing. You will want to read the booklet more closely on your own. Let's now consider spiritual breathing."

Have everyone silently read page 15 of the Holy Spirit booklet.

> 2. How to breathe spiritually

SAY:

"There are two situations that help us to understand what this page is saying. The first paragraph explains that there will be times when the Holy Spirit will reveal sin in our lives when we are not aware of having sinned. Let's look at an example of this situation in your study guides."

> 3. Two examples of spiritual breathing
>
> Example 1:
> Bill and his friend, Jon, were talking one Saturday while working on their cars. They both enjoyed the time together. However, later in the day, as Bill was thinking about their conversation, he realized that he had made a rather inconsiderate comment, which probably had hurt Jon's feelings.
>
> What should Bill do according to what we learned on page 15 of the booklet?

Have a group member read Example 1.

DISCUSSION:

Direct the group in a discussion of the questions. Share the suggested answers only if necessary. Summarize the group's answers after discussing each question and encourage group members to write the conclusions in their study guides.

> He should agree with God that he had said something inconsiderate to Jon. He should simply thank God that He has forgiven him for it on the basis of Christ's death on the cross. Bill should thank God for His love for him and continue to have fellowship with Him. At the first opportunity he should apologize to Jon for his inconsiderate comment.

RELATE:

"The second paragraph explains what we should do when we knowingly disobey God and retake the thrones of our lives."

Have a group member read Example 2.

(25)

Example 2:
Bill got up on the "wrong side of the bed" one morning. Just as he was ready to leave the house for work, the phone rang. It was Jon calling. Even though he knew that it would hurt Jon's feelings, Bill showed his irritation and complained that Jon was making him late. Even as he was talking to Jon, the Holy Spirit showed him that his manner of conversation was sin.

ASK:

What should Bill do according to God's Word?

See also I John 1:9; Ephesians 5:18

> He should exhale by confessing his sin, thanking God for His forgiveness, and inhale by appropriating the fulness of the Holy Spirit by faith. After the Holy Spirit is in control of his life, he will see the importance of apologizing to Jon.

SAY:

"Now let's look at Psalm 32 and see what David said about confessing sin when God revealed sin in his life."

Leader's Guide

Ask someone to
read the passage.

Discuss the study
questions. Follow
the same proce-
dure as before.

PSALM 32:1-5

4. What are some things David said about
    himself when he did not confess his sin?

    He felt as though his body was wasting
    away because his vitality was drained and
    he experienced a loss of energy. Also, he
    groaned all day since God's hand was
    heavy upon him, causing him to feel
    downhearted.

Application

5. What else do you see in these verses that
    should motivate us to confess sin when
    God shows it to us?

    God covers our sin. He does not impute
    iniquity to us. We see how God responded
    favorably to David when he confessed his
    sin. God also forgives the guilt of the sin.

SAY:

"We must remember that merely confessing our
sins will not provide the power to keep from sin-
ning. We must appropriate (receive) the filling of
the Holy Spirit so that the Holy Spirit will empower
us to live differently.

"Another important thing to remember is that we should not become overly introspective by constantly looking for sin in our lives. We deal with sin as the Holy Spirit shows us. He will make it clear when we need to confess, so we do not need to do His work for Him.

"Quite possibly, as we have talked, the Holy Spirit has made you aware of some unconfessed sin in your life, and you know that you are not filled with the Holy Spirit. I'd like to give you an opportunity to apply what we've just talked about. Let's spend a few minutes in silent prayer. If you know that there is unconfessed sin in your life, now is the time to deal with it. You may want to open the Holy Spirit booklet to the prayer on page 12. In a couple of minutes, I'll close our time in prayer."

Wait for four or five minutes and then close in prayer, thanking God for his forgiveness and for the filling of His Spirit.

TRANSITION: "The second key principle of walking in the Spirit is to be prepared for spiritual conflict."

Observ./Interp.

C. TO WALK IN THE SPIRIT, WE MUST BE PREPARED FOR SPIRITUAL CONFLICT

SAY: "In our last lesson, we talked about conflict with the flesh."

Briefly explain these first two conflicts--the flesh and the world.

1. Conflict with the flesh (Galatians 5:17; Romans 7:14-25).

    The solution--walk in the Spirit (Galatians 5:16; Romans 8:1-4).

SAY: "The second source of conflict for the Christian is the world system today."

Ask a group (26)
member to read the
verses.

> 2. Conflict with the world (I John 2:15,16).
>
> The solution--our faith (I John 5:1,4).

ASK:

"What are some things in our own culture that are obviously a part of the world?"

Suggest the answers if no one mentions them.

Pornography, the cult of materialism, the blatant emphasis on sex and immorality, the philosophy of pleasure first and the emphasis on doing what you feel like doing, etc.

SAY:

"I John 5:4 says, 'For whatever is born of God overcomes the world; and this is the victory that has overcome the world--our faith.' As we live by faith in God and His Word, we will overcome the desire to yield to the pressures from the world to sin.

"The third conflict is with Satan."

Have someone read the verses.

> 3. Conflict with Satan (Ephesians 6:11,12).
>
> The solution--spiritual armor (Ephesians 6:10-17).

EXPLAIN:

"We will be spending a whole lesson on our conflict with Satan, so we will not discuss our conflict
with him at length right now. The main thing to
remember is Ephesians 6:10: 'Be strong in the
Lord, and in the strength of His might.' As long as
we rely on the Lord's strength and obey God, we
have nothing to fear from Satan.

TRANSITION:

"Another principle of walking in the Spirit is to
know your rights as children of God."

**D. TO WALK IN THE SPIRIT, WE MUST KNOW
OUR RIGHTS AS CHILDREN OF GOD**

SAY:

"Time will not allow us to develop this concept in
depth, but the Bible has thousands of promises we
can claim as God's children. As God's sons and
daughters, we have rights and privileges that others do not have."

Ask a group
member to read the
verses.

Discuss the
questions.

ROMANS 8:16,17
1. How does Romans 8:16,17 describe us
    and why is this description significant?

    We are children of God and co-heirs with
    Christ, heirs of God. It is significant
    because it demonstrates that we have a
    special relationship with God.

    _____

    _____

MATTHEW 7:7-11
2. What do these verses say about our privi-
    leges as children of God?

    We can ask our Heavenly Father for things
    that we need and expect Him to give them
    to us.

    _____

    _____

SAY:

"Remember the story of the cheese and cracker
Christian we talked about in our last study? At first
he did not enjoy his voyage on the ship because
he did not take full advantage of the privileges that
were his. He did not know what was his for the
asking.

"There are many promises and privileges in the Christian life that we need to know about. Our lives can be an adventure of discovering those things in God's Word.

TRANSITION:

"The final principle of walking in the Spirit is to live by faith."

Ask a group member to read the verses.

Discuss:

COLOSSIANS 2:6
E. TO WALK IN THE SPIRIT, WE MUST LIVE BY FAITH

1. How does a person receive Christ?

By faith.

(27)

2. How should a Christian walk with Christ?

A Christian should walk in the same manner—by faith.

SAY:

"Let's look at a story that is told by a well-known Christian speaker."

Have the group read the story silently or have someone read it aloud.

3. Story of a bitter Christian

Some time ago, a young woman came to Arrowhead Springs, the International Headquarters of Campus Crusade for Christ, for a conference. After one of my lectures, she came for counsel. Through her tears she shared her story of the loss of her dearest friend who had been killed in an accident. She had been driving the car when he was killed. They were coming home from their engagement party, and an oncoming automobile crossed the center line, forcing her off the road into a telephone pole.

The sadness and the tragedy of losing her dearest friend were compounded by the guilt of knowing that she had been driving the car. Her heart was broken. "What shall I do?" she pleaded.

Months had passed, and she had gone to psychiatrists, psychologists, ministers and many others, seeking cousel. She said, "If you can't help me, I fear for my sanity." I asked her if she were a Christian, and she said, "Yes." We read Romans 8:28 and I asked, "Do you believe that all things work together for good?" She said, "Yes, I belive that."

We turned to I Thessalonians 5:18. She read it aloud: "In everything give thanks; for this is God's will for you in Christ Jesus." I said to her, "Have you thanked God for the loss of your loved one?" She was shocked and could hardly believe that she heard me correctly. She looked at me in disbelief as she said, "How can I ever thank God for such a tragic loss?"

"You do not trust God, do you?" I asked. "Yes, I trust God," she insisted. "Then why not show that you do?" I asked. "Will you pray and tell God that you trust Him and give thanks in everything?" As we knelt together, she prayed through her tears, "God, I don't understand, but I know that I can trust You; and I do say 'thank You.'"

(28) When she said "thank You" she was saying to God, "I trust You." The Bible says that without faith we cannot please God and the best way to demonstrate faith is to say "thank You." You may hate God because you have lost a loved one, or your inheritance, or your money, or your business, or your health. You may ask, "Why did God do this to me?" But God says, "In everything give thanks." Unbelief is sin and displeases God, according to Hebrews 3:17-4:2 and Romans 14:23.

That young lady came to my office early the next morning bubbling over with joy.

She said, "Last night I slept without medication for the first time since the accident. And this morning when I awakened, my heart was filled with praise and thanksgiving to God. I just cannot understand it, but I know that it has something to do with what you taught me about saying 'thank You' to God."*

Application

4. Colossians 2:7 says we should be overflowing with gratitude to God. Considering the preceding story and your own experience, what are some reasons that thankfulness is essential for living the Christian life?

Thankfulness expresses faith. It is impossible to be filled with the Holy Spirit and have a bitter attitude because it grieves God and is sin. Lack of thankfulness expresses distrust in God.

You would greatly benefit from reading Transferable Concept 4, "How to Walk in the Spirit," by Dr. Bill Bright.

SAY:

"Galatians 5:22,23 describes qualities that the Holy Spirit will produce in our lives when we are filled with the Spirit. They are love, joy, peace, patience, kindness, goodness, faithfulness, gentleness and self-control.

"We have the choice of being unthankful and bitter or being thankful and allowing the Holy Spirit to produce peace and joy in our lives."

*Bill Bright, How to Walk in the Spirit, Copyright © 1971, pp. 43-45: Used by permission of Campus Crusade for Christ, Inc., Arrowhead Springs, California.

Prayer
(5 Minutes)

SAY:

"Let's spend just a few minutes in prayer. Possibly, you have been bitter toward God because of a broken relationship or some other problem area in your life. If we want to experience God's best, we need to live by faith and say 'thank You.' Let's pray silently about these areas and I will close in a few moments. Thanking God demonstrates faith."

Close the prayer time after several minutes.

Do this if time allows.

SAY:

"Would one or two of you like to share something for which you thanked God for the first time?

"I trust that our study on how to walk in the Spirit has been profitable for you."

Arrange time and place for the next meeting.

5
Becoming People
══of Action══

OVERVIEW GOAL

The goal of this lesson is to motivate and equip group members to share their faith in Christ, using the Four Spiritual Laws booklet.

LEARNING OBJECTIVES

By the end of this lesson, group members will be able to:

1. Explain Christ's purpose and His purpose for us.

2. Explain the related responsibilities of the Christian and the Holy Spirit in evangelism.

3. Read through the Four Spiritual Laws booklet with someone.

Time/Section	Outline/Questions and Learning Activities
10	**Sharing** Have group members share any experiences they had in applying the principles of walking with Christ that they studied in the previous lesson.
20	**Bible Study**

Motivation

A. THE MOST IMPORTANT TASK IN LIFE

   1. What are some words you would use to describe a research scientist who discovered the cure for cancer, but never told anyone about it?

   2. What would you say is the cure for the spiritual cancer of sin?

   3. What words would you use to describe a person who knew the cure for the spiritual cancer of sin and started telling others about it?

   TRANSITION: "We need to understand that man's helplessness is one reason we should share our faith. Another reason for sharing is that it is Christ's purpose for our lives. First, let's consider what purpose Christ had and how it relates to us."

Observ./Interp.

B. CHRIST'S PURPOSE AND HIS PURPOSE FOR US

John 17:1-4

   1. What are some things that you see in these verses concerning the purpose and desires Christ had for His life?

   2. In verse 4, what did Jesus do to glorify the Father in His life?

Luke 19:10;
John 17:18,20
Application

   3. How would you describe "the work" that God the Father gave Jesus to do?

   4. If we allowed Jesus to live His life through us today, what are some things He would be doing?

Time/Section	Outline/Questions and Learning Activities
Matthew 28:18-20	5. According to Matthew 28:18-20, what is the scope or boundary of our task of seeking and saving the lost? TRANSITION: "Let's now consider the Holy Spirit's responsibility as He seeks and saves a lost world through us."
Observ./Interp.	C. THE HOLY SPIRIT'S RESPONSIBILITY IN FULFILLING THE TASK
Acts 1:8	1. What does Jesus promise concerning the Holy Spirit?
Application John 16:8-10	2. Suppose a person who was skeptical of witnessing asked you, "How can you expect to go around telling people about Christ and, in just a few minutes, convince them to receive Christ?" TRANSITION: "Despite the obvious commands to share our faith, and the available power to do so, many people don't share their faith regularly. A very common reason people do not share their faith is that they don't know how. In our remaining time, we'll be discussing one method for communicating our faith that has been proven to be effective."
25	**Practical Ministry**
(3-5)	A. WHY USE THE FOUR SPIRITUAL LAWS BOOKLET? 1. It helps you begin the conversation. 2. It begins with a positive note: God loves you. 3. It presents the claims of Christ clearly. 4. It includes an invitation to receive Christ. 5. It offers suggestions for growth and emphasizes the importance of the church. 6. It helps you to stay on the subject. 7. It enables you to be brief, prepared and confident.

Time/Section	Outline/Questions and Learning Activities
	8. It provides a transferable method for presenting Christ to others.
	9. It can be left with the individual after you have shared with him.
	10. It is an immediate follow-up tool.
(10)	B. DEMONSTRATION OF SHARING THE FOUR SPIRITUAL LAWS BOOKLET THROUGH PAGE 10
(10)	C. TWO-BY-TWO PRACTICE OF SHARING THE FOUR SPIRITUAL LAWS BOOKLET

Action Point   Read through the entire Four Spiritual Laws booklet with a friend this week. You will also greatly benefit from reading Transferable Concept 6, "How to Introduce Others to Christ."

5

Prayer

Close by praying for opportunities to share the Four Spiritual Laws this week. Ask the Lord for results as the gospel is presented.

60

Preparation

PERSONAL PERSPECTIVE

Set aside at least half an hour when you won't be disturbed. Have your Bible, Discovery Group study guide and a Four Spiritual Laws booklet with you. Begin your time by asking the Lord to give you His heart for the world and to see individuals the way He does. Answer all the questions in the study guide and become completely familiar with the Four Spiritual Laws booklet. Put yourself in the place of the group members and remember the first time you were trained in sharing the Four Spiritual Laws booklet. This lesson should be a natural transition to an actual witnessing situation in Lesson 6. Unless your group is unusually mature, do not tell them in advance that they will go witnessing the next week.

INTRODUCTION TO JOHN

The purpose of the fourth Gospel, written by the beloved apostle John between 85 and 90 A.D., is to set forth the deity of Jesus, as stated in John 20:30,31. John gives irrefutable proof of Jesus' deity in order to produce faith in men's hearts that they might receive eternal life. Many sections of the book (e.g. all of Chapter 3) deal primarily with being born spiritually through faith.

INTRODUCTION TO ACTS

Luke, the physician, has been given credit for the authorship of Acts, written about 63 A.D. The book of Acts bridges the period between the four Gospels and the Epistles and deals with the history of the first-century Church. Chapter 1 is the beginning point as our Lord prepares His men for the coming of the Holy Spirit.

SUPPLIES

Four Spiritual Laws booklets for group members.

RESOURCES

Unger's Bible Handbook
Transferable Concept 5, "How to Witness in the Spirit"
Transferable Concept 6, "How to Introduce Others to Christ"

The greatest work a Christian can do is to introduce Jesus Christ to a friend.

Sharing
(10 Minutes)

Have the group members share any experiences they had in applying the principles of walking with Christ that they studied in the previous lesson.

ASK:

"In what ways were you able to apply the principles concerning how to walk with Christ that we discussed last week?"

If only a little sharing takes place, say:

"Let's spend a few minutes sharing what God has been doing in our lives this week. Maybe there is something each of you would like to share with the rest of us."

Bible Study
(20 Minutes)

Open the bible study in a brief prayer, asking God to teach the group.

Motivation (30)

DISCUSSION:

Direct the group in a discussion of the following questions. Share the suggested answers only if necessary. Summarize the group's answers after discussing each question and encourage group members to write the conclusions in their study guides.

A. THE MOST IMPORTANT TASK IN LIFE

1. What are some words you would use to describe a research scientist who discovered the cure for cancer, but never told anyone about it?

   Irresponsible, selfish, crazy, inhumane.

2. What would you say is the cure for the spiritual cancer of sin?

   Knowing Christ personally, trusting in Him for forgiveness of sin and having Him live through us to make us new.

Clarifying
Questions:

2a. What do some others of you think?
2b. What is the only way a man can be forgiven of his sins?
2c. Why did Christ have to die?

3. What words would you use to describe a person who knew the cure for the spiritual cancer of sin and started telling others about it?

Loving, concerned, compassionate

RELATE:

"We have the cure for man's sin and the heart-aches of the world. It really is inconceivable that we would not share Christ with a sick and dying world. We have the incredible privilege of seeing lives changed because of our witness for Christ.

TRANSITION:

"We need to understand that man's helplessness is one reason we should share our faith. Another reason for sharing is that it is Christ's purpose for our lives. First, let's consider what purpose Christ had and how it relates to us."

Observ./Interp.   (31)

Ask a group member to read the Scripture.

Discuss the follow-ing questions. Fol-low the same procedure as before.

B. CHRIST'S PURPOSE AND HIS PURPOSE FOR US

JOHN 17:1-4
1. What are some things that you see in these verses concerning the purpose and desires Christ had for His life?

He wanted to glorify the Father, to give eternal life to men and to accomplish the work the Father gave Him to do.

2. In verse 4, what did Jesus do to glorify the Father in His life?

He accomplished the work the Father gave Him to do.

Direct group members to look at the Scripture verses and continue the discussion.

> **LUKE 19:10; JOHN 17:18,20**
> 3. How would you describe "the work" that God the Father gave Jesus to do?
>
> <u>To give eternal life to men; also implied is</u> <u>discipling His men to help bring His mes-</u> <u>sage to a lost world.</u>
> _____
> _____

Application

> 4. If we allowed Jesus to live His life through us today, what are some things He would be doing?
>
> <u>He'd use us to seek and save the lost and</u> <u>develop men to go to the world.</u>
> _____
> _____

Clarifying Questions:

4a. What does Luke 19:10 say that could help us know what Jesus would be doing through us today?
4b. Therefore, what should we be doing?

> **MATTHEW 28:18-20**
> 5. According to Matthew 28:18-20, what is the scope or boundary of our task of seeking and saving the lost?
>
> <u>Every nation, our goal is the whole world.</u>
> _____
> _____

TRANSITION:

"Let's now consider the Holy Spirit's responsibility as He seeks and saves a lost world through us."

Observ./Interp. (32)

> C. THE HOLY SPIRIT'S RESPONSIBILITY IN FULFILLING THE TASK

Have the verse read.

Discuss the study questions. Share the suggested answers if necessary.

> ACTS 1:8
> 1. What does Jesus promise concerning the Holy Spirit?
>
>   <u>To empower, to enable Christians to be</u>
>   <u>His witnesses throughout the whole</u>
>   <u>world.</u>
>   _____
>   _____

EXPLAIN:

"A witness is someone who testifies about something he has seen or experienced personally. He is called upon to speak the truth. The Holy Spirit enables us to be witnesses for Christ.

"However, some may be scared about sharing Christ."

Application

> JOHN 16:8-10
> 2. Suppose a person who was skeptical of witnessing asked you, "How can you expect to go around telling people about Christ and, in just a few minutes, convince them to receive Christ?"
>
>   <u>It is our responsibility to tell others and it</u>
>   <u>is the Holy Spirit's responsibility to con-</u>
>   <u>vict men of their need. Even before we go</u>
>   <u>out to share, God is preparing men.</u>
>   _____
>   _____

EXPLAIN:

"When Christ promised that the Holy Spirit would empower us to be witnesses for Him, He also meant that the Holy Spirit would give us the confidence and boldness as well as the words to speak. And as we share the gospel, the Holy Spirit also opens the hearts and minds of those with whom we talk so they can understand and receive Christ.

"Because God is at work in the hearts of men, drawing them to Himself, we know that the victory is already ours and we need only to collect the fruit which He has prepared. The Holy Spirit is preparing men even as we go. The victory is the

Lord's in the hearts of men and we have the privilege of seeing God work.

TRANSITION:

"Despite the obvious commands to share our faith, and the available power to do so, many people don't share their faith regularly. A very common reason people do not share their faith is that they don't know how. In our remaining time, we'll be discussing one method for communicating our faith that has been proven to be effective."

Practical Ministry
(25 Minutes)

Ask a group member to read part A. Instruct the others to follow along in their study guides.

A. WHY USE THE FOUR SPIRITUAL LAWS BOOKLET?

1. It helps you to begin the conversation.
2. It begins with a positive note: God loves you.
3. It presents the claims of Christ clearly.
4. It includes an invitation to receive Christ.
5. It offers suggestions for growth and emphasizes the importance of the church.
6. It helps you to stay on the subject.
7. It enables you to be brief, prepared and confident.
8. It provides a transferable method for presenting Christ to others.
9. It can be left with the individual after you have shared with him.
10. It is an immediate follow-up tool.

SAY:

"I would like to demonstrate how we can use this booklet to share Christ with someone else."

Choose a partner for the demonstration.

RELATE:

"(Name), please pretend that you are a person who has not received Christ, but you are open to the gospel.

"Let's assume that my partner and I have been talking for a little while and are getting to know each other. In the course of the conversation, I say something like, 'I've been sharing this booklet with some people and getting their opinions on it. It explains how a person can have a personal relationship with God through Jesus Christ. Would you mind if I took a few minutes and shared it with you?'

"You may want to take notes in your study guides as you observe."

Share the Four Spiritual Laws booklet through page 10. Read the booklet directly to your partner without additional explanations. Don't pause and say, "This is how I would do it." Give your demonstration as though you were really sharing with a non-Christian. Hold the booklet so your partner can see it. Go slowly. Ask him to read a verse occasionally.

(33)

B. DEMONSTRATION OF SHARING THE FOUR SPIRITUAL LAWS BOOKLET THROUGH PAGE 10

Notes:

After the demon-
stration, ask the
group members if
they have any
questions about it.

Pause and answer
any relevant ques-
tions. Don't get
side-tracked.

Continue with the
two-by-two
practice.

SAY: "Now I would like everyone to choose a partner.

"Let's practice sharing the Four Spiritual Laws with
each other. Look at the instructions in your study
guides for this practice."

READ:

C.   TWO-BY-TWO PRACTICE OF SHARING THE
     FOUR SPIRITUAL LAWS BOOKLET

1.   Introduce the booklet (use a or b).

    a.   "I'm involved in a six-week study. One
       of my assignments is to get some
       individuals' opinions on a booklet
       we've been studying. Would you have
       a few minutes to help me with this
       assignment?" (Wording of this may
       vary with your situation.)
    b.   "We're getting some opinions on this
       booklet called The Four Spiritual
       Laws. Would you have a few minutes
       to help me?"

2.   Read the booklet directly to your partner
    without additional explanations.
3.   Give the presentation as though you were
    really sharing with a non-Christian.
4.   Hold the booklet so your partner can see
    it.
5.   Go slowly. Have your partner read a verse
    occasionally.
(34)   6.   After reading page 10, conclude with a
    personal invitation to receive Christ.

RELATE:

"One of you should pretend that you are a non-Christian who is open and interested. The person who is the Christian should read the booklet just as it is. Stop after leading the person in prayer at the bottom of page 10. I'll tell you when to switch parts."

Allow 10 minutes for the two-by-two practice. After five minutes, have them switch parts, continuing to read the booklet through page 10.

RELATE:

"For next week I would like each of you to practice sharing your faith using the method we discussed today."

Action Point Read through the entire Four Spiritual Laws booklet with a friend this week. You will also greatly benefit from reading Transferable Concept 6, "How to Introduce Others to Christ."

Prayer
(5 Minutes)

Close by praying for opportunities to share the Four Spiritual Laws this week. Ask the Lord for results as the Gospel is presented.

DISCIPLESHIP HINTS FOR THE LEADER

By this time, the people who are "fruitful" should begin to show themselves. Those who are not interested, or who have not resolved the issue of Christ's lordship in their lives, will be resisting the group meetings and/or meeting with you.

We might define a faithful person as one who has a teachable spirit, a heart for God and who gives beginning indications of desiring to pass on to others what he/she is learning.

There are some leaders who feel responsible for those who are not interested. Therefore, they spend their time trying to build interest in those who are resisting spiritual things. The result is usually disappointing. Very few, if any, vital spiritual movements have been built by leaders who spend their time with those who are not ready to move for God.

Jesus provided numerous examples of philosophy for discipleship which might be summarized in the phrase, "Move with the movers." In other words, "Disciple those who want to be discipled."

In Matthew 19:21, Jesus challenged the rich young man to follow Him. However, the young man declined the challenge. Jesus did not run after the young man and beg him to "follow Me." The challenge and conditions were clearly stated and the opportunity was given, but the final decision was always left with the potential disciple.

Each of Jesus' 12 disciples, in contrast with the rich young man, willfully followed Him. Jesus invested three years of His time with these men—men who wanted to follow Him and desired to be discipled.

It is interesting that during this period of time, Christ moved with perfect clarity of purpose. His objective was clear—to seek and to save the lost.

His disciples, though they were often hesitant and disloyal, and eventually betrayed Him, were never allowed by the Master to lose sight of His objective. Therefore, a group leader must never be afraid to set high standards and call his disciples to those standards.

Also, group leaders must never be afraid to lose people. If everyone is responding positively, it is likely that a low commitment level is being demonstrated by both the group leader and the members. On the other hand, if there is little positive response, you must evaluate whether you are building relationships effectively.

6
Sharing Christ
══With Others══

As the leader, you have two options for this Discovery Group lesson.

OPTION ONE:

This option demonstrates the use of a survey to introduce the Four Spiritual Laws booklet.

OPTION TWO:

This option demonstrates how to initiate a conversation to share the Four Spiritual Laws booklet without the use of a survey.

OPTION ONE

OVERVIEW GOAL

The goal of this lesson is to provide a successful witnessing experience for group members as they use a survey in introducing the Four Spiritual Laws booklet.

LEARNING OBJECTIVES

By the end of this lesson, group members will be able to:

1. State how Paul's purpose in life should affect our lives today.

2. Use a survey to introduce the Four Spiritual Laws.

3. Share their faith in Christ with non-Christians.

Time/Section	Outline/Questions and Learning Activities
5	## Sharing Have the group members share any opportunities they had to read through the Four Spiritual Laws booklet with a friend.
20-25	## Bible Study
Motivation	A. J. HUDSON TAYLOR—GOD'S MAN IN CHINA TRANSITION: "Although God is ultimately responsible for bringing people to Himself, He desires to use Christians to be a part of communicating the good news. Let's look at Paul's life as an example of how we can be a part of reaching those who do not know Christ."
Observ./Interp. Acts 20:17-27 **Application**	B. A REVOLUTIONARY PURPOSE 1. How would you summarize Paul's purpose in life as expressed in this passage? 2. What are some things Paul did and endured in order to see that purpose fulfilled? 3. Do you think Paul's purpose is representative of what ours should be? If so, what are some things that we should be doing to see that purpose fulfilled in our lives?
75	## Practical Ministry C. HINTS ON USING THE FOUR SPIRITUAL LAWS BOOKLET

192

Time/Section	Outline/Questions and Learning Activities

(15)	D. USING THE SURVEY TO INTRODUCE THE FOUR SPIRITUAL LAWS BOOKLET
	
	    1. Demonstration of how to use the survey and the transition to the Four Spiritual Laws
	    2. Hints for witnessing with a survey
	    3. Two-by-two practice

(60)	E. WITNESSING EXPERIENCE
15-30	F. SHARING TIME **Action Point** Read Transferable Concept 7, "How to Help Fulfill the Great Commission."
5	# Prayer Close in prayer for the various individuals with whom the group members shared. Emphasize again that the Lord is responsible for the results. We are simply to follow Him.
──────── 2 hrs. to 2 hrs. and 20 min.	

Preparation

PERSONAL PERSPECTIVE

Set aside at least one half hour when you will not be disturbed. Study the leader's guide and the Discovery Group study guide for the lesson. Pray for your group members that their hearts would be prepared to walk in obedience to Christ. Consider ways to make the meeting profitable for the group members.

This lesson is devoted to motivating the group members to apply their Christian faith in witnessing. The group leader must determine the best situation for exposing his group to evangelism.

This lesson will require two hours. If you have less time, designate the witnessing time as priority. You may omit both the Sharing time at the beginning and point B of the Bible Study. Also the praise time after witnessing may be shortened to 15 minutes rather than 30.

In order to save time, familiarize yourself with the motivation story and be prepared to tell it briefly to the group.

Choose the best places for the group members to go witnessing. Random witnessing does not always provide the most fruitful contacts for follow-up. However, random contacts can provide excellent opportunities to see the Lord work in miraculous ways. Random witnessing often stretches a person's faith as no other kind of witnessing does. The total time for travel and witnessing should be no more than one hour. Plan your location to fit this limit.

SUPPLIES

Surveys—Either the Community Religious Survey or the University Religious Questionnaire (See IV Practical Ministry—Training Appendix for samples)
Four Spiritual Laws booklet for each group member
Transferable Concept 7, "How to Help Fulfill the Great Commission" for each group member.

"There is no greater honor than to be the instrument in God's hands of leading one person out of the kingdom of Satan into the glorious light of Heaven."*

D.L. Moody

Sharing
(5 Minutes)

Have the group members share any opportunities they had to read through the Four Spiritual Laws booklet with a friend.

ASK:

"Did anyone have an opportunity to share the Four Spiritual Laws with a friend during the week?"

Your attitude about witnessing will be very important in setting the tone for the group members. Let them know that you are excited because of the significance this experience could have in their lives and in the lives of those with whom they share.

If no one responds, say:

"Let's spend a few minutes sharing what God has been doing in our lives this week. Maybe there is something you would like to share with us."

*Bill Bright, *Teacher's Manual for the Ten Basic Steps Toward Christian Maturity*, Copyright © 1965, p. 342: Used by permission of Campus Crusade for Christ, Inc., Arrowhead Springs, California.

Bible Study
(20-25 Minutes)

Open the Bible
study in a brief
prayer, asking God
to teach the group.

Motivation (36)

Summarize this
story in your own
words:

A. J. HUDSON TAYLOR—GOD'S MAN IN CHINA

". . . the missionary came at once to the heart of his message. Back again in thought in the land of his adoption, he was traveling by native junk from Shanghai to Ningpo. Among his fellow-passengers, one Chinese, who had spent some years in England and went by the name of Peter, was much upon his heart, for, though not unacquainted with the Gospel, he knew nothing of its saving power. Simply he told the story of this man's friendliness and of his own efforts to win him to Christ. Nearing the city of Sungkiang, they were preparing to go ashore together, when Taylor in his cabin was startled by a sudden splash and cry that told of a man overboard. Springing at once on deck he looked around and missed Peter.

'Yes,' exclaimed the boatmen unconcernedly, 'it was over there he went down!'

To drop the sail and jump into the water was the work of a moment; but the tide was running out, and the low, shrubless shore afforded little landmark. Searching everywhere in an agony of suspense, Taylor caught sight of some fishermen with a drag-net—just the thing needed.

'Come,' he cried as hope revived, 'come and drag over this spot. A man is drowning!'

'*Veh bin*,' was the amazing reply: 'It is not convenient.'

'Don't talk of convenience! Quickly come, or it will be too late.'

'We are busy fishing.'

'Never mind your fishing! Come—only come *at once*! I will pay you well.'

'How much will you give us?'

'Five dollars! only don't stand talking. Save life without delay!'

'Too little!' they shouted across the water. 'We will not come for less than thirty dollars.'

'But I have not so much with me! I will give you all I've got.'

'And how much may that be?'

'Oh, I don't know. About fourteen dollars.'

(37) Upon this they came, and the first time they passed the net through the water brought up the missing man. But all Taylor's efforts to restore respiration were in vain. It was only too plain that life had fled, sacrificed to the callous indifference of those who might easily have saved it.

A burning sense of indignation swept over the great audience. Could it be that anywhere on earth people were to be found so utterly callous and selfish! But as the earnest voice went on, conviction struck home all the more deeply that it was unexpected:

Is the body, then, of so much more value than the soul? We condemn those heathen fishermen. We say they were guilty of the man's death—because they could easily have saved him, and did not do it. But what of the millions whom we leave to perish, and that eternally? What of the plain command 'Go ye into all the world and preach the gospel to every creature,' and the searching question inspired by God Himself, 'If thou forbear to deliver them that are drawn unto death and those that are ready to be slain; if thou sayest, Behold, we knew it not; doth not he that pondereth the heart consider it? and he that keepeth thy soul, doth not he know it? and shall he not render to every man according to his works?'"*

TRANSITION:

"Although God is ultimately responsible for bringing people to Himself, He desires to use Christians to be a part of communicating the good news. Let's look at Paul's life as an example of how we can be a part of reaching those who do not know Christ."

Observ./Interp.

Ask a group member to read the passage.

DISCUSSION:

Direct the group in a discussion of the questions. Share the suggested answers only if necessary.

ACTS 20:17-27
B. A REVOLUTIONARY PURPOSE

Summarize the group's answers after discussing each question and encourage the group members to write the conclusions in their study guides.

1. How would you summarize Paul's purpose in life as expressed in this passage?

To testify of the gospel of the grace of God (vs. 24)

---

*Dr. and Mrs. Howard Taylor, *J. Hudson Taylor: God's Man in China*, Copyright © 1977, pp. 165,166: Used by permission of Moody Press, Chicago, Illinois.

Clarifying
Questions:

1a. What do some of the rest of you think?
1b. What ministry had God given according to vs. 24?

(38)

2. What are some things Paul did and endured in order to see that purpose fulfilled?

He spent time with one group of men, serving them in tears and trials. He taught all that was profitable. He went out publicly, even house-to-house, testifying repentence toward God and faith in Christ. He was willing to face imprisonment. He didn't see his life as being of any value to himself. He preached the kingdom and declared the purpose of God.

Application

3. Do you think Paul's purpose is representative of what ours should be? If so, what are some things that we should be doing to see that purpose fulfilled in our lives?

We should count our lives as having no value to ourselves. We should be actively involved in telling people about Christ and helping them to tell others.

Clarifying
Questions:

3a. What do others of you think?
3b. What are some ways we can be involved in seeing others come to Christ?

SAY:

"As we mentioned last week, the Four Spiritual Laws booklet is one method that God uses to draw men to Himself. Let's take a few minutes to look at some helpful hints on how to effectively use the Four Spiritual Laws."

Practical Ministry
(75 Minutes)

READ:

> C. HINTS ON USING THE FOUR SPIRITUAL
>   LAWS BOOKLET
>
> 1. Simply read aloud the Four Spiritual Laws
>   booklet, slowly and in a natural way.
> 2. When questions come up that would
>   change the subject, explain that most
>   questions are answered as you go
>   through the booklet. Or say, "That's a
>   good question. Let's talk about it after we
>   have read through the Four Spiritual
>   Laws."
> 3. Occasionally stop and ask, "Is this making
>   sense?"
> 4. Hold the booklet so that it can be seen
>   clearly. You may wish to use a pen to
>   focus on key points. This will help to hold
>   the person's attention.
> 5. Avoid arguing. Trust the Holy Spirit to use
>   the Word of God to convince men.
> 6. When you finish sharing the Four Spiritual
>   Laws and have answered all questions as
>   best you can, be sure to give the person
>   an opportunity to receive Christ.
> 7. Give the booklet to the person and
>   encourage him to refer to it later.
> 8. Always be gracious and express apprecia-
>   tion to the person for giving his time to
>   allow you to share the Four Spiritual Laws
>   with him.

(39)

RELATE:

"During our last lesson we discussed that the Holy
Spirit is preparing men to receive Christ. As we are
filled with the Holy Spirit and we talk about Christ,
we can expect God to use us as He used the first
century Church. Before we begin looking at some
'How-to's,' let's look at one more hint for sharing
the Four Spiritual Laws—the definition of successful witnessing."

READ:

> 9. Remember, successful witnessing is taking the initiative to share Christ in the power of the Holy Spirit and leaving the results to God.

SAY:

"It is our responsibility to go in the power of the Spirit. It is God's responsibility to produce the fruit.

"Now, let's talk about what we will actually be saying as we seek to share our faith today. Some of this will be a review from last week."

D. USING THE SURVEY TO INTRODUCE THE FOUR SPIRITUAL LAWS BOOKLET

1. Demonstration of how to use the survey and the transition to the Four Spiritual Laws

RELATE:

"One of the tools that we can use to help us as we share our faith is called a Community Religious Survey (or a University Religious Questionnaire). The survey helps us to determine the religious thinking of the people in any particular community. It's also an effective way for us to begin to relate to people and then to share our faith. For a few minutes I would like to demonstrate how to use the survey."

Ask two group
members to help
you in the demon-
stration. One will
be your witnessing
partner and the
other will be the
person with whom
you are sharing.

Demonstrate how
to use the survey as
if you were actually
using it with a non-
Christian. Do not
pause during your
demonstration to
give hints to the
group members.

SAY:

"Hello, my name is _____. This is _____. We are
conducting a survey to help determine the religious thinking of the people in this community,
and we are sharing some helpful information with
those who are looking for fulfillment in the spiritual dimension of their lives. Would you help us by
giving us your opinions in answer to a few
questions?"

Ask the first ques-
tion on the survey.
Then skip to the
last question and
ask it.

THEN SAY:

"Thank you, this ends the survey. By the way, what
is your name? Are you working (studying) here?"
(Establish rapport.)

"As I mentioned, we are also sharing some helpful
information called the Four Spiritual Laws. It
explains how Christ can be known personally.
Have you ever heard of it? . . . Would you mind if I
took a few minutes to share it with you? . . . Just as
there are physical laws . . .

Do not continue
reading the
booklet.

SAY: "Look at your study guides under the section entitled 'Hints for witnessing with a survey.' Follow along in your study guides as I read them."

READ:

2. Hints for witnessing with a survey
a. Move through the survey quickly and do not get off on tangents.
b. If a person is unable or unwilling to answer a question, move graciously to the next question rather than press the issue.
c. If a person desires more information as to why you are taking the survey, be honest and open with him and simply say that you are taking the survey because you are interested in the spiritual lives of individuals, and the survey helps you to be aware of the needs of people and how you can be of help to them.
d. Be certain to maintain a neutral attitude during the survey. Do not give any help or any approval or disapproval of the answers given.

RELATE: "At this point I would like for you to copy the simple introduction that I used at the top of one of the surveys which you are about to receive. Also, copy the transition to the Four Spiritual Laws at the bottom of the same survey.

Distribute surveys to the group members.

SAY: "You will see the following introduction in your study guides, but please copy it onto the top of the survey sheet."

203

(40)

> e. Introduce the survey: "Hello, my name is _____. This is _____. We are conducting a survey to help determine the religious thinking of the people in this community and we are sharing some helpful information with those who are looking for fulfillment in the spiritual dimension of their lives. Would you help us by giving us your opinions in answer to a few questions?"

RELATE:

"At the end of the survey, attempt to establish rapport with the person. Ask him appropriate questions like: 'Where are you from?' 'Are you studying here?' or others. After a short time of establishing rapport, you can say something like I said during my demonstration. Even though it's in your study guides, please copy this transition at the bottom of one of your surveys."

> f. Transition to the Four Spiritual Laws: "As I mentioned, we are also sharing some helpful information called the Four Spiritual Laws. It explains how Christ can be known personally. Have you ever heard of it? Would you mind if I took a few minutes to share it with you?"

RELATE:

"At this time, let's take a few minutes to practice using the survey. Choose a partner and let's practice with one another. Use the introduction that I just shared with you and then proceed through the entire survey. Do not give your partner a difficult time. Answer the questions normally. At the conclusion of the survey, make the transition to the Four Spiritual Laws, using the statement that you wrote at the bottom of your survey. It's not necessary to go through the Four Laws booklet at this time."

Allow five minutes for practice.

SAY:

Lead a short time of prayer centered on God's faithfulness or the verses studied earlier in Acts.

Give directions on the location for witnessing.

SAY:

Send the group members out in pairs to spend an hour sharing their faith at a predetermined place. Before they go, review the definition of successful witnessing.

When everyone returns, lead a time of sharing.

ASK:

Wait for responses.

SAY:

---

3. Two-by-two practice

"Before we go out to share our faith, let's spend a few minutes praying together."

"In about an hour, let's meet here (or another appropriate place). We can share some of the things that happened and how the Lord has worked."

"How many of you had success in witnessing?

"Remember, our success in witnessing is not measured by what we saw happen. If we went in the power of the Holy Spirit and we took the initiative to share Christ, then we were successful in our witnessing. If we were filled with the Holy Spirit, we have no right to take credit for any results we saw. Neither can we blame ourselves if there were no visible results."

Ask group members to share their experiences. Use these experiences as a training time. After each group member speaks, make comments on what he shared. Comments should be instructive and helpful for the particular individual as well as for the rest of the group.

Emphasize how God is pleased with their faith and obedience in going. Do not let anyone feel guilty if he did not see fruit. Point them again to the definition of successful witnessing if needed.

The effectiveness of the sharing time depends upon your ability to discover exactly what happened and to relate to your group members in an instructive, loving manner.

READ THE
ACTION POINT:

Action Point "As you consider making an impact for Christ in this world, read Transferable Concept 7, 'How to Help Fulfill the Great Commission.'"

Prayer
(5 Minutes)

Close in prayer for the various individuals with whom the group members shared. Emphasize again that the Lord is responsible for the results. We are simply to follow Him.

OPTION TWO

OVERVIEW GOAL

The goal of this lesson is to provide a successful witnessing experience for the group members as they use conversation in introducing the Four Spiritual Laws booklet.

LEARNING OBJECTIVES

By the end of this lesson, group members will be able to:

1. State how Paul's purpose in life should affect our lives today.

2. Use initiating conversation to introduce the Four Spiritual Laws.

3. Share their faith in Christ with non-Christians.

Time/Section	Outline/Questions and Learning Activities
5	## Sharing
	Have the group members share any opportunities they had to read through the Four Spiritual Laws booklet with a friend.
20-25	## Bible Study
Motivation	A. J. HUDSON TAYLOR—GOD'S MAN IN CHINA
	TRANSITION: "Although God is ultimately responsible for bringing people to Himself, He desires to use Christians to be a part of communicating the good news. Let's look at Paul's life as an example of how we can be a part of reaching those who do not know Christ."
Observ./Interp.	B. A REVOLUTIONARY PURPOSE
Acts 20:17-27	1. How would you summarize Paul's purpose in life as expressed in this passage?
	2. What are some things Paul did and endured in order to see that purpose fulfilled?
Application	3. Do you think Paul's purpose is representative of what ours should be? If so, what are some things that we should be doing to see that purpose fulfilled in our lives?
75	## Practical Ministry
	C. HINTS ON USING THE FOUR SPIRITUAL LAWS BOOKLET

Time/Section	Outline/Questions and Learning Activities
(15)	**D. INTRODUCING THE FOUR SPIRITUAL LAWS BOOKLET WITHOUT USING A SURVEY**
	1. Demonstration of the introduction and transition to the Four Spiritual Laws booklet
	2. Hints for witnessing without using a survey
	3. Two-by-two practice
(60)	**E. WITNESSING EXPERIENCE**
15-30	**F. SHARING TIME**
	Action Point Read Transferable Concept 7, "How to Help Fulfill the Great Commission."
5	# Prayer
	Close in prayer for the various individuals with whom the group members shared. Emphasize again that the Lord is responsible for the results. We are simply to follow Him.
2 hrs. to 2 hrs. and 20 min.	

Preparation

PERSONAL PERSPECTIVE

Set aside at least one half hour when you will not be disturbed. Study the leader's guide and the Discovery Group study guide for the lesson. Pray for your group members that their hearts would be prepared to walk in obedience to Christ. Consider ways to make the meeting profitable for the group members.

This lesson is devoted to motivating the group members to apply their Christian faith in witnessing. The group leader must determine the best situation for exposing his group to evangelism.

This lesson will require two hours. If you have less time, designate the witnessing time as priority. You may omit both the Sharing time at the beginning and point B of the Bible Study. Also the praise time after witnessing may be shortened to 15 minutes rather than 30.

In order to save time, familiarize yourself with the motivation story and be prepared to tell it briefly to the group.

Choose the best places for the group members to go witnessing. Random witnessing does not always provide the most fruitful contacts for follow-up. However, random contacts can provide excellent opportunities to see the Lord work in miraculous ways. Random witnessing often stretches a person's faith as no other kind of witnessing does. The total time for travel and witnessing should be no more than one hour. Plan your location to fit this limit.

SUPPLIES

Four Spiritual Laws booklet for each group member
Transferable Concept 7, "How to Help Fulfill the Great Commission" for each group member

> "There is no greater honor than to be the instrument in God's hands of leading one person out of the kingdom of Satan into the glorious light of Heaven."*
>
> D.L. Moody

Sharing
(5 Minutes)

Have the group members share any opportunities they had to read through the Four Spiritual Laws booklet with a friend.

ASK:

"Did anyone have an opportunity to share the Four Spiritual Laws with a friend during the week?"

Your attitude about witnessing will be very important in setting the tone for the group members. Let them know that you are excited because of the significance this experience could have in their lives and in the lives of those with whom they share.

If no one responds, say:

"Let's spend a few minutes sharing what God has been doing in our lives this week. Maybe there is something you would like to share with us."

*Bill Bright, *Teacher's Manual for the Ten Basic Steps Toward Christian Maturity*, Copyright © 1965, p. 342: Used by permission of Campus Crusade for Christ, Inc., Arrowhead Springs, California.

Bible Study
(20-25 Minutes)

Open the Bible study in a brief prayer, asking God to teach the group.

Motivation

Summarize this story in your own words:

A. J. HUDSON TAYLOR—GOD'S MAN IN CHINA

". . . the missionary came at once to the heart of his message. Back again in thought in the land of his adoption, he was traveling by native junk from Shanghai to Ningpo. Among his fellow-passengers, one Chinese, who had spent some years in England and went by the name of Peter, was much upon his heart, for, though not unacquainted with the Gospel, he knew nothing of its saving power. Simply he told the story of this man's friendliness and of his own efforts to win him to Christ. Nearing the city of Sungkiang, they were preparing to go ashore together, when Taylor in his cabin was startled by a sudden splash and cry that told of a man overboard. Springing at once on deck he looked around and missed Peter.

'Yes,' exclaimed the boatmen unconcernedly, 'it was over there he went down!'

To drop the sail and jump into the water was the work of a moment; but the tide was running out, and the low, shrubless shore afforded little landmark. Searching everywhere in an agony of suspense, Taylor caught sight of some fishermen with a drag-net—just the thing needed.

'Come,' he cried as hope revived, 'come and drag over this spot. A man is drowning!'

'*Veh bin*,' was the amazing reply: 'It is not convenient.'

'Don't talk of convenience! Quickly come, or it will be too late.'

'We are busy fishing.'

'Never mind your fishing! Come—only come *at once*! I will pay you well.'

'How much will you give us?'

'Five dollars! only don't stand talking. Save life without delay!'

'Too little!' they shouted across the water. 'We will not come for less than thirty dollars.'

'But I have not so much with me! I will give you all I've got.'

'And how much may that be?'

'Oh, I don't know. About fourteen dollars.'

Upon this they came, and the first time they passed the net through the water brought up the missing man. But all Taylor's efforts to restore respiration were in vain. It was only too plain that life had fled, sacrificed to the callous indifference of those who might easily have saved it.

A burning sense of indignation swept over the great audience. Could it be that anywhere on earth people were to be found so utterly callous and selfish! But as the earnest voice went on, conviction struck home all the more deeply that it was unexpected:

Is the body, then, of so much more value than the soul? We condemn those heathen fishermen. We say they were guilty of the man's death—because they could easily have saved him, and did not do it. But what of the millions whom we leave to perish, and that eternally? What of the plain command 'Go ye into all the world and preach the gospel to every creature,' and the searching question inspired by God Himself, 'If thou forbear to deliver them that are drawn unto death and those that are ready to be slain; if thou sayest, Behold, we knew it not; doth not he that pondereth the heart consider it? and he that keepeth thy soul, doth not he know it? and shall he not render to every man according to his works?'"*

TRANSITION:

"Although God is ultimately responsible for bringing people to Himself, He desires to use Christians to be a part of communicating the good news. Let's look at Paul's life as an example of how we can be a part of reaching those who do not know Christ."

Observ./Interp.

ACTS 20:17-27
B.   A REVOLUTIONARY PURPOSE

Ask a group member to read the passage.

DISCUSSION:

Direct the group in a discussion of the questions. Share the suggested answers only if necessary.

Summarize the group's answers after discussing each question and encourage the group members to write the conclusions in their study guides.

1.   How would you summarize Paul's purpose in life as expressed in this passage?

To testify of the gospel of the grace of God (vs. 24)

*Dr. and Mrs. Howard Taylor, *J. Hudson Taylor: God's Man in China*, Copyright © 1977, pp. 165,166: Used by permission of Moody Press, Chicago, Illinois.

Clarifying
Questions:

1a. What do some of the rest of you think?

1b. What ministry had God given Paul according to vs. 24?

---

2. What are some things Paul did and endured in order to see that purpose fulfilled?

He spent time with one group of men, serving them in tears and trials. He taught all that was profitable. He went out publicly, even house-to-house, testifying repentence toward God and faith in Christ. He was willing to face imprisonment. He didn't see his life as being of any value to himself. He preached the kingdom and declared the purpose of God.

Application

3. Do you think Paul's purpose is representative of what ours should be? If so, what are some things that we should be doing to see that purpose fulfilled in our lives?

We should count our lives as having no value to ourselves. We should be actively involved in telling people about Christ and helping them to tell others.

Clarifying
Questions:

3a. What do others of you think?

3b. What are some ways we can be involved in seeing others come to Christ?

SAY:

"As we mentioned last week, the Four Spiritual Laws booklet is one method that God uses to draw men to Himself. Let's take a few minutes to look at some helpful hints on how to effectively use the Four Spiritual Laws."

Practical Ministry
(75 Minutes)

READ:

> C. HINTS ON USING THE FOUR SPIRITUAL LAWS BOOKLET
>
> 1. Simply read aloud the Four Spiritual Laws booklet, slowly and in a natural way.
> 2. When questions come up that would change the subject, explain that most questions are answered as you go through the booklet. Or say, "That's a good question. Let's talk about it after we have read through the Four Spiritual Laws."
> 3. Occasionally stop and ask, "Is this making sense?"
> 4. Hold the booklet so that it can be seen clearly. You may wish to use a pen to focus on key points. This will help to hold the person's attention.
> 5. Avoid arguing. Trust the Holy Spirit to use the Word of God to convince men.
> 6. When you finish sharing the Four Spiritual Laws and have answered all questions as best you can, be sure to give the person an opportunity to receive Christ.
> 7. Give the booklet to the person and encourage him to refer to it later.
> 8. Always be gracious and express appreciation to the person for giving his time to allow you to share the Four Spiritual Laws with him.

RELATE:

"During our last lesson we discussed that the Holy Spirit is preparing men to receive Christ. As we are filled with the Holy Spirit and we talk about Christ, we can expect God to use us as He used the first century Church. Before we begin looking at some 'How-to's,' let's look at one more hint for sharing the Four Spiritual Laws—the definition of successful witnessing."

READ:

> 9. Remember, successful witnessing is taking the initiative to share Christ in the power of the Holy Spirit and leaving the results to God.

SAY:

"It is our responsibility to go in the power of the Spirit. It is God's responsibility to produce the fruit.

"Now, let's talk about what we will actually be saying as we seek to share our faith today. Some of this will be a review from last week."

Direct group members to turn in their study guides to the section titled, "Option Two."

SAY:

"When you open a conversation with a person, it is always essential that you demonstrate interest in him and seek to establish rapport. Introduce yourself and explain why you wish to talk with him."

Ask two group members to help you in the demonstration. One will be your witnessing partner and the other will be the person with whom you are sharing.

D. INTRODUCING THE FOUR SPIRITUAL LAWS BOOKLET WITHOUT USING A SURVEY

> 1. Demonstration of the introduction and transition to the Four Spiritual Laws booklet.

RELATE:

"Assume I am approaching this person who is sitting on a bench in the shopping mall."

READ:

Depending on the witnessing location you have planned, offer them several appropriate questions they might use to establish rapport. Use one or two in a demonstration.

> "Hello, my name is _____. This is my friend, _____. What's your name? . . . Do you come here very often? (or another question to establish rapport) . . . We're spending some time today getting individuals' opinions on this little booklet called the Four Spiritual Laws. It explains how Christ can be known personally. Have you ever heard of it? . . . Would you help us by letting us share it with you and getting your opinion on it?"

SAY:

"At this time I would like you to look at your study guides and follow along as I read the 'Hints for witnessing without using a survey.'"

READ: (41)

> 2. Hints for witnessing without using a survey
>
> a. Introduce yourself and your partner, and ask the person for his name.
> b. Establish rapport.
> c. Explain that you are spending some time with a group that is involved in sharing a booklet called the Four Spiritual Laws. Ask if he has seen it. Then ask if you may share the booklet with him.

EXPLAIN:

"At this time I would like for you to take a few minutes to practice opening a conversation. Choose a partner and use the introduction I shared with you. Remember not to give your partner a difficult time. It is not necessary to go through the entire booklet now."

Allow five minutes for practice.

> 3. Two-by-two practice

SAY:

"Before we go out to share our faith, let's spend a few minutes praying together."

Lead a short time of prayer centered on God's faithfulness or the verses studied earlier in Acts.

Give directions on the location for witnessing.

SAY:

"In about an hour, let's meet here (or another appropriate place). We can share some of the things that happened and how the Lord has worked."

Send the group members out in pairs to spend an hour sharing their faith at a predetermined place. Before they go, review the definition of successful witnessing.

When everyone returns, lead a time of sharing.

ASK:

"How many of you had success in witnessing?

Wait for responses.

SAY:

"Remember, our success in witnessing is not measured by what we saw happen. If we went in the power of the Holy Spirit and we took the initiative to share Christ, then we were successful in our witnessing. If we were filled with the Holy Spirit, we have no right to take credit for any results we saw. Neither can we blame ourselves if there were no visible results."

Ask group
members to share
their experiences.
Use these expe-
riences as a train-
ing time. After each
group member
speaks, make
comments on what
he shared. Com-
ments should be
instructive and
helpful for the par-
ticular individual as
well as for the rest
of the group.

Emphasize how
God is pleased with
their faith and obe-
dience in going. Do
not let anyone feel
guilty if he did not
see fruit. Point
them again to the
definition of suc-
cessful witnessing
if needed.

The effectiveness
of the sharing time
depends upon your
ability to discover
exactly what hap-
pened and to relate
to your group
members in an
instructive, loving
manner.

READ THE
ACTION POINT:

Action Point "As you consider making an impact
for Christ in this world, read Transferable Concept
7, 'How to Help Fulfill the Great Commission.'"

Prayer
(5 Minutes)

Close in prayer for the various individuals with whom the group members shared. Emphasize again that the Lord is responsible for the results. We are simply to follow Him.

Division:
Discipleship Group
Lesson Plans 7-20

7
Developing My Relationship
═With My Heavenly Father═

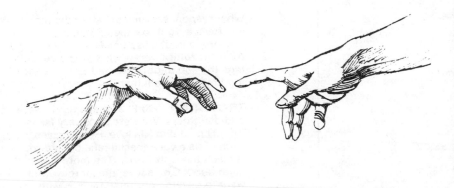

OVERVIEW GOAL

The goal of this lesson is to motivate group members to make their relationships with God a priority through having daily quiet times.

LEARNING OBJECTIVES

1. Explain why they should want to develop their relationships with God.

2. Identify five elements of a profitable quiet time as demonstrated in Psalm 143.

Time/Section	Outline/Questions and Learning Activities

10-15

Sharing

Have the group members share any opportunities they had to tell others about Christ during the past week.

30-40

Bible Study

Motivation

A. STORY OF A YOUNG MAN

   1. What responses from his father did the son have a right to expect? What responses might he hope for?

   2. After his return home, what are some feelings the son might have had about spending time with his father?

     TRANSITION: "God has made us His sons and daughters. We were once very far from Him; but in His love, He has given each of us a very special relationship with Himself through Christ. The more we learn about God's love, the more we will want to develop our relationships with Him. Let's look at Ephesians 1 and discover the special relationship we have with Him."

Observ./Interp.

B. DISCOVERING THE LOVE OF MY HEAVENLY FATHER

Ephesians 1:3-8a

   1. According to this passage, what are some things that God has done for us?

   2. Since God has chosen us to know Him (vs. 4) and has adopted us as His children (vs. 5), what are some conclusions we can draw about His love for us?

   3. What are some things that our heavenly Father desires us to have as His adopted children?

Application

   4. Although we don't deserve it, our heavenly Father has adopted us and has forgiven us all our sins. In response, what

Time/Section	Outline/Questions and Learning Activities
	should be some of our desires concerning our relationships with Him?
	TRANSITION: "Since we should want to spend time with God and develop our relationships with Him, let's look at some ways we can spend time with God through quiet times or devotional times. In Psalm 143, we can identify some characteristics of the psalmist's devotional time."
Observ./Interp.	C. SPENDING TIME WITH MY HEAVENLY FATHER
Psalm 143	1. What are some things that David might have felt as he wrote this prayer to God?
	2. Why do you think David was able to communicate his attitudes so openly to God?
Application	3. What do you see in David's relationship with God that you would like to see present in your relationship with your heavenly Father?
	4. What are some elements in this prayer that we could use in our time with God each day?
	5. What are some ways that we can consider what God has said and done in the past?
	6. What are some ways we can make our relationships with our heavenly Father a priority this week?
	7. Five things to remember in our quiet times
	Action Point Develop a plan for beginning a regular quiet time with your heavenly Father.
15-25	## Practical Ministry
	A. HOW TO DEAL WITH THE RESPONSES TO THE TWO QUESTIONS FOLLOWING THE CIRCLES
	1. The questions
	2. Responses to the circles

Time/Section	Outline/Questions and Learning Activities
	B. TWO-BY-TWO PRACTICE
5-10	**Prayer**
60-90	Close in conversational prayer. Ask God to help you develop a deeper relationship with Him.

Preparation

PERSONAL PERSPECTIVE

Set aside at least one-half hour when you will not be disturbed. Take your Bible and Discipleship Group study guide and be especially aware of the presence of God during this time. As you study Ephesians 1:3-8, ask your heavenly Father to communicate to you how much He loves you. Use the study questions on Psalm 143 to help you consider how David spent time with God. Ask God to show you how you can use David's psalm as a model for your daily quiet times.

There is potential in this lesson to get off on a tangent concerning predestination versus the free will of men. Although that is an interesting and important issue, the concern of this lesson is how to develop our relationship with our heavenly Father. If the group does begin to discuss an issue not pertaining directly to the lesson, it would be good to say something like this: "This is an issue which has fascinated men for centuries. Actually there are many Scriptures which talk about God choosing us and many others which talk about us choosing God. I think that there are some things about the Christian life that we just won't understand until we get to heaven! Predestination emphasizes God's perspective on our salvation, while our discussion today is more concerned with man's response as he develops his relationship with his heavenly Father." Then continue with the lesson.

INTRODUCTION TO EPHESIANS

This letter was written to the church at Ephesus about 61 or 62 A. D. The theme of the book is right living in light of our new position in Christ. Chapter 1 focuses on the blessings of God in Christ.

INTRODUCTION TO PSALM 143

Apparently this psalm was written as part of David's quiet time one day when he had a specific need. The Psalms as we have them today fall into two basic categories. Some were written for use in corporate worship. These generally are a call to worship God for His faithfulness. The second category, of which Psalm 143 is a part, is much like a quiet time journal we might have today. Psalm 143 was David's written prayer to God after he had spent time with Him and had considered His past faithfulness (vs. 5).

231

SUPPLIES

Four Spiritual Laws booklets

RESOURCES

Unger's Bible Handbook
Transferable Concept 9, "How to Pray"

Developing a relationship with God is the greatest adventure in life.

Sharing
(10-I5 Minutes)

Have the group members share any opportunities they had to tell others about Christ during the past week. Be sure to keep it positive.

Bible Study
(30-40 Minutes)

Open the Bible study in a brief prayer, asking God to teach the group.

Motivation

(2)

Have a group member read the story.

A. STORY OF A YOUNG MAN

The story is told of a young man who wanted to leave home and seek his fortune. Although his parents felt that he was too immature to leave home, the son insisted that he should be able to go. The son was aware of the contents of his father's will; and not wanting to wait around for his father's death, he asked for his part of the inheritance in advance. Although the parents didn't think this was wise, they decided to let the son go and gave him his share of the estate.

As soon as the son moved to another city, he spent all his money and became involved with a rough crowd. Eventually, he ended up in jail. The judge was willing to release him if he would pay a $500 fine. Since he didn't have any money, the son realized that his only hope was to write to his folks and ask for help, even though he had not written or communicated

with them for an entire year. The son was particularly concerned about his father's reaction,
since he had strongly warned the son that
something like this might happen. "Will my
father send the money?" he wondered. The
young man wrote a letter asking for understanding and help.

DISCUSSION:

Direct the group in
a discussion of the
questions. Share
the suggested
answers only if
necessary. Sum-
marize the group's
answers after dis-
cussing each ques-
tion, and en-
courage group
members to write
the conclusions in
their study guides.

1. What responses from his father did the
    son have a right to expect? What
    responses might he hope for?

    He had no right to expect anything
    positive—maybe a letter lecturing him that
    his time in jail would teach him a lesson!
    He might hope for a check to bail him out
    and for his father's forgiveness.

READ:

Much to the son's surprise, his father showed
up at the jail a few days later. He paid the fine
and hugged his son. With tears in his eyes,
the father told the son how much he had
missed him and that he had prayed each day
for his safe return. A large party was planned to
welcome the son home and to celebrate his
becoming a partner in his father's business.

(3)
2. After his return home, what are some feelings the son might have had about spending time with his father?

He would have felt privileged to spend time with him because he would have realized that his father loved him unconditionally. He would have a greater respect for his father's wisdom and values and would realize that his father had much to teach him. Therefore, he would greatly appreciate each hour spent with him.

_____
_____

Clarifying Questions:

2a. What are some other feelings the son might have experienced?
2b. What are some things the son probably learned about his father through this situation?
2c. Do you think the son would want to spend time with someone who loved him as much as his father did?

SAY:

"The story we have just looked at is a modern day version of the parable of the prodigal son in Luke 15."

If your group members are relatively young Christians, you may want to take time to read the parable.

TRANSITION:

"God has made us His sons and daughters. We were once very far from Him; but in His love, He has given us a very special relationship with Himself through Christ. The more we learn about God's love, the more we will want to develop our relationships with Him. Let's look at Ephesians 1 and discover the special relationships we have with Him."

Observ./Interp.

RELATE:

"The book of Ephesians is a letter written by the apostle Paul to the church in Ephesus around 61 or 62 A. D. It was circulated to other churches in the vicinity. The theme of this book is right living in light of all God has done for us in Christ. Chapter 1 especially tells us about what God has done for us."

Have a group member read the verses.

Discuss the following questions. Follow the same procedure as before.

EPHESIANS 1:3-8a
B. DISCOVERING THE LOVE OF MY HEAVENLY FATHER

1. According to this passage, what are some things God has done for us?

    He has given us every spiritual blessing in Christ. He has chosen us before the foundation of the world that we should be holy and blameless before Him. He predestined us to adoption as sons. He has given us grace, redemption, forgiveness of sins.

2. Since God has chosen us to know Him (vs. 4) and has adopted us as His children (vs. 5), what are some conclusions we can draw about His love for us?

    His love doesn't depend upon our behavior; it's unconditional, it's bountiful. It is prompted solely by Him.

Clarifying Questions:

2a. Any other ideas?
2b. What are some things we've done to deserve God's love?

3. What are some things that our heavenly Father desires us to have as His adopted children?

Our heavenly Father wants us to be happy
and fulfilled. He wants us to be holy and
blameless before Him. He wants us to
respond to Him with love and gratitude.
He wants us to live as adopted children
with the full rights and privileges that are
afforded true children.

Clarifying
Questions:

3a. What does it mean to be adopted?

3b. What are some things that parents
would provide for an adopted child?

3c. How do you think God wants us to
respond to Him?

3d. Do you think it pleases God when we
are afraid of Him? Why not?

Application

4. Although we don't deserve it, our heavenly Father has adopted us and has forgiven us all our sins. In response, what
should be some of our desires concerning
our relationship with Him?

(4)

We should want to develop the most inti-
mate relationship with Him that we can.
We should want to delight Him rather than
bring Him grief. We should respond to His
love and love Him with all our hearts.

Clarifying
Questions:

4a. What are some ways that we might please our heavenly Father?
4b. Since God already owns the entire universe, what can we give Him that He doesn't already have?

We can give Him ourselves. We can desire to spend time with Him.

TRANSITION:

"Since we should want to spend time with God and develop our relationships with Him, let's look at some ways we can spend time with God through quiet times or devotional times. In Psalm 143, we can identify some characteristics of the psalmist's devotional time."

Observ./Interp.

RELATE:

"The Psalms, as we have them today, fall into two basic categories. Some were written to be used by a large group of people in worshipping God. Psalm 143, however, is a psalm which falls into the second category. It is a prayer that was written down by an individual, David, as he spent time with the Lord."

Ask someone to read the psalm.

DISCUSS:

PSALM 143
C. SPENDING TIME WITH MY HEAVENLY FATHER

1. What are some things that David might have felt as he wrote this prayer to God?

He might have felt humble, desperate, overwhelmed and appalled by his situation. He probably felt hungry for God. He was confident in God's faithfulness, was teachable and yielded to God.

Clarifying
Questions:

1a. What attitudes did David express toward his circumstances?
1b. What attitudes did David express about his God?

> 2. Why do you think David was able to communicate his attitudes so openly to God?
>
> He evidently had a close, open relation-
> ship with God. He seemed to know God.
> _____
> _____

Clarifying
Questions:

2a. By looking at this prayer, what kind of relationship do you think David had with God?

2b. Does prayer seem to be awkward to David?

RELATE:

"Let's consider for a few moments how we might profit from observing David's walk with God. He obviously had a close walk with God."

Application

> 3. What do you see in David's relationship with God that you would like to see present in your relationship with your heavenly Father?
>
> I see in David openness, honest commun-
> ication, confidence in God's interest in his
> problems and His willingness to do some-
> thing about them.
> _____
> _____

Clarifying
Questions:

3a. What do some of the rest of you think?

3b. What impresses you most about David's walk with God?

RELATE:

"Actually, we can have the same kind of relationship with God that David had—the kind that we are observing in this Psalm. In fact, our heavenly Father longs for us to develop our relationships with Him. Let's look at Psalm 143 and discuss how we can spend time with God on a regular basis."

READ AND DISCUSS: (5)

4. What are some elements in this prayer that we could use in our time with God each day?

   We could focus on what God is like and review what He's done in the past. We could talk with Him honestly about what's happening in our lives and express trust in Him. We could yield our lives to Him.

   _____

   _____

Clarifying Questions:

4a. What are some things that David did in his quiet time that we might do in ours?

4b. What was David doing in verse 5?

5. What are some ways that we can consider what God has said and done in the past?

   We can think about God's faithfulness to us in the past and the prayers He has answered. We can study God's Word to learn what God is like and see what He's done in the past for others.

   _____

   _____

Clarifying Questions:

5a. Any other thoughts?

5b. What is a good way to remind yourself about all that God has done for you?

6. What are some ways we can make our relationships with our heavenly Father a priority this week?

   We can spend time with Him, reading what He's written to us in His Word. We can talk to Him throughout the day and trust Him with our problems.

   _____

   _____

Clarifying
Questions:

6a. What are some practical ways we can express our love to God?
6b. How can we get to know God better?

RELATE:

"Let me summarize five things that will help us get the most out of our time with the Lord. Most of these are just a rephrasing of the things you have already mentioned."

7. Five things to remember in our quiet times

Be sure to read these slowly allowing time for group members to write them in their study guides.

a. Learn what God is like.
b. Learn what God does and says (through Scripture).
c. Express your needs honestly to God.
d. Express your trust in Him.
e. Yield your will to Him.

READ AND
EXPLAIN:

(6) **Action Point** Develop a plan for beginning a regular quiet time with your heavenly Father.

1. Choose a quiet place where you will not be disturbed.

2. Choose a time of day when you are alert and responsive to God.

3. Begin by setting a reasonable goal such
    as:

    _____ minutes in Bible study to learn
    what God is like and what He
    promises.

    _____ minutes in praise/thanksgiving and
    expressing your trust in God.

    _____ minutes making requests of God to
    meet your needs, to guide you for
    the day and to express yieldedness
    to His will.

RELATE:

"In our next lesson we'll be discussing 'Our New
Life in Christ.' The main passage we'll be looking
at is Colossians 3:1-17. To get the most out of our
discussion, I'd encourage you to read over this
passage beforehand and even spend some time
studying it.

Practical Ministry
(15-25 Minutes)

Vision

Share a witnessing
experience that you
had when you were
first learning to
share your faith.
Seek to encourage
your group
members by mak-
ing the point that
God can use us in
spite of our lack of
experience.

Strategy

RELATE:

"For the next few weeks we will concentrate on
learning techniques that will make us more effective in sharing Christ with our friends and
acquaintances.

"During our last several times together, you have learned how to share the Four Spiritual Laws booklet and have received some training in actual witnessing situations. Now, let's talk more about how to handle various responses to the two questions following the circles."

Pass out the booklets if they don't have them.

Training

Have group members turn to page 9 of the Four Spiritual Laws booklet. Begin with, "These two circles represent two kinds of lives:" Have them follow along as you read to the bottom of the page.

A. HOW TO DEAL WITH THE RESPONSES TO THE TWO QUESTIONS FOLLOWING THE CIRCLES (Page 9 of the Four Spiritual Laws booklet.)

1. The questions:
   Question one—Which circle best represents your life?
   Question two—Which circle would you like to have represent your life?

RELATE:

"The purpose of these two questions is to help an individual identify and understand where he is spiritually. Remember, though, that one of the main objectives of sharing the Four Spiritual Laws is to show a person how to receive Christ and to give him an opportunity to do so. This is accomplished after reading the prayer on page 10. Therefore, you will want to continue your presentation no matter what the responses to these two questions are. Now, let's consider the various responses that might occur."

2. Responses to the circles.

Self-directed life

Christ-directed life

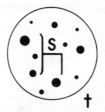
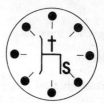

Discuss each answer and its appropriate response with your group. You may choose to demonstrate the first three responses. Stop after asking, "Which circle would you like to have represent your life?"

Demonstrate what to say when a person answers, "The circle on the right." Stop after responding to his answer concerning whether he has prayed a similar prayer.

(7)

Which circle best represents your life?

If a person answers	Appropriate Response
"The circle on the left."	"Which circle would you like to have represent your life?"
"Not sure."	"Which circle would you like to have represent your life?"
Silence	"Which circle would you like to have represent your life?"
"The circle on the right."	"That's good! I'd like to finish reading the booklet so that you can use it to share your faith with someone else." Then read through the prayer and ask, "Have you ever prayed a prayer similar to this, trusting Christ to come into your life?"

Discuss each answer and its appropriate response.

Use a group member as a partner and demonstrate the three responses to the second question. Continue reading through the prayer.

If "no": Give him an opportunity to pray.

If "yes": Ask how it happened.

Which circle would you like to have represent your life?

If a person answers	Appropriate Response
"The circle on the right."	"The following explains how you can receive Christ." Continue to read through the prayer.
"Not sure."	"The following explains how you can receive Christ." Continue to read through the prayer.
(8) "The circle on the left."	"Let me explain how you can invite Christ into your life when you decide to do so in the future." Continue to read through the prayer.

B.   TWO-BY-TWO PRACTICE

Have members pair up and practice the various answers and responses. Let them practice for a couple of minutes and then have them switch roles.

Prayer
(5-10 Minutes)

Close in conversational prayer. Ask God to help you develop a deeper relationship with Him.

Arrange the time and place for the next meeting.

8
Our New Life
══in Christ══

OVERVIEW GOAL

The goal of this lesson is to enable each member to have a new perspective in life because of his union with Christ and to motivate him to a new lifestyle as a Christian.

LEARNING OBJECTIVES

By the end of this lesson, each group member will be able to:

1. Describe a new perspective in life as a result of his union with Christ.

2. Explain his responsibility in making a willful decision to put on the new self.

3. Describe various character qualities which result from having a new lifestyle.

Time/Section	Outline/Questions and Learning Activities
10-15	**Sharing**
	Have group members share any success they have had in beginning regular quiet times with God during the week.
30-40	**Bible Study**
Motivation	A. CHARACTERISTICS OF A CHRIST-CENTERED CHRISTIAN
	1. List as many characteristics as you can that you would expect to see in the life of a person who has Christ living in and through him.
	2. Contrast the characteristics you listed with your own life and check the areas in which you would like to see changes.
	TRANSITION: "Because Christ lives in us, we have brand new lives. We can choose to allow Christ to produce exciting new qualities in our lives. Let's look at how we can view life differently as a result of being united with Christ."
Observ./Interp.	B. A NEW PERSPECTIVE
Colossians 3:1-4 Ephesians 2:5,6	1. Romans 6 explains that we have been united with Christ in His death, burial and resurrection. In Colossians 3:1-4 and Ephesians 2:5,6, what are some other things that you see are true of our union with Christ?
	2. What are some ways Paul describes the focus we each should have (Colossians 3:1-4)?
Application Matthew 6:19-21,31-34	3. Picture yourself raised up to heaven and seated with Christ. Read Matthew 6:19-21, 31-34. What are some ways that your position in heaven should affect your desires and values in life?

Time/Section	Outline/Questions and Learning Activities
Ephesians 5:15,16 Matthew 28:18-20	4. Read Ephesians 5:15,16 and Matthew 28:18-20. Since we will spend eternity with Christ, in what ways should our position in Christ affect the way we spend our time on earth? TRANSITION: "Let's look now at how we can decide between the two lives that we can live and how we can choose to experience God's best for us."
Observ./Interp. Colossians 3:5-11 Ephesians 4:22-25 **Application**	C. A NEW DECISION 1. What are some ways that these verses in Colossians describe our old manner of life? 2. Read Ephesians 4:22-25 and Colossians 3:8-10 and explain what you think it means to put off the "old self" and put on the "new self." 3. Because of God's great love toward us, He gave each of us a free will. What are some ways our having a free will relates to our "old self" and "new self"? TRANSITION: "It is obvious from this passage in Colossians that Paul was urging the believers to live new lives as a result of putting on the 'new self.' Let's look at some of the characteristics of that new lifestyle Paul was talking about."
Observ./Interp. Colossians 3:12-17 Galatians 5:22,23	D. A NEW LIFESTYLE 1. What are some of the character qualities you see in the Colossians passage? 2. What do you think the relationship is between the work of the Spirit in Galatians 5:22,23 and the character qualities you found in Colossians 3:12-17? 3. In Colossians 3:16, what do you think it means to "Let the word of Christ richly dwell within you"?

Time/Section	Outline/Questions and Learning Activities
Application	4. What are some ways our new lifestyle would be affected if we didn't allow the Word of Christ to richly dwell within us? 5. What are some steps you want to take to begin "putting on your new self"?
15-25	**Practical Ministry**
Matthew 9:36	A. DEVELOPING COMPASSION 1. What are some ways we can demonstrate compassion for people? 2. What would be some opportunities we might have to share Christ this week? B. RESPONDING TO THE QUESTION, "DOES THIS PRAYER EXPRESS THE DESIRE OF YOUR HEART?" 1. If the person answers "yes": 2. If the person answers "yes, but I'm not ready to pray" or "no," the prayer doesn't express the desire of his heart:
5-10	**Prayer** Lead the group members in conversational prayer. Encourage group members to ask God for wisdom and direction in how to respond to people they have opportunities to share Christ with this week.
60-90	

Preparation

PERSONAL PERSPECTIVE

Set aside at least one half hour when you will not be disturbed. Take your Bible and Discipleship Group study guide. Pray that God will give you insights into what it means to be united with Christ in His death, burial, resurrection and ascension to the heavenly places. Answer all the questions in the study guide, and then go back and compare your answers with the suggested answers in the leader's guide.

Be sure you are Spirit-filled. Anticipate questions group members will have in understanding their "old" and "new" selves. Be sensitive to those members who may not be growing as fast as others and be sure not to make them feel embarrassed or uncomfortable by the application of the lesson.

INTRODUCTION TO EPHESIANS

This letter was written by Paul to the church at Ephesus about 61 or 62 A.D. The theme is the believer's union with Christ in His death, burial and resurrection. Chapter 4 encourages the believer to live a life that reflects his new position in Christ.

INTRODUCTION TO COLOSSIANS

This letter, also written by Paul around 61 or 62 A.D., was written to combat various false doctrines that were threatening the church. To combat these errors, Paul exalts Christ in His person and work and describes the believer's union with Him.

RESOURCES

Unger's Bible Handbook

> "When someone becomes a Christian he becomes a brand new person inside. He is not the same any more. A new life has begun!"
>
> II Corinthians 5:17 (The Living Bible)

Sharing
(10-15 Minutes)

Have the group members share how their quiet times were during the past week, along with any particular thing they may have discovered from the Word. See I. Sharing Appendix for additional ideas.

Bible Study
(30-40 Minutes)

Open the Bible study in a brief prayer, asking God to teach the group.

Motivation (10)

Have the group members list the character qualities and give them three minutes to do personal evaluations.

Do not attempt to make them share the contrasts they found unless they choose to do so.

A. CHARACTERISTICS OF A CHRIST-CENTERED CHRISTIAN

1. List as many characteristics as you can that you would expect to see in the life of a person who has Christ living in and through him.

_____
_____
_____

2. Contrast the characteristics you listed with your own life and check the areas in which you would like to see changes.

_____
_____
_____

252

Clarifying
Questions:

2a. What are some of the characteristics that you came up with?

2b. Would any of you like to share how you would like to see your lives change in light of the characteristics we just listed?

TRANSITION:

"Because Christ lives in us, we have brand new lives. We can choose to allow Christ to produce exciting new qualities in our lives. Let's look at how we can view life differently as a result of being united with Christ."

Observ./Interp.

COLOSSIANS 3:1-4
EPHESIANS 2:5,6
B.   A NEW PERSPECTIVE

Briefly give some background information on Paul's letters to the Colossians and the Ephesians. See your Preparation page and your Bible handbook.

1.   Romans 6 explains that we have been united with Christ in His death, burial and resurrection. In Colossians 3:1-4 and Ephesians 2:5,6, what are some other things that you see are true of our union with Christ?

We have been raised up with Him and made alive with Him; we are seated in the heavenly places with Christ. Our lives are now hidden with Christ in God and we will one day be revealed with Him in glory.

Allow your group several minutes to answer the first question on their own.

DISCUSSION:

Direct the group in a discussion of the questions. Share the suggested answers only if necessary.

Summarize the group's answers after discussing each question, and encourage group members to write the conclusions in their study guides.

SAY:

"Christ not only died for our sins and forgave us, but He also delivered us from sin's power and made His Spirit to dwell within us."

---

2. What are some ways Paul describes the focus we each should have (Colossians 3:1-4)?

   We should set our minds on heavenly things and not on earthly or material things.

Clarifying Questions:

2a. In what ways does this attitude differ from that of the average non-Christian?

2b. What do others of you think?

Application (11)

3. Picture yourself raised up to heaven and seated with Christ. Read Matthew 6:19-21,31-34. What are some ways that your position in heaven should affect your desires and values in life?

We will want to do things that store up treasures in heaven rather than trying to accumulate possessions on earth. We won't be anxious for the things that we need on earth but we will seek the kingdom of God first and desire His righteousness.

Clarifying
Questions:

3a. What does anyone else think?
3b. How should our position in Christ affect our goals in life?

4. Read Ephesians 5:15,16 and Matthew 28:18-20. Since we will spend eternity with Christ, in what ways should our position in Christ affect the way we spend our time on earth?

We should make the most of our time to win men to Christ. We should be actively involved in helping to fulfill the Great Commission—helping men and women come to Christ and then discipling them.

TRANSITION: "Let's look now at how we can decide between the two lives that we can live and how we can choose to experience God's best for us."

Observ./Interp.

COLOSSIANS 3:5-11
C. A NEW DECISION

Ask a group member to read the verses. Discuss the following questions. Follow the same procedure as before.

1.   What are some ways that these verses describe our old manner of life?

Qualities like anger, wrath, malice, slander and abusive speech are all evidences of the old manner of life along with the desire to be immoral, impure, passionate, evil and greedy.

(12)

EPHESIANS 4:22-25; COLOSSIANS 3:8-10
2.   Explain what you think it means to put off the "old self" and put on the "new self."

It means laying aside, by a decision of the will, the old, corrupt nature of our lives before Christ; and putting on our new man. It is as if we are taking off dirty garments. Christ has given us clean garments, characterized by renewed minds and increasingly righteous and holy lives.

Clarifying Questions:

2a. What are some other things you think it means?

2b. Can you think of an example or illustration which would describe what it means to lay aside the old self and put on the new self?

2c. What are some similarities between this passage and laying aside old clothes and putting on new ones?

Application

3. Because of God's great love toward us, He gave each of us a free will. What are some ways our having a free will relates to our "old self" and our "new self"?

We each have a free choice: we can either allow our old manner of life to control us, or we can apply the truth of our new lives in our daily experiences.

Clarifying
Questions:

3a. Are there any other ideas?
3b. What does it mean to have a free will?
3c. If we count as true the fact that we have new natures, do you think God will give us new lifestyles as well?

SAY:

"Romans 8 and Galatians 5:16 explain that the problem of the flesh (the 'old self') can be solved by allowing the Spirit of God to direct and empower our lives. To put on the 'new self' means to make a decision to allow God's Spirit to give us direction and to empower us.

TRANSITION:

"It is obvious from this passage in Colossians that Paul was urging the believers to live the kinds of life that result from putting on the 'new self.' Let's look at some of the characteristics of that new lifestyle Paul was talking about."

Observ./Interp.

COLOSSIANS 3:12-17
D. A NEW LIFESTYLE

DISCUSS:

1. What are some of the character qualities you see in this passage?

It mentions compassion, kindness, humility, gentleness, patience, forgiveness, love, peacefulness, thankfulness to God, and understanding of and an ability to wisely teach God's Word, joy and excellence in work.

GALATIANS 5:22,23
2. What do you think the relationship is between the work of the Spirit in Galatians 5:22,23, and the character qualities you found in Colossians 3:12-17?

The work of the Holy Spirit in our lives naturally produces the qualities referred to in Colossians 3:12-17.

Clarifying Questions:

2a. Would anyone else like to add anything?
2b. According to Colossians 3:12-17, what are some qualities the Holy Spirit will produce in us to enable us to minister to others?

(13)

3. In Colossians 3:16, what do you think it means to "Let the word of Christ richly dwell within you"?

It means to spend time studying, understanding, memorizing and meditating upon God's Word.

Clarifying Questions:

3a. Does anyone have any other ideas?
3b. What do you think the word "dwell" means?
3c. How would you define "richly"?

Application

4. What are some ways our new lifestyle would be affected if we didn't allow the Word of Christ to richly dwell within us?

We would have little way of knowing what our new lifestyles should be like and we would not know how to let the Holy Spirit produce it in our lives, etc.

Clarifying
Questions:

4a. What would you expect to happen to a Christian who never read God's Word?

4b. Do you think he could live consistently in his new nature?

SAY:

"Let's spend a few minutes answering the next questions in our own study guides."

READ THE
QUESTION:

Give them two or three minutes to answer in their study guides.

5. What are some steps you want to take to begin "putting on your new self"?

Use my time better, be involved in winning men to Christ, have heavenly values, be careful what I spend my time looking at or thinking about (i.e., magazines, T.V.), etc.

RELATE:

"The Christian life is a life that is progressive. It involves growing in our knowledge of Christ and all the benefits He has provided for us. Everyday, make sure that you are allowing your 'new self' to characterize your life.

"Prayer plays an important part in seeing our lives changed. Let's spend a couple of minutes asking God to make our lives what He wants them to be. Maybe several of you would like to pray, then I'll close in a couple minutes."

Take two or three minutes to pray.

RELATE:

"In our next lesson, we'll be discussing 'The Christian's Walk and Warfare.' The main passage we'll be looking at is Ephesians 6:10-18. To get the most out of the discussion, I'd encourage each of you to read over the passage beforehand and even spend some time studying it."

Practical Ministry
(15-25 Minutes)

Vision

Have someone read the verse.

Ask the following questions and discuss the answers.

MATTHEW 9:36
A. DEVELOPING COMPASSION

1. What are some ways we can demonstrate compassion for people?

Share the life-saving message of Jesus Christ, provide spiritual leadership.

Strategy

2. What would be some opportunities we might have to share Christ this week?

Students—with people in the dorms, fraternities, sororities, classes, clubs, cafeteria, etc. Laymen—with neighbors, business associates, club members, friends, relatives, etc.

Clarifying Questions:

2a. Are there any other opportunities you can think of?
2b. Where would be some places you could typically meet people throughout the day?

SAY:

"In order to help us share Christ, we will learn what to do with different responses at the point of the prayer on page 10 in the Four Spiritual Laws booklet."

Training

RELATE:

"In presenting the Four Spiritual Laws, there is no way that you can adequately judge whether the person is ready to receive Christ unless you give him a specific opportunity to do so. Many times, someone who seems indifferent will want to pray when he is given a definite opportunity to ask Jesus Christ to be Savior and Lord of his life.

"Last week we received training on how to handle various responses to the circles. We used the questions to help the person understand and identify his spiritual status and then continued reading the booklet through the prayer on page 10. Now we are going to talk about how to handle the person's responses to the questions following the prayer."

Have the group follow along in their study guides as you read.

B. RESPONDING TO THE QUESTION, "DOES THIS PRAYER EXPRESS THE DESIRE OF YOUR HEART?"

1. If the person answers "yes":

   a. Read the next sentence: "If it does, pray this prayer right now, and Christ will come into your life as He promised."
   b. Then say: "I'll read back through the prayer and you can pray it phrase by phrase after me. Let's pray." Then lead the person through the prayer.
   c. Should he not want to pray the prayer after you, suggest that he either:

      1) Pray the prayer himself aloud.
      2) Pray the prayer silently, saying "amen" aloud when he has finished.

Roleplay:

Choose a group
member as a
partner and
demonstrate this
section. Lead him
through the prayer
on page 10. Then
have group
members practice
two-by-two. Have
them switch roles
after two minutes.

Have group
members follow
along as you read
through this
section.

2. If the person answers "yes," but is not
    ready to pray; or "no," the prayer doesn't
    express the desire of his heart:

    a. Be loving.
    b. Be positive.
    c. Say: "Let me show you what will
        happen when you decide to ask
        Christ into your life." Then turn to
        page 13 and read the introductory
        sentence and five points using the fu-
        ture tense. For example, point 3
        would read: "You will become a child
        of God." After reading, "Can you
        think of anything more wonderful that
        could have happened to you than
        receiving Christ?" Turn back to the
        prayer and give him another
        opportunity to receive Christ.
    d. If the person still doesn't invite Christ
        into his life, ask, "If later you want to
        receive Christ, what would you have
        to do?" Be sure he knows that he
        would have to invite Christ into his life
        as Savior and Lord.

Roleplay:

Choose another group member as a partner and demonstrate a situation in which a person desires to pray but says he isn't ready.

Read through page 13 and give your partner another opportunity to receive Christ.

Also demonstrate a situation in which a person says the prayer does not express the desire of his heart. After you give your partner an opportunity to pray the second time, (instruct him to decline) ask him what he would have to do if he wanted to receive Christ later.

Prayer
(5-10 Minutes)

Lead the group members in conversational prayer. Encourage group members to ask God for wisdom and direction in how to respond to people they have the opportunity to share Christ with this week. Encourage group members to pray short, sentence prayers. Each person may pray as often as he wants to or not at all. See V. Prayer Appendix for additional ideas.

Arrange the time and the place of the next meeting.

9
The Christian's Walk
══and Warfare══

OVERVIEW GOAL

The goal of this lesson is to equip group members to live victoriously in spiritual battle.

LEARNING OBJECTIVES

By the end of this lesson, each group member will be able to:

1. List the weapons used in spiritual battle.

2. Explain the use of each weapon.

3. Explain how he can use these weapons in spiritual battle.

Time/Section	Outline/Questions and Learning Activities
10-15	## Sharing
	Have group members share what they have been learning in their quiet times during the past week.
30-40	## Bible Study
Motivation	A. STORY OF A SOLDIER
	1. What are some similarities between this soldier and the Christian who does not know about his victory?
	2. What are some ways that a soldier's attitude might change if he began to realize his side was winning?
	TRANSITION: "Let's see what God's Word says about how to experience victory in our battle against Satan."
Observ./Interp.	B. PREPARING FOR BATTLE
Ephesians 6:10-18	1. What are some ways we can describe the battle Christians face?
	2. What are the various forms of protection the Lord has given us against these spiritual forces of wickedness?
	3. What are some meanings of the phrase "be strong in the Lord, and in the strength of His might" (vs. 10)?
	C. EXAMINING THE ARMOR
	1. What are some things that "to gird your loins with truth" might mean (vs. 14)?
	2. What are some meanings of "put on the breastplate of righteousness" (vs. 14)?
	3. What are some reasons why it would be important to have righteousness as a breastplate?

Time/Section	Outline/Questions and Learning Activities
	4. You need to "shoe" your feet with the knowledge that the battle with Satan has been won and we have peace with God. What would be some actions you would expect from the kind of person Paul is describing in verse 15?
	5. What are some ways faith is used in a spiritual battle (vs. 16)?
	6. What do you think Paul means by using the term "helmet of salvation" (vs. 17)?
	7. In what ways is the Word of God used in a spiritual battle (vs. 17)?
Application	D. USING THESE WEAPONS DAILY
	1. What things do you think we can do to be better equipped to use the sword of the Spirit, the Word of God?
	2. What are some of the consequences of not using these pieces of armor?
15-25	**Practical Ministry**
Luke 10:1,2	A. DISCIPLES CALLED TO THE HARVEST
	B. FINDING NEW HARVESTERS
	C. QUESTIONS FROM PAGE 11 OF THE FOUR SPIRITUAL LAWS BOOKLET
	D. QUESTIONS TO ASK A PERSON IF HE IS UNSURE THAT CHRIST IS IN HIS LIFE, REFERRING TO REVELATION 3:20
	E. PRINCIPLES TO EMPHASIZE AFTER READING PAGES 12 AND 13 TO THE NEW BELIEVER
5-10	**Prayer**
60-90	Close in conversational prayer.

Preparation

PERSONAL PERSPECTIVE

Plan a time when you can concentrate on Ephesians 6:10-18 and this lesson for at least 45 minutes. Work through your Discipleship Group study guide using only your Bible as a resource for answering the questions. Spend plenty of time on the application questions, sincerely seeking God and asking Him how you can use your weapons more effectively. Think through the spiritual battles in which you are presently engaged. Decide on at least one personal application you can share with the group. Fill in the blanks under the application section. Then carefully study your leader's guide, especially the explanations given regarding the weapons. Make sure you clearly understand each weapon and its role in the battle. Be prepared to do a role-play in the training section; determine who you will ask to assist you.

INTRODUCTION TO EPHESIANS

While imprisoned in Rome, Paul wrote this letter to the church at Ephesus about 61-62 A.D. The theme of this book is right living, in light of our new position in Christ. Chapter 6 speaks of the spiritual battle in which Christians are engaged.

SUPPLIES

Artist's pad and colored markers

RESOURCES

Balancing the Christian Life, Charles Ryrie, pp. 133,134
Satan is Alive and Well on Planet Earth, Hal Lindsey, pp. 220-228
Ten Basic Steps Teacher's Manual pp. 179-186
Unger's Bible Handbook

"The night is almost gone, and the day is at hand. Let us therefore lay aside the deeds of darkness and put on the armor of light" (Romans 13:12).

Sharing
(10-15 Minutes)

Have group members share what they have been learning in their quiet times during the past week.

Bible Study
(30-40 Minutes)

Open the Bible study in a brief prayer, asking God to teach the group.

Motivation

READS: (16) A. STORY OF A SOLDIER

There was a soldier who had been wounded and separated from the rest of his company in the jungles of a South Seas island. The soldier had to hunt for food, water and shelter and was in constant fear of being captured or killed by enemy patrols. For two years he avoided the enemy. Finally he stumbled upon some soldiers from his own country near the edge of a village. With joy, he quickly told them his story and asked if the enemy had finally been driven off the island. The men were amazed and saddened by the man's story. They told him that the war had been over for a long time and that his country had won.

SAY:

"This story is similar to what could happen in the life of a Christian. Like the soldier, he may be living in defeat and fear because he doesn't know the victory has been won in the conflict with Satan."

DISCUSSION:

Direct the group in a discussion of the questions. Share the suggested answers only if necessary. Summarize the group's answers after discussing each question and encourage group members to write the conclusions in their study guides.

1. What are some similarities between this soldier and the Christian who does not know about his victory?

He lives in fear of Satan. He tries to fight the battle alone and becomes separated from God and needs fellowship. He can feel defeated. He can experience freedom when he finds out that the war has already been won.

2. What are some ways that a soldier's attitude might change if he began to realize his side was winning?

He would be more confident in fighting: he would have more confidence in his leadership.

270

RELATE:

"The Bible teaches very clearly that the Christian life is not only a walk, but also a warfare. Many Christians do not realize this. They think that living the Christian life means escaping all trials, difficulties and temptations, and they expect to glide through their years on earth with scarcely a problem. As a matter of fact, we are strangers and pilgrims of this earth (I Peter 2:11 (KJV), living in a world ruled by Satan, and we must continually face opposition and difficulty. The Christian life should be a victorious one, but it's not always an easy one. We must continually be strengthened 'In the Lord, and in the strength of His might' (Ephesians 6:10). We cannot expect to win the battle unless we allow Christ to fight the battle for us. We have all that it takes to be good soldiers; we have Jesus Christ."

TRANSITION:

"Let's see what God's Word says about how to experience victory in our battle against Satan."

Observ./Interp.

EPHESIANS 6:10-18
B.   PREPARING FOR BATTLE

Ask a group member to read the passage. Relate the following background material.

"Paul wrote this letter to the church at Ephesus about 61 or 62 A.D. He was a prisoner in Rome at the time. A Roman guard was always stationed at his side. The theme of this book is right living, in light of our new position in Christ. We are looking at his concluding remarks regarding the Christian's walk. Here he talks about the Christian's warfare."

Discuss the following questions. Follow the same procedure as before. (17)

1.   What are some ways we can describe the battle Christians face?

The battle is against the devil and against spiritual forces of wickedness. It is not against flesh and blood.

Clarifying
Questions:

1a. What else do you see?
1b. Against whom are we battling?

You may want to
use an artist's pad
and colored
markers. Write a list
of the various parts
of the uniform so
they will stand out
to the group when
you refer to them.

2. What are the various forms of protection
that the Lord has given us against these
spiritual forces of wickedness?

The armor of protection includes the belt
of truth, the breastplate of righteousness;
shod with the gospel of peace; the shield
of faith, the helmet of salvation and the
sword of the Spirit (Word of God).

Clarifying
Questions:

2a. Are there any more?
2b. There are six forms of protection. Did
we miss any?

3. What are some meanings of the phrase
"be strong in the Lord, and in the strength
of His might" (vs. 10)?

It means to trust the Lord to give me His
power to resist the enemy. It is impossible
to fight supernatural powers in my own
human strength; the battle is God's.

Clarifying
Questions:

3a. Does anyone have any other ideas?
3b. Whose battle is it?

SAY:

"Let's examine in more detail the various parts of the armor.

"The Roman soldier was girded (strapped) with a belt síx to eight inches wide around his waist. Everything he wore was held together by this belt. His skirt was caught up in it to allow freedom of movement and his sword hung from it. It was the foundational piece of his armor."

Continue discussing the study questions.

(18)

See also John 17:17

C. EXAMINING THE ARMOR

1. What are some things that "to gird your loins with truth" might mean (vs. 14)?

   It means to wrap the truth around your-self. Abide in Jesus Christ and the Word and have a growing knowledge and under-standing of the Word and how it relates to your life.

Clarifying
Questions:

1a. What does the word "truth" mean?
1b. What is our source of truth as Christians?

See also
Ephesians 4:24;
Galatians 3:6

---

2. What are some meanings of "put on the breastplate of righteousness" (vs. 14)?

   A breastplate is important because it pro-tects the chest area, especially the heart. The "breastplate of righteousness" is the righteousness of Christ. Righteousness means "right standing before God." We identify ourselves with Christ's righteous-ness, therefore we are righteous. Putting on the breastplate of righteousness helps us to remember where we stand before God and to realize we already have victory.

273

Clarifying
Questions:

2a. What is a breastplate?
2b. What does it protect?

See also I John
1:7-9

3. What are some reasons it would be important to have righteousness as a
breastplate?

The breastplate is very important because
it protects the vital organs in our bodies.
Paul is saying that knowing our right
standing before God is vital in order to
stand firm against Satan. Unrighteousness
is fatal to the Christian's walk. Unconfessed sin destroys our fellowship with
God.

Clarifying
Questions:

3a. What do others of you think?
3b. How important is it for us to know our
right standing before God?

RELATE:

"'Having shod your feet with the preparation of the
gospel of peace' refers to a part of the armor which
might be difficult to describe unless we turn to the
part of the Old Testament that Paul was referring
to. The bold letters in the verse refer to something
he was quoting. Turn to Isaiah 52:7."

Ask a group
member to read the
verse.

SAY:

"The reference to the 'gospel' or 'good news' of
peace comes from a time when the Jews were
taken captive by the Babylonians. The gospel of
peace was that the war was over. It came to signify
the good news that a war was over and the victory
was won. The good news in Ephesians is that the
battle with Satan has already been won.

"This passage in Ephesians is not necessarily talking about evangelism, but as we share Christ we
have the news that the victory over Satan has been
won by Christ's death and resurrection."

Read verse 15 and continue the discussion.

4. You need to "shoe" your feet with the knowledge that the battle with Satan has been won and we have peace with God. What would be some actions you would expect from the kind of person Paul is describing in verse 15?

   A person would tell non-Christians about how to have a personal relationship with Christ. The person would tell Christians that Christ has victory over their troubles, concerns and hurts.

5. What are some ways faith is used in a spiritual battle (vs. 16)?

   Just as a shield protects us from attacks by the enemy, our faith protects us from attacks by Satan (i.e., temptations, impure thoughts, confusion, etc.).

Clarifying Questions:

5a. How would you describe faith?
5b. What are some ways that faith protects us?

RELATE:

"The helmet of the Roman soldier was hard, solid, impenetrable; it couldn't be broken."

(19)

6. What do you think Paul means by using the term "helmet of salvation" (vs. 17)?

    It is the knowledge and facts about the truth of Christ. Having this protection for our heads means our thoughts are protected from doubt. Being secure in our right relationship with God is our greatest protection.

7. In what ways is the Word of God used in a spiritual battle (vs. 17)?

    This is the only offensive weapon. It's used to attack Satan to keep him away. As Satan attacks, we can quote Scripture to defeat him. It's also used defensively as protection. When we fill our hearts, minds and mouths with the Word of God, Satan has less opportunity to tempt or attack us.

Clarifying Questions:

7a. How does the Word of God differ from the other parts of the armor listed?

7b. How does the Word help in defending against Satan's attacks?

RELATE:

"An interesting observation to make here is that the Greek word used for the Word of God is *rhema*. This word refers to a spoken proclamation of a specific occasion, rather than simply a written word. In other words, it means to quote or proclaim the Word of God for a specific purpose.

"Now that we've looked at the kind of battle in which we're engaged and the weapons available to us, let's spend some time talking about how we can use our weapons."

Application

ASK:

D. USING THESE WEAPONS DAILY

1. What things do you think we can do to be better equipped to use the sword of the Spirit, the Word of God?

   Study the Bible in groups and individually so we will know what it really says. Memorize it so our minds will be filled with it and our lips will be ready to speak it. Meditate on it. That means to think about different parts of a passage and determine its meaning and application to our lives.

Lead the group in a discussion of the following chart. Share personal applications.

2. What are some of the consequences of not using these pieces of armor?

Weapons	Consequences of Not Using Weapons
a. Belt of truth	a. Follow false teaching, live an ungodly life-style. Believe wrong doctrine.
b. Breastplate of righteousness	b. Live an ungodly life. Feel unnecessary guilt. Forget we have the righteousness of Christ.
(20) c. Shod with the gospel of peace	c. Miss out on blessings by not telling people about Christ.
d. Shield of faith	d. Feel discouraged and defeated. Lives become ineffective and impotent in spiritual things. Don't experience victory God has provided.

Weapons	Consequences of Not Using Weapons
e. Helmet of salvation	e. Lack of security in our relationship with God.
f. Sword of the Spirit	f. No power in our witness. Inability to counsel others effectively. Lack of aggressiveness in our lives (no confidence in the Word).

RELATE:

"In our next lesson, we'll be discussing the 'Ministry of Reconciliation.' The main passage we'll be looking at is II Corinthians 5. To get the most out of the discussion, I'd encourage you to read over this passage beforehand and even spend some time studying it."

Practical Ministry
(15-25 Minutes)

Vision

Read the verses.

LUKE 10:1,2
A. DISCIPLES CALLED TO THE HARVEST

DISCUSS:

1. Where has our discipleship group been sent?

   _____

   _____

2. What should our prayer as a group be?

   _____

   _____

SAY:

"Let's expect God to answer our prayers as we look for potential harvesters to join us in the harvest. God will provide individuals who will help you form your own discipleship groups."

Leader's Guide

Strategy   (21)

READ:

> **B. FINDING NEW HARVESTERS**
>
> 1. List all evangelistic contacts you have had in the last two weeks.
>
> _____
> _____
>
> 2. Circle the ones who are potential members for your discipleship group.

You want to help your group understand that evangelism is also designed to help them find people whom they can disciple. Think about how you can help them find people to disciple.

Training

RELATE:

"As a person learns to share his faith in Christ, he can sometimes find himself in a situation he does not know how to handle. That is why these training times are so important. Most successful athletic coaches believe that a team can only function well when it has mastered the fundamentals of the sport. In the same way, if we want to function well as a team of individuals, influencing our world for Christ, we'll need to become masters of the fundamentals.

"This week we want to practice sharing with each other the basic elements of assurance that we would want to communicate with people immediately after they receive Christ.

"I am going to roleplay a situation with _____ and we are going to assume that he has just prayed to receive Christ. As I cover page 11 in the Four Spiritual Laws booklet, read along in your study guides. The series of questions I will use are presented there."

Leader's Guide

Roleplay:

Ask each question at the top of page 11. Have your partner respond as though he understands that Christ is in His life.

C. QUESTIONS FROM PAGE 11 OF THE FOUR SPIRITUAL LAWS BOOKLET

1. Did you receive Christ into your life?

2. According to His promise in Revelation 3:20, where is Christ right now in relation to you?

3. Christ said that he would come into your life. Would He mislead you?

4. On what authority do you know that God has answered your prayer?

Read the verses. Emphasize the words "has" and "know" in verses 12 and 13. Ask these questions.

I JOHN 5:11-13
5. What has God given us?

6. Where is this life found?

7. Do you have the Son in your life?

8. If you have the Son, what else do you have?

9. When did your eternal life begin?

Read the verse and the question.

HEBREWS 13:5
10. How many times will you have to invite Christ into your life?

Thank the one who helped in the roleplay.

EXPLAIN:

"In the Greek language there are double and triple negatives used here. He was saying 'I will never, no never leave you and I will never, never, never forsake you.'"

ASK:

"What are some of your observations and questions concerning the roleplay?"

Have group members practice two-by-two, sharing assurance from page 11 with each other.

EXPLAIN: "Sometimes a person will not be sure Christ is in his life. If that happens, turn back to Revelation 3:20 and ask these questions."

(22) **D. QUESTIONS TO ASK A PERSON IF HE IS UNSURE THAT CHRIST IS IN HIS LIFE, REFERRING TO REVELATION 3:20**

1. What does the door represent?
2. According to this verse, what is our responsibility?
3. What is Christ's responsibility?
4. Were you sincere when you invited Christ into your life?

RELATE: "After you share assurance with an individual, there are several other principles that are important for this new believer to know. They are contained on pages 12 and 13 of the Four Spiritual Laws booklet. You will want to read through these pages with him and then explain the following principles."

Read through the principles with them, answering any questions.

E. PRINCIPLES TO EMPHASIZE AFTER READING PAGES 12 AND 13 TO THE NEW BELIEVER

1. Explain the importance of not depending on feelings.
2. Explain the train diagram.
3. Explain that at the moment he, as an act of faith, received Christ, many things happened, including the following:
   a. Christ came into his life (Revelation 3:20; Colossians 1:27).
   b. His sins were forgiven (Colossians 1:14).

c. He became a child of God
(John 1:12).
d. He received eternal life (John 5:24).
e. He began the great adventure for
which God created him (John 10:10;
II Corinthians 5:17; I Thessalonians
5:18).

4. Then suggest that you bow together and
thank God for what He has done. The very
act of thanking God demonstrates faith
and obedience, which often results in
Christ manifesting Himself to the new
Christian in a special way (John 14:21).

Prayer
(10-15 Minutes)

Close in conversa-
tional prayer.

Arrange the time
and place of the
next meeting.

10
The Ministry of
=Reconciliation=

OVERVIEW GOAL

The goal of this lesson is to motivate group members to carry out a ministry of reconciliation by giving them an eternal perspective as ambassadors for Christ.

LEARNING OBJECTIVES

By the end of this lesson, group members will be able to:

1. Explain Paul's view of men.

2. List several ways our lives should be affected by having an eternal perspective.

3. Explain what it means to have the ministry of reconciliation as ambassadors of Christ.

283

===Leader's Guide===

Time/Section	Outline/Questions and Learning Activities
10-15	## Sharing Have group members share what God has been teaching them about their identity in Christ in the last week.
30-40	## Bible Study
Motivation	A. THE STORY OF A DOCTOR AND HIS ASSISTANT 1. What are some of the reasons why the task was such a privilege for the young assistant? 2. What are some of the reasons why the task was such an awesome responsibility for him? 3. What are some ways that this story would apply to the Christian life? TRANSITION: "Let's take a look at Paul's perspective concerning the awesome task he had been given."
Observ./Interp. II Corinthians 5:1-17	B. PAUL'S ETERNAL PERSPECTIVE 1. What are some insights we gain from Paul's desire in life as seen in verses 1-10? 2. What do you think some of Paul's plans for accomplishing these desires might have been? C. PAUL'S VIEW OF PEOPLE; THE RESULT OF HIS ETERNAL PERSPECTIVE 1. According to verse 11, how did Paul's knowledge that all people will eventually appear before the Lord affect his actions? 2. What are some other things from these verses that motivated Paul to action? 3. Based on this passage, what are some ways that an eternal perspective affected Paul's view of people?

Time/Section	Outline/Questions and Learning Activities
Application	4. In what ways would our view of people affect our willingness to share Christ with them? TRANSITION: "In the light of how Paul viewed people let's now look at how he viewed his ministry as well as the implications it might have for our own lifestyle."
Observ./Interp. II Corinthians 5:18-21	D. OUR MINISTRY OF RECONCILIATION AS AMBASSADORS FOR CHRIST 1. According to verses 18 and 19, what is the ministry of reconciliation? 2. What are some things that are true of an ambassador? 3. How should we conduct ourselves as ambassadors for Christ? 4. Remembering the perspective Paul had in verse 16, is there anyone you now view as "having it all together," yet who doesn't know Christ? 5. How would Paul view this person? 6. What steps can you take this week to share with someone the Lord has placed in your life? **Action Point** Make a list of people with whom you want to share and decide how you plan to contact them.
15-25	**Practical Ministry** A. ARRANGING THE FIRST FOLLOW-UP APPOINTMENT 1. Try to set up the appointment within 24 to 48 hours. 2. Set a specific time and place to meet. 3. Help the new believer become aware of his need to know God and to grow in his relationship with Him.

Time/Section	Outline/Questions and Learning Activities
	4. Give the new believer follow-up booklet 1, "Beginning Your New Life!" Encourage him to review the Four Spiritual Laws contained in the booklet and to read the first three chapters of the Gospel of John, also reprinted in the booklet.
	B. DEMONSTRATION DIALOGUE
	C. FIRST FOLLOW-UP APPOINTMENT WITHOUT USING THE BOOKLET
	1. Have the new believer review the Four Spiritual Laws booklet.
	2. Encourage the new believer to read the first three chapters of the Gospel of John.
	3. Be prepared to give the new believer follow-up booklet 1 at the beginning of the first follow-up appointment.
5-10	## Prayer
	Begin with silent prayer for individuals the Lord has impressed each group member to share with. Then pray conversationally for everyone in the group to be strong ambassadors for Christ this week and for results in the ministry of reconciliation.
60-90	

Preparation

PERSONAL PERSPECTIVE

Set aside at least one-half hour when you will not be disturbed. Take your Bible, Discipleship Group study guide and Bible study helps for II Corinthians 5:1-21. Begin the time in prayer, asking God to give you His eternal perspective as you study the passage in II Corinthians. Be thoroughly familiar with the definitions of an ambassador and the ministry of reconciliation. Complete all the questions in the study guide and be prepared to share with the group some of your experiences as an ambassador for Christ as well as the results of people you personally have seen trust Christ as their Savior and Lord.

You will need to ask a group member to help you with the demonstration. You may want to practice the dialogue beforehand.

INTRODUCTION TO II CORINTHIANS

This letter was written by Paul to the church at Corinth about 56 A.D. from Macedonia. In the first seven chapters, Paul presents a defense for his life and ministry. As he is forced to lay open his life because of being attacked by some brethren, he includes both instruction and inspiration to those called to be ministers of Christ.

Chapter 5 challenges us to have an eternal perspective while living here on earth. It reminds us that the gospel message is the message of reconciliation and challenges us to actively participate as Christ's ambassadors.

RESOURCES

Bible dictionary.
Disciples Are Made Not Born, by Walter A. Henrichsen.
Matthew Henry's Commentary.
Unger's Bible Handbook.

> There are few things that are more important for a man to understand than how his life can affect others.

Sharing
(10-15 Minutes)

Have the group members share only opportunities they had to apply the things learned last week about their identity in Christ. See I. Sharing Appendix for additional ideas.

Open the Bible study in a brief prayer asking God to teach the group.

Bible Study
(30-40 Minutes)

Motivation

READER: (24)   A. THE STORY OF A DOCTOR AND HIS
                                       ASSISTANT

The story is told of a doctor who dedicated his entire life to finding a cure for a disease that was killing millions of people. There were many others who were also searching for a cure, but this man was using very different methods from the rest. Often the others would simply laugh at him and his unconventional ways. At the end of his life, to his great joy, he discovered the cure! But he knew that ahead of him was the task of convincing his colleagues that this unconventional and simple treatment would actually work, and he did not have the time or the strength left to do the job. The old doctor explained to his young assistant that he would have to be the one to carry out the work. There was no one else. The young assistant was overwhelmed by the awesome privilege and responsibility of this task.

DISCUSSION:

Direct the group in a discussion of the questions. Share the suggested answers only if necessary. Summarize the group's answers after discussing each question and encourage group members to write the conclusions in their study guides.

1. What are some of the reasons why the task was such a privilege for the young assistant?

He was not the one who had worked hard to discover the cure. Others had much more knowledge and experience, yet he was the one who had the privilege of telling the world about it. He would have the ultimate satisfaction of knowing that he had helped to save million of lives.

2. What are some of the reasons why the task was such an awesome responsibility for him?

He would have to go against the popular philosophies and try to convince others who were more experienced and knowledgeable in this area. If he did not get the cure out, many more people would needlessly die. The old doctor had entrusted his entire life's work into his hands; if he didn't carry it out, the doctor's work would have been for nothing.

(25)

3. What are some ways that this story would apply to the Christian life?

We as Christians have the same type of privilege and responsibility as this young man, but ours is much more awesome. We did nothing to develop it, but we have the cure for spiritual death; our message of the gospel will literally give those who receive it eternal life! Often we have to go against the popular way of thinking to present our discovery; yet the rewards are great—both for us, and for those who are saved.

Clarifying Questions:

3a. Can you think of any special responsibilities and privileges with which we as Christians have been entrusted?

3b. Who does the doctor represent? Who does the assistant represent?

Give the following brief background information on the book of II Corinthians. For additional information see *Unger's Bible Handbook*.

RELATE:

"II Corinthians was written by Paul to the church at Corinth about 56 A.D. The first seven chapters contain thoughts on his personal ministry as well as challenges believers to be faithful servants of Christ. Chapter 5 deals particularly with these eternal perspectives on presenting Christ to others.

TRANSITION:

"Let's take a look at Paul's perspective concerning the awesome task he had been given."

A

Observ./Interp.

Ask a group member to read the verses.

Discuss the following questions. Follow the same procedure as before.

T

C

II CORINTHIANS 5:1-17
B.   PAUL'S ETERNAL PERSPECTIVE

1.   What are some insights we gain from Paul's desires in life as seen in verses 1-10?

Paul's desire was to be pleasing to the Lord, realizing that everything he did would some day be judged by God. His thoughts were directed to the eternal. He was looking forward to going home to heaven.

_____

_____

2.   What do you think some of Paul's plans for accomplishing these desires might have been?

He wanted to live courageously. He wanted to please God.

_____

_____

E

I
r
v
t
v
g
u
a
r

Clarifying
Questions:

RELATE:

2a.   Any other thoughts?
2b.   What are some ways Paul lived his life?

"It's obvious that Paul's desires in life were governed by an eternal viewpoint. Let's see how this affected his perspective of others."

READ AND CON-
TINUE TO
DISCUSS:

2. What are some things that are true of an ambassador?

An ambassador is the highest-ranking diplomatic representative appointed to represent a country or government. He lives in the country to which he is an ambassador, but it is not his home. He is a foreigner, being different from the people who live there. He must be faithful to his own country and represent it accurately. Even though his heart's desire may be to return to his home, his job is to stay and represent his country to these people. He is the unifying link between the two.

Clarifying
Questions:

2a. What are some responsibilities of an ambassador?
2b. What are some privileges of an ambassador?

Application

3. How should we conduct ourselves as ambassadors for Christ?

We should take our position and respon-sibility seriously and view our task as the highest calling in the world. We should demonstrate by our actions and attitudes that we know the King whom we repres-ent. We should reflect His attitude toward men. We should expect to be different from those who are not of God's kingdom, those who don't know Christ.

(28)

4. Remembering the perspective Paul had in verse 16, is there anyone you now view as "having it all together" yet who doesn't know Christ.

5. How would Paul view this person?

As lost for eternity apart from Christ, in
need of the gospel regardless of outward
appearance.

Allow time for
group members to
think about
answers to this
question. If there is
enough time, you
may want to ask
group members to
share their
responses.

6. What steps can you take this week to
share with someone the Lord has placed
in your life?

READ AND
EXPLAIN THE
ACTION POINT

Action Point Make a list of people with whom you
want to share and decide how you plan to contact
them.

RELATE:

"In our next lesson, we'll be discussing 'Expanding
Your Circle of Confidence.' The main passage we'll
be looking at is I Samuel 17:1-54. To get the most
out of the discussion, I'd encourage each of you to
read over this passage beforehand and even spend
some time studying it."

Practical Ministry
(15-25 Minutes)

SAY:

"As you are faithful to be ambassadors for Christ,
you will come across people who trust Christ as a
result of your witness and others who are young
Christians who need to be followed up. I would
like to prepare you to help these Christians grow
in their faith."

Joe: "By spending time with the person, I guess. You know, talking with each other and doing things together."

You: "That's right. In other words, we need to learn how to communicate with Christ and allow Him to communicate with us. We need to learn how to spend time with Him so our friendship with Him can grow. You know, Joe, I would like to get together with you and share how you can build your friendship with Christ. Would you be interested?"

Joe: "Sure."

You: "Are you free tomorrow about this time?"

Joe: "Yes."

You: "That's great! Why don't we meet right here at ＿＿ o'clock tomorrow? Is that alright?"

Joe: "Yes, that's fine."

You: "Joe, why don't you read through the Four Spiritual Laws booklet on your own tonight and thank Christ that He has come into your life. By thanking God, you communicate faith, which pleases Him. There is a little booklet entitled, 'Beginning Your New Life!' that I would like to give you. It has a reprint of the Gospel of John in it. I want to encourage you to read the first three chapters because I found it very helpful to me when I prayed to receive Christ. Also, if you have time, you might want to fill in some of the questions in the booklet."

Joe: "O.K."

You: "Great! It's been good talking and sharing these things with you, Joe. I'll look forward to meeting you tomorrow at ＿＿ o'clock right here. See you later."

(30)

RELATE:

"There will be times when someone receives Christ with you and you don't have booklet 1. What do you do then?"

Refer the group members to the next section in their study guides.

C. FIRST FOLLOW-UP APPOINTMENT WITH-OUT USING THE BOOKLET.

1. Have the new believer review the Four Spiritual Laws booklet.
2. Encourage the new believer to read the first three chapters of the Gospel of John.
3. Be prepared to give the new believer follow-up booklet 1 at the beginning of the first follow-up appointment.

Divide the group into pairs and have them do a two-by-two practice using the demonstration dialogue as a guide.

Prayer
(5-10 Minutes)

Begin with silent prayer for individuals the Lord has impressed each group member to share with. Then close in conversational prayer for one another. Pray for everyone in the group to be strong ambassadors for Christ this week and to be able to see results in the ministry of reconciliation He has given. See V. Prayer Appendix for additional ideas.

Arrange the time and place for the next meeting.

11
Expanding Your Circle of === Confidence ===

OVERVIEW GOAL

The goal of this lesson is to motivate group members to begin aggressively enlarging their circles of confidence as a way of life.

LEARNING OBJECTIVES

By the end of this lesson, group members will be able to:

1. Identify their circles of confidence.

2. Explain principles of enlarging their circles of confidence.

3. Implement a plan to enlarge their circles of confidence.

Time/Section	Outline/Questions and Learning Activities
10-15	## Sharing
	Share about quiet times or opportunities they have had to be Christ's ambassadors in evangelism.
30-40	## Bible Study
Motivation	A. DEFINING CIRCLE OF CONFIDENCE
	1. The meaning of the circle of confidence.
	2. How to expand the circle of confidence.
	B. OUR PRESENT AND FUTURE CIRCLE OF CONFIDENCE
	1. List a few things for which you are now trusting Christ that you would consider part of your circle of confidence.
	2. List a few things that you would consider outside of your circle of confidence.
	TRANSITION: "Tension and fear are a normal part of the exciting Christian life because they allow us to experience the life of faith which is pleasing to God. Hebrews 11:6 tells us that without faith it is impossible to please God. Let's see how David pleased God by trusting Him to overcome a faith barrier and to enlarge his circle of confidence."
Observ./Interp.	C. DAVID'S CONFIDENCE IN GOD'S CHARACTER
I Samuel 17:1-54	1. What were some of the obstacles David faced?
	2. What were some of David's responses to the obstacles he faced?
	3. What were some of the ways David could have responded to the challenge?
Application	4. What are some principles that you see in this passage that will help you expand your circle of confidence?

302

Time/Section	Outline/Questions and Learning Activities
	D. EXPANDING YOUR CIRCLE OF CONFIDENCE

D. EXPANDING YOUR CIRCLE OF CONFIDENCE

1. Take a moment and list one area in your personal ministry that presently is not a part of your circle of confidence, but which you would like to see become an area of confidence.
2. What are some steps you could take to allow God's character to help you gain confidence in this area?
3. Take a moment before the Lord and commit this area to His sufficiency. Ask Him to reveal to you a plan of action to allow you to place this area into your circle of confidence.

Action Point   List the specific action you will take in the power of the Holy Spirit within the next week or two to expand your circle of confidence in this particular area.

15-25

Practical Ministry

5-10

Prayer

Pray for each group member's action plan for enlarging his circle of confidence in the next week.

60-90

Preparation

PERSONAL PERSPECTIVE

Set aside at least one-half hour when you can be undisturbed. Take your Bible and Discipleship Group study guide. Complete the study guide and become thoroughly familiar with the lesson and the story of David and Goliath in I Samuel 17. Ask the Lord to help you discover your circle of confidence as well as several areas that exist outside of your circle of confidence. Develop a plan of action which will enable you to see the Lord demonstrate faithfulness in overcoming this area. Be sure that the area you choose is a faith stretcher and not something that can be done without trusting God. Follow the same instructions with your group members. You may want to consider doing something as a group to stretch your faith and build unity (i.e., an evangelistic meeting, a group outreach, etc.).

You will need to develop your own Practical Ministry time. Consult Appendices II, III and IV.

INTRODUCTION TO I SAMUEL 17

I and II Samuel contain some of the finest historical writing in all literature. While largely historical and biographical, the narratives are unique in that they stress moral and spiritual repercussions. Samuel is not said to be the only author of the books but may have had joint authorship with Nathan and Gad. I Samuel 17 deals with the rise of David and the decline of Saul.

SUPPLIES

Optional: Transferable Concept 6, "How to Introduce Others to Christ"

RESOURCES

Unger's Bible Handbook

> "The man who never takes steps of faith because
> of fear of failure has failed already."*
>
> J. Kent Hutcheson

Sharing
(10-15 Minutes)

Have the group members share how their quiet times have been coming along. They may also share any opportunities they have had to be Christ's ambassadors in evangelism. See I. Sharing Appendix for further suggestions.

ASK:

"Have any of you been able to consistently spend time with the Lord this week by having quiet times? What have you been learning?

"Last week, we discussed what it means to be an ambassador. Have any of you been able to talk with some of your friends about Christ this week? How did it go?"

Bible Study
(30-40 Minutes)

Open the Bible study in a brief prayer, asking God to teach the group.

*J. Kent Hutcheson, A personal interview with James Kent Hutcheson at Arrowhead Springs, California, 1979.

Motivation

READS: (32)   A.   DEFINING CIRCLE OF CONFIDENCE

Circle of Confidence

1.   Everyone has a circle of confidence. It is a person's circle of activities in which he feels comfortable and in which he is able to trust God with little or no fear or tension. Basically, these are things he is confident in doing.

RELATE:

"For some of us, sharing the Four Spiritual Laws or giving our personal testimonies is within our circles of confidence. However, the thought of being involved in doing an evangelistic meeting may bring considerable fear or insecurity."

ASK MEMBERS TO
FOLLOW ALONG
AS YOU READ:

2.   The Lord never desires our faith to remain static. He wants to expand our circle of confidence by breaking our faith barriers. He is constantly placing us in various situations, urging us to take steps of faith which will allow Him to enlarge our circle of confidence. He wants to give us a greater knowledge of His faithfulness in our daily experiences.

As we believe Him for areas outside of our circle of confidence, we find that our ability to trust God increases.

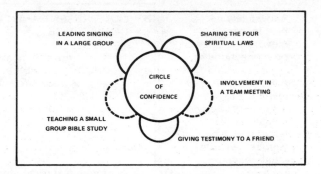

RELATE:

"In this circle, the individual's circle of confidence has expanded in three new areas: sharing the Four Spiritual Laws, leading singing in a large group and giving his personal testimony to a friend. He has taken steps of faith and has seen God demonstrate His faithfulness and sufficiency by allowing these areas of confidence. However, teaching a small group Bible study and being involved in a team meeting are still outside the circle of confidence and cause him fear or unwillingness to trust God. He will need to trust God and step out in faith in order for his circle of confidence to include these areas."

Ask group members if they have any questions about the circle of confidence and how to enlarge it. Make sure everyone has at least a general understanding before proceeding.

SAY:

"Let's spend a few moments looking at some of the areas of our lives that have become part of our circles of confidence because of God's faithfulness, as well as those areas that presently are outside our circles of confidence."

Allow a few min-
utes for group
members to answer
both questions.

Ask the group
members to share
with the group, the
areas they listed.
Avoid criticism;
keep the environ-
ment positive.

(33)

You may want to
share a few areas
that have become
part of your circle
of confidence as
well as those areas
which you have yet
to entrust to God.

TRANSITION:

Observ./Interp.

Give a brief over-
view of the chapter,
including a sum-
mary of the first 20
verses. Have each
group member read
four verses, begin-
ning at verse 20
and continuing
through verse 50.
Summarize the last
of the chapter.

B. OUR PRESENT AND FUTURE CIRCLE OF
    CONFIDENCE

  1. List a few things for which you are now
      trusting Christ that you would consider
      part of your circle of confidence.

      _____
      _____
      _____
      _____

  2. List a few things that you would consider
      outside of your circle of confidence.

      _____
      _____
      _____
      _____

"Tension and fear are a normal part of the exciting
Christian life because they allow us to experience
the life of faith which is pleasing to God. Hebrews
11:6 tells us that without faith it is impossible to
please God. Let's see how David pleased God by
trusting Him to overcome a faith barrier and to
enlarge his circle of confidence."

I SAMUEL 17:1-54
C. DAVID'S CONFIDENCE IN GOD'S
    CHARACTER

Leader's Guide

Don't spend excess time getting through the verses—move on to the discussion questions.

DISCUSSION:

Direct the group in a discussion of the following questions. Share the suggested answers only if necessary. Summarize the group's answers after discussing each question, and encourage group members to write the conclusions in their study guides.

1. What were some of the obstacles David faced?

   He was ridiculed by family, friends and the enemy. He was inexperienced with using the proper equipment. He was young. He faced an overwhelming opposition against Goliath's size and experience.

Clarifying Questions:

1a. What were some things that could have caused David to fear?

1b. Why did everyone try to discourage David from fighting Goliath?

Give group members a few minutes to observe the passage and individually list their findings. Continue the discussion.

(34)

2. What were some of David's responses to the obstacles he faced?

   He recognized that the battle was the Lord's—His name was at stake. He went with His present resources. He based his future on God's past faithfulness. He separated himself from those who would

309

hold him back. He trusted God's character, power and sufficiency. He was
obedient.

Clarifying
Questions:

2a. What are some ways to describe David's perspective?
2b. On what was his confidence based?
2c. Who was he depending upon to provide for his lack of experience, age,
size, etc.?

3. What were some of the ways David could
have responded to the challenge?

He could have agreed with the opinions of
others and not become involved because
of his age and inexperience. He could
have refused to relate God's past faithfulness to this situation. He could have
allowed Goliath's size to intimidate him
and cause him to be afraid instead of
bold.

Clarifying
Questions:

3a. What do some of the others of you
think?
3b. What are some ways you might have
responded in this situation?

Application

4. What are some principles you see in this
passage that will help you expand your
circle of confidence?

Develop an eternal perspective in which
God's faithfulness and sufficiency is the
object of our faith. Focus on and trust
God's character, who He is and His trustworthiness. Respond to His attributes and
not our fears.

Clarifying
Questions:

4a. What should be the focus of our
     attention?
4b. What are some aspects of God's
     character in which we should trust?

Give group
members a few
minutes to write
their own answers.

Ask if anyone
would like to share
his ideas with the
group.

D. EXPANDING YOUR CIRCLE OF
    CONFIDENCE

1. Take a moment and list one area in your
    personal ministry that presently is not part
    of your circle of confidence, but which
    you would like to see become an area of
    confidence.

    _____
    _____

(35)

2. What are some steps you could take to
    allow God's character to help you gain
    confidence in this area?

    _____
    _____
    _____

Give group
members a few
minutes for quiet
prayer and medita-
tion to allow the
Lord to speak to
their hearts about a
specific plan of
action.

3. Take a moment before the Lord and
    commit this area to His sufficiency. Ask
    Him to reveal to you a plan of action that
    will allow you to place this area into your
    circle of confidence.

READ:

Action Point List the specific action you will take
in the power of the Holy Spirit within the next
week or two to expand your circle of confidence in
this particular area.

_____
_____

RELATE:

"In our next lesson, we'll be discussing motivation to witness. The main passage we'll be looking at is Romans 10:11-17. To get the most out of the discussion, I'd encourage you to read over this passage beforehand and even spend some time studying it."

You may assign your group to read Transferable Concept 6 in preparation for next week.

Practical Ministry
(15-25 Minutes)

To develop the Practical Ministry (Vision, Strategy, Training) Section of this lesson, complete the following steps:

____ 1. Turn to the "Strategy Chart for Student and Adult Ministries" (Point B of the III. Practical Ministry—Strategy Appendix) (see p. 528).

____ 2. On the left hand side of the chart, identify the ministry strategy your group is now or soon will be pursuing.

____ 3. On the right hand side of the chart, choose the training unit which you could best teach this week to prepare your group to be involved in the ministry strategy.

____ 4. Turn in the IV. Practical Ministry—Training Appendix to the number of the training unit you have chosen and prepare to teach the content from the outline given.

____ 5. Now turn to the II. Practical Ministry—Vision Appendix and choose the "Resource Idea" (point B) or a "Vision Passage" (point C) that would best motivate your group toward the strategy and training you have chosen.

___ 6. When you reach the Practical Ministry portion of your discipleship group meeting, teach the Vision portion first, then discuss your local strategy in light of that vision. Then teach the Training portion. (For some topics, you may prefer to go from Vision into Training and then end with a discussion of your local strategy suggesting action points for the coming week.)

Prayer
(5-10 Minutes)

Pray for each group member's action plan for enlarging his circle of confidence in the next week.

Arrange the time and place of the next meeting.

12
Witnessing
═══Experience═══

OVERVIEW GOAL

The goal of this lesson is to enable group members to have a positive witnessing experience.

LEARNING OBJECTIVES

By the end of this lesson, group members will be able to:

1.   Relate a scriptural motivation for sharing their faith in Christ.

2.   Share the results of an actual witnessing experience.

Time/Section	Outline/Questions and Learning Activities
5	**Sharing** Have the group members share their experiences in breaking personal faith barriers last week. Have them share anything they found helpful in Transferable Concept 6, "How to Introduce Others to Christ."
15	**Bible Study**
Motivation	A. THE STORY OF TWO ROOMMATES 1. If you asked the young man who was already a Christian why he didn't share Christ with his roommate, what are some reasons you think he might give? 2. What problems do you see in this Christian's thinking? TRANSITION: "Now we're going to take a few minutes to look at the apostle Paul's attitude toward talking about Christ."
Observ./Interp. Romans 10:11-17 **Application**	B. THE NEED TO WITNESS 1. What are some things these verses say that should make Christians want to tell others about Christ? 2. What are some things this passage tells us about God's attitude toward us when we share our faith?
60	**Practical Ministry** A. WITNESSING ASSIGNMENTS B. WITNESSING C. GROUP SHARING

Time/Section	Outline/Questions and Learning Activities
10	# Prayer
90	Reassemble the group to share their experiences and close the time with conversational prayer for those contacted.

Preparation

PERSONAL PERSPECTIVE

Set up appointments for your group members if possible. Random witnessing is an alternative if you choose an appropriate location. (See Lesson 6 for specific guidelines on selecting a location.) You will want to review Lessons 5 and 6 and have your group members do the same. If you use surveys, alert them so that they can come prepared with the opening and transition to the Four Spiritual Laws booklet.

Plan the time carefully because it will be easy to go overtime. Plan your assignments and transportation in advance to avoid last minute delays. Do not plan to travel more than a few minutes, since your time will be limited. Plan for both people in each pair to share the Four Spiritual Laws booklet if possible.

INTRODUCTION TO ROMANS

Romans is the first great work of Christian theology. It was written by the apostle Paul about 57 A.D. from Corinth. He wrote it to the Roman Church to enlist their aid in fulfilling the Great Commission, to instruct them and to announce his forthcoming visit.

SUPPLIES

Four Spiritual Laws booklets for each person.
Optional: Surveys—Refer to IV. Practical Ministry—Training Appendix for samples of effective surveys.
Optional: If you decide to have your group members read Transferable Concept 5, "How to Witness in the Spirit," you should have copies available for them.

RESOURCES

Transferable Concept 5, "How to Witness in the Spirit"
Transferable Concept 6, "How to Introduce Others to Christ"

> "Father, make of me a crisis man. Bring those I contact to decision. Let me not be a milepost on a single road; make me a fork, that men must turn one way or another on facing Christ in me."*
>
> Jim Elliot

Sharing
(5 Minutes)

Have the group members share any experiences they had in breaking personal faith barriers during the previous week. Have them share anything they found helpful in Transferable Concept 6, "How to Introduce Others to Christ."

If any missed a chance to witness, encourage them and identify specific steps that they may take next week.

Bible Study
(15 Minutes)

Open the Bible study in a brief prayer, asking God to teach the group.

*Elizabeth Elliot, *Shadow of the Almighty*, Copyright © 1959, p. 59: Used by permission of Harper and Brothers Publishers, New York, New York.

Motivation

SAY: "Let's begin with a story of two roommates."

(38) A. THE STORY OF TWO ROOMMATES

READ:

A young man rushed back to his apartment after a Billy Graham meeting. He and his roommate had lived and worked together for several years. "I must tell you something," he said to his friend. "Tonight I invited Christ to be my Savior, and He has changed my life." His friend smiled and said, "Wonderful! I have been hoping you would do that. I have been living the Christian life for several years, all the time hoping that you would trust Christ as your Savior." Being surprised, the new Christian said, "You lived such a perfect life that I kept trying to do it without Christ, since you seemed to be doing it without Christ. Tonight I invited Him to become my Lord and Savior because I failed to live up to your standards. You should have told me why you live the way you live. Why didn't you tell me how I could know Christ, too?"*

*Bill Bright, *Teacher's Manual for the Ten Basic Steps Toward Christian Maturity*, Copyright © 1965, p. 343: Used by permission of Campus Crusade for Christ, Inc., Arrowhead Springs, California.

DISCUSSION:

Direct the group in a discussion of the questions. Share the suggested answers only if necessary. Summarize the group's answers after discussing each question and encourage group members to write the conclusions in their study guides.

(39)

1. If you asked the young man who was already a Christian why he didn't share Christ with his roommate, what are some reasons you think he might give?

   Just living the life is enough. He didn't want to offend. He felt his roommate would not be interested.

2. What problems do you see in his thinking?

   People won't give Christ the credit for living a godly life unless you tell them about Him. People really are hungry for God. It is contrary to the Word and will of God to withhold the gospel from non-believers.

TRANSITION:

"Now we're going to take a few minutes to look at the apostle Paul's attitude toward talking about Christ."

Observ./Interp.

Ask someone to read the passage.

Discuss the following questions. Follow the same procedure as before.

ROMANS 10:11-17
B. THE NEED TO WITNESS

   1. What are some things these verses say that should make Christians want to tell others about Christ?

      He abounds in riches for all who call on Him. Whoever will call upon the name of the Lord will be saved. People shall not hear without a preacher. Christians shall not preach unless they are sent. They must share the gospel for people to be saved.

Clarifying
Questions:

1a. Any other ideas?
1b. According to this passage, can merely living the Christian life lead someone to Christ? Why or why not?

Application

2. What are some things this passage tells us about God's attitude toward us when we share our faith?

   We are appreciated by and are beautiful to God. He desires and delights to work through us.

Clarifying
Questions:

2a. How do you think God feels when someone shares Christ?
2b. What does verse 15 say about God's attitude?

RELATE:

"One of the ways we can be prepared to witness is through training. We can be trained as we take time to go out, two by two, like the disciples did in Mark 6:7-13. That's what we're going to do today. This gives us a chance not only to share Christ with someone, but also to practice sharing our faith so that we'll know what to do when we have an unexpected opportunity to talk with someone about Christ.

"Let's pray silently for a few minutes and make sure that there's no unconfessed sin in our lives and that we're controlled by the Holy Spirit."

Close in prayer. Ask God to lead each pair to those who are ready to hear the gospel, and that He would speak through them and make them good representatives of Him.

322

Practical Ministry
(60 Minutes)

A. WITNESSING
   ASSIGNMENTS

Consider
beforehand:
Location
Appointments
Transportation
Meeting place and
   time upon
   completion
Any additional
   guidelines

Check to be sure
people know the
introduction and
the transitions to
the Four Spiritual
Laws. If they don't
know them, have
them write them
down and review
them on the way to
their appointment.

Review the defini-
tion of successful
witnessing. Ask
someone to quote
it. If necessary,
relate:

Successful witnessing is simply taking the initiative to share Christ in the power of the Holy Spirit
and leaving the results to God.

Remind them to
give each person a
chance to share the
Four Spiritual Laws
if possible.

Complete these
assignments in five
minutes or less.
Tell the group what
time to meet back
together to share
what happened.

B. WITNESSING

C. GROUP
   SHARING

Have the group
members share
their experiences in
witnessing.

After 5-10 minutes,
review the defini-
tion of successful
witnessing, espe-
cially if several
people had neutral
or negative
responses.

RELATE:

Successful witnessing is simply taking the initiative to share Christ in the power of the Holy Spirit
and leaving the results to God.

"In our next lesson, we'll be discussing 'Biblical
Strategy for Multiplication.' The main passages
we'll be looking at are Matthew 28:18-20 and
II Timothy 2:1-10. To get the most out of the discussion, I'd encourage you to read over these passages beforehand and even spend some time
studying them."

You may want to
have group
members read
Transferable Con-
cept 7, "How to
Help Fulfill the
Great Commis-
sion," by next
week.

Prayer
(10 Minutes)

Close with about
five minutes of
conversational
prayer for those
contacted.

Arrange the time
and place for the
next meeting.

13
The Biblical Strategy for
═══Spiritual Multiplication═══

OVERVIEW GOAL

The goal of this lesson is to motivate group members to increase their commitments to reach the world for Christ through spiritual multiplication.

LEARNING OBJECTIVES

By the end of this lesson, group members will be able to:

1. Identify God's strategy for fulfilling the Great Commission.

2. List two qualities that are desirable in people they choose to disciple.

3. Explain some commitments one needs to make in order to be a strong spiritual multiplier.

Time/Section	Outline/Questions and Learning Activities
10-15	**Sharing**
	Lead the group members in a time of sharing any opportunities they had to witness for Christ during the previous week.
30-40	**Bible Study**
Motivation	A. BUZZ GROUPS: Why hasn't the Great Commission been fulfilled during the past 100 years?
	TRANSITION: "Let's see what kind of solution the Lord has for overcoming these barriers that have prevented the Great Commission from being fulfilled."
Observ./Interp.	B. OUR OBJECTIVE
Matthew 28:18-20	1. What are some of the main ideas mentioned in this passage?
Application	2. What are some different ways that we as Christians could try to fulfill this command?
	TRANSITION: "Do you think that God would give us a command that He knew we couldn't fulfill? Of course not! He certainly isn't trying to frustrate us. God has given us a goal, but He's also outlined the most effective method that we can use to reach that goal."
Observ./Interp.	C. OUR METHOD
II Timothy 2:2	1. What are some similarities that you can see between the strategies of Jesus and Paul?
Application	2. What are some ways that we could apply the principle of multiplication to our individual ministries?

Time/Section	Outline/Questions and Learning Activities
	TRANSITION: "It is crucial for us to be expecting a multiplied return from the people to whom we are entrusting spiritual things. Let's examine two qualities that are desirable in those whom we expect to be multipliers."
Observ./Interp.	D. OUR EXAMPLE
II Timothy 2:2	1. What are some of the qualities that Timothy was to look for in the people with whom he worked?
Application	2. What are some of the long range consequences we will face if we work with people who do not have these qualities?
	TRANSITION: "In the next few verses Paul continues to describe the sort of commitment a spiritual multiplier should have. He delivers quite a challenge!"
Observ./Interp.	E. OUR COMMITMENT
II Timothy 2:3-10	1. What are some ways that these three illustrations (the soldier, the athlete and the farmer) relate to becoming strong spiritual multipliers?
	2. How does commitment to becoming a strong spiritual multiplier, as described in II Timothy 2:3-10, determine our success or failure in spiritual multiplication?
	3. What are some things which entangle people in our culture? In what ways do these things lessen their effectiveness as spiritual multipliers?
Application	4. In light of our discussion today, what are some things you might want to do to have a more effective ministry of multiplication?
	Action Point Steps I want to take to become a more effective spiritual multiplier.
15-25	**Practical Ministry**

Time/Section	Outline/Questions and Learning Activities
5-10	# Prayer
	Lead the group members in conversational prayer for each other's objectives listed in their action points.
60-90	

Preparation

PERSONAL PERSPECTIVE

Set aside at least 45 minutes when you will not be disturbed. Take your Bible and Discipleship Group study guide with you. Ask God to communicate to you His desire to reach the world through spiritual multiplication as you study Matthew 28:18-20 and II Timothy 2:2-10. Ask Him to develop in you a firm conviction of your personal responsibility to be involved in a ministry of multiplication.

You will need to develop clarifying questions for question B1. You will also need to develop your own Practical Ministry time. Consult Appendices II, III and IV.

INTRODUCTION TO MATTHEW 28

As you read this chapter you will notice that the Great Commission in verses 18-20 was given to the disciples after Jesus had completed His earthly ministry. These were quite likely the last words Jesus said to His disciples while He was bodily present with them. This alone should be enough reason to cause us to consider this passage extremely important.

INTRODUCTION TO II TIMOTHY

The book of II Timothy contains the last recorded words of Paul. It is addressed to Timothy, his "dearly beloved spiritual son" who was the pastor of a church. The letter was written to outline the course of a true servant of Christ in a time of doctrinal dissension.

RESOURCES

Disciples are Made—Not Born, Walter A. Henrichsen
Transferable Concept 7, "How to Help Fulfill the Great Commission"
Unger's Bible Handbook

> "If I fear to hold another to the highest goal because it is so much easier to avoid doing so, then I know nothing of Calvary love."*
>
> Amy Carmichael

Sharing
(10-15 Minutes)

Lead the group members in a time of sharing any opportunities they had to witness for Christ during the previous week.

Bible Study
(30-40 Minutes)

Open the Bible study in a brief prayer, asking God to teach the group.

Motivation (42)

Ask group members to get a partner. Have them list as many reasons as they can to answer the question in their study guides. Allow three minutes only. Then have each buzz group share what they have found.

A. BUZZ GROUPS: Why hasn't the Great Commission been fulfilled during the past 100 years?

_____
_____
_____
_____
_____

TRANSITION:

"Let's see what kind of solution the Lord has for overcoming these barriers that have prevented the Great Commission from being fulfilled."

*Amy Carmichael, *If*, Copyright © 1966, p. 34: Used by permission of Christian Literature Crusade, Fort Washington, Pennsylvania.

Observ./Interp.

Read the verses.

DISCUSSION:

Direct the group in a discussion of the questions. Share the suggested answers only if necessary. Summarize the group's answers after discussing each question and encourage group members to write the conclusions in their study guides.

Develop Clarifying Questions:

Application

This question is for the purpose of stimulating discussion and causing each group member to think about how he would personally help to fulfill the Great Commission. The purpose is not to give group members the solution immediately.

MATTHEW 28:18-20
B. OUR OBJECTIVE

1. What are some of the main ideas mentioned in this passage?

   Jesus has all authority in heaven and on earth. He commanded his disciples to make disciples of all the nations to reach the world.
   _____
   _____

1a. (Wide-open)
1b. (Open or limiting)

2. What are some different ways that we as Christians could try to fulfill this command?

   Mass evangelism, sharing Christ one-on-one, evangelistic television programs, small group multiplication, etc.
   _____
   _____

Clarifying
Questions:

The methods group
members suggest
will fall into two
basic categories:
addition strategy
(individually win-
ning multitudes to
Christ through var-
ious means) and
multiplication stra-
tegy (building qual-
itatively into the
lives of a few who
will in turn disciple
others).

2a. If Jesus were to tell you today that it
was your responsibility to reach the
world of over four billion people, how
would you begin?
2b. What are some of the methods that
we might use?

RELATE:

"Let's say that (name of group member) is unusually effective in evangelism. Since our lesson on
sharing Christ last week, he's been leading an
average of 1,000 people per day to Christ! If he
continues at this rate, moving from country to
country, how long do you think it would take him
to reach the world for Christ?"

Wait for their
responses.

SAY:

"Assuming that the population didn't grow at all, it
would take him over 11,000 years!

TRANSITION:

"Do you think that God would give us a command
that He knew we couldn't fulfill? Of course not! He
certainly isn't trying to frustrate us. God has given
us a goal, but He's also outlined the most effective
method that we can use to reach that goal."

Observ./Interp.

Ask a group member to read the verse. Discuss the following questions. Follow the same procedure as before.

II TIMOTHY 2:2
C. OUR METHOD

1. What are some similarities that you can see between the strategies of Jesus and Paul?

    <u>They both entrusted their messages to</u>
    <u>other men and expected them to teach</u>
    <u>still others (or make disciples of them).</u>
    _____
    _____

Clarifying
Questions:

1a. What are some other similarities?
1b. According to Matthew 28:19, what method did Jesus command His disciples to use?
1c. What were the men who heard Timothy's message supposed to do with it?

READ: (43)

"Some time ago there was a display at the Museum of Science and Industry in Chicago. It featured a checkerboard with one grain of wheat on the first square, two on the second, four on the third, then 8,16,32,64,128, etc. Somewhere down the board, there were so many grains of wheat on the square that some were spilling over into neighboring squares—so here the demonstration stopped. Above the checkerboard display was a question, 'At this rate of doubling every square, how much grain would you have on the checkerboard by the time you reached the 64th square?'

To find the answer to this riddle, you punched a button on the console in front of you, and the answer flashed on a little screen above the board: 'Enough to cover the entire subcontinent of India 50 feet deep.'

=Leader's Guide=

> Multiplication may be costly and, in the initial stages, much slower than addition, but in the long run, it is the most effective way of accomplishing Christ's Great Commission... and the only way."*

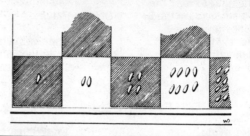

RELATE: "This quote refers to multiplication as the only feasible way to fulfill Christ's Great Commission. Let's consider more fully why the multiplication of disciples is so effective."

Application

DISCUSS:

2. What are some ways that we could apply the principle of multiplication to our individual ministries?

   <u>We need not only to win people to Christ, but also to help them grow and multiply by teaching them to teach others.</u>

Clarifying Questions:

2a. What are some other ideas?
2b. We saw how long it took (*same group member's name*) to reach the world by simply reaching 1,000 people per day. How could he have been involved in multiplication?

RELATE: "Let's suppose that you selected three men to disciple for one year with the expectation that they each would choose three men and repeat the process the following year. How long do you think it would take you to reach the world?"

*Walter A. Henrichsen, *Disciples Are Made—Not Born*, Copyright © 1974, p. 143: Used by permission of Victor Books, Wheaton, Illinois.

336

Have the group
members suggest
answers.

RELATE: "Our group could actually reach the world for
                           Christ in 21 years by discipling faithful disciplers.

                           "At that rate, isn't it amazing that the world hasn't
                           been reached yet? The natural question is, 'Why
                           hasn't this extensive spiritual multiplication taken
                           place?' Let's look at II Timothy 2:2 for some bibli-
                           cal specifics on why we haven't yet seen the world
                           reached through spiritual multiplication.

                           "The word 'entrust' in II Timothy 2:2 means 'to
                           commit to.' In the Greek, the word has the implied
                           meaning of making a deposit in a bank; that is,
                           committing or entrusting money to a bank. The
                           implication is that the deposit is made with an
                           expectation of a multiplied return.

                           "So when Paul used the word 'entrust,' he was fully
                           expecting a multiplied return on Timothy's life (i.e.,
                           there would be many disciples as the result of
                           Paul's discipleship of Timothy).

TRANSITION: "It is crucial for us to be expecting a multiplied
                           return from the people to whom we are entrusting
                           spiritual things. Let's examine two qualities that
                           are desirable in those whom we expect to be
                           multipliers."

Observ./Interp.   (44)

Ask someone to
read the verse
again.

Discuss:

| II TIMOTHY 2:2 |
| D. OUR EXAMPLE |
| |
| 1. What are some of the qualities that Timothy was to look for in the people with whom he worked? |
| |
| He was to seek those who were faithful and able to teach others. |

Application

Emphasize the possible consequences of one person in your group not multiplying himself (potential millions not being reached in our generation). Emphasize the contribution that each group member would make by being a multiplier the rest of his life (the world will be reached).

2. What are some of the long range consequences we will face if we work with people who do not have these qualities?

We will make no significant contribution to reaching the world. Potential millions will not be discipled. We will be frustrated by working with unfaithful people who do not reproduce their lives into the lives of others, etc.

_____

_____

Clarifying Questions:

2a. Any other thoughts?
2b. If we disciple unfaithful people who don't teach others, what would be the results?

TRANSITION:

"In the next few verses Paul continues to describe the sort of commitment a spiritual multiplier should have. He delivers quite a challenge!"

Observ./Interp.

Ask a group member to read the passage.

II TIMOTHY 2:3-10
E. OUR COMMITMENT

Discuss:

Emphasize that discipleship is not easy and many

1. What are some ways that these three illustrations (the soldier, the athlete and the farmer) relate to becoming strong spiritual multipliers?

obstacles will keep a person from multiplying spiritually. However, the consequences of not multiplying are overwhelming.

The soldier does not entangle himself in the affairs of everyday life. He is motivated to please the one who enlisted him. The athlete competes according to the rules and has a competitive spirit. We are competing for the purpose of winning the world for Christ. The farmer is able to enjoy the fruit of his hard work. We need to be primarily motivated by a desire to please God and must avoid entanglement in the affairs of everyday life in order to become strong spiritual multipliers. We need to follow God's "rules" of reaching the world through multiplication. Hard work is going to be necessary in order to have an effective and fruitful ministry.

Clarifying Questions:

1a. Why do you think Paul used these examples right after describing the multiplication strategy?
1b. Why are the character qualities of a soldier, athlete and farmer important to spiritual multiplication?

(45)

2. How does commitment to becoming a strong spiritual multiplier, as described in II Timothy 2:3-10, determine our success or failure in spiritual multiplication?

If we do not have the sort of commitment described in this passage, we as individuals will never become strong spiritual multipliers and thus we will be weak links (or breaks) in the chain of multiplication. If we in the Body of Christ do have that sort of commitment, we could reach the world for Christ in a short time.

Clarifying
Questions:

2a. What are some other ways that this sort of commitment will affect the strategy of multiplication?

2b. What will happen if we are not committed?

2c. What would be the result if we in the Body of Christ had this type of commitment?

---

3. What are some things which entangle people in our culture? In what ways do these things lessen their effectiveness as spiritual multipliers?

People may waste too much time in such activities as watching too much television, unnecessary conversation and un-profitable reading. People can be tied down by materialism and pursue ambi-tions that are not in line with God's will, etc.

Clarifying
Questions:

3a. Any other ideas?

3b. Do you think something has to be evil in nature to be an entanglement?

No, the good is often the enemy of the best.

Application

4. In light of our discussion today, what are some things you might want to do to have a more effective ministry of multiplication?

I can choose to work with faithful people who will be able to teach others. I can avoid entanglements (be specific) by obeying God and working hard. I can learn how to lead my own discipleship group and teach members to do the same.

Clarifying
Questions:

4a. Any other ideas?
4b. What are some characteristics you should look for in the disciples you choose?
4c. Which entanglements are you most prone to?

RELATE:

"We've considered quite a few things that would help us become more effective multipliers. Let's take a few minutes to think about which ones we want to trust God to make real in our lives."

READ: (46)

Action Point   Steps I want to take to become a more effective spiritual multiplier

1. Two things I want to begin incorporating into my ministry:

2. Two entanglements I want to trust God to help me avoid:

RELATE:

"In our next lesson we'll be discussing 'Our Identification With Christ.' The main passages we'll be looking at are Romans 6:1-16 and Romans 8:12-17. To get the most out of the discussion, I'd encourage you to read over those passages beforehand and even spend some time studying them."

Practical Ministry
(15-25 Minutes)

To develop the Practical Ministry (Vision, Strategy, Training) Section of this lesson, complete the following steps:

_____ 1. Turn to the "Strategy Chart for Student and Adult Ministries" (Point B of the III. Practical Ministry—Strategy Appendix) (see p. 528).

_____ 2. On the left hand side of the chart, identify the ministry strategy your group is now or soon will be pursuing.

_____ 3. On the right hand side of the chart, choose the training unit which you could best teach this week to prepare your group to be involved in the ministry strategy.

_____ 4. Turn in the IV. Practical Ministry— Training Appendix to the number of the training unit you have chosen and prepare to teach the content from the outline given.

_____ 5. Now turn to the II. Practical Ministry— Vision Appendix and choose the "Resource Idea" (point B) or a "Vision Passage" (point C) that would best motivate your group toward the strategy and training you have chosen.

_____ 6. When you reach the Practical Ministry portion of your discipleship group meeting, teach the Vision portion first, then discuss your local strategy in light of that vision. Then teach the Training portion. (For some topics, you may prefer to go from Vision into Training and then end with a discussion of your local strategy suggesting action points for the coming week.)

Prayer
(5-10 Minutes)

Have group members share one or two things they listed in their action points. After all have shared, instruct each group member to pray specifically concerning the objectives of the person on his right. Pray conversationally. Ask a group member to close in prayer after 5-10 minutes.

See V. Prayer Appendix for additional ideas.

Arrange the time and place for the next meeting.

14
Our Identification
=With Christ=

OVERVIEW GOAL

The goal of this lesson is to show group members how their identification with Christ means freedom from the power of sin.

LEARNING OBJECTIVES

By the end of this lesson, group members will be able to:

1. Explain the meaning of their identification with Him.

2. Explain the source of power for living out their identity.

3. State a four-step process for living out their identity.

================== **Leader's Guide** ==================

Time/Section	Outline/Questions and Learning Activities
10-15	## Sharing Have group members share opportunities they had to witness during the past week or applications they have made of their own strategies for multiplication.
30-40	## Bible Study
Motivation	A. THE STORY OF A PARDONED PRISONER You will need to develop the method to present the given motivational ideas as well as a transitional statement to take you into the Bible study.
Observ./Interp. Romans 6:1-16	B. OUR IDENTIFICATION WITH CHRIST 1. According to this passage, what are some things that are true of us in our union with Christ? 2. Explanation of baptism 3. What are some ways you could explain what "dead to sin" means? 4. Look at verses 3,6,9,11,13 and 16. What are some things Paul tells us to do to make our position in Christ affect our daily experiences? 5. Example of a pilot 6. What are some things Romans 6:12-16 says about presenting our bodies as instruments of righteousness?
Romans 8:12-17	C. THE POWER TO LIVE OUT OUR IDENTITY 1. What are some things this passage tells us about the key to experiencing our identity with Christ? 2. What do you think verse 13 means when it says, "by the Spirit you are putting to death the deeds of the body"?

346

Time/Section	Outline/Questions and Learning Activities
Application	D. OUR IDENTITY MADE REAL
	1. When you consider yourself to be dead to sin, what are some things that you might think or do when you are tempted?
	2. Are there some sins in your life to which you could now consider yourself dead?
The Four-Step Process	3. What are some steps that you need to take so you can have victory over sin?
	4. How should your identification with Christ affect your relationships with the opposite sex?
	5. How should your identification with Christ affect your relationships with members of your families?
15-25	**Practical Ministry**
5-10	**Prayer**
	Pray for each other—that you will successfully apply the ideas detailed in the discussion of Romans 6:1-16 and Romans 8:12-17.
60-90	

Preparation

PERSONAL PERSPECTIVE

Set aside at least 30 minutes when you will not be disturbed. Take your Bible, leader's guide and Discipleship Group study guide. Pray that the Holy Spirit will give you insight into God's Word. Study Romans 6:1-16 and 8:12-17 carefully, noting key words and ideas. Answer the questions in the study guide, then refer to the leader's guide to prepare for the group lesson.

The main idea is given for the Motivation section of this lesson. However, you will need to develop the method of presenting it. You will need to prepare two sets of clarifying questions for parts BI and B6. Also, you will need to develop your own Practical Ministry time. Consult Appendices II, III and IV.

INTRODUCTION TO ROMANS

Romans is the first great work of Christian theology. It was written by Paul about 57 A.D. from Corinth. He wrote it to the Roman Church to enlist their aid in fulfilling the Great Commission, to instruct them and to announce his forthcoming visit. Chapter 6 is one of the key portions of Scripture explaining our identity in Christ.

RESOURCES

Unger's Bible Handbook
Romans 5-8
Ephesians 1,2

Have you ever wondered whether you would have obeyed God if you were in Adam and Eve's place in the Garden of Eden? We need to realize that in Christ, we are as free to choose to obey as they were.

Sharing
(10-15 Minutes)

Have group members share opportunities they had to witness during the past week or applications they have made of their own strategies for multiplication. Keep the time positive. Where members have had difficulty or missed opportunities, emphasize solutions rather than dwelling on the problems they have had.

Bible Study
(30-40 Minutes)

Open the Bible study in a brief prayer, asking God to teach the group.

Motivation (48)

Develop your own method of presenting the Motivation as well as a transitional statement to take you into the Bible study.

A. THE STORY OF A PARDONED PRISONER

There was a prisoner condemned to death who received a pardon for his crime. Upon being released, he returned to a normal lifestyle—if you can call it that. It seems he adjusted very well to working, and he assumed the responsibility for his home and personal affairs very well. The unusual problem this man experienced was that he frequently returned to the prison and would assume the role of a prisoner. This would be discovered at roll call, and he would be sent home. But somehow he would always return to the prison.

TRANSITION:

This story seems a little too unusual to be true—and in fact, is not true. But how many Christians act the same way toward their relationship with sin?

Observ./Interp.

ROMANS 6:1-16
B. OUR IDENTIFICATION WITH CHRIST

Direct the group in a discussion of the questions. Share the suggested answers only if necessary. Summarize the group's answers after discussing each question and encourage group members to write the conclusions in their study guides.
Develop Clarifying Questions:

1. According to this passage, what are some things that are true of us in our union with Christ?

   We are baptized into Christ's death, buried with Him, crucified with Him, united with Him in His death, resurrection and ascension. We walk in newness of life; our life comes from Him.
   _____
   _____

1a. (Wide-open)
1b. (Open)

Have a group member read the explanation of baptism. Do not get involved in a discussion on the different methods of water baptism should the subject arise. If necessary, relate that it is not our purpose to discuss the mode of baptism and that many different viewpoints are held by churches on this

2. Explanation of baptism

   The Greek word at the root of our word "baptize" is *baptizo*, meaning "to dip into." It is the same word that is used in I Corinthians 12:13 and Romans 6:3. It was used in Greek military jargon to describe the rite in which a soldier preparing for battle would dip his sword into blood, identifying his sword with the battle. It was also a common household term used to describe the dying of a garment by dipping it into a dye.

350

topic. The focus of this study is our identification with Christ. Review Romans 6:1-16, emphasizing the statements that identify us with Christ. For example: Christ died, you died; Christ was buried, you were buried; etc.

(49) Baptize: To identify with

RELATE:

"Suppose you had a white shirt that you wanted to be red. You would baptize or place the shirt into a tub of red dye. The shirt would forever be identified with that red dye and you would never call it white again. The shirt would receive a new identity.

"The word 'baptize' in Romans 6 means to be identified with Christ. When we received Christ, the Holy Spirit baptized us into the Body of Christ and united us with Him to give us a new identity and a new life.

"Do you see how these things relate to our position in Christ, but may not be necessarily true in our daily experiences? We are going to examine how our position affects our experiences."

DISCUSS:

3. What are some ways that you could explain what "dead to sin" means?

It means we do not have to sin. We have been released from having to sin ever again. We no longer have to be overcome by sin's power. We have a choice to yield to its power or to walk in the Spirit and obey God.

Clarifying
Questions:

3a. What would the rest of you say?
3b. What are some other phrases in this passage that mean the same thing as "dead to sin"?
3c. What does the verse mean when it says that sin is no longer to be master over you?

Ask group
members to explain
the diagram in light
of Romans 6:11.

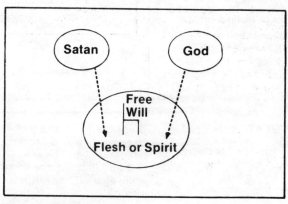

SUMMARIZE:

"God has given us the choice of obeying or disobeying Him. Before we receive Christ, we have no choice but to disobey. But when Christ comes into our lives, the Holy Spirit lives in us and we have a choice to obey or not to obey. If freedom of choice had not been restored to us, it would be impossible for us to be 'alive to God' (vs. 11). But Jesus Christ now lives in us, therefore, we can experience new life in Him.

"When we choose to follow our desires to do wrong rather than obey Christ, we do not experience the freedom of Romans 6. We are free to make the decision to sin. But we are also free to be unresponsive to the desire to sin. It is possible for sin to have no more power over us than it has over a dead man.

"Romans 6 tells us that we died to the power of sin when Christ died. In other words, we were released from having to sin. Romans 7 makes it clear that we can be overcome by our desires to do evil if we choose to live in our own strength. Romans 8 explains that in our day-to-day lives, we can experience freedom from the power of sin when we walk by the Spirit."

DISCUSS:

4. Look at verses 3,6,9,11,13 and 16. What are some things Paul tells us to do to make our position in Christ affect our daily experience?

If "know" does not come out, point it out as a last resort. Because it is not a command, it is not necessarily a logical answer to the question. You could explain that "know" means to be aware of what is true about our identity. As a result of our knowing we "consider" (believe as fact) our identity. Be certain group members grasp these four points.

know	verses 3,6,9
consider	verse 11
present	verse 13
obey	verse 16

Clarifying Questions:

4a. What do the rest of you see?
4b. What are some words used with the word "you"?

Have a group member read the "Example of a Pilot."

5. Example of a Pilot

    Airplanes are equipped with instrument panels which indicate to the pilot the position that the plane is in and the course that it is following. These panels are particularly important when it is dark or when there is low visibility. A strange thing happens to pilots when they are not able to see: their senses can become very disoriented; they can experience vertigo. The plane can be right side up and straight on course, yet if the pilot cannot see, he can feel like the plane is on its side or even upside down. He has a choice to make: he can trust his instrument panel even though his feelings and senses don't

(50)

353

agree with what it says; or, he can believe his feelings, turn the plane, and probably lose control and crash.

SAY: "In the same way, we as Christians have an accurate guide for life which is the Word of God. There will be times when we don't feel as though we are dead to sin or that we have a new identity in Christ, but we need to trust in God's Word, not our feelings. Like the pilot who trusts his instruments, we trust God's Word as our guide above all else. As we do this, we are able to take positive steps of obedience rather than being overcome by sin's power."

DISCUSS:

6. What are some things Romans 6:12-16 says about presenting our bodies as instruments of righteousness?

   We are to present ourselves to God as those alive from the dead. To whomever we present ourselves, we are slaves for obedience. As "instruments of righteousness," we are tools in the hand of God.

Develop Clarifying Questions:

6a. (Wide-open)
6b. (Open)
6c. (Limiting)

EXPLAIN:
"We present ourselves to God as a result of considering ourselves to be free from the power of sin. Many are often confused at this point. We do not present ourselves as instruments of righteousness in order to gain or keep God's blessing. We already have God's blessing, a new position, and all the resources of God. Because we are identified with Christ, we now are able to present ourselves as instruments of righteousness."

Read the verses:
ROMANS 8:12-17
C. THE POWER TO LIVE OUT OUR IDENTITY

ASK:
1. What are some things this passage tells us about the key to experiencing our identity in Christ?

We are not obligated or required to sin (or to live in the power of the flesh). We are to be led by the Spirit (filled, directed and empowered). We are not slaves to sin but sons of God and fellow-heirs with Christ.

_____

_____

Clarifying
Questions:
1a. How many times is "Spirit" mentioned in Romans 8:12-17?
1b. Where do we get the power to know, consider, present and obey?

2. What do you think verse 13 means when it says, "by the Spirit you are putting to death the deeds of the body"?

See also
Galatians 5:16
As we walk in the power of the Holy Spirit, we will experience victory over sins of our flesh.

_____

_____

RELATE:
"Let's consider how our identity is made real to us."

Application (51)

DISCUSS:

Give them a couple
minutes to answer
in their study
guides. Then ask
several to share
their answers.

Clarifying
Questions:

Invite group
members to share,
but have them
acknowledge to
themselves the sins
that they may be
unwilling to admit
to the group. Give
them a few minutes
of silence to iden-
tify these.

D. OUR IDENTITY MADE REAL

1. If you consider yourself to be dead to sin,
    what are some things that you might think
    or do when you are tempted?

Know my identity and realize I do not
have to sin. Knowing Scripture enables
me to know what is true about my identity
which helps me to resist temptation.
Leave the scene and get my mind on
obeying God and doing something positive. Say to myself, 'I don't have to sin. I
have a choice and I choose to obey God.'
Tell God I want my life to be an instrument of righteousness for Him, etc.

1a. How does considering yourself to be
     dead to sin help you resist
     temptation?
1b. When tempted, how can you make
     your life an instrument of
     righteousness?

2. Are there some sins in your life to which
    you could now consider yourself dead?

Continue the discussion:

The Four-Step Process:
Make sure the group members understand the importance of each step. You might discuss what would happen if you left out one step. The best way to know is to meditate on the particular passage. Then result will be a natural progression of steps two, three and four.

3. What are some steps that you need to take so you can have victory over sin?

First, know what God's Word says about your identity with Christ. Second, consider yourself to be dead to sin. Third, stop its reign by presenting yourself to Christ, acknowledging His Lordship. Fourth, as an act of your will, obey God. All of this has to be done in the power of the Holy Spirit.

4. How should your identification with Christ affect your relationships with the opposite sex?

We should not be compelled to live for our own selfish desires but we should live in a way to glorify God and to make our lives instruments of righteousness and love.

Clarifying Questions:

4a. What do others think?
4b. How does being free from the power of sin enable us to love others?

(52)

5. How should your identification with Christ affect your relationships with members of your family?

SAY:

"In our next lesson, we will be discussing 'Effective Prayer.' The main passage is Matthew 6:9-13. To get the most out of the discussion, I'd encourage you to read over that passage beforehand and even spend some time studying it."

Practical Ministry
(15-25 Minutes)

To develop the
Practical Ministry
(Vision, Strategy,
Training) Section
of this lesson,
complete the steps
explained in Les-
sons 11 and 13.

Prayer
(5-10 Minutes)

Pray for each
other—that you will
successfully apply
the ideas detailed
in the discussion of
Romans 6:1-16 and
Romans 8:12-17.
See V. Prayer
Appendix for addi-
tional ideas.

Arrange time and
place of next
meeting.

15
Effective
══Prayer══

OVERVIEW GOAL

The goal of this lesson is to develop the group members' personal convictions for having effective and regular prayer lives.

LEARNING OBJECTIVES

By the end of this lesson, group members will be able to:

1. Explain the significance and meaning of each part of the Lord's Prayer.

2. Desire more consistent prayer lives through seeing what some of the results would be if God's kingdom truly reigned in our nation.

Time/Section	Outline/Questions and Learning Activities
10-15	**Sharing**
	Lead an informal sharing time in which group members share how they were able to apply the previous lesson, "Our Identification With Christ," in their lives.
30-45	**Bible Study**
Motivation	A. (You will need to develop your own motivation.)
	TRANSITION: "With that in mind, we're going to spend the rest of our time gaining a better understanding of the Lord's perspective on prayer, and also do some praying ourselves."
Observ./Interp.	B. REASONS TO PRAY
Jeremiah 33:3	1. What are some promises God gives concerning our prayers?
Mark I:35; Luke 5:16; John 5:30	2. What are some reasons Jesus prayed?
Matthew 6:9-13	C. THE LORD'S PRAYER
	1. What are some reasons Jesus addressed God as Father, rather than by some other name?
	2. In what ways could we rephrase "hallowed be Thy name" to help us better understand what Jesus meant?
	3. What are some things that come to mind when you think of the word "kingdom"?
	4. What are some possible meanings of the phrase "Thy kingdom" in verse 10?
	5. What are some reasons Jesus said, "Thy kingdom come" instead of "Thy kingdom will come"?

Time/Section	Outline/Questions and Learning Activities
	6. In what ways would you describe the relationship between "Thy kingdom come" and "Thy will be done"?
	7. What are some things Jesus was referring to when He said to ask the Father to provide their "daily bread" (vs. 11)?
	8. What would be some reasons Jesus thought it important to include verse 12 in His prayer?
	9. How would you describe the Lord's responsibilities concerning the temptation and evil around us (vs. 13)?
	10. In what ways is the last part of verse 13 a significant closing for the Lord's prayer?
Application	D. A KINGDOM MENTALITY
	Direct the group in a very brief discussion of what our nation would be like if the kingdom of God were truly reigning in our government, our media and our families. Spend as much time as possible praying for these realities to come true.
	Action Point (You will need to develop an action point.)
15-25	## Practical Ministry
5	## Prayer
	Close in a brief time of thanking and praising the Lord for what He has taught you about the elements of effective prayer.
60-90	

Preparation

PERSONAL PERSPECTIVE

Spend at least one uninterrupted half hour to prepare for this lesson. You will need your Bible and Discipleship Group study guide. Ask the Lord to personalize this lesson and develop your own conviction for effective prayer. Prepare the Motivation, Application and Action Point sections in terms of your group members' needs. You will also be developing the clarifying questions for three of the main questions (C-3, C-7, C-10). Be sure to have a watch so you can time the periodic prayer times.

RESOURCES

Ten Basic Steps Toward Christian Maturity, Step 4, "The Christian and Prayer"
Power Through Prayer, E.M. Bounds
Transferable Concept 9, "How to Pray"
With Christ in the School of Prayer, Andrew Murray

> "You can do more than pray, after you have prayed, but you can never do more than pray until you have prayed."*
>
> Unknown Author

Sharing
(10-15 Minutes)

Lead an informal sharing time in which group members share how they were able to apply the previous lesson, "Our Identification With Christ," in their lives. See I. Sharing Appendix for other ideas.

Bible Study
(30-45 Minutes)

Open the Bible study in a brief prayer, asking God to teach the group.

Motivation (54)

Develop a motivation that will capture the group members' interests and create a need for more effective prayer.

A.

TRANSITION: (You may want to develop another transition which relates to your motivation.)

"With that in mind, we're going to spend the rest of our time gaining a better understanding of the Lord's perspective on prayer, and also do some praying ourselves."

*Unknown Author, *The Kneeling Christian*, Copyright © 1971, p. 30: Used by permission of Zondervan Publishing House, Grand Rapids, Michigan.

Observ./Interp.
Read the verse.

DISCUSSION:

Direct the group in a discussion of the questions. Share the suggested answers only if necessary. Summarize the group's answers after discussing each question and encourage group members to write the conclusions in their study guides.

JEREMIAH 33:3
B.   REASONS TO PRAY

1.   What are some promises God gives concerning our prayers?

   <u>God promises to answer us, to tell us</u>
   <u>great things, and to reveal to us things we</u>
   <u>do not know.</u>
   _____
   _____

RELATE:

"God not only tells us to pray, but He also gives us an example to follow in the prayer life of our Lord."

Read the verses. Discuss the question, following the same procedure as before.

MARK 1:35; LUKE 5:16; JOHN 5:30
2.   What are some reasons Jesus prayed?

   <u>Jesus wanted to spend time alone with</u>
   <u>His Father. He was dependent on the</u>
   <u>Father for everything, particularly for</u>
   <u>decisions and judgments He had to make.</u>
   _____
   _____

Clarifying Questions:

2a.   What attitudes were demonstrated by Jesus toward His Father when He prayed?

2b. What attitude toward the Father did Jesus demonstrate in John 5:30?

EXPLAIN:

"Obviously, prayer was a significant part of Jesus' life. Prayer wasn't so much an act of obedience as it was an expression of His constant dependence on His Father. Because of His continual prayer life, the disciples asked Him to teach them to have an effective prayer life, too."

Read the Scripture. Discuss the study questions.

(55)

MATTHEW 6:9-13
C. THE LORD'S PRAYER

1. What are some reasons Jesus addressed God as Father, rather than by some other name?

The word "Father" represented one to whom He had submitted. It also gives a good picture of their close family relationship as well as Jesus' dependence on Him.

Clarifying Questions:

1a. What would be some other reasons?
1b. What are some qualities of a father that are also true of God?

2. In what ways could we rephrase "hallowed be Thy name" (vs. 9) to help us better understand what Jesus meant?

Webster's dictionary defines "hallowed" as "made holy or sacred, honored as holy." This could be rephrased as "holy or sacred be Thy name."

Clarifying Questions:

2a. What are some other ways to rephrase that statement?
2b. What does the word "hallowed" mean?

Direct the group in one or two minutes of conversational prayer, focusing on thanking God for being our Father and praising Him for His holiness.

DISCUSS:

3. What are some things that come to mind when you think of the word "kingdom"?

A kingdom is a government or country ruled by a king or queen; a realm or domain. There is one who rules and many who are ruled. The king is given the responsibility of leading and caring for his kingdom.

Develop Clarifying Questions:

3a. (Wide-open)
3b. (Open)

(56)

4. What are some possible meanings of the phrase "Thy kingdom" in verse 10?

It refers to God's present, future and continuous reign on earth and in heaven.

Clarifying
Questions:

4a. To what else could Christ have been referring in that phrase?

4b. When did God's kingdom start and when will it end?

---

5. What are some reasons Jesus said, "Thy kingdom come" instead of "Thy kingdom will come"?

It is stated in the present progressive tense, meaning that God's kingdom is coming and reigning in the various areas of our lives and world. God's kingdom is not just something to look forward to in the future. We must pray for His kingdom to reign everywhere now.

Clarifying
Questions:

5a. What would be some other reasons?

5b. What is the difference between the two verb tenses used in this question?

5c. How does the verb tense Jesus used tell us when His kingdom will arrive?

---

6. In what ways would you describe the relationship between "Thy kingdom come" and "Thy will be done"?

As God's kingdom comes, His will is being done. As He is in control, His will is accomplished.

Clarifying
Questions:

6a. What other ways are there to explain the relationship?

6b. How is one dependent on the other?

---

7. What are some things Jesus was referring to when He said to ask the Father to provide their "daily bread" (vs. 11)?

> Throughout the Bible this principle is
> taught, and it can refer to such things as
> food, clothing, protection, proper atti-
> tudes, emotional strengths or any other
> human need.

Develop Clarifying
Questions:

7a. (Wide-open)
7b. (Open)
7c. (Limiting)

> 8. What would be some reasons Jesus
>   thought it important to include verse 12 in
>   His prayer?
>
>   Jesus knew that in order to experience
>   abundant fellowship with God, we need to
>   be free from the guilt of sin—both toward
>   God and others.

Clarifying
Questions:

8a. What else is significant about this
    verse being included in the prayer?
8b. How would forgiving others and being
    forgiven affect our prayers?

DISCUSS: (57)

> 9. How would you describe the Lord's
>   responsibilities concerning the temptation
>   and evil around us (vs. 13)?
>
>   He will not direct us toward temptation
>   and He will deliver us from evil. Satan is
>   the one who tempts us, and God is the
>   one who delivers us.

Clarifying
Questions:

9a. What can we trust God to do as we
    face temptation and evil?
9b. What other ideas do you have?

If time allows, direct the group in one or two minutes of conversational prayer focusing on specific requests for God's deliverance from the evils around them.

ASK:

> 10. In what ways is the last part of verse 13 a significant closing for the Lord's prayer?
>
> After making some specific requests of God, it is always good to spend some more time worshipping Him. This is an active demonstration of our faith in God to accomplish what concerns us, and also leaves our focus on God instead of the needs or problems.

Develop Clarifying Questions:

10a. (Wide-open)
10b. (Open)
10c. (Limiting)

SAY:

"Having a kingdom mentality—focusing on God's kingdom—will have a dynamic impact on our prayer lives, as well as on our commitments and ministries."

Application

Develop an open question to direct the group in a very brief discussion of what our nation would be like if the kingdom of God were truly reigning in our government, our media and our families. Spend as much time as possible praying for these realities to come true.

D. A KINGDOM MENTALITY

Develop an action point in which your group members can apply the model of Jesus' prayer life and kingdom mentality to their own lives.

Action Point

SAY:

"In our next lesson, we will be discussing 'Dealing With Temptation.' The main passages we'll be looking at are James 1:12-15 and Psalm 119:9-16. To get the most out of the discussion, I'd encourage you to read over these passages beforehand and even spend some time studying them."

Practical Ministry
(15-25 Minutes)

To develop the Practical Ministry (Vision, Strategy, Training) Section of this lesson, complete the steps explained in Lessons 11 and 13.

Prayer
(5 Minutes)

Close the group in prayer, thanking and praising God for what He has taught you about the elements of effective prayer.

SAY:

"Since we've spent much of our time in prayer, I'll just close us in prayer myself."

Arrange the time and place of the next meeting.

16
Dealing With
═══Temptation═══

OVERVIEW GOAL

The goal of this lesson is to enable group members to deal with temptation.

LEARNING OBJECTIVES

By the end of this lesson, group members will be able to:

1.   Explain the progression from temptation to sin.

2.   Explain how to resist temptation.

371

Time/Section	Outline/Questions and Learning Activities
10-15	## Sharing
	Ask group members to share ways they were able to apply the principles of prayer which they learned last week.
30-40	## Bible Study
Motivation	A. (Develop your own motivational idea, method of presentation and transitional statement.)
Observ./Interp.	B. HOW DOES TEMPTATION BECOME SIN?
James 1:12-15	1. What relationship do you see in this passage between temptation and sin? 2. What do you think the word "lust" means? 3. What are some other areas of life besides male-female relationships where we might experience lust? 4. What are some situations in which we are most often tempted?
	C. HOW TO DEAL WITH TEMPTATION
	1. Apply your identity. 2. Walk in the Spirit. 3. Treasure God's Word in your heart.
Psalm 119:9-16	4. What are some of the attitudes the psalmist has toward God's Word? 5. How do we treasure God's Word in our hearts (vs. II)? 6. How are these three concepts related: being filled with the Spirit, knowing our identity in Christ and meditating upon God's Word?
Application	D. (Prepare an application step with appropriate question(s) that will help group members deal with temptation.)
15-25	## Practical Ministry

Time/Section	Outline/Questions and Learning Activities
5-10	## Prayer
	Close in conversational prayer, asking the Lord to apply the principles of dealing with temptation to your lives.
60-90	

Preparation

PERSONAL PERSPECTIVE

Set aside at least one hour of uninterrupted time. Consider the needs of your group members as you prepare this lesson. Tailor it to meet their needs. You will need to develop three sets of clarifying questions (for questions B-3, B-4 and C-6). Take some time to develop these questions as you study. You will also need to develop the Application and Motivation sections.

INTRODUCTION TO JAMES

The book of James could be described as an interpretation of the Old Testament and the Sermon on the Mount in light of the gospel of Christ. The epistle deals with the necessity of having a living faith. This may be the earliest of the epistles and was written by James, a half-brother of Jesus, as early as 45 A.D. James 1 deals with faith as tested by trial.

INTRODUCTION TO PSALMS

The Hebrew title for the Psalter is "Book of Praises!" Praise, worship, confession and the outpouring of prayer characterize the Psalms. There are several authors of the Psalms, the most prominent being David, who wrote 73 of them. Psalm 119 exalts the Word of God.

SUPPLIES

A dictionary

RESOURCES

Unger's Bible Handbook

> "As I see it, some Christians resemble a pressure cooker with the lid ready to blow off. They have permitted the satanic world system to pump more and more pressure into their thought lives: selfish ambitions, worry, lust, anger, resentment, fear. They suppose that adding heavier lids will keep these things from exploding into their behavior. They are mistaken, of course, because eventually the heaviest lid will blow and the blast will be enormous."*
>
> Earl Radmacher

Sharing
(10-15 Minutes)

Ask group members to share ways they were able to apply the principles of prayer which they learned last week. See I. Sharing Appendix for additional ideas.

Bible Study
(30-40 Minutes)

Open the Bible study in a brief prayer, asking God to teach the group.

Motivation (60)

A.

Develop a motivational idea and method of presentation. Be sure to include a transitional statement to lead into the next point.

*Earl D. Radmacher, *You and Your Thoughts*, Copyright © 1977, pp. 28,32: Used by permission of Tyndale House, Wheaton, Illinois.

TRANSITION:

Observ./Interp.

Give some brief background information on the book of James. (See Preparation page.) Have a group member read the verses.

DISCUSSION: Direct the group in a discussion of the questions. Share the suggested answers only if necessary. Summarize the group's answers after discussing each question and encourage group members to write the conclusions in their study guides.

Clarifying Questions:

Have someone find the word "lust" in the dictionary and read the definition to the group.

JAMES 1:12-15
B. HOW DOES TEMPTATION BECOME SIN?

1. What relationship do you see in this passage between temptation and sin?

   When we give in to temptation (thoughts of lust), it turns into sin.
   _____
   _____

1a. What takes place in your life between the temptation and the sin?
1b. What is the source of temptation?

2. What do you think the word "lust" means?

   It is a desire to gratify the senses: bodily appetite.
   _____
   _____

> 3. What are some other areas of life besides male-female relationships where we might experience lust?
>
> Lust can be any strong desire for prestige, material possessions, position or even food.

Develop Clarifying
Questions:

3a. (Wide open)
3b. (Open)

> 4. What are some situations in which we are most often tempted?
>
> Some situations are when someone criticizes us, when we hear a rumor, when it seems that avoiding the truth would gain us an advantage, etc.

Develop Clarifying
Questions:

4a. (Wide-open)
4b. (Open)

Relate the explana-(61)
tions after reading
each point.

> C. HOW TO DEAL WITH TEMPTATION
>
> 1. Apply your identity.

SAY:

"Do you remember our study of Romans 6:1-16? We discussed how our identity with Christ should affect our response to temptation. Remember we discussed a four-step process. We found that we should: know who we are in Christ, consider ourselves dead to sin, present ourselves to Christ and begin to obey God as an act of our will."

> 2. Walk in the Spirit.

SAY:

"Remember our study of the Spirit-filled life in Lesson 3? Galatians 5:16 says, 'Walk by the Spirit, and you will not carry out the desire of the flesh.' If we try to win the battle with temptation in our own strength we are doomed to lose."

3. Treasure God's Word in your heart.

RELATE:

"There is another important area that we need to consider if we are to stop temptation from becoming sin. It is the area of our mind. Often we try to change our actions without changing our thoughts. On the front of your lesson is this quote by Earl Radmacher:

"'As I see it, some Christians resemble a pressure cooker with the lid ready to blow off. They have permitted the satanic world system to pump more and more pressure into their thought lives: selfish ambitions, worry, lust, anger, resentment, fear. They suppose that adding heavier lids will keep these things from exploding into their behavior. They are mistaken, of course, because eventually the heaviest lid will blow and the blast will be enormous.'"

RELATE:

"Let's look at a passage in Psalm 119 that will help us know how to deal with our thoughts."

Give some brief background information on the book of Psalms. (See Preparation page.) Have a group member read the verses.

Discuss the following questions. Follow the same procedure as before.

PSALM 119:9-16

4. What are some of the attitudes the psalmist has toward God's Word?

He treasures it in his heart, he wants God's teaching and he rejoices in God's Word. He meditates on it, delights in it, and does not want to forget it.

_____

_____

5. How do we treasure God's Word in our hearts (vs. II)?

Another word for heart is mind; we treasure God's Word in our heart by meditating on it, by memorizing it and by applying it to our lives.

_____

_____

(62)

6. How are these three concepts related: being filled with the Spirit, knowing our identity in Christ and meditating upon God's Word?

Knowing our identity tells us we don't have to sin, while being filled gives us the power not to sin. Meditating on God's Word gives us the desires and will not to sin and to live godly, obedient lives.

_____

_____

Develop Clarifying Questions:

6a. (Wide-open)
6b. (Open)
6c. (Limiting or leading)

Application

Prepare an application step with appropriate question(s) that will help group members deal with temptation.

D.

_____

_____

_____

_____

_____

_____

_____

RELATE:

"In our next lesson, we'll be discussing 'Discovering God's Will.' The main passages we'll be looking at are Romans 12:1,2; Psalm 119:97-105 and Daniel 1. To get the most out of the discussion, I'd encourage you to read over these passages beforehand and even spend some time studying them."

Practical Ministry
(15-25 Minutes)

To develop the
Practical Ministry
(Vision, Strategy,
Training) Section
of this lesson com-
plete the steps
explained in Les-
sons 11 and 13.

Prayer
(5-10 Minutes)

Close in conversa-
tional prayer, ask-
ing the Lord to
apply the principles
of dealing with
temptation to your
lives. See V. Prayer
Appendix for addi-
tional ideas.

Arrange the time
and place of the
next meeting.

17
Discovering
═══God's Will═══

OVERVIEW GOAL

The goal of this lesson is to motivate group members to know and to do God's will.

LEARNING OBJECTIVES

By the end of this lesson, group members will be able to:

1. State two prerequisites for knowing God's will.

2. Explain how their minds can be renewed and their lives transformed.

3. Explain Daniel's example of obedience to God's will and the results of his obedience.

Leader's Guide

Time/Section	Outline/Questions and Learning Activities
10-15	## Sharing
	Have group members share ways they experienced victory over temptation during the past week.
30-40	## Bible Study
Motivation	A. (Develop your own motivational idea, method of presentation and transitional statement.)
Observ./Interp.	B. EXAMINATION OF GOD'S WILL
Romans 12:1,2	1. According to these verses, what are some things we need to do in order to prove or demonstrate that the will of God is good, acceptable and perfect? 2. What are some things you think Paul meant when he described God's will as good, acceptable and perfect?
Psalm 119:97-105	C. EXPLANATION OF "TRANSFORMATION" 1. In what ways did the psalmist see his life transformed by God's Word? 2. Since it is apparent that the transformation of the psalmist's life was related to God's Word, what are some things you notice about how he used God's Word?
Daniel 1:1-21	D. EXAMPLE OF "PRESENTATION" 1. In what ways did Daniel's refusal to eat the king's choice food demonstrate a total yieldedness to God's will? 2. It is evident that Daniel was ready and willing to do God's will. What are some of the results you see in his life concerning God's good, acceptable and perfect will?

384

Time/Section	Outline/Questions and Learning Activities
Application	E. EXPERIENCE GOD'S BEST

 1. If you had been Daniel, what are some reasons you might have chosen to conform to the world?
 2. What are some steps we should be willing to take in order to experience God's good, acceptable and perfect will for our lives?
 3. What are some areas in your life in which you need to present yourself to God as a living sacrifice? (Areas in which you know God's will but have not been willing to do it)
 4. God's Word brings transformation in our lives. (Develop as a question.)
 5. God has a good, acceptable and perfect will for me. (Develop as a question.)

Action Point   Carefully read the Paul Brown letter. Using a Pro-Con Chart, apply the principles shared in this letter to a particular area of your life in which you are seeking God's direction (for example: occupation, marriage, purchases).

Time/Section	
15-25	**Practical Ministry**
5-10	**Prayer**

Close in conversational prayer, asking God to direct each member in decisions he must make.

60-90

385

Preparation

PERSONAL PERSPECTIVE

Since it is your objective to motivate the group to know and to do God's will, read through Daniel 1, visualizing yourself in Daniel's position and identifying as many reasons as possible why you would or would not do what Daniel did. This will help you as a leader to better understand the dilemma an individual often faces in doing God's will. Be prepared to relate instances in your life when you were faced with similar difficult decisions and the results of those decisions. Both positive and negative examples would be good.

To better understand the passages being studied, read Romans 11 and Daniel 2-6 if time allows.

If necessary, spend some extended time with the Lord recommitting yourself to go anywhere He asks you to go, to do anything He asks you to do, to say anything He asks you to say and to give anything He asks you to give. That which will communicate most to the group members will be your own willingness to know and to do God's will.

You will need to develop your own Practical Ministry time. Consult Appendices II, III and IV. Also, you will need to develop a Motivation section for the beginning of the Bible study, two main questions (E-4, E-5) in the Application section and the clarifying questions for the entire lesson.

Take time to read and study the Paul Brown letter. Then fill out the Pro-Con Chart applying the principles discussed in the letter. Use a real situation in your life or make up an example that will apply to the group members. The Pro-Con chart is not included in the study guide, so you may want to provide copies for your group members.

INTRODUCTION TO ROMANS 12

Paul wrote this letter to the Church in Rome which was comprised primarily of Gentile believers. At this point in his letter he begins to exhort them to act in accordance with the principle he has shared in the preceding chapters (i.e. God's mercy to the Gentiles).

INTRODUCTION TO PSALM 119

Each section of eight verses in this entire Psalm begins with successive letters of the Hebrew alphabet. This wisdom psalm communicates the truth that the Word of God contains everything man needs to know.

INTRODUCTION TO DANIEL

Daniel was alive before, during and after the 70 year captivity of Judah by Babylon. His lifespan closely aligns with those of Jeremiah and Ezekiel. As a youth, he was taken captive by Nebuchadnezzar, king of Babylon and ruler of the entire world. Throughout his life, Daniel constantly saw God's favor as a result of his uncompromising obedience.

RESOURCES

Affirming the Will of God, Paul Little (Inter-Varsity Press booklet)
Getting to Know the Will of God, Alan Redpath (Inter-Varsity Press booklet)
Halley's Bible Handbook
The Ryrie Study Bible

SUPPLEMENTARY THOUGHTS ABOUT GOD'S WILL

Jim Elliot was 28 years old when he died at the hands of the Auca Indians in Ecuador. He and four others were taking the life-saving message of Jesus Christ to these people who had never heard it. Yet he was able to experience what he had written in his journal six years earlier. "He is no fool who gives what he cannot keep to gain what he cannot lose."*

Nathan Brown of Burma wrote this prayer:

"And shall I pray Thee change Thy will, my Father,
Until it be according unto mine?
But no, Lord, no; that never shall be, rather
I pray Thee, blend my human will with Thine."**

---

*Elizabeth Elliot, *Shadow of the Almighty*, Copyright © 1959, p. 15: Used by permission of Harper and Brothers Publishers, New York, New York.

**Shadow of the Almighty*, p. 151.

HIS PLAN FOR ME

"When I stand at the judgment seat of Christ,
    And He shows me His plan for me,
The plan of my life as it might have been
    Had He had His way, and I see how
I blocked Him here and checked Him there,
    And I would not yield my will,
Will there be grief in my Savior's eyes,
    Grief though He loves me still?
He would have me rich, but I stand there poor
    Stripped of all but His grace,
While memory runs like a hunted thing,
    Down the paths I cannot retrace.
Then my desolate heart will well-nigh
    Break with the tears I cannot shed.
I shall cover my face with my empty hands,
    And bow my uncrowned head.
Lord, of the years that are left to me,
    I give them to Thy hand.
Take me and break me, mold me,
    To the pattern Thou hast planned."*

Author Unknown

Sharing
(10-15 Minutes)

Have group members share ways they experienced victory over temptations during the past week. See I. Sharing Appendix for additional ideas.

* Bill Bright, *Teacher's Manual for the Ten Basic Steps Toward Christian Maturity*, Copyright © 1965, p. 402: Used by permission of Campus Crusade for Christ, Inc., Arrowhead Springs, California.

Bible Study
(30-40 Minutes)

Open the Bible
study in a brief
prayer, asking God
to teach the group.

Motivation   (64)

Remember that
your objective is to
motivate group
members to know
and to do God's
will. Design your
motivation with that
in mind. Also,
develop a transi-
tional statement
that will lead into
section B.

TRANSITION:

A.

Observ./Interp.

Give some back-
ground material if
necessary. Be
familiar with the
Introduction to
Romans on the
Preparation page.

Read the verses.

Explain that the
word "prove" in
verse 2 means to
demonstrate, or live
out God's will for
our lives.

ROMANS 12:1,2
B.   EXAMINATION OF GOD'S WILL

1.   According to these verses, what are some
things we need to do in order to prove or
demonstrate that the will of God is good,
acceptable and perfect?

We need to present our bodies as living
sacrifices. We should not be conformed to

DISCUSSION:
Direct the group in a discussion of the questions. Share the suggested answers only if necessary. Summarize the group's answers after discussing each question and encourage group members to write the conclusions in their study guides.

the world, but rather transformed by the renewing of our minds.

2. What are some things you think Paul meant when he described God's will as good, acceptable and perfect?

It is all good for me: it contains no bad things. It will be something I can enjoy. It is perfect: there is no plan that could be better.

Develop Clarifying Questions:

2a. (Wide-open or rephrase)
2b. (Open or limiting)
2c. (Limiting or leading)

RELATE:

"Two major aspects of these verses are the presentation of our bodies as living sacrifices and the transformation of our lives by the renewing of our minds. The passages we're now going to discuss deal specifically with these two aspects."

Relate the background material on Psalm 119 from the Preparation page. Have a group member read the passage.

Discuss the following questions. Follow the same procedure as before.

PSALM 119:97-105
C. EXPLANATION OF "TRANSFORMATION"

1. In what ways did the psalmist see his life transformed by God's Word?

> He developed a love for the Word. The
> Word of God made him wiser than his
> enemies, gave him more insight than his
> teachers and gave him more understand-
> ing than the aged. By it, he was restrained
> from doing evil. He became obedient to
> the Word, and the Word became sweet
> and not bitter to him. It became a light
> that showed him the proper path.

Develop Clarifying Questions:

Notice the answers are in the first line of each verse.

1a. (Wide-open)
1b. (Limiting)

(65)

2. Since it is apparent that the transformation of the psalmist's life was related to
   God's Word, what are some things you
   notice about how he used God's Word?

   > He meditated on it; he spent continual
   > time in it; he observed the commands; he
   > obeyed it; he spent time alone with the
   > Lord allowing Him to use the Word to
   > teach him; he used it to discern right from
   > wrong and to determine direction for his
   > life.

Develop Clarifying Questions:

Notice the answers are in the second line of each verse.

Indicate that since you have now looked at Scripture relating to the transforming of our

2a. (Wide-open or rephrase)
2b. (Open or limiting)
2c. (Limiting or leading)

lives by God's Word, the next passage of our study gives an example of how one man yielded himself to what he knew was God's will; and as a result, experienced God's good, acceptable and perfect will for his life.

To introduce this passage, be familiar with the background material from the Preparation page.

Divide the 21 verses by the number of people in the group and have each member read a portion aloud.

Discuss the study questions.

DANIEL 1:1-21

D. EXAMPLE OF "PRESENTATION"

1. In what ways did Daniel's refusal to eat the king's choice food demonstrate a total yieldedness to God's will?

Daniel was willing to risk everything in order to follow God's will. There was a possibility that he was risking his life. He might have been put in prison, or reassigned to do manual labor as a slave; or he might have starved to death.

Develop Clarifying
Questions that
focus on things
Daniel may have
been giving up by
refusing to eat the
food.

1a. (Open or rephrase)
1b. (Wide-open)

ASK: (66)

2. It is evident that Daniel was ready and willing to do God's will. What are some of the results you see in his life concerning God's good, acceptable and perfect will?

The results of Daniel's obedience were supernatural. He gained knowledge, intelligence and the ability to interpret dreams. He and his friends were found to be ten times better than anyone else in the kingdom. God also granted him a long life.

Develop Clarifying
Questions:

2a. (Rephrase)
2b. (Wide-open)
2c. (Limiting)

Application

DISCUSS:

E. EXPERIENCE GOD'S BEST

1. If you had been Daniel, what are some reasons you might have chosen to conform to the world?

I might conform because of peer pressure, fear for my life or fear that the test would fail. I might have thought that God no longer cared for me and might have become bitter against Him about my captivity. I might feel if I could keep the king's favor, I'd be in a better position to help my people, etc.

Develop Clarifying
Questions:
Help group
members consider
some reasons why
they conform to
this world.

1a. (Rephrase)
1b. (Wide-open)

(67)

> 2. What are some steps we should be willing
>   to take in order to experience God's good,
>   acceptable and perfect will for our lives?
>
>   We should be willing to offer our bodies
>   as a living sacrifice, renew our minds with
>   God's Word, be transformed by God's
>   Word, obey His Word and yield to His will.

Explain that if an
individual wishes to
experience God's
best plan for his
life, it is clear that
he needs to live a
live that is continu-
ally transformed by
God's Word. He
also must demon-
strate a complete
willingness to yield
to God's will no
matter what it may
be.

Continue the
discussion.

Be sensitive if
group members
don't want to share.

> 3. What are some areas in your life in which
>   you need to present yourself to God as a
>   living sacrifice? (Areas in which you know
>   God's will but have not been willing to do
>   it.)

Develop an open question which will cause group members to think of ways they can use God's Word to bring about transformations in their lives.

4. _____
   _____
   _____
   _____
   _____
   _____

Develop an open question which will cause group members to visualize what they think might be God's good, acceptable and perfect will for them.

5. _____
   _____
   _____
   _____
   _____
   _____

SAY:

"Now that we have talked in general about how a person can know and experience God's will for his life, there are other biblical principles to help us in determining God's specific will for us in vocation, marriage, finances, etc. Not only Is God's Word important, but we also need the counsel of mature Christians who know the Word and can apply it to our situations. Prayer and sometimes providential circumstances can also help us to determine God's will for our lives.

"The Paul Brown letter is a tool that explains these principles and is designed to help Spirit-filled Christians make decisions about God's specific will for their lives."

READ:

Action Point

1. Carefully read the Paul Brown letter.
2. Using a Pro-Con Chart, apply the principles shared in this letter to a particular area of your life in which you are seeking God's direction (for example: occupation, marriage, purchases).

EXPLAIN:

If you have made copies of the Pro-Con Chart, pass out the copies to group members.

After reading the Paul Brown letter in your study guides, take your Pro-Con Chart and fill in three (or more) different options you might have regarding a decision you are currently facing. Before you begin to fill in the grid, ask yourself if you are willing to do whatever God reveals to you. List the options you can think of, not just the options you want to do.

"The left hand column lists the major criteria on which our decisions need to be based: God's Word, the Holy Spirit, the Great Commission, counsel of others, and circumstances. Each of the areas listed in the left column are discussed in the Paul Brown letter included in this lesson. For example, as you seek God's guidance for your decision, ask yourself, 'How will this option help in the fulfillment of the Great Commission?' Then record your thoughts in the boxes."

If you have not made copies for your group members, help them develop their own by using the example chart provided in the Leader's Guide, or from the illustration in the Paul Brown letter.

CAMPUS CRUSADE FOR CHRIST INTERNATIONAL ⊕⊕

Arrowhead Springs, San Bernardino, CA 92414 · Telephone (714) 886-5224 · William R. Bright, Founder and President

> Though not actually written to Paul Brown, this
> letter contains the basic counsel which
> Dr. Bright gives students and adults concerning,
> "How to know the will of God for your life":

Mr. Paul V. Brown
The Graduate House
University of California
Los Angeles, California 90024

     Re: How to Know the Will of God for your Life
         according to the "Sound-Mind Principle" of Scripture.

Dear Paul:

Thank you for your recent letter sharing some of the exciting experiences
which you are having in your new and adventuresome life with Christ.

When I read that part of your letter in which you expressed the desire to
invest your life fully for Christ, I paused to give thanks to the Lord: first, for
His great love and faithful direction of the lives of all who will trust Him; and
second, for your response to His love and your willingness to trust Him with
every detail of your life.

It is at this crucial point that many Christians deprive themselves of the full,
abundant and purposeful life which the Lord Jesus promised in John 10:10.
Failing to comprehend the true character and nature of God, His absolute
love, grace, wisdom, power and holiness, many Christians have foolishly
chosen to live according to their own plans rather than consider and do the
will of God. Some have such a distorted view of God that they think of Him
as a tyrant whom one must either appease, or experience His wrath, as
those who worship a pagan god. Since they are afraid of Him, they cannot
love and trust Him. This is sometimes true of individuals who have transferred to God their fear of an earthly father who may have been overly strict,
unduly demanding, or even tyrannical.

In all fairness I should say that there are many sincere Christians who want
to do the will of God but do not know how to go about discovering His will
for their lives.

A choice young college graduate came recently for counsel concerning
God's will for his life. "How can I know what God wants me to do?" he
asked. Briefly I explained the safest approach to knowing the will of God—
to follow what I have chosen to call the "Sound-Mind Principle" of Scripture.

In less than an hour, by following the suggestions contained in this letter, this young man discovered what he had been seeking for years. He knew not only the work which God wanted him to do, but the very organization with which he was to be affiliated.

Now you may ask, "What is the 'Sound-Mind Principle' of Scripture?" In II Timothy 1:7 we are told that "God has not given us the spirit of fear; but of power, and of love and of a sound mind." The sound mind referred to in this verse means a well-balanced mind: a mind that is under the control of the Holy Spirit, "remade" according to Romans 12:1,2: "Therefore, my brothers, I implore you by God's mercies to offer your very selves to Him, a living sacrifice, dedicated and fit for His acceptance, the worship offered by mind and heart. Adapt yourselves no longer to the pattern of the present world, but let your minds be remade and your whole nature thus transformed. Then you will be able to discern the will of God and to know it is good, acceptable, and perfect." (NEB)

There is a vast difference between the inclination of the natural or carnal man to use "common sense" and that of the spiritual man to follow the "Sound-Mind Principle." One, for understanding, depends upon the wisdom of man without benefit of God's wisdom and power; the latter, having the mind of Christ, receives wisdom and guidance from God moment by moment through faith.

Are your decisions as a Christian based upon unpredictable emotions and chance circumstances, the "common sense" of the natural man? Or do you make your decisions according to the "Sound-Mind Principle" of Scripture?

Through the years, as I have counselled with many Christians, the question most frequently asked has been, "How can I know the will of God for my life?" Inevitably, the majority of Christians who come for counsel are looking for some dramatic or cataclysmic revelation from God by which they will know God's plan. Without minimizing the importance of feelings, which Jesus promised in John 14:21 as a result of obedience, more emphasis needs to be placed upon the importance of the sound mind which God has given. Multitudes of sincere Christians are wasting their lives, immobile and impotent, as they wait for some unusual or dramatic word from God.

The Scripture assures us that "God has not given us a spirit of fear, but of power, and of love, and of a sound mind." Thus, a Christian who has yielded his life fully to Christ can be assured of sanctified reasoning, and a balanced, disciplined mind. Also, God has promised to give His children wisdom according to James 1:5-7. Further, we can know with "settled and absolute assurance" that when we pray according to the will of God, He will always hear and grant our petitions. (I John 5:14,15.) Since the Christian is to live by faith, and faith comes through an understanding of the Word of God, it is impossible to over-emphasize the importance of the Scripture in the lives of those who would know and do the will of God.

If you would like to know the will of God for your life according to the "Sound-Mind Principle" of Scripture, may I suggest that you follow this bit of logic. First, consider these questions: "Why did Jesus come?" He came "to seek and save the lost." (Luke 19:10). Then "What is the greatest experience of your life?" If you are a Christian, your answer quite obviously will be: "To know Christ personally as my Savior and Lord." Finally, "What is the greatest thing that you can do to help others?" The answer is again obvious, "Introducing them to Christ."

Jesus came to seek and to save the lost, and every Christian is under divine orders to be a faithful witness for Christ. Jesus said, "Herein is my Father glorified, that ye bear much fruit; so shall ye prove that ye are my disciples." It logically follows that the most important thing I can possibly do as a Christian is to allow the Lord Jesus Christ in all of His Resurrection power to have complete, unhindered control of my life, otherwise he cannot continue seeking and saving the lost through me.

Thus, every sincere Christian will want to make his God-given time, talents and treasure available to Christ so that his fullest potential will be realized for Him. For one Christian, this talent which God has given him may be prophetic preaching, evangelism or teaching; for another, it may be business; for another, the ministry or missions; for another, homemaking, as expressed in Rom. 12:5, I Cor. 12, I Cor. 14, Eph. 4, and other scriptures.

As you evaluate the talents that God has given you in relation to your training, personality, and other qualities, may I suggest that you take a sheet of paper and make a list of the most logical ways through which your life can be used to accomplish the most for the glory of God. With the desire to put His will above all else,

Campus Crusade		Teaching		Church Ministry		Business or Profession	
Pro	Con	Pro	Con	Pro	Con	Pro	Con

list the pros and cons of each opportunity. Where or how, according to the "Sound-Mind Principle," can the Lord Jesus Christ through your yielded life accomplish the most in continuing His great ministry of "seeking and saving the lost?" Like my young friend, you will find that such a procedure will inevitably result in positive actions leading to God's perfect will for your life. But note a word of caution: The "Sound-Mind Principle" is not valid unless certain factors exist.

1. There must be no unconfessed sin in your life; following I John 1:9 takes care of that: "If we confess our sins, God is faithful and just to forgive us our sins and to cleanse us from all unrighteousness."

2. Your life must be fully dedicated to Christ according to Romans 12:1,2, and you must be filled with the Holy Spirit in obedience to the command of Ephesians 5:18. As in the case of our salvation, we are filled and controlled by the Spirit through faith.

3. In order to know the will of God, you must walk in the Spirit (abiding in Christ) moment by moment. You place your faith in the trustworthiness of God with the confidence that the Lord is directing and will continue to direct your life according to His promise that the "steps of a righteous man are ordered of the Lord." For "as you have therefore received Christ Jesus the Lord, so walk in Him." How? By faith, by placing your complete trust in Him. Now, you must go on walking by faith. Remember, "that which is not of faith is sin," and "the just shall live by faith," and "without faith it is impossible to please God." Faith is the catalyst for all our Christian relationships.

The counsel of others should be prayerfully considered, especially that of mature, dedicated Christians who know the Word of God and are able to relate the proper use of Scripture to your need. However, care should be taken not to make the counsel of others a "crutch." Although God often speaks to us through other Christians, we are admonished to place our trust in Him. In Psalm 37 we are told to delight ourselves in the Lord and He will give us the desires of our hearts, to commit our ways unto the Lord, to trust Him and He will bring it to pass. Also, in Proverbs 3 we are told "Trust in the Lord with all thine heart; and lean not unto thine own understanding. In all thy ways acknowledge Him, and He shall direct thy paths."

God never contradicts Himself. He never leads us to do anything 'contrary' to the commands of His Word; for according to Philippians 2:13, "It is God who is at work within you, giving you the will and the power to achieve His purpose." (Phillips)

Through the centuries sincere religious men have suggested spiritual formulas for discovering the will of God. Some are valid; others are unscriptural and misleading. For example, a young seminary graduate came to see me. He was investigating various possibilities of Christian service and had come to discuss the ministry of Campus Crusade for Christ. Applying the "Sound-Mind Principle" approach to his quest, I asked him, "In what way do you expect God to reveal His place of service for you?" He replied, "I am following the 'closed door' policy. A few months ago I began to investigate several opportunities for Christian service. The Lord has now closed the door on all but two, one of which is Campus Crusade for Christ. If the door to accept a call to a particular church closes, I shall know that God wants me in Campus Crusade." Many sincere Christians follow this illogical and unscriptural method, often with most unsatisfactory and frustrating consequences. Don't misunderstand. God may and often closes doors in the life of every active, Spirit-controlled Christian. This was true in the experience of the Apostle Paul. As recorded in Acts 16:6-11, he was forbidden by the Spirit to go into Bithynia because God wanted him in Macedonia. My reference to 'closed door' policies does not preclude such experiences, but refers to a careless "hit or miss" attitude without the careful evaluation of all the issues.

This approach is illogical because it allows elements of chance to influence a decision rather than a careful intelligent evaluation of all the factors involved. It is unscriptural in that it fails to employ the God-given faculties of reason that are controlled by the Holy Spirit. Further, the 'closed door policy' is in error because it seeks God's will through the process of elimination rather than seeking God's best first. It should be understood that true faith is established on the basis of fact. Therefore, vital faith in God is emphasized rather than minimized through employing Spirit-controlled reason. In making decisions some sincere Christians rely almost entirely upon impressions, or hunches, fearful that if they use their mental faculties they will not exercise adequate faith and thus will grieve the Holy Spirit.

There are those who assume that a door has been closed simply because of difficulties that have been encountered. Yet, experience has taught and Scripture confirms that God's richest blessings often follow periods of greatest testing. This might include financial needs, loss of health, objection of loved ones and criticism of fellow Christians. God's blessing is promised, however, only to those who are obedient, who keep on trying, who demonstrate their faith in God's faithfulness. The apparent defeat of the Cross was followed by the victory of the Resurrection.

An acceptable consideration for discussing God's will contains four basic factors somewhat similar to "Sound-Mind Principle." God's will is revealed in: 1. The Authority of Scripture; 2. Providential circumstances; 3. Conviction based upon reason; 4. Impressions of the Holy Spirit upon our minds. However, such an appraisal is safer with a mature Christian than with a new or carnal Christian, and there is always danger of misunderstanding "impressions."

You must know the source of "leading" before responding to it. To the inexperienced, what appears to be the leading of God may not be from Him at all but from "the rulers of darkness of this world." Satan and his helpers often disguise themselves as "angels of light" by performing "miracles, signs, foretelling events," etc. The enemy of our souls is a master counterfeiter.

Remember, just as the turning of the steering wheel of an automobile does not alter its direction unless it is moving, so God cannot direct our lives unless we are moving for Him. I challenge you to begin employing the "Sound-Mind Principle" today in all your relationships. Apply it to the investment of your time, your talents and your treasure; for this principle applies to everything you do in this life. Every Christian should take spiritual inventory regularly by asking himself these questions: Is my time being invested in such a way that the largest possible number of people are being introduced to Christ? Are my talents being invested to the full to the end that the largest possible number of people are being introduced to Christ? Is my money, my treasure, being invested in such a way as to introduce the greatest number of people to Christ?

Every Christian is admonished to be a good steward of his God-given time, talents and treasure. Therefore, these investments must not be dictated by tradition, habit or by emotions. Every investment of time, talent, and treasure, unless otherwise directed by the Holy Spirit, should be determined by the "Sound-Mind Principle" of Scripture according to II Timothy 1:7.

Regarding the questions asked by your girl friend, the same principle applies to her. How does this "Sound-Mind Principle" apply in the case of a secretary, homemaker, an invalid, or one who, because of circumstances beyond her control, does not have direct contact with men and women who are in need of Christ.

First, each Christian must be a witness for Christ; this is simply an act of obedience for which one need not possess the gift of evangelism. If normal day-to-day contacts do not provide opportunities to witness for Christ, an obedient Christian will make opportunities through personal contacts, church calling, letter writing, etc. Two of the most radiant, effective and fruitful Christians whom I have known were both bed-ridden invalids who, though in constant pain, bore a powerful witness for Christ to all—stranger and friend alike. "That which is most on our hearts will be most on our lips," was demonstrated in their lives. Second, a careful evaluation should be given to determine if God may not have a better position for one. Again, "Sound-Mind Principle" applies. For example, a secretary in a secular organization may have less opportunity to make her life count for the Lord. It may be that God wants to use one's talents in a Christian organization. One should be very careful, however, not to run from what appears to be a difficult assignment. A careful appraisal of one's present responsibilities, with this new understanding of God's leading, may well reveal a great potential for Christ.

(I happen to know that there is a great scarcity of qualified secretarial help in many Christian organizations, including Campus Crusade for Christ.) Quite obviously, members of an office staff do not have as much contact with men and women who are in need of our Savior as those who are actually working on the campus or conducting evangelistic meetings. However, according to the "Sound-Mind Principle," if their lives are fully dedicated to Christ, they can make a vital contribution to the effectiveness of any Christian ministry. By relieving others who have the gift of evangelism without the talent for business or secretarial responsibilities, the overall ministry for Christ in such an organization is strengthened greatly. In this way, they can more fully utilize their talents in helping to seek and save the lost.

For example, a dedicated member of the secretarial staff of the world-wide ministry of Campus Crusade for Christ is just as vital to the success of this campus strategy as those who are working on the campus. My own personal ministry has been greatly increased by the dedicated efforts of several secretaries who are more concerned about winning students to Christ than their own personal pleasure.

One further word of explanation must be given. It is true that God still reveals His will to some men and women in dramatic ways, but this should be considered the exception rather than the rule. God still leads men today as He has through the centuries. Philip, the deacon, was holding a successful campaign in Samaria. "Sound-Mind Principle" would have directed him to continue his campaign. However, God overruled by a special revelation, and Philip was led by the Holy Spirit to preach for Christ to the Ethiopian eunuch. According to tradition, God used the Ethiopian eunuch to communicate the message of our living Lord to his own country.

Living according to the "Sound-Mind Principle" allows for such dramatic leadings of God. But, we are not to wait for such revelations before we start moving for Christ. Faith must have an object. A Christian's faith is built upon the authority of God's Word supported by historical fact, and not upon any shallow emotional experience. However, a Christian's trust in God's will revealed in His Word will result in the decisions which are made by following the "Sound-Mind Principle." The confirmation may come in various ways according to many factors including the personality of the individual involved. Usually, the confirmation is a quiet, peaceful assurance that you are doing what God wants you to do, with expectancy that God will use you to bear "much fruit."

As any sincere Christian gives himself to a diligent study of the Scripture and allows a loving, all-wise, sovereign God and Father to control his life, feelings will inevitably result. Thus, the end result of a life that is lived according to the "Sound-Mind Principle" is the most joyful, abundant, and fruitful life of all. Expect the Lord Jesus Christ to draw men to Himself through you. As you begin each day, acknowledge the fact that you belong to Him. Thank Him for the fact that He lives within you. Invite Him to use your mind to think His thoughts, your heart to express His love, your lips to speak His truth. Ask Jesus to be at home in your life and to walk around in your body in order that He may continue seeking and saving souls through you.

It is my sincere prayer, Paul, that you may know this kind of life, that you may fully appropriate all that God has given to you as your rightful heritage in Christ. I shall look forward to hearing more from you concerning your personal application of the "Sound-Mind Principle."

Warmly in Christ,

Bill Bright

Pro-Con Chart

	OPTION I		OPTION II		OPTION III	
	Corporation		Teaching		Full-Time Christian Work	
AM I WILLING? (Yes or No)	Yes		Yes		Yes	
	PRO	CON	PRO	CON	PRO	CON
THE WORD (What does the Bible say? Give references.)		Job pressures me to do things I do not want to do. (James 4:17)	Opportunities to share my faith in the classroom (Luke 19:10)		Commission to make disciples (Matthew 28:18-20)	
HOLY SPIRIT (Impressions of the Holy Spirit on your heart through prayer)	I sense that God has given me talent for the job.		Holy Spirit has shown me how I can influence others for Christ with this job.	I feel I am somewhat inadequate.	I am convinced that God can use me to influence others.	
GREAT COMMISSION (How does it relate to the fulfillment of the Great Commission?)	Able to contribute to missionary efforts financially	Very little time to develop ministry	Able to influence education in the state of Michigan.	Limited by law as to what I can do and say	Directly related to seeing the Great Commission fulfilled	

Pro-Con Chart

	OPTION I Corporation		OPTION II Teaching		OPTION III Full-Time Christian Work	
AM I WILLING? (Yes or No)	Yes		Yes		Yes	
	PRO	CON	PRO	CON	PRO	CON
COUNSEL (Mature Christians who know the Word, me and the situation)		My best friend thinks I will be unfulfilled in this job.	My father thinks this would be a good opportunity to build credibility.		My pastor thinks I have the aptitude for this work.	
CIRCUMSTANCES (Usually confirmation of action already taken)	I can stay in Texas. Pay is excellent.		Pay is more than adequate.	I would have to move to Michigan.		Not sure I can get any support
DECISION (Based upon the above factors, reason and a sound mind)	From what I know about God's will and the above factors, I will disregard this option.		From what I know about God's will and the above factors, I will consider this if God prevents me from my first option.		From what I know about God's will, I will pursue this option.	

Pro-Con Chart

	OPTION I		OPTION II		OPTION III	
AM I WILLING? (Yes or No)	Yes		Yes		Yes	
	PRO	CON	PRO	CON	PRO	CON
THE WORD (What does the Bible say? Give references.)						
HOLY SPIRIT (Impressions of the Holy Spirit on your heart through prayer)						
GREAT COMMISSION (How does it relate to the fulfillment of the Great Commission?)						

Pro-Con Chart

	OPTION I		OPTION II		OPTION III	
AM I WILLING? (Yes or No)	Yes		Yes		Yes	
	PRO	CON	PRO	CON	PRO	CON
COUNSEL (Mature Christians who know the Word, me and the situation)						
CIRCUMSTANCES (Usually confirmation of action already taken)						
DECISION (Based upon the above factors, reason and a sound mind)						

RELATE:

"In our next lesson, we'll be discussing 'Becoming a World Christian.' The main passages we'll be looking at are Matthew 9:36-38; 28:19,20; Philippians 4:14-19 and Acts 1:8. To get the most out of the discussion, I'd encourage you to read over these passages beforehand and even spend some time studying them."

Practical Ministry
(15-25 Minutes)

To Develop the Practical Ministry (Vision, Strategy, Training) Section of this lesson, complete the steps explained in Lessons 11 and 13.

Prayer
(5-10 Minutes)

Close in conversational prayer, asking God to direct each member in decisions he must make.

See V. Prayer Appendix for additional ideas.

Arrange the time and place of the next meeting.

18
Becoming a
===World Christian===

OVERVIEW GOAL

The goal of this lesson is to enable group members to understand how they can have an impact on the world by helping to fulfill the Great Commission.

LEARNING OBJECTIVES

By the end of this lesson, group members will be able to:

1. Explain specific ways they can have an impact on the world by helping to fulfill the Great Commission.

2. Explain what a world Christian is.

Time/Section	Outline/Questions and Learning Activities
10-15	## Sharing
	Conduct an informal sharing time on ways they were able to personally apply the previous Bible study topic, "Discovering God's Will."
30-40	## Bible Study
Motivation	A. QUOTE FROM C. T. STUDD:
	"If Jesus Christ be God and died for me, then no sacrifice can be too great for me to make for Him."*
	TRANSITION: "Not only C.T. Studd's words, but also his life, should be a tremendous challenge to us. Right now we're going to discuss four aspects of becoming a world Christian."
Observ./Interp.	B. A WORLD CHRISTIAN AND PRAYER
Matthew 9:36-38	1. Various observations of Jesus' heart for the lost can be made in this passage. (Develop a question.)
	2. What are some reasons Jesus told His disciples to pray for workers rather than for souls?
	3. What are some consequences of not praying for the fulfillment of the Great Commission?
Philippians 4:14-19	C. A WORLD CHRISTIAN AND GIVING
	1. Those who receive a gift experience many benefits. (Develop as a question.)
	2. What are some benefits experienced by the one who gives a gift?
	3. What are some consequences of not being involved financially in helping to fulfill the Great Commission?

*Norman Grubb, *C. T. Studd*, Copyright © 1972, p. 141: Used by permission of Christian Literature Crusade, Fort Washington, Pennsylvania.

Time/Section	Outline/Questions and Learning Activities
Matthew 28:19,20	**D. A WORLD CHRISTIAN AND DISCIPLESHIP** 1. There is a great significance in our role and in the benefits of making disciples. (Develop as a question.) 2. What do you think would be some of the consequences of not being involved in building disciples to help fulfill the Great Commission?
Acts 1:8	**E. A WORLD CHRISTIAN AND AVAILABILITY** 1. Jesus described where the disciples needed to go in order to fulfill the Great Commission. (Develop as a question.) 2. What do you think would be some of the consequences of not being willing to go anywhere to help fulfill the Great Commission?
	F. DEFINING A WORLD CHRISTIAN In what ways would you define a world Christian?
Application	**G. BECOMING A WORLD CHRISTIAN** The four aspects of ministry (prayer, giving, discipleship and availability) are essential to becoming a world Christian. (Develop as a question.) **Action Point** Lead group members to make personal applications of the principles taught and definite plans to implement them.
15-25	# Practical Ministry
5-10	# Prayer
	Pray for the fulfillment of the Great Commission, emphasizing the involvement of each group member.
60-90	

411

Preparation

PERSONAL PERSPECTIVE

Set aside at least one half hour when you will not be disturbed. You will need your Bible, your Discipleship Group leader's guide and study guide. Ask the Lord to make the material fresh and personal for you as you think through it. Ask Him to show you special areas of need that your group members might have and how you can draw those out with questions.

You will be developing four main questions (B-1, C-1, D-1, and E-1), all the clarifying questions, the Application and the Action Point for this lesson. You will also need to develop your own Practical Ministry time. Consult Appendices II, III and IV.

RESOURCES

Transferable Concept 7, "How to Help Fulfill the Great Commission."

A. Quotes:

  1. A.W. Tozer, *The Pursuit of God*.

     "In this hour of all-but-universal darkness one cheering gleam appears: within the fold of conservative Christianity, there are to be found increasing numbers of persons whose religious lives are marked by a growing hunger after God Himself . . . this is the only harbinger of revival which I have been able to detect anywhere on the religious horizon."*

  2. Francis Schaeffer, *Death in the City*.

     "We live in a post-Christian world. God has turned away in judgment as our generation turned away from Him and He is allowing cause and effect to take its course in history. God can bring His judgment in one of two ways: either by direct intervention in history or by the turning of the wheels of history . . . We must be realistic. The place to begin is to understand that you and I live in a post-Christian world."**

*A.W. Tozer, *The Pursuit of God*, Copyright © 1958, p. 7: Used by permission of Tyndale Publishers, Wheaton, Illinois.

**Francis Schaeffer, *Death in the City*, Copyright © 1969, pp. 20,21: Used by permission of Inter-Varsity Press, Downer's Grove, Illinois.

"Thus it is not the will of your Father who is in heaven that one of these little ones perish" (Matthew 18:14).

Sharing
(10-15 Minutes)

Conduct an informal sharing time on ways they were able to personally apply the previous Bible study topic, "Discovering God's Will." Determine a set of questions to draw them out. See I. Sharing Appendix for other ideas.

Bible Study
(30-40 Minutes)

Open the Bible study in a brief prayer, asking God to teach the group.

Motivation

READ: (76) A. QUOTE FROM C.T. STUDD:

Ask group members what personal significance this quote has for them.

"If Jesus Christ be God and died for me, then no sacrifice can be too great for me to make for Him."*

TRANSITION: "Not only C.T. Studd's words, but also his life, should be a tremendous challenge to us. Right now we're going to discuss four aspects of becoming a world Christian."

*Norman Grubb, *C.T. Studd*, Copyright © 1972, p. 141: Used by permission of Christian Literature Crusade, Fort Washington, Pennsylvania.

Observ./Interp.

Ask a group member to read the verses.

MATTHEW 9:36-38
B. A WORLD CHRISTIAN AND PRAYER

Develop an open question to discuss observations of Jesus' heart for the lost.

1. _____
_____
_____
_____
_____

DISCUSSION: Direct the group in a discussion of the questions. Share the suggested answers only if necessary. Summarize the group's answers after discussing each question and encourage group members to write the conclusions in their study guides.

Develop Clarifying Questions:

1a. (Wide-open)
1b. (Open)

2. What are some reasons Jesus told His disciples to pray for workers rather than for souls?

Because Jesus said the fields were white for harvest, the need was for men to reap the ready souls for the kingdom. As it is today, men and women are ready to receive Christ because God has prepared them. The need is for laborers.

Develop Clarifying Questions:

2a. (Open)
2b. (Limiting)

3. What are some consequences of not praying for the fulfillment of the Great Commission?

Some of the consequences are that more workers are not sent, people do not hear the gospel and needs are not met.

Develop Clarifying Questions:

3a. (Wide-open)
3b. (Open)

SAY:

"Prayer is not the only important aspect of becoming a world Christian; giving is also important."

Ask a group member to read the passage.

(77) PHILIPPIANS 4:14-19
C. A WORLD CHRISTIAN AND GIVING

Develop an open question to discuss the benefits experienced by one who receives a gift.

1. _____
   _____
   _____
   _____
   _____

Discuss the following questions. Follow the same procedure as before. Be sure the answers relate not only to general situations but also the members own particular situations.

2. What are some benefits experienced by the one who gives a gift?

   He is encouraged by the recipient, his accounts profit, he pleases God and his needs are provided.

3. What are some consequences of not being involved financially in helping to fulfill the Great Commission?

   Some consequences are that God is not pleased, needs aren't met, the fulfillment of the Great Commission is hindered, and we miss out on the blessings of being involved in a helpful way.

Develop Clarifying Questions:

3a. (Wide-open)
3b. (Open)

SAY:

"Another aspect of becoming a world Christian is discipleship. It is important for us to be involved in making disciples."

Read the verses. (78)

MATTHEW 28:19,20
D. A WORLD CHRISTIAN AND DISCIPLESHIP

Develop an open question to discuss their role and the benefits of making disciples.

1. _____
   _____
   _____
   _____
   _____

Develop Clarifying Questions:

1a. (Wide-open)
1b. (Open)
1c. (Limiting)

2. What do you think would be some of the consequences of not being involved in building disciples to help fulfill the Great Commission?

   Some consequences are that God is not pleased, we miss out on the blessings and fulfillment of a discipleship ministry, others miss out on being disciples, many will not hear the good news.
   _____
   _____

Develop Clarifying Questions:

2a. (Wide-open)
2b. (Open)
2c. (Limiting)

SAY:

"Availability is another aspect that we must consider as we discuss becoming a world Christian."

Ask a group member to read the verse.

ACTS 1:8
E. A WORLD CHRISTIAN AND AVAILABILITY

Develop an open
question to discuss
the fact that Jesus
told them to be
witnesses not only
to their home
areas, but also to
the world.

1. _____
_____
_____
_____

Develop Clarifying
Questions:

1a. (Open)
1b. (Limiting)

2. What do you think would be some of the
consequences of not being willing to go
anywhere to help fulfill the Great
Commission?

Certain parts of the world remain
unreached, we stagnate where we are and
miss out on God's best for our lives.
_____
_____

Develop Clarifying
Questions:

2a. (Wide-open)
2b. (Open)
2c. (Limiting)

SUMMARIZE BY
SAYING:

"So, as we've seen here, a world Christian involves
himself in helping to fulfill the Great Commission
by praying, giving, discipling and going."

ASK:

F. DEFINING A WORLD CHRISTIAN

In what ways would you define a world
Christian?
_____
_____
_____

Develop Clarifying
Questions:

1a. (Wide-open)
1b. (Open)

RELATE THE DEFINITION:

"So a world Christian could be defined as a person who evaluates the use of his time, talents and treasure in light of the fulfillment of the Great Commission. He is willing to use his time in prayer and discipleship. He is available to use his abilities and talents for God's glory. And he is privileged to be able to invest his financial resources into God's kingdom."

Application (79)

Develop an open question that applies to the entire lesson. Challenge them to make the four aspects of a world Christian's ministry (prayer, giving, discipleship and availability) real in their own lives.

Develop an Action Point. Lead group members to make personal applications of the principles taught and definite plans to implement them.

G. BECOMING A WORLD CHRISTIAN

_____
_____
_____
_____
_____
_____

Action Point

RELATE:

"In our next lesson, we'll be discussing 'Making My Life Count.' The main passages we'll be looking at are Mark 8:34-38 and Luke 12:15-21. To get the most out of the discussion, I'd encourage you to read over these passages beforehand and even spend some time studying them."

Practical Ministry
(15-25 Minutes)

To develop the
Practical Ministry
(Vision, Strategy,
Training) Section
of this lesson,
complete the steps
explained in Les-
sons 11 and 13.

Prayer
(5-10 Minutes)

Direct the group in
praying for the ful-
fillment of the
Great Commission,
emphasizing the
involvement of
each group
member.

Arrange the time
and place for the
next meeting.

19
Making My
══Life Count══

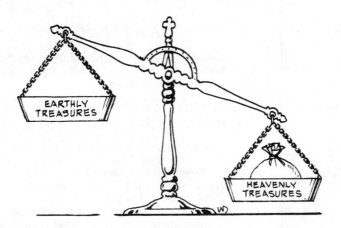

OVERVIEW GOAL

The goal of this lesson is to enable each group member to evaluate his life in view of God's values and then to take steps to make his life count in terms of those values.

LEARNING OBJECTIVES

At the end of this lesson, group members will be able to:

1. Describe the value God places on one human soul.

2. Relate God's perspective to their decisions in life.

3. Evaluate whether their present lifestyles and future goals are aimed at making an optimum impact in light of the value God places on the human soul.

Time/Section	Outline/Questions and Learning Activities

10-15

Sharing

Ask your group if, during the week, they were able to act on any of the principles of becoming world Christians.

30-40

Bible Study

Motivation

A. QUOTE BY A CHRISTIAN LEADER

(Develop a means to present the given motivational statement. You will also need to develop a transitional statement.)

Observ./Interp.

B. GOD'S PERSPECTIVE ON THE INVESTMENT OF OUR LIVES

Mark 8:34-38

1. According to this passage, there are several things involved in following Jesus. (Develop as a question.)
2. Verses 36 and 37 note the value of one soul. (Develop as a question.)
3. The human soul is the most valuable thing you can invest in. What are some ways to invest in a human soul?

Luke 12:15-21

C. RELATING GOD'S PERSPECTIVE TO OUR DECISIONS IN LIFE

1. Have your group members count the number of times "I" and "my" are used by the rich man. There are several things we can say about his values. (Develop as a question.)
2. There are some similarities between the rich man's life and our lives today. (Develop as a question.)
3. According to verses 15,20 and 21, in what ways did God's values differ from the rich man's?

Time/Section	Outline/Questions and Learning Activities
Application	D. (Prepare an application step with appropriate question(s) that will cause group members to evaluate whether or not they are making an optimum impact on human lives today. Also have each of them evaluate his life's direction in light of the value God places on the human soul.)
15-25	**Practical Ministry**
5-10	**Prayer**
	Ask God to help the group experience His values concerning human souls and to enable your lives to count for him.
60-90	

Preparation

PERSONAL PERSPECTIVE

Set aside a time when you can work through this lesson undisturbed. Read the passages, and then work through the leader's guide, developing four main questions (B-1, B-2, C-1, and C-2) and all the clarifying questions necessary to bring your group members to the desired conclusions. Also, develop ideas to present the Motivation, the Application and the Practical Ministry sections. Pray that the Lord will use this Bible study to help your group members determine to make their lives count for God.

INTRODUCTION TO MARK 8

This book was written sometime between A.D. 64 and 68 by John Mark, an associate of Paul and Barnabas. It is the shortest of the gospels and contains approximately 93% of the material also found in the books of Matthew and Luke. Chapter 8 deals with Jesus' prediction of His death.

INTRODUCTION TO LUKE 12

This book was written about A.D. 58 by Luke the physician, who was also a co-worker of Paul. The theme of the book is the life of Christ. Chapter 12 deals with parables and warnings.

RESOURCES

Unger's Bible Handbook, pp. 493,502,511 and 528

SUPPLEMENTAL MATERIAL

A. The following is an excerpt from an article written by an atheist. It was this author who spurred C.T. Studd to all-out dedication to Christ.

"If I firmly believed, as millions say they do, that the knowledge and practice of religion in this life influences destiny in another, then religion would mean to me everything. I would cast away earthly enjoyments as dross, earthly cares as follies, and earthly thoughts and feelings as vanity. Religion would be my first waking thought, and my last image before sleep sank me into unconsciousness. I should labor in its cause alone. I would take thought for the morrow of Eternity alone. I would esteem one soul gained for heaven worth a life of suffering. Earthly consequences would never stay my head, or seal my lips. Earth, its joys and its griefs, would occupy no moment of my thoughts. I would strive to look upon Eternity alone, and on the immortal souls around me, soon to be everlastingly happy or everlastingly miserable. I would go forth to the world and preach to it in season and out of season, and my text would be, WHAT SHALL IT PROFIT A MAN IF HE GAIN THE WHOLE WORLD AND LOSE HIS OWN SOUL?"*

B. Others are willing to pay the price to get their message before the people. A student at an eastern university recently went to Mexico, where in the process of time he discovered true dedication to some cause in Communist workers. He became a Communist. Shortly afterward, he wrote to his fiancee, breaking off their engagement. This letter was given to Billy Graham by a Presbyterian minister in Montreat, North Carolina. This is what it says:

"We Communists have a high casualty rate. We're the ones who get shot and hung and lynched and tarred and feathered and jailed and slandered and ridiculed and fired from our jobs, and in every other way made as uncomfortable as possible. A certain percentage of us get killed or imprisoned. We live in virtual poverty. We turn back to the Party every penny we make above what is absolutely necessary to keep us alive.

"We Communists don't have the time or the money for many movies or concerts or T-bone steaks or decent homes or new cars. We've been described as fanatics. We are fanatics. Our lives are dominated by one great overshadowing factor—*the struggle for world Communism.* We Communists have a philosophy of life, which no amount of money could buy. We have a cause to fight for, a definite purpose in life. We subordinate our petty, personal selves into a great movement of humanity, and if our personal lives seem hard or our egos appear to suffer through subordination to the Party, then we are adequately compensated by the thought that each of us in his small way is contributing to something new and true and better for mankind.

"There is one thing in which I am dead in earnest about and that is the Communist cause. It is my life, my business, my religion, my hobby, my sweetheart, my wife and my mistress, my bread and meat. I work at it in the day time and dream of it at night. Its hold grows on me, not lessens, as time goes on. Therefore I cannot carry on a friendship, a love affair, or even a conversation without relating it to this force which both drives and guides my life. I evaluate people, books, ideas, and actions according to how they affect the Communist cause and by their attitude toward it. I've already been in jail because of my ideas and, if necessary, I'm ready to go before a firing squad."***

*Norman Grubb, *C.T. Studd,* Copyright © 1972, p. 36: Used by permission of Christian Literature Crusade, Fort Washington, Pennsylvania.

**Billy Graham, *Call to Commitment,* Copyright © 1960, pp. 1-2: Used by permission of Billy Graham Evangelistic Association, Minneapolis, Minnesota.

C. The following is an excerpt from "On Breeding Spotted Mice," an editorial by A.W. Tozer.

"The Associated Press lately carried an interesting if somewhat depressing story out of London about a certain British peer who had died a few days short of his 89th birthday.

"A man of means and position, it had presumably not been necessary for him to work for a living, so at the time of his death he had had about 70 adult years in which he was free to do whatever he wished, to pursue any calling or to work at anything he felt worthy of his considerable abilities.

"And what did he choose to do? According to the story he had devoted his life to trying to breed the perfect spotted mouse.

"Now I grant every man the right to breed spotted mice if he wants to and can get the cooperation of the mice. It is his business and not mine. Not being a mouse lover (nor a mouse hater for that matter; I am just neutral about mice) I do not know but that a spotted mouse might be more useful and make a more affectionate pet than a common mouse-colored mouse. But still I am troubled.

"The mouse breeder in question was a lord, and I was born in the hill country of Pennsylvania, but since a cat can look at a king I suppose a farm boy can look at a lord, even look at him with disapproval if circumstances warrant. Anyway, I feel a certain kinship for every man born of woman; so I cannot but grieve for my brother beyond the seas.

"Made in the image of God, equipped with awesome powers of mind and soul, called to dream immortal dreams and to think the long thoughts of eternity, he chooses the breeding of a spotted mouse as his reason for existing. Invited to walk with God on earth and to dwell at last with the saints and angels in the world above, called to serve his generation by the will of God, to press with holy vigor the mark for the prize of the high calling of God in Christ Jesus, he dedicates his life to the spotted mouse--not just evenings or holidays, mind you, but his entire life. Surely this is a tragedy worthy of the mind of an Aeschylus or Shakespeare.

"The story points up a stark human tragedy that is being enacted before our eyes daily, not by make-believe play actors, but by real men and women who *are* the characters they portray. These should be concerned with sin and righteousness and judgment; they should be getting ready to die and live again; but instead they spend their lives breeding spotted mice."*

*David J. Fant, Jr., *A.W. Tozer—A Twentieth Century Prophet*, Copyright © 1964, p. 142: Used by permission of Christian Publications, Inc., Harrisburg, Pennsylvania.

> "He is no fool who gives what he cannot keep to gain what he cannot lose."*
>
> Jim Elliot

Sharing
(10-15 Minutes)

Ask your group if, during the week, they were able to act on any of the principles of becoming world Christians. See I. Sharing Appendix for other ideas.

Bible Study
(30-40 Minutes)

Open the Bible study in a brief prayer, asking God to teach the group.

Motivation (82)

Develop a means to present the motivational statement to the group. Be sure to include a transitional statement to lead into the next point.

TRANSITION:

> A. QUOTE BY A CHRISTIAN LEADER
>
> "Whether or not we are Christians, we are going to have problems in this life. Christians or not, we will one day die. If I am going to be a Christian, I want all that God has for me and I want to be all that He wants me to be. If I am to suffer at all, and one day die, why not suffer and die for the highest and best, for the Lord Jesus Christ and His Gospel!"**

*Elizabeth Elliot, *Shadow of the Almighty*, Copyright © 1959, p. 15: Used by permission of Harper and Brothers Publishers, New York, New York.

**Bill Bright, *The Christian and the Holy Spirit*, Copyright © 1968, p. 18: Used by permission of Campus Crusade for Christ, Inc., Arrowhead Springs, California.

Observ./Interp.

Read the verses. You may give some brief background to the book of Mark (see Preparation page). Discuss the following questions.

Develop an open question which brings out the idea that there are several things involved in following Jesus—a total commitment and an unashamed willingness in proclaiming the Gospel.

Develop Clarifying Questions:

Develop an open question from verses 36 and 37 which brings out the value of one human soul—the whole universe would not be enough to give in exchange for its redemption.

MARK 8:34-38

B. GOD'S PERSPECTIVE ON THE INVESTMENT OF OUR LIVES

1. _____
    _____
    _____
    _____
    _____

1a. (Wide-open)
1b. (Open)

2. _____
    _____
    _____
    _____
    _____

READ: (83)   The point is that if you took all the wealth of the world—gold, silver, jewels, coal, oil, money, houses—and put it on one side of a scale, and then put the soul of the most humanly insignificant person in the world on the other, the value of that one soul would outweigh all else in God's eyes.

DISCUSS: 3. The human soul is the most valuable thing you can invest in. What are some ways to invest in a human soul?

                Witness to others, disciple others, be a friend, etc. _____

Develop Clarifying Questions: 3a. (Wide-open)

                3b. (Open or limiting)

Ask someone to read the passage. Have your group members count the number of times "I" and "my" are used by the rich man in

LUKE 12:15-21
C.   RELATING GOD'S PERSPECTIVE TO OUR DECISIONS IN LIFE

1. _____
     _____
     _____

this passage. Then ask a question which brings to light the rich man's values—he valued himself and his comforts more than others.

2. _____

Develop a question which challenges the group members to find the similarities between their lives and the rich man's life.

Develop Clarifying Questions:

2a. (Wide-open)
2b. (Limiting or leading)

ASK:

3. According to verses 15,20 and 21, in what ways did God's values differ from the rich man's?

God valued his soul; the man valued his riches. The man ended up with nothing because he placed his values in the wrong thing. _____

Application (84)

D. _____

Prepare an application step with appropriate question(s) that will cause group members to evaluate whether or not they are making an optimum impact on human lives today. Also have each of them evaluate his life's direction in light of the value God places on the human soul.

RELATE:

"In our next lesson, we'll be discussing 'Learning to Study God's Word.' The main passages we'll be looking at are Psalm 119:9-16 and Luke 9:57-62. To get the most out of the discussion, I'd encourage you to read over these passages beforehand and even spend some time studying them."

Practical Ministry
(15-25 Minutes)

To develop the Practical Ministry (Vision, Strategy, Training) Section of this lesson, complete the steps explained in Lessons 11 and 13.

Prayer
(5-10 Minutes)

Ask God to help the group experience His values concerning human souls and to enable your lives to count for Him. See V. Prayer Appendix for other ideas.

Arrange time and place of the next meeting.

20
Learning to Study
═══God's Word═══

OVERVIEW GOAL

The goal of this lesson is to motivate group members to study the Bible by training them to use one method of inductive Bible study.

LEARNING OBJECTIVES

By the end of this lesson, group members will be able to:

1. Identify some benefits of personal Bible study.

2. Explain the steps of observation, interpretation and application in studying the Bible.

Time/Section	Outline/Questions and Learning Activities
10-15	## Sharing
	Ask your group to share any ways in which their perspectives have become more like Jesus' perspective in regard to the value of others' souls.
30-40	## Bible Study
Motivation	A. (Develop and present a motivational introduction, emphasizing the benefits of personal Bible study and how the inductive Bible study method will help them reap these benefits. You will also need to develop a transitional statement.)
Observ./Interp.	B. OBSERVATION: WHAT DO I SEE?

1. Definition: Observation may be defined as seeing and noting carefully what is contained in a passage of Scripture. It uses the questions, "Who?", "What?", "Where?", "When?" and "How?"
2. Example:

Psalm 119:9-16

Verse & Question		Observation
v. 9	Who?	—young man
	What?	—keep his way pure
	How?	—by keeping it according to Thy Word

3. Have the group members practice writing observations on Luke 9:57-62 (five minutes).
4. Develop an open question to determine if they understand observation.
5. Develop an open question to draw out their observations of the passage.

Time/Section	Outline/Questions and Learning Activities
	C. INTERPRETATION: WHAT DOES IT MEAN? 1. Definition: Interpretation is determining what the author intended to say to his readers. There is only one correct interpretation for any passage. We can ask, "Why?" to help discover the meaning of a passage. For example, "Why did the author describe it this way?" 2. Example: Psalm 119:9-16

Observation	Interpretation
—young man —keep his way pure —by keeping it according to Thy Word	A young person can live a pure life by living according to the principles of the Bible.

3. Have them practice interpretation on Luke 9:57-62 (five minutes).
4. Develop an open question to determine if they understand interpretation.
5. Develop an open question to draw out their interpretations of the passage.

Application

D. APPLICATION: WHAT DIFFERENCE DOES IT MAKE TO ME?

1. Definition: Application is determining what things you need to do as a result of learning these truths. There can be many applications for one truth. Ask, "How does the Holy Spirit want me to apply this to my life?"

Time/Section	Outline/Questions and Learning Activities

2. Example:

Psalm 119:9-16

Interpretation	Application
A young person can live a pure life by living according to the principles of the Bible.	1. I can live a pure life if I follow God's Word. 2. I will begin today by determining to know His Word and to obey it. 3. I will start a regular Bible study time.

3. Have them write out applications for their observations and interpretations on Luke 9:57-62 (five minutes).

Action Point   From the above Application portion of Psalm 119, schedule a plan for regular Bible study using the method you have learned in this lesson. Study the Bible passage your leader gives you by filling in the Sample Chart at the end of this lesson.

E. EXAMPLE

1. Psalm 1:1-3
2. Sample Chart

15-25

Practical Ministry

5-10

Prayer

Ask God to give the group members special wisdom in their personal Bible study times.

60-90

Preparation

PERSONAL PERSPECTIVE

Set aside a half hour when you will not be disturbed. Take your Bible, paper, a pen and your Discipleship Group leader's guide. Pray and ask God to give you direction and wisdom in preparing the lesson. Work through the passage assigned for the lesson, doing observation, interpretation and personal application using the provided charts. You will need to develop the Motivation and your own questions (B-4, B-5, C-4 and C-5) in leading the discussions of what the group members find in each step. You will also need to develop your own Practical Ministry time. Consult Appendices II, III and IV.

What you are doing in this lesson is simply helping your group members to use the Bible study method you have been using for the past 19 group lessons. Make sure you understand the method clearly. In the lesson, define observation, interpretation and application; and explain how to record each step using a sample chart. Next, you will have a workshop in which the group members will practice doing each step. Develop your own discussion questions to have them share their work. Finally, choose another passage for your group to study on their own as an Action Point. Help them to develop a simple plan for implementing the Action Point, including when and where you will see their filled-in Bible study charts.

RESOURCES

Independent Bible Study, Irving Jensen
The Joy of Discovery, Oletta Wald

> "God's Word is truer than anything I feel. God's Word is truer than anything I experience. God's Word is truer than any circumstance I will ever face. God's Word is truer than anything in the world."*
>
> Ney Bailey

Sharing
(10-15 Minutes)

Ask your group to share any ways in which their perspectives have become more like Jesus' perspective in regard to the value of others' souls. See I. Sharing Appendix for other ideas.

Bible Study
(30-40 Minutes)

Motivation   (86)

Develop and present a motivational introduction, emphasizing the benefits of personal Bible study and how the inductive Bible study method will help them reap these benefits.

A.

*Ney Bailey, *Faith Is Not a Feeling*, Copyright © 1978, p. 24: Used by permission of Here's Life Publishers, San Bernardino, California.

TRANSITION:

Explain that today
they will be learn-
ing a three-step
inductive Bible
study method to
help them get into
the Word on their
own. The first step
is observation.

Observ./Interp.

READ THE
DEFINITION.

Look at the example
together. See if they have
any questions about it.

B. OBSERVATION: WHAT DO I SEE?

1. Definition: Observation may be defined as
    seeing and noting carefully what is con-
    tained in a passage of Scripture. It uses
    the questions, "Who?", "What?",
    "Where?", "When?" and "How?"
2. Example: Psalm 119:9-16

Verse and Question		Observation
vs. 9	Who?	—young man
	What?	—keep his way pure
	How?	—by keeping it accord-ing to Thy Word

Have them write
observations on
Luke 9:57-62. Allow
five minutes.

3. Practice: Luke 9:57-62

Verse and Question	Observation

DISCUSS:

Develop open
questions to
determine if they
understand obser-
vation and to draw
out their observa-
tions of the
passage.

(87)

4. _____
_____
_____
_____

5. _____
_____
_____
_____

Explain that inter-
pretation is the
second step of this
inductive method.

READ THE
DEFINITION.

Look at the exam-
ple together and
see if there are any
questions about it.

C. INTERPRETATION: WHAT DOES IT MEAN?

1. Definition: Interpretation is determining
what the author intended to say to his
readers. There is only one correct interpretation for any passage. We can ask,
"Why?" to help discover the meaning of a
passage. For example, "Why did the
author describe it this way?"

2. Example: Psalm 119:9-16

Observation	Interpretation
—young man —keep his way pure —by keeping it according to Thy Word	A young person can live a pure life by living according to the principles of the Bible.

440

Have them practice(88)
interpretation on
the passage. Allow
five minutes.

3. Practice: Luke 9:57-62	
Observation	Interpretation
(Refer back to your observation in B-3.)	

DISCUSS:

Develop open
questions to
determine if they
understand inter-
pretation and to
draw out their
interpretations of
the passage.

4. _____
_____
_____
_____
_____
_____

5. _____
_____
_____
_____
_____
_____

Explain that appli-
cation is the third
step of this method.

Application

READ THE
DEFINITION.

D. APPLICATION: WHAT DIFFERENCE DOES
IT MAKE TO ME?

   1. Definition: Application is determining
what things you need to do as a result of
learning these truths. There can be many
applications for one truth. Ask "How does
the Holy Spirit want me to apply this to
my life?"

(89)

2. Example: Psalm 119:9-16

Interpretation	Application
A young person can live a pure life by living according to the principles of the Bible.	1. I can live a pure life if I follow God's Word. 2. I will begin today by determining to know His Word and to obey it. 3. I will start a regular Bible study time on Tuesday and Thursday at 7:00 A.M. for a half hour.

Have them write out applications for their observations and interpretations. Allow five minutes and ask several members to share.

3. Practice: Luke 9:57-62

Interpretation	Application
(Refer back to your interpretation in C-3.)	

SAY:

"Now by personalizing the Application of Psalm 119, you can develop a Bible study plan that is best for you."

READ:

Emphasize the importance of each group member having a specific time for Bible study.

Action Point From the above Application portion of Psalm 119, schedule a plan for regular Bible study using the method you have learned in this lesson. Study the Bible passage your leader gives you by filling in the Sample Chart at the end of this lesson.

Allow 5-10 minutes for them to initiate their plans. You may offer assistance if needed.

EXPLAIN:

"You will notice a completed example of another passage, Psalm 1:1-3, reproduced in your study guides. It's provided for your additional reference."

If you have time, (90) you may want to begin to work through the example

E. EXAMPLE			
1. Psalm 1:1-3			
Verse and Question	Observation	Interpretation	Application
v. 1 Who?	Man that does not walk in the counsel of the wicked, stand in the path of sinners, or sit in the seat of scoffers	Man who does not follow evil advice and does not put himself in a place where he can be influenced by sin	I could be happier and less influenced by sin and worldly advice if I let God's Word fill my mind.
What?	Is blessed	He is happy.	
v. 2 How?	His delight is in the law of the Lord. He meditates on it day and night.	He satisfies himself with God's Word and spends time filling his mind with it.	I will spend one half hour a day studying and meditating on God's Word so I will be directed by it.

SAY: "You will notice a blank sample chart is provided for you. You can reproduce it to use in your future personal Bible studies."

2. Sample Chart			
Verse and Question	Observa-tion	Interpreta-tion	Applica-tion

Leader's Guide

READ:
Ask a group
member to read the
characteristics
from the diagram.   (91)

As we grow in our knowledge of and obedience to
God's Word, the Holy Spirit causes growth in
many areas of our lives.

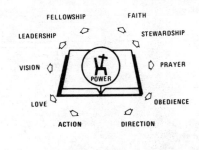

FELLOWSHIP   FAITH

LEADERSHIP   STEWARDSHIP

VISION   PRAYER

POWER

LOVE   OBEDIENCE

ACTION   DIRECTION

RELATE:

"The diagram in your study guides shows how the
Holy Spirit increasingly uses the Word of God to
cause us to grow in many areas of our lives. We
become conformed to the image of Christ as we
begin to explore what the Bible teaches about
some of these qualities."

Practical Ministry
(15-25 Minutes)

To develop the
Practical Ministry
(Vision, Strategy,
Training) Section
of this lesson,
complete the steps
explained in Les-
sons 11 and 13.

Prayer

(5-10 Minutes)

Ask God to give the
group members
special wisdom in
their personal Bible
study times.

See V. Prayer
Appendix for other
ideas.

Arrange the time
and place of the
next meeting.

Note: The following
information is for
the leader only.

What to do after Lesson 20

Here is a partial list of resources you may want to use in developing future
Bible study portions of your group meetings. This resource is topical in
nature and provides hundreds of pages of ideas for the Bible study section
of your discipleship groups. Some adaptation of these materials may be
necessary in order to put them into a guided discussion format.

Faith

Agape Group sessions:

20. The God in Whom We Trust

21. How God's Attributes Relate to Me

22. Reaching Out to Others Through Faith

Love

Agape Group sessions:

24. God's Love: How to Understand and Experience It

25. How to Love by Faith

28. The Loving Relationship

29. How to Become Free to Love and Edify the Body of Christ

Transferable Concept 8, "How to Love by Faith"

Prayer

Agape Group sessions:

31. Praying Like Jesus

32. Expanding our Prayer Vision

34. Intercessory Prayer

Transferable Concept 9, "How to Pray"

Ten Basic Steps Toward Christian Maturity, Step 4, "The Christian and Prayer"

Obedience

Ten Basic Steps, Step 6, "The Christian and Obedience"

Stewardship

Ten Basic Steps, Step 8, "The Christian and Stewardship"

Vision

Agape Group session:

18. Developing a Great Commission Mentality

Power (more study on the ministry of the Holy Spirit)

Ten Basic Steps, Step 3, "The Christian and the Holy Spirit"

Direction (more information on studying God's Word)

Ten Basic Steps, Step 5, "The Christian and the Bible"

Ten Basic Steps, Step 9, "Highlights of the Old Testament"

Ten Basic Steps, Step 10, "Highlights of the New Testament"

Action (more training in ministry skills)

Agape Group sessions:

19. Strategy for Building *Agape* People

23. How to Initiate Friendships and Establish Rapport

26. Motivating New Christians for Further Commitment

27. How to Help New Christians Begin Their New Life

30. Spiritual Adoption

33. Discipleship by Natural Groups

35. Fellowship in the Church—I

36. Fellowship in the Church—II

Study guide for *Evidence that Demands a Verdict*, by Josh McDowell

Ten Basic Steps, Step 7, "The Christian and Witnessing"

Division:
Leadership Group
Lesson Plans 1-5

When Do I Use the Leadership Group Lessons?

The Leadership Group Lesson Plans 1-5 are five lessons which help prepare your group members to begin and lead groups of their own. These lessons would generally come after Lesson 20. By that time most members should have been involved in personal evangelism and follow-up to the point where they are ready to begin leading a Discovery Group. (Some members may have already begun their groups.)

There are also several other options for using the Leadership Group lesson plans to train your leaders.

A.   Insert the Leadership Group lessons in the middle of the Discipleship Group lessons. If several of your members are ready to begin their groups before you complete Lesson 20, you may want to suspend the regular series for five weeks and cover the Leadership Group lesson plans.

B.   Teach them on a weekend. When several of your group members are ready to begin their groups you could ask them to read all five Articles in advance and hold the five discussions on a week-end retreat (actually they could all be completed in a single day if necessary.)

C.   Orient a group of leaders. If your campus or church has a number of groups starting at the same time you may want to bring together all the leaders and orient them at the same time (a week-end or an all-day retreat.) This would also be a useful approach if there are groups in existence that have previously been using other materials.

How Do I Use the Leadership Group Lesson Plans?

These lesson plans are to be used in conjunction with the Leadership Group articles 1-5 on pages 27 through 75 of this book. The Articles are also found in the Leadership Group Study Guides. The questions and activities in the Leadership Group Leader's Guides are based on Articles 1-5.

The Biblical Basis for ===Discipleship Groups===

OVERVIEW GOAL

The goal of this lesson is to enable group members to understand the biblical basis of discipleship and to motivate them to be involved in the objective of discipleship, which is to build a movement of Spirit-filled Christians who are obedient to God's Word and are actively involved in helping to fulfill the Great Commission.

LEARNING OBJECTIVES

By the end of this lesson, group members will be able to:

1.   Explain how Jesus fulfilled the objective of discipleship.

2.   Identify some of the results of applying and not applying the principles Jesus demonstrated.

3.   List some practical steps they can take with their groups to begin reaching the objective of discipleship.

453

Time/Section	Outline/Questions and Learning Activities
10-15	**Sharing**
30-40	**Study**
Motivation	A. PRODUCT OF A SMALL GROUP
	TRANSITION: "Ed Kimball's proper perspective on the importance of individuals and their potential led to an unending chain of results. As you'll recall from the Article, Jesus had a similar perspective."
Observ./Interp.	B. PRINCIPLES OF JESUS' MINISTRY
	1. Jesus was a model of the spiritual multiplication principle. In what ways can we pattern our ministries after His in order to insure that our disciples multiply?
	2. What are some things Jesus would probably say if we asked Him why He discipled His men?
	3. In the Article, we read that Jesus was committed to building a movement of Spirit-filled Christians who were obedient to God's Word and who were actively involved in helping to fulfill the Great Commission. What were some ways this commitment was demonstrated in His ministry?
	4. In what ways would our ministries be hurt if we used only Jesus' model before Pentecost as our model for discipleship?
	5. In what ways will our ministries improve if we also keep in mind the model of how Jesus discipled His men after Pentecost?
Application	6. What are some practical steps you can take with your group or your future group to insure that they are reaching Jesus' objective of discipleship?

Time/Section	Outline/Questions and Learning Activities
15-25	**Practical Ministry**
5-10	**Prayer**
60-90	

Preparation

PERSONAL PERSPECTIVE

In order to really understand the content of Leadership Group Article 1, you should read it thoroughly before leading a discussion on it. Ask the Lord to deepen your understanding of the principles taught and to give you practical and creative ways to apply them. Think through the points of the Article and how they relate to your group members and the members of their groups.

If the Leadership Group lessons are being taught in a weekly Discipleship Group meeting, develop and include the Practical Ministry and Prayer sections. However, if the lessons are being taught in another setting, such as a retreat, you will need to decide which of the above sections to delete, based on your teaching objectives.

> "And He went up to the mountain and summoned those whom He Himself wanted, and they came to Him. And He appointed twelve, that they might be with Him, and that He might send them out to preach" (Mark 3:13,14).

Sharing
(10-15 Minutes)

See I. Sharing Appendix for ideas to develop this section of study if you choose to use it.

Study
(30-40 Minutes)

Open the study with a brief prayer, asking God to teach the group.

Motivation　(12)

Have a group member read this story aloud.

A. PRODUCT OF A SMALL GROUP

Almost every person involved in small group discipleship wonders at one time or another whether or not his efforts are all in vain. Often, a group is made up of untrained, uninformed and even unattractive individuals. Yet God, in His marvelous plan, allows us to have a worldwide impact through the lives and influence of those very same group members. The following is a short sequence of events that tells the story of how one individual, working with a small group, was ultimately able to make an impact on the world.

One day a shy, nervous Sunday school teacher named Ed Kimball went to visit one of his students who worked in a shoe store. God had impressed Ed to share the gospel with each member of his small group, but he had hesitated to share with this overweight, unattractive shoe salesman. There had even been times when he wished this young man would stop coming to his class. In obedience to God, however, this very ordinary Sunday school teacher was used in an extraordinary way to lead the young shoe salesman, Dwight L. Moody, to Christ.

Moody later became a famous revivalist who traveled throughout the United States and Europe. While in Europe, immediately following one of his revivals, he personally led to Christ the father of C.T. Studd. Seeing his father's changed life, C.T. Studd responded to Christ and went on to spend his entire life in pioneer missionary efforts in China, India and Africa.

Mordacai Ham was another individual who responded to Christ through this chain of evangelism begun by Ed Kimball. Ham was the evangelist who, during one of his revivals, led a young athlete by the name of Billy Graham to Christ.

Obviously, the chain now has many links. At one of Billy Graham's Crusades, a man responded to the invitation to receive Christ by making his way to the front from the very back of the auditorium. This man was later able to influence Chuck Colson, the author of *Born Again*, to receive Christ. Through his prison ministry, Chuck Colson helps to reach and disciple many inmates through the United States.

It becomes clear that the ultimate impact our small groups can have on the world is a never-ending chain of individuals who influence many others for Christ.

TRANSITION:

"Ed Kimball's proper perspective on the importance of individuals and their potential led to an unending chain of results. As you'll recall from the Article, Jesus had a similar perspective."

Observ./Interp.

DISCUSSION:
Direct the group in
a discussion of the
questions. Share
the suggested
answers only if
necessary. Sum-
marize the group's
answers after dis-
cussing each ques-
tion and encourage
group members to
write the conclu-
sions in their study
guides.

See also II Timothy
2:2

Clarifying
Questions:

(13)

See also
Mark 3:13,14;
Matthew 5:16

Clarifying
Questions:

B. PRINCIPLES OF JESUS' MINISTRY

1. Jesus was a model of the spiritual multiplication principle. In what ways can we
pattern our ministries after His in order to
insure that our disciples multiply?

<u>We can concentrate on discipling a few,</u>
<u>sending them out to minister to others</u>
<u>and training them to continue their minis-</u>
<u>tries long after we are gone.</u>

1a. What other things can we do?
1b. What emphasis would Jesus have us
develop in our ministries?

2. What are some things Jesus would probably say if we asked Him why He discipled
His men?

<u>He would probably say He discipled His</u>
<u>men so that they would learn how to know</u>
<u>and love God. He wanted to build their</u>
<u>character; He wanted to teach them how</u>
<u>to walk in obedience to God and depend-</u>
<u>ence on Him; He wanted to show them</u>
<u>how they could reach the world with the</u>
<u>gospel and glorify God.</u>

2a. We read in the Article that Jesus did
not disciple men just for the purpose
of having love relationships in the
Spirit. How do you think Jesus would
answer the question, "Why are you
discipling men?"
2b. What are some other answers He
would give?

3. In the Article, we read that Jesus was committed to building a movement of Spirit-filled Christians who were obedient to God's Word and who were actively involved in helping to fulfill the Great Commission. What were some ways this commitment was demonstrated in His ministry?

See also Matthew 28:18-20; Acts 1:8

He helped His disciples to learn to depend on God's power. He taught them to obey God's Word, and He trained and sent them to have a ministry in others' lives.

_____

_____

Clarifying Questions:

3a. In what other ways did He show this commitment?
3b. How were Jesus' convictions related to His actions?

SAY:

"The Article stated that Jesus not only discipled His men in person for three years, as seen in the gospels, but He also discipled them through the power of the Holy Spirit after Pentecost, as seen in the Book of Acts."

Continue the discussion:

4. In what ways would our ministries be hurt if we used only Jesus' model before Pentecost as our model for discipleship?

We would have a discipleship philosophy without power, without vision, without movement and momentum. We would tend to focus only on our small group. We would also tend to become introspective (turned inward).

_____

_____

Clarifying Questions:

4a. What is the major difference between Jesus' ministry before and after Pentecost?
4b. What happens to our ministries if we begin thinking we are solely responsible for our disciples' growth?

5. In what ways will our ministries improve if we also keep in mind the model of how Jesus discipled His men after Pentecost?

Our discipleship ministries will be characterized by the explosive power of the Holy Spirit. Our philosophy of discipleship will not be exclusively small group-oriented, but will also take into consideration the fact that the Spirit can awaken Christians by the millions if they only know how to walk in the Spirit.

Clarifying Questions:

5a. What do some of the rest of you think?

5b. What were some characteristics of the disciples' ministry after Jesus' ascension which could model characteristics of our ministries?

5c. How will knowing that discipleship is the Holy Spirit's responsibility keep our ministries in balance?

RELATE:

"We've seen that Jesus' objective wasn't merely to build a close-knit group of men. He wanted men who were filled with the Holy Spirit and committed to the Great Commission."

Application (14)

DISCUSS:

6. What are some practical steps you can take with your group, or your future group, to insure that they are reaching Jesus' objective of discipleship?

Model aggressive evangelism and teach the ministry of the Holy Spirit. Do not let the group become an end in itself.

SAY:

"In our next lesson, we'll be discussing the disciple-ship principles which Jesus used in His ministry."

Tell group
members to read
Leadership Group
Article 2 before the
next meeting.

Practical Ministry
(15-25 Minutes)

To develop the Practical Ministry (Vision, Strategy, Training) Section of this lesson, complete the following steps:

_____ 1. Turn to the "Strategy Chart for Student and Adult Ministries" (Point B of the III. Practical Ministry—Strategy Appendix) (p. 528).

_____ 2. On the left hand side of the chart, identify the ministry strategy your group is now or soon will be pursuing.

_____ 3. On the right hand side of the chart, choose the training unit which you could best teach this week to prepare your group to be involved in the ministry strategy.

_____ 4. Turn in the IV. Practical Ministry— Training Appendix to the number of the training unit you have chosen and prepare to teach the content from the outline given.

_____ 5. Now turn to the II. Practical Ministry— Vision Appendix and choose the "Resource Idea" (point B) or a "Vision Passage" (point C) that would best motivate your group toward the strategy and training you have chosen.

_____ 6. When you reach the Practical Ministry portion of your discipleship group meeting, teach the Vision portion first, then discuss your local strategy in light of that vision. Then teach the Training portion. (For some topics, you may prefer to go from Vision into Training and then end with a discussion of your local strategy suggesting action points for the coming week.)

Prayer
(5-10 Minutes)

See V. Prayer Appendix for ideas to develop this section of study if you choose to use it.

Arrange the time and place for the next meeting.

Discipleship Principles
===of the Master===

OVERVIEW GOAL

The goal of this lesson is to enable group members to apply Jesus' discipleship principles to their lives.

LEARNING OBJECTIVES

By the end of this lesson, group members will be able to:

1. Explain how they can apply eight principles of small group discipleship to their own ministries.

2. Explain how to avoid pitfalls in selecting their disciples.

3. State one personal strategy goal and one group strategy goal and begin planning for the accomplishment of these goals.

Time/Section	Outline/Questions and Learning Activities
10-15	**Sharing**
30-40	**Study**
Motivation	A. THE BOY WITH A DREAM
Observ./Interp.	B. APPLICATION CHARTS

Application	1. Eight principles of small group discipleship
	       a. Principles involved in small group discipleship
	       b. As a discipler of others, how can I apply this principle to my ministry?
	
	    2. Potential pitfalls in the selection process
	       a. Pitfalls to avoid in the selection process
	       b. What are some ways that I can avoid these pitfalls?
	
	    3. Specific strategy goals and plans
	       a. Group strategy
	       b. Personal strategy

15-25	**Practical Ministry**
5-10	**Prayer**
60-90	

Preparation

PERSONAL PERSPECTIVE

Set aside a half hour or more when you can be alone, taking Leadership Group Article 2 and the study guide with you. Read the Article thoroughly, then fill in the charts. Make notes of things you would like to stress to your group members during the discussion time. Also, take time to pray for your group members, that they would not only understand this material but that they also would be able to apply it. Pray that God will use you to guide the discussion in such a way that it will produce the maximum impact on everyone (including you). Before beginning, be sure you are filled with the Holy Spirit.

Take time to think through a group goal you would like to work toward; for example, reaching Smith dorm or a three block radius of your church for Christ in the next three months. Using the strategy chart (B-3) as an example, work out, before your meeting, the details of accomplishing your goal. This will give you an idea of how to direct the group. When you reach the strategy chart in the lesson, encourage your group members to suggest group goals. They may come up with yours or they may not. In order to guide them in reaching a goal which is compatible with the overall objective of the group, think through several goals of your own.

Be sure to remind group members to read the Article before the group meets. If the Leadership Group lessons are being taught in a weekly discipleship meeting, include the Practical Ministry and Prayer sections. However, if the lessons are being taught in another setting, such as a retreat, you will need to decide which of the above sections to delete, based on your teaching objectives.

RESOURCES

Disciples Are Made—Not Born, Walter A. Henrichsen
Master Plan of Evangelism, Robert E. Coleman

> "And the things which you have heard from me in the presence of many witnesses, these entrust to faithful men, who will be able to teach others also" (II Timothy 2:2).

Sharing
(10-15 Minutes)

See I. Sharing Appendix for ideas to develop this section of study if you choose to use it.

Study
(30-40 Minutes)

Open the study with a brief prayer, asking God to teach the group.

Motivation (24)

Have a group member read Point A.

A. THE BOY WITH A DREAM

Let's take a moment to reflect on the story at the beginning of the Article about the boy who wanted to become a great pianist. He read biographies, listened to records, even practiced on his own, yet he could only get so far in his achievement.

Then he enrolled in a music class taught by a master pianist. This made all the difference. Under the expert guidance of this great teacher, the boy improved dramatically and eventually became a master pianist himself.

SAY:

"The principle drawn from this example is that the key to our effectiveness as disciplers is becoming like the Master. As believers who want to see our lives maximized in the fulfillment of the Great Commission, we also need to develop our practical skills in discipling others to the highest quality. Just as the aspiring young pianist needed training and advice from an expert in his field, we also need to get to know and become like the expert in the field of discipleship—Jesus Christ."

Observ./Interp.

Application

As a group, discuss
briefly each princi-
ple mentioned in
Chart 1, "Eight
Principles of Small
Group Disciple-
ship." Lead them to
draw simple, prac-
tical applications.
Spend no longer
than 15 minutes
discussing this
chart. Have each
member fill in his
chart as the discus-
sion progresses.

B. APPLICATION CHARTS

1. Eight Principles of Small Group Discipleship	
a. Principles involved in small group discipleship.	b. As a discipler of others, how can I apply this principle to my ministry?
1) Build qualitatively into the lives of a few.	1)
2) Spend time with them.	2)
3) Require commitment.	3)
4) Teach in the context of real life experiences.	4)
5) Teach by example.	5)
6) Give practical assignments.	6)
7) Watch and supervise.	7)
8) Commission your disciples to reproduce spiritually.	8)

Continue the discussion using Chart 2, "Potential Pitfalls in the Selection Process." Ask group members to quickly look over the list of pitfalls and put a star by the one that may

give them the most
difficulty. Then
proceed to discuss
each one briefly.
Allow 5 to 10 min-
utes. Some sugges-
tions are given, but
the group will come
up with other ideas.

(25)

2. Potential Pitfalls in the Selection Process	
a. Pitfalls to avoid in the selection process	b. What are some ways that I can avoid these pitfalls?
1) Losing sight of my objective to reach the world for Christ	1) Expose myself to challenging meetings and conferences, stay in the Word, read missionary biographies, be aware of current events, correspond with and pray for missionaries.
2) Choosing disciples who are not "full of faith"	2) Notice whether or not a person is willing to break personal faith barriers, no matter how small they seem.
3) Ignoring elements of maturity (social, emotional, personal) which are crucial in a spiritual multiplier	3) Be aware of whether or not a person is able to maintain close friendships and follow through on small commitments.
4) Ignoring the ability and sphere of influence of a potential disciple	4) Seek to share Christ with and disciple those in leadership positions. Begin to pray for spiritual leaders in my city and on my campus.
5) Having an imbalance in group affinity	5) Maintain a continual emphasis on outreach, including others in social activities, inviting others to Christian activities.

Pause for a brief prayer; ask God to guide you as you fill in the chart.

Read down to Point a. (26)

Guide the group members to choose one group goal and one personal goal. Then work through Point a of this chart as a group, making a specific plan and goal and committing yourselves to work toward that goal together. Be accountable to one another in moving toward meeting these goals.

The chart is filled in here to show you how much detail you may want to include in your plan.

3. Specific Strategy Goals and Plans

Goal	Plan	Implementation
What do I want to see by when?	How am I going to get there?	What are the specific steps I have to take?
a. Group strategy		
Reach every girl in Smith Hall by Christmas break.	Assign: 1) Each group member to be responsible for two floors. 2) Take surveys. 3) Have evangelistic popcorn parties. 4) Make friends with the girls.	1) Make a list of the girls on my floor. 2) Pray for each girl. 3) Find out who the leaders are. 4) Start immediately.

Allow group members 5-10 minutes to work on Point b. by themselves. At the end of that time, have each person share, if he wants to, what his personal strategy is.

b. Personal strategy		
By February, I want to see God raise up a group of women for me to work with.	1) Make a list of potential disciples. 2) Seriously pray for God's guidance and wisdom in choosing the right people. 3) Spend time with those potential disciples to see their heart and to get to know them. 4) After steps 1-3, challenge those whom God impresses upon me.	Sally Gellespie Dorothy Planas Mary Nettles Lois Gaston Betty DeGreef Joanne Bovy

RELATE:

Tell your group members to read Leadership Group Article 3 before the next meeting.

"In our next lesson we'll be discussing the characteristics of a discipleship group."

Practical Ministry
(15-25 Minutes)

To develop the
Practical Ministry
(Vision, Strategy,
Training) Section
of this lesson,
complete the steps
explained in Les-
son I.

Prayer
(5-10 Minutes)

See V. Prayer
Appendix for ideas
to develop this sec-
tion of study if you
choose to use it.

Arrange time and
place of the next
meeting.

Characteristics of a ═══Discipleship Group═══

OVERVIEW GOAL

The goal of this lesson is to enable group members to understand the characteristics of a Discipleship Group and to develop these characteristics within a group.

LEARNING OBJECTIVES

By the end of this lesson, group members will be able to:

1. Explain three main characteristics of a Discipleship Group.

2. Explain specific ways to develop these characteristics within the group.

Time/Section	Outline/Questions and Learning Activities
10-15	## Sharing
30-40	## Study
Motivation	A. CASE STUDY

A. CASE STUDY

1. What are some words and phrases you would use to describe this group?
2. What are some ways this group could improve?

   TRANSITION: "Unfortunately, some of these characteristics are too common in Discipleship Groups. That's why we're spending some time discussing three important characteristics of a Discipleship Group. The first important characteristic is our growing dependence upon and love for Christ. The second one is our growing love and concern for our group members and the third characteristic is our growing compassion and concern for the lost world. Let's look now at the first characteristic."

Observ./Interp.

B. OUR GROWING DEPENDENCE UPON AND LOVE FOR CHRIST

I Thessalonians 1:3,8-10

1. What are some reasons that dependence upon and love for Christ are so crucial to the development of the other two characteristics (Points C and D)?
2. If our Leadership Group were growing in this characteristic, what would be some specific evidences of that growth?
3. When the members of your group are focusing on problems, what are some things that we can do to point them to Christ?

Acts 2:42-47

C. OUR GROWING LOVE AND CONCERN FOR DISCIPLESHIP GROUP MEMBERS

1. What are some reasons we sometimes hesitate to get involved in the lives of

Time/Section	Outline/Questions and Learning Activities
	other Christians, such as those in our group?
	2. What are some practical, meaningful and creative ways we can demonstrate love and concern for those in our group?
Matthew 9:36-38	D. OUR GROWING COMPASSION AND CONCERN FOR THE LOST WORLD
	1. In what ways can we develop and demonstrate compassion for the lost?
	2. What are some of the dangers of a Discipleship Group not reaching out to others?
Application	3. If you were dying at the age of 85 and a Christian magazine was going to write an article about you, how would you like your life to be described?
	Action Point As you discuss the questions below, record your specific thoughts concerning our Leadership Group and the group you are leading.
	1. What are some things that we can begin doing that would have an impact on the quality and effectiveness of our Leadership Group?
	2. What are some things we can begin doing immediately within groups we are leading to implement some of the principles and applications we have been discussing?
15-25	**Practical Ministry**
5-10	**Prayer**
60-90	

Preparation

PERSONAL PERSPECTIVE

Set aside at least an hour when you will not be disturbed. You will need your Bible, Leadership Group study guide and the related Leadership Group Article. Take time to carefully and thoughtfully read through the Article. Ask God to use the preparation time, not only to prepare you to discuss the material, but also to increase your own understanding of the key characteristics of a Discipleship Group. Think through the specific needs of your own group members and relate the questions to them. Study the chart used under Application so that you will be familiar with it and able to explain it. Use the questions and the chart under the Action Point to evaluate your group. This will help prepare you to discuss your plans when you complete the chart together during the lesson. Also, be sure to remind the group members to read the Article before the group meets.

If the Leadership Group lessons are being taught in a weekly Discipleship Group meeting, develop and include the Practical Ministry and Prayer sections. However, if the lessons are being taught in another setting, such as a retreat, you will need to decide which of the above sections to delete, based on your teaching objectives.

"And the glory which Thou hast given Me I have given to them; that they may be one, just as We are one; I in them, and Thou in Me, that they may be perfected in unity, that the world may know that Thou didst send Me, and didst love them, even as Thou didst love Me" (John 17:22,23).

Sharing
(10-15 Minutes)

See I. Sharing Appendix for ideas to develop this section of study if you choose to use it.

Study
(30-40 Minutes)

Open the study with a brief prayer, asking God to teach the group.

Motivation   (40)

A. CASE STUDY

A group of students formed a Bible study and began meeting every week in one member's home. Each person in the group was from a different background and all of them had extremely different personalities and interests. Because they each enjoyed separate activities, it was difficult for them to spend time together outside of their weekly meetings. However, they always looked forward to this weekly time because they were able to discuss their personal problems in detail with each other. Since they were all experiencing some similar daily problems, they found it easy to understand each other. One difficulty that they discussed frequently was their attitude toward non-Christians at school and work.

DISCUSSION:

Direct the group in a discussion of the questions. Share the suggested answers only if necessary. Summarize the group's answers after discussing each question and encourage group members to write the conclusions in their study guides.

1. What are some words and phrases you would use to describe this group?

    The members seemed to be selfish in that they were unwilling to do what the others enjoyed doing. They were problem-centered, introverted and had no vision for the lost people.

    _____

    _____

2. What are some ways this group could improve?

    They could focus on praising God for positive things that He's doing. They could have more structure in their Bible study to stay on the subject. To focus on others instead of themselves, they could have social times and invite their non-Christian friends from school and work.

    _____

    _____

TRANSITION:

"Unfortunately, some of these characteristics are too common in Discipleship Groups. That's why we're spending some time discussing three important characteristics of a Discipleship Group. The first important characteristic is our growing dependence upon and love for Christ. The second one is our growing love and concern for our group members, and the third characteristic is our growing compassion and concern for the lost world. Let's look now at the first characteristic."

Observ./Interp.

Ask a group member to read the verses. Continue to discuss the study questions following the same procedure.

I THESSALONIANS 1:3,8-10
B. OUR GROWING DEPENDENCE UPON AND LOVE FOR CHRIST

1. What are some reasons that dependence upon and love for Christ are so crucial to the development of the other two characteristics (Points C and D)?

    It is the foundation of the group and the source of the other two characteristics.

Without it, the group will become introverted because members will depend on
each other rather than on Christ. The
members will lack power in their lives
because they do not depend on God's
Spirit to change their lives and their
problems.

Clarifying
Questions:

1a. What are some other reasons?
1b. What would happen in the group if
this characteristic did not exist?

(41)

2. If our Leadership Group were growing in
this characteristic, what would be some
specific evidences of that growth?

Some specific evidences would be praise
and thanksgiving to God for everything,
focus on Christ instead of problems, quality times of prayer, positive and believing
hearts, respect for God's Word and steps
toward breaking faith barriers.

Clarifying
Questions:

2a. What would be some other specific
evidences?
2b. What are some attitudes and activities
that would be present?

See also
Hebrews 12:1-13;
Philippians 4:4-8

3. When the members of your group are focusing on problems, what are some things
we can do to point them to Christ?

We can share promises and examples of
Christ's sufficiency from the Bible as well
as personal examples. We can pray
together concerning the biblical promise
that relates to the problem. We can exhort
them to take their eyes off the problem
and encourage them to give thanks.

3a. What are some other things we can do?

3b. What are some things that help you to change your focus from problems to solutions in Christ?

Ask a group member to read the verses.

DISCUSS:

ACTS 2:42-47
C. OUR GROWING LOVE AND CONCERN FOR DISCIPLESHIP GROUP MEMBERS

1. What are some reasons we sometimes hesitate to get involved in the lives of other Christians, such as those in our group?

Self-sacrifice is required when we make commitments to be involved with other people, and we are not willing to make the sacrifice of time and effort. Also, we must live our lives so that they stand up under the scrutiny of others. The more time spent with disciples, the more clearly one's strengths and weaknesses are seen. We do not like to be that vulnerable. Often it is because we do not want to give of ourselves to others. As we grow spiritually and become more committed to Christ, we will desire to give of ourselves to others and be their example.

Clarifying Questions:

1a. What would be some other reasons?

1b. What are some desirable and undesirable results of getting involved in the lives of others?

1c. Why do these potentially undesirable results keep us from getting involved with others, even though we know we should be?

2. What are some practical, meaningful and creative ways we can demonstrate love and concern for those in our group?

We can do for them what we appreciate others doing for us—joyfully meeting their needs by being a good listener, spending time outside of the ministry with them and doing what demonstrates love and concern to them (it varies with the individual).

Clarifying Questions:

2a. What are some other ideas?
2b. What things communicate love and concern to you?
2c. What are some ways you demonstrate love and concern to your friends?

Ask a group member to read the verses. (42)

MATTHEW 9:36-38
D. OUR GROWING COMPASSION AND CONCERN FOR THE LOST WORLD

DISCUSS:

1. In what ways can we develop and demonstrate compassion for the lost?

We can pray that we will grow in our love for Christ so that His heart's burden will become ours, that we will realize people are dying without Christ, that reaching the lost will be the goal of the Discipleship Group. Praying for the lost, as well as sharing our faith in Christ with them, are the means of reaching our goal.

Clarifying Questions:

1a. What else can we do?
1b. What kinds of situations bring out the response of compassion in our hearts?
1c. What things do we need to realize about non-Christians in order to respond to them with heart-felt compassion?

2. What are some of the dangers of a Discipleship Group not reaching out to others?

Some dangers would be that they would lack vision for reaching the world for Christ. The group would become introverted. The members would depend on each other instead of Christ, and there would be a lack of focus on Christ. Non-Christians would not be won to Christ.

Clarifying
Questions:

2a. What are some other dangers?

2b. What typically happens when we lose sight of, or never really understand, our purpose for doing something?

2c. What things would probably happen if a Discipleship Group lost sight of its purpose?

RELATE:

"You remember reading in the Article about Adoniram Judson, how God used the life of this one man who stepped out in faith. Now think about your own life and how you would like God to use you."

Application

Allow group members several minutes to respond, then ask if anyone would like to share his thoughts.

3. If you were dying at the age of 85 and a Christian magazine was going to write an article about you, how would you like your life to be described?

RELATE:

"If we want our lives to count with maximum impact for Christ by the time we're 85, there are specific steps of action we should begin taking now."

READ:

Complete the
Action Point as a
group. Explain that
group members
should use the fol-
lowing chart to
record their spe-
cific thoughts as
you discuss the two
questions.

(43) **Action Point** As you discuss the questions below,
record your specific thoughts concerning our
Leadership Group and the group you are leading.

1. What are some things that we can begin
doing that would have an impact on the
quality and effectiveness of our Leadership Group?
2. What are some things we can begin doing
immediately within groups we are leading
to implement some of the principles and
applications we have been discussing?

Characteristics of a Discipleship Group	Weak or Strong		Plans for Improvement		When to Implement These Plans	
	Our Group	Your Group	Our Group	Your Group	Our Group	Your Group
Growing dependence upon and love for Christ						
Growing love and concern for Discipleship Group members						
Growing com-passion and concern for the lost world						

RELATE:

Tell group
members to read
Leadership Group
Article 4 before the
next group
meeting.

"In our next lesson, we'll be discussing some principles for discipling your group members."

Practical Ministry
(15-25 Minutes)

To develop the
Practical Ministry
(Vision, Strategy,
Training) Section
of this lesson,
complete the steps
explained in Les-
son I.

Prayer
(5-10 Minutes)

See V. Prayer
Appendix for ideas
to develop this sec-
tion of study if you
choose to use it.

Arrange the time
and place of the
next meeting.

Discipling your
Group Members

OVERVIEW GOAL

The goal of this lesson is to enable group members to understand some underlying principles that will help them improve their discipleship ministries.

LEARNING OBJECTIVES

By the end of this lesson, group members will be able to:

1. Identify the five underlying principles of discipleship.

2. Explain the significance of having a well-planned strategy for discipleship.

3. List the four elements of the proper environment for discipleship.

4. Explain how circumstances relate to the discipleship process.

487

Time/Section	Outline/Questions and Learning Activities

10-15   **Sharing**

30-40   **Study**

Motivation

A. THE FOOTBALL TEAM WITHOUT A PLAN

   1. What are some possible parallels between this story and our ministry situations?
   2. If we had a "Pug Jones" type of leader here, what would be some of the results?

B. THE OBJECTIVE AND PRINCIPLES OF DISCIPLESHIP

   1. The objective of discipleship is to build a movement of Spirit-filled Christians who are obedient to God's Word and are actively involved in helping to fulfill the Great Commission in their generation.
   2. Five underlying principles of discipleship
     a. Have clearly defined objectives.
     b. Teach biblical content.
     c. Have a game plan.
     d. Provide the proper context.
     e. Allow circumstances to disciple us.

TRANSITION: "As we evaluate the process of discipleship today, it becomes obvious that some of these principles are being neglected, preventing dynamic spiritual movements from being developed. Earlier Articles have covered the first two principles (objectives and biblical content). Now let's look at the remaining three principles in detail, with the hope that we will each be catalysts of strong discipleship ministries."

Observ./Interp.

C. THE SIGNIFICANCE OF STRATEGY AND MINISTRY TOOLS

   1. What are some ways that structure and guidance (game plans) give value to an athletic team?

488

Time/Section	Outline/Questions and Learning Activities
	2. What are some reasons why it would be important for players to play according to the rules in athletics and not to make up their own rules as they go along?
	3. What are some parallels between using a well-thought-through game plan in athletics and using strategy and ministry tools in building a discipleship movement?
Luke 10:1-11	4. In what ways does this passage relate to our previous discussion?
	5. This diagram shows how strategy and ministry tools are used in discipleship.
	D. ELEMENTS OF THE PROPER ENVIRONMENT FOR DISCIPLESHIP
Philippians 4:9; I Corinthians 11:1 I Thessalonians 2:8	1. What are some ways that our actions speak louder than our words?
	2. What are some ways that strong personal relationships can enhance discipleship?
Matthew 9:36-38	3. What are some ways that a personal vision can be built into other disciples?
Acts 2:47 Acts 5:42	4. What are some reasons why a strong evangelistic emphasis is important in creating a proper environment for discipleship?
Application	**E. GOD'S USE OF CIRCUMSTANCES TO DISCIPLE US**
James 1:2-4	1. These verses tell us to rejoice in our trials because of the results those trials produce in our character development. What are some ways in which you have experienced this principle in your life?
Romans 8:28,29	2. What are some circumstances in your life right now that you need to relate to these verses?
	Action Point List some ways on the chart that you can improve the context of your discipleship ministry.
15-25	**Practical Ministry**

Time/Section	Outline/Questions and Learning Activities
5-10	**Prayer**
60-90	

Preparation

PERSONAL PERSPECTIVE

Set aside at least one half hour when you will not be disturbed. Take your Bible and Leadership Group study guide. Read through the related Leadership Group Article twice before preparing this lesson. Be sure group members also have read the Article before the meeting. Study the Scriptures mentioned in the Article and in the leader's guide. Answer each discussion question personally and develop the implementation steps required in the Action Point. Remember you are to be a model, setting the example for your group members. As you prepare, pray that your group members will be willing to actively take steps of action in discipling others.

If the Leadership Group lessons are being taught in a weekly discipleship meeting, develop and include the Practical Ministry and Prayer sections. However, if the lessons are being taught in another setting, such as a retreat, you will need to decide which of the above sections to delete, based on your teaching objectives.

> "A leader is one who knows where he's going and is able to persuade others to go along with him."*
> Howard Hendricks

Sharing
(10-15 Minutes)

See I. Sharing Appendix for ideas to develop this section of study if you choose to use it.

Study
(30-40 Minutes)

Open the study in a brief prayer, asking God to teach the group.

Motivation

READ:

(54)

A. THE FOOTBALL TEAM WITHOUT A PLAN

Pug Jones, a football coach, wanted to win the big game badly. He met with his team day after day. Being a gifted speaker, he exhorted his team to win for the glory of old Pine Needle U. Each time the team heard him speak they were ecstatic. Team members would say, "Man, when he speaks, he really delivers the goods! Am I ever charged up!" But the coach never designed a game plan for his team or taught them any plays.

DISCUSSION: Direct the group in a discussion of the

1. What are some possible parallels between this story and our ministry situations?

*Howard Hendricks, "How to Lead I," in *The Ministry of Management*, Steven B. Douglass and Bruce E. Cook, Copyright © 1972: Used by permission of Campus Crusade for Christ, Inc., Arrowhead Springs, California.

questions. Share the suggested answers only if necessary. Summarize the group's answers after discussing each question and encourage group members to write the conclusions in their study guides.

> We as leaders may really motivate our disciples, but then we often stop there. We must go beyond motivation to give them some plans and tools to aid them in their ministries.

> 2. If we had a "Pug Jones" type of leader here, what would be some of the results?
>
>   Our movement would dwindle because it would be all talk and no action. Needs possibly would not be met, goals would probably be vague and no practical plan of action for reaching the goals would develop.

RELATE:

"We want victory for the Gospel of Christ. We don't want our team to be frustrated and confused. Let's look at the objective behind discipleship to help us form a strategy that will bring victory."

Ask a group member to read Point 1.

> B. THE OBJECTIVE AND PRINCIPLES OF DISCIPLESHIP
>
>   1. The objective of discipleship is to build a movement of Spirit-filled Christians who are obedient to God's Word and are actively involved in helping to fulfill the Great Commission in their generation.

SAY:

"In order to understand this movement, we need to look at five underlying principles of discipleship."

READ:

> 2. Five underlying principles of discipleship
>
>   a. Have clearly defined objectives. You must know where you are going in order to take others with you.

b. Teach biblical content. God's Word is more true than our feelings.

(55)

c. Have a game plan. A well-planned strategy is the only way to reach your objective.

d. Provide the proper context. Modeling, personal relationships, vision and evangelism are the dynamics of the discipleship context.

e. Allow circumstances to disciple us. The Lord has a uniquely designed set of circumstances for our growth.

TRANSITION:

"As we evaluate the process of discipleship today, it becomes obvious that some of these principles are being neglected, preventing dynamic spiritual movements from being developed. Earlier Articles have covered the first two principles (objectives and biblical content). Now let's look at the remaining three principles in detail, with the hope that we will each be catalysts of strong discipleship ministries.

RELATE:

"The story of Pug Jones illustrates that it isn't enough to have motivational objectives. We need a well-thought-through game plan to show our discipleship 'team' how to win."

Observ./Interp.

Discuss the following questions. Follow the same procedure as before.

C. THE SIGNIFICANCE OF STRATEGY AND MINISTRY TOOLS

1. What are some ways that structure and guidance (game plans) give value to an athletic team?

Team members are able to work together because they understand the duties and responsibilities of their positions. At the same time, they are able to play within the official rules, therefore avoiding penalties which would hinder their efforts to win.

2. What are some reasons why it would be important for players to play according to the rules in athletics and not to make up their own rules as they go along?

The results would be chaos with a slim chance of victory, if any at all. Team unity would be broken because of individual performances. Penalties would be numerous as a result of team members not observing the official rules.

Explain that a "game plan" refers to structure and ministry tools that have been developed from biblical content and are arranged in logical sequence. This insures that we disciple others in the basics of the Christian life.

3. What are some parallels between using a well-thought-through game plan in athletics and using strategy and ministry tools in building a discipleship movement?

We need strategy and ministry tools in order to create unity and quality in a discipleship ministry, just like athletic team members need a game plan in order to play together effectively. Without a definite plan, everyone does his own thing, hindering progress growth toward God's plan for us.

Ask a group (56) member to read the verses.

LUKE 10:1-11
4. In what ways does this passage relate to our previous discussion?

Jesus gave them directions in how they were to go (in pairs), where they were to go, what to say when they got there and when to return. This shows that He was concerned with structure in ministry. He didn't just send them out; He equipped them for the task first.

RELATE:

"The following diagram shows a simple plan for discipling Christians. Ministry tools have been developed from biblical content and are arranged in a sequence of lesson plans to help us reach our goal of fulfilling the Great Commission.

"In the diagram we find that our basic tools in evangelism are the Four Spiritual Laws and the Holy Spirit booklets; our tools in individual follow-up are the "Beginning Your New Life" booklets 1-5; in small group follow-up we use the Discovery Group Lessons 1-6 and in discipleship training we use the Discipleship Group Lessons 7-20."

Explain how Spirit-filled Christians who are obedient to God's Word can utilize structure as a means of actively helping to fulfill the Great Commission in their generation.

Attempt to answer questions relating to the diagram to help everyone understand.

5. This diagram shows how strategy and ministry tools are used in discipleship.

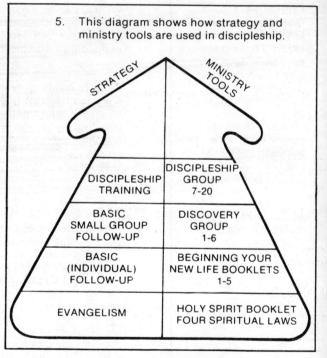

STRATEGY | MINISTRY TOOLS

DISCIPLESHIP TRAINING	DISCIPLESHIP GROUP 7-20
BASIC SMALL GROUP FOLLOW-UP	DISCOVERY GROUP 1-6
BASIC (INDIVIDUAL) FOLLOW-UP	BEGINNING YOUR NEW LIFE BOOKLETS 1-5
EVANGELISM	HOLY SPIRIT BOOKLET FOUR SPIRITUAL LAWS

RELATE:

"Simply having a good strategy and good ministry tools will not insure discipleship. The spiritual environment to which our disciples are being exposed is also crucial. Let's look at four important elements that are included in a healthy spiritual environment."

(57)

D. ELEMENTS OF THE PROPER ENVIRON-MENT FOR DISCIPLESHIP

Ask a group member to read the verses before discussing each study question. Share the suggested answers only if necessary.

PHILIPPIANS 4:9; I CORINTHIANS 11:1
1. What are some ways that our actions speak louder than our words?

Modeling: People watch our actions to see if they back up our words. If what we do does not match what we say, then people will not be likely to follow us. If our actions match our words, people will more likely follow us. Whatever we are is reproduced into the lives of others, because "like produces like."

I THESSALONIANS 2:8
2. What are some ways that strong personal relationships can enhance discipleship?

Relationships: Commitment to each other builds trust. Having a relationship of trust creates an avenue for easy transfer of information and vision. Discipleship is more effective when you spend personal and informal time together.

MATTHEW 9:36-38
3. What are some ways that a personal vision can be built into other disciples?

Vision: If we set an example of commitment to reaching a particular area for Christ, and if we plan and pray together about it, vision will be transferred. It is important to remember that vision is "caught" not "taught."

(58)   ACTS 2:47; 5:42
4.   What are some reasons why a strong
     evangelistic emphasis is important in
     creating a proper environment for
     discipleship?

Evangelism: The atmosphere of consistent
evangelism creates momentum for the
movement and provides new potential
disciples continually, allowing new generations of disciples to be built.

RELATE: "Often, we as disciples can forget that it is the
Lord who actually does the discipling through His
own set of situations and circumstances. Let's
spend a few minutes looking at how the Lord is
actively involved in the discipleship process."

Application

DISCUSS:

E.   GOD'S USE OF CIRCUMSTANCES TO DIS-
     CIPLE US

JAMES 1:2-4
1.   These verses tell us to rejoice in our trials
     because of the results those trials produce
     in our character development. What are
     some ways in which you have expe-
     rienced this principle in your life?

Ask a group
member to read the
verses.

ROMANS 8:28,29
2.   What are some circumstances in your life
     right now that you need to relate to these
     verses?

SAY:

"Let's take some time to develop an action plan to apply the principles of this lesson."

READ AND
EXPLAIN:

(59)

Action Point Take five minutes and list ways that you can improve the context of your discipleship ministry—modeling, relationships, vision and evangelism. Include how and when you plan to implement these improvements.

Ways to Improve Your
Context of Discipleship

Area	What to Improve	How to Improve	When to Implement
Modeling			
Personal Relationships			
Vision			
Evangelism			

Allow time for group members to begin the chart, encouraging them to finish it during the week. Have them work either in pairs or individually.

RELATE:

"In our next lesson we'll be discussing the elements of an effective movement."

Tell group members to read Leadership Group Article 5 before the next meeting.

Practical Ministry
(15-25 Minutes)

To develop the
Practical Ministry
(Vision, Strategy,
Training) Section
of this lesson,
complete the steps
explained in
Lesson 1.

Prayer
(5-10 Minutes)

See V. Prayer
Appendix for ideas
to develop this sec-
tion of study if you
choose to use it.

Arrange the time
and place of the
next meeting.

Being Involved in a
═Spiritual Movement═

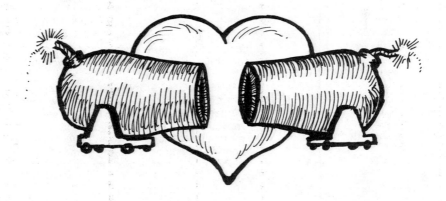

OVERVIEW GOAL

The goal of this lesson is to motivate group members to become actively involved in their own personal ministries and to take personal responsibility for the overall movement of which they are a part.

LEARNING OBJECTIVES

By the end of this lesson, group members will be able to:

1.   Identify the characteristics of an effective movement.

2.   Explain how effective personal ministries contribute to the overall effectiveness of the movement of which they are a part.

Time/Section	Outline/Questions and Learning Activities
10-15	**Sharing**
30-40	**Study**

Motivation

A. OUR OBJECTIVE

 1. Write down what you feel is the primary objective of the movement we are involved in and how your having a personal ministry relates to it.
 2. What are some of your thoughts on the objective of our movement?
 3. What do you think are some ways your personal ministry fits into our movement?

 TRANSITION: "Along with understanding our primary objective, knowing how your personal ministry fits into the overall movement is one of the most important motivational factors we can have. Let's spend some time reviewing some of the elements of an effective movement."

Observ./Interp.

B. AN EFFECTIVE MOVEMENT

 1. What are some things that you think make the difference between a movement with high momentum and a gathering of Christians simply carrying on "spiritual" activities?
 2. What are some reasons multiplication might turn to addition?
 3. What are some differences we might experience in our ministry if we saw a more effective movement?

Application

C. INCREASING THE EFFECTIVENESS OF OUR MOVEMENT

 1. Momentum
   a. What do you think are some things we could do to increase the momentum of our ministry?

Time/Section	Outline/Questions and Learning Activities
	b. When do you think would be a good time to do some of these things?
	2. Multiplication a. What are some of your personal goals for seeing multiplication take place? b. What do you think are some things we could be doing to increase the multiplication process?
	3. Management a. What are some things regarding management that you feel we are now doing effectively? b. What are some of your thoughts on positive management factors that we could be implementing to increase our effectiveness?
	4. Movement in General a. What do you think are some ways we could improve our movement? b. What are some of your thoughts on when we should implement some of these ideas?
	Action Point Complete the Ministry Evaluation and Planning Chart.
15-25	**Practical Ministry**
5-10	**Prayer**
60-90	

Preparation

PERSONAL PERSPECTIVE

Set aside at least one half hour when you will not be disturbed. Take your Leadership Group study guide and any ministry plan you may have for your area of responsibility. Make sure you have read the corresponding Leadership Group Article to this lesson and answered the questions in the study guide. Be sure you are thoroughly familiar with the overall objective of your ministry and understand how your group members' ministries fit into that objective. Decide which area of your movement needs improvement to increase its effectiveness. Determine which set of questions to pursue in the Application section based on your decision. Plan steps of action. Make sure that group members read the Leadership Group Article before the group meeting.

If the Leadership Group Lessons are being taught in a weekly discipleship meeting, include the Practical Ministry and Prayer sections. However, if the lessons are being taught in another setting, such as a retreat, you will need to decide which of the above sections to delete, based on your teaching objectives.

RESOURCES

Area of responsibility plan, if available (i.e., campus plan, city plan, church plan, etc.).

===== **Leader's Guide** =====

> "Only one life t'will soon be past, only what's done for Christ will last."*
>
> C.T. Studd

Sharing
(10-15 Minutes)

See I. Sharing Appendix for ideas to develop this section of study if you choose to use it.

Study
(30-40 Minutes)

Open the study in a brief prayer, asking God to teach the group.

Motivation　　(70)

Have group members take 3 minutes to answer part A.

DISCUSSION:

Direct the group in a discussion of the questions. Share the suggested answers only if necessary. Summarize the group's answers after discussing each question and encourage

A.　OUR OBJECTIVE

1.　Write down what you feel is the primary objective of the movement we are involved in and how your having a personal ministry relates to it.

_____
_____
_____
_____

*Norman Grubb, *C.T. Studd*, Copyright © 1972, p. 141: Used by permission of Christian Literature Crusade, Fort Washington, Pennsylvania.

505

group members to
write the conclu-
sions in their study
guides.

If group members
have trouble identi-
fying the primary
objective, refer to
Article 5 for
clarification.

2. What are some of your thoughts on the objective of our movement?

_____

_____

_____

_____

3. What do you think are some ways your personal ministry fits into our movement?

My small group is a part of one multiplication element of our movement. My disciples also need to be involved in some
larger momentum producing activities,
etc.

_____

_____

TRANSITION:

"Along with understanding our primary objective, knowing how your personal ministry fits into the overall movement is one of the most important motivational factors we can have. Let's spend some time reviewing some of the elements of an effective movement."

Observ./Interp.

Continue the dis-
cussion following
the same
procedure.

B. AN EFFECTIVE MOVEMENT

1. What are some things you think make the difference between a movement with high momentum and a gathering of Christians simply carrying on "spiritual" activities?

Enthusiasm, excitement and action gen-
erated from leaders and passed down to
others involved; common goal; unity of
members; commitment and dedication of
people; and many people at all levels of
commitment. Overall, spiritual multiplication is taking place.

(71) 2. What are some reasons multiplication
          might turn to addition?

          Group members cease to have as their
          actual goal building their own group of
          multiplying disciples and instead want to
          be part of a comfortable Bible study;
          emphasis on building men in Christ with-
          out effort to win or send.

Clarifying
Questions:

2a. Have you ever seen a ministry of mul-
     tiplication turn to addition? What are
     some things you may have noticed
     that caused it to happen?
2b. Any other ideas of how a ministry
     could end up addition-minded?

3. What are some differences we might
    experience in our ministry if we saw a
    more effective movement?

    Excited, enthusiastic meetings; people
    who have a vision to reach the world
    through their personal ministries; stronger
    evangelistic efforts coupled with breaking
    personal faith barriers more consistently.

SAY: "Let's take some time now to discuss more specifi-
      cally how we might increase the effectiveness of
      our movement here."

Application

Choose between
the four sections:
momentum, multi-
plication, manage-
ment or movement
in general, deter-
mining which set of
questions best fits
the needs of your
ministry.

Have group
members look at
the appropriate
section in their
study guides.

Discuss the study
questions under
the appropriate
section. Be sure to
keep the group on
target, constructive
and solution-
oriented. Many
suggestions are
given as possible
answers, but your
group should come
up with most of
their own.

(72)

C. INCREASING THE EFFECTIVENESS OF OUR MOVEMENT

1. Momentum
   a. What do you think are some things we could do to increase the momentum of our ministry?

   Change format of main meeting to create more enthusiasm; have a retreat to build unity; have a major evangelistic outreach or event to generate excitement and increase vision.

   b. When do you think would be a good time to do some of these things?

   Sometime in the fall would be a good time for a retreat. A major event would build momentum mid to end of year. A special series of evangelistic outreaches in the community for church members could be planned preceding the week of Easter, etc.

2. Multiplication
   a. What are some of your personal goals for seeing multiplication take place?

   To see two generations of multiplying disciples below me, with three or more disciples in each group in addition to the leader.

   b. What do you think are some things we could be doing to increase the multiplication process?

Increase standards for discipleship groups; have an outreach to develop responsibility and leadership of present leaders; generate additional contacts for groups.

3. Management
   a. What are some things regarding management that you feel we are now doing effectively?

      Making yearly plans, delegating major responsibilities, weekly planning and evaluation meetings.

   b. What are some of your thoughts on positive management factors that we could be implementing to increase our effectiveness?

      Keep better ministry records; plan activities sooner; have evaluation meetings; let people give input in the planning process; develop a strategy to systematically reach our area.

(73)
4. Movement in General
   a. What do you think are some ways we could improve our movement?

      Have training classes; plan a conference; have a classic; do team meetings; speak in classrooms.

509

b.   What are some of your thoughts on
     when we should implement some of
     these ideas?

_____
_____
_____

SAY:

"Let's take a few minutes to individually fill out the
evaluation and planning chart."

Give group
members the
remaining time to
get started on the
chart; then suggest
they finish it at
home.

Action Point   Evaluate your ministry using this
chart.

Encourage
members to choose
two or three of
these actions to
implement in the
next few weeks. Set
up a means for
them to be accoun-
table to you.

Ministry Evaluation and Planning Chart			
	Yes No	Plan of Action	Target Date for Implementation
1. Are you praying specifically?			
2. Are you involved in personal evangelism and follow-up?			
3. Are you meeting personally and in small groups with those who have indicated an interest for further involvement?			

		Yes No	Plan of Action	Target Date for Implementation
(74)	4. Are you spending priority time with people who are eager to grow and be involved?			
	5. Are you challenging people for further commitment and involvement?			
	6. Are you involved in continuous evangelism?			
	7. Do your disciples see you model evangelism?			
	8. Are you building multiplying disciples?			
	9. Are you building disciples in small groups?			
	10. Are you giving disciples specific and thorough biblical teaching and training?			
	11. Is the Discipleship Group you lead characterized by relationships of love?			
	12. Are you involving disciples in personal and group evangelism, follow-up and discipleship of others?			
	13. Are those under you who are leading groups (if any) demonstrating the Spirit-filled life and ministry skills to their group members?			
(75)	a. Are they regularly taking them to do personal and group evangelism, follow-up and discipleship?			

	Yes No	Plan of Action	Target Date for Implementation
b. Do they have a healthy balance between demonstration and observation of those they are discipling?			
14. Do you have second and third generation disciples?			

Practical Ministry
(15-25 Minutes)

To develop the Practical Ministry (Vision, Strategy, Training) Section of this lesson, complete the steps explained in Lesson I.

Prayer
(5-10 Minutes)

See V. Prayer Appendix for ideas to develop this section of study if you choose to use it.

Arrange the time and place of the next meeting.

Division:
Appendices I-V

I. Sharing Appendix

Use the ideas in this Sharing Appendix to supplement the suggestions given in the **Sharing** section of the actual lesson plans.

Time Frame: 10-15 minutes

OUTLINE

I. **SHARING APPENDIX**
   A. **Purpose of Group Sharing**
   B. **Conducting a Sharing Time**

A. Purpose of Group Sharing

Group sharing was an element of the Lord's ministry with the early disciples. For example, we read in Luke 10:17 that "the seventy returned with joy, saying, 'Lord, even the demons are subject to us in Your name.'" Such spontaneous sharing is the natural result of God's working in the lives of your group members, as He had been doing in the case of the seventy recorded in Luke 10:17.

Early in the book of Acts, we read that interaction between the Christians played just as vital a role as Bible study and prayer. "They were continually devoting themselves to the apostles' teaching and to fellowship, to the breaking of bread and to prayer" (Acts 2:42).

One sign of a healthy, vital group is a quality time of sharing and interaction among the members. This should become a matter of prayer for you as you plan your group time together. You will not be able to force group members into sharing. However, through prayer and the use of proper techniques, God will use you as a catalyst for quality Sharing times. Among the results of a good Sharing time are the following:

A1. Creates a sense of spontaneity
A2. Creates a sense of informality
A3. Creates a sense of freedom to speak out
A4. Creates a sense of freedom to be one's self
A5. Creates a sense that others in the group, especially the leader, care about the group member's personal life
A6. Enables group members to get to know one another better
A7. Enables group members to encourage one another as they share what God has done in their lives
A8. Enables group members to challenge one another to greater things as they share how God has used their lives
A9. Creates a sense of excitement and group momentum

515

I. Sharing Appendix

B. Conducting a Sharing Time

B1. Pre-arranged sharing

Pre-arranged sharing requires that the leader be aware of what is taking place in the lives and ministries of his members. As he learns of things that take place, or of lessons that God has taught someone, he then asks that person to share these things with the group during the next group time together.

B2. Spontaneous sharing

Spontaneous sharing may occur in two ways:

2a. The group naturally becomes involved in a sharing time during the normal course of conversation before the meeting begins. In this case, the leader need not do anything to stimulate sharing, although he may wish to verbalize specific questions to help guide it. Perhaps his biggest problem in this situation will be to turn the setting from sharing to the Bible Study or Prayer time.

2b. The group becomes involved in sharing in response to simple questions posed by the leader. Some examples of questions are:

bl. "What has God been teaching you this past week?"
b2. "What has God been doing in your life this past week?"
b3. "Has anything happened this past week that you would like to share with the group?"
b4. "Does anybody have anything to share?"

B3. Sharing by topics

Ask the members of your group to share about specific areas of their lives. Some examples are:

3a. Their favorite Bible verses and explain why they have become their favorites
3b. How they came to know Christ
3c. Something God has taught them from the Word
3d. Something they've learned from circumstances
3e. Their ministry of evangelism and discipleship
3f. The person who has influenced their life the most (outside their family)
3g. What they want to see when they are 70 years old and look back on their life
3h. What they want to be doing five years and ten years from now
3i. The time when God seemed closest to them
3j. What they would do on a day that was perfect for them

I. Sharing Appendix

B4. Providing the example for sharing

The leader can help stimulate group sharing by becoming a model to the group members. As the leader shares freely from his own life, others will be encouraged to share.

II. Practical Ministry—Vision Appendix

The Vision Appendix is to be used to complement the other two Practical Ministry Appendices (Strategy and Training). See Lessons 11 and 13 for a step-by-step plan to develop the **Practical Ministry** section of your group meeting.

Time Frame: 2-5 minutes

OUTLINE

II. PRACTICAL MINISTRY-VISION APPENDIX
   A. Purpose
   B. Resource Ideas
   C. Vision Passages

A. Purpose

This section is to help you, the leader, instill a sense of momentum into your group. It is to be a brief but exciting, convicting motivation for the Strategy and Training times.

This appendix provides ideas for the group leader in preparing for this time. You should try several kinds of things during the Vision portion of each lesson. You might share current Christian events from various sources and use them as an encouragement. Or you might use a magazine article, highlights of a Scripture passage or some other idea.

It is not necessary to use a Bible passage, since you will have just finished a Bible study. Definitely do not lead another discussion. When you do use a Bible passage, several suggestions have been provided for your use. Be brief. Read the passage, highlight major ideas and draw your conclusion. This is not a sermon, but a motivational introduction to Strategy and Training.

B. Resource Ideas

B1. Example one: Articles

After the Bible study content, you might want your Vision section to involve reading articles about what God is doing around the world. The news sections of *Worldwide Challenge*, *Christianity Today*, *Moody Monthly* (one or more may be available in your library) or *The Church Around the World* (Tyndale Publishers) are good sources. The following are some examples:

II. Vision Appendix

1a. "World events often are just a clue as to what God is doing today. For example:

"'Christian broadcasters to China report a dramatic upsurge in letter responses. Far Eastern Broadcasting Company reported receiving more than fifty-six hundred letters from the People's Republic in its Hong Kong office this year through mid-April. This compares with fifty-eight letters received in all of 1978, and an average of eighteen letters received annually over the past ten years. In previous years it was obvious that the letters had been opened and censored; this year the envelopes are arriving intact. The Christian Broadcasting Association of Hong Kong also reports an upswing. Both groups say that 90 percent or more of the mail is coming from non-Christians.' (from *Christianity Today*, June 8, 1976, p. 61)

"Let's pray for those in China and Russia to see the Great Commission fulfilled in those countries."

1b. "Sometimes God answers prayer in unusual ways. For instance, after sharing a hard life and simple food with Venezuelan villagers during a rural evangelism project, Juan Miguel prayed on the concluding evening, 'Lord, if this project hasn't been enough to make me the quality of Christian you want, do whatever else you need to do.'

"Twenty-four hours later, Juan and two others found themselves in jail, victims of a visa mix-up. But they used their unexpected imprisonment to launch a brief 'jail house ministry.' Held in jail for three days, the three men saw 12 people indicate decisions for Christ." (from *Worldwide Challenge*, June, 1979, p. 4)

"We ask God to use us and He will. We just need to take advantage of the opportunities He gives us. We need to look past our circumstances and see God's hand at work."

1c. You may want to share the impact of this man's life:

Elmer Lappen
A Life of Impact

"When Elmer Lappen was in college, he began to pray that he would see 100 people enter full-time Christian work as a result of his ministry. God answered that prayer overabundantly.

"Lappen died recently at age 55 from a massive heart attack, which followed pneumonia. In his life he influenced more than 400 students and lay people to serve God full time.

II. Vision Appendix

Thousands of people trusted Christ as their Savior and grew in their faith through his 23-year ministry as Campus Crusade for Christ area director for Arizona and campus director at Arizona State University in Tempe. In addition, Lappen trained more than 200 Campus Crusade staff, many of whom serve Christ throughout America and overseas.

"For anyone to have such a fruitful ministry would be notable. For Lappen, it was a special testimony of God's power. He served despite constant pain from rheumatoid arthritis and was confined to a wheelchair after 1965. Lappen's physical struggles, which included learning to walk four times, revealed his strong trust in God. He was also known for his emphasis on memorizing Scripture—during one long hospital stay he learned more than 300 verses.

"Approximately 1,000 people attended a praise and worship service honoring Lappen's faith and ministry at Grace Community Church in Tempe, Arizona. The service emphasized Lappen's commitment to discipleship and evangelism.

"Four men shared testimonies and memories of Lappen's impact on their lives. All four—André Kole, Carl Heath, Don Orvis and Doug Broyles—have developed dynamic ministries of their own—Kole and Broyles as Campus Crusade staff members, Orvis as a seminary professor of evangelism and Heath as a layman. Kole is probably the best known of those Lappen encouraged to enter Christian service. As a traveling representative for Campus Crusade, Kole has used illusions to present the gospel to millions of people in 73 countries.

"At the end of the service, Dr. Bill Bright, founder and president of Campus Crusade, played a short tape of Lappen's testimony. Bright then briefly went through the Four Spiritual Laws (each person was given a booklet with the service's program) and gave an invitation to receive Christ. Bright also asked those who wished to commit themselves to following God's will to stand. Almost everyone present stood.

"Perhaps André Kole best summed up the challenge of Lappen's life: 'I think what God wants each of us to know through the life of Elmer Lappen is this fact: If He could use Elmer Lappen to do what he did—with the limitations and the suffering that he went through—then He can use you and me if we're simply willing to be totally committed to Him.'" (from *Worldwide Challenge*, June, p. 41)

II. Vision Appendix

B2. Example two: Current happenings

Listen for current happenings in your community or campus and share how Christ is changing men.

B3. Example three: "Dreaming dreams"

Another idea is to have a time of "dreaming dreams" for your campus or city. You might pose the question: "What might this campus/ city look like if there were 400 discipleship groups in it?" or "What would this campus/city be like if 10% of the students were witnessing, Spirit-filled believers?"

B4. Example four: Quotations

Quotations are also an excellent way to produce vision and commitment. Share the quotation and then briefly give a motivational conclusion. For example, say: "The man who fails to attempt great things for God for fear of failure has failed already." After sharing a quotation, you can use it as a basis for giving a challenge like this: "Many people today are immobile because of fear. Yet we have the privilege of attempting great things for God and seeing Him use us in great ways. Jesus said in John 14:12, 'Truly, truly, I say to you, he who believes in Me, the works that I do shall he do also; and greater works than these shall he do; because I go to the Father.' Let's be sure that we do not fail by failing to attempt great things for God."

B5. Example five: Tapes and books

Tapes and books are also good resources for quotes. You may want to play a short portion of a tape or read a paragraph from a Christian book or biography you are reading. Missionary biographies are excellent resources.

C. Vision Passages

When using a biblical passage for motivation and vision, you may want to read it if it is a short passage of no more than five or six verses. However, if the story or concept is longer than six verses, you will need to paraphrase the passage and then state the motivating statements you desire to give. In some cases, application questions may help your group members apply the passage to their lives. Remember, the time for this Vision section is five minutes. Anything you do must be done with this time limit in mind. The first two examples below give the process you should use in thinking through a Vision time. The other examples are given to stimulate your own thinking and creativity.

II. Vision Appendix

C1. Example one: Acts 5:14,42

    1a. Example of introduction: "We all would like to see God do great things through us to win others to Christ. Let's look at two verses in Acts 5 that give us an example of what God can do through us."

    1b. Read Acts 5:14

    "Notice that the early church was constantly seeing multitudes won to Christ. We all would like that to happen in our community/campus, and it can. Let's see what they did in order for this to happen."

    1c. Read Acts 5:42

    "What did the early church do to see people won to Christ? Everyday they taught and preached Jesus as the Christ. They went from house to house and they went to the temple—where people were."

    1d. Give a motivational vision statement: "If we are willing to be daily involved in evangelism by saturating our area of influence and going where people are, we too will see multitudes won daily to Christ."

C2. Example two: II Kings 6:15-17

    2a. Example of introduction: "Many times we as Christians fail to see the awesome power of God at work. If we watch the news we may think God is no longer sovereign and that we are hopeless in helping to change the world."

    2b. Read II Kings 6:15-17 and give some brief background information on the passage.

    2c. Give a motivational vision statement: "We do not see or understand all that God is doing today to bring men and nations to Himself. There is a great spiritual battle taking place. We need to pray and ask God to open our eyes as He did for the servant in this passage. Then we need to step out, knowing that God is going before us, and that the gates of hell will not prevail against us."

C3. Example three: Prayer power and miraculous answers (Acts 12:5,7)

    3a. Summarize the story of Peter's imprisonment, how the church prayed fervently for his release, and how the Lord released him from prison.

II. Vision Appendix

3b. Focus of application: "Often when we pray we don't really expect the Lord to answer us, so our prayers become half-hearted. But look at the unlimited abilities the Lord has to answer our prayers according to His will and for His glory. What are some opportunities that you now have to pray and ask the Lord to intervene miraculously? Let's unite our hearts now and continue to be in fervent prayer and expect Him to answer our requests."

C4. Example four: God's ability to do the impossible in saving men (Matthew 19:26)

4a. Summarize Jesus' teaching on how difficult it is for men to be saved (by their own efforts) and how God has the ability to do anything—even save a rich man.

4b. Focus of application: "Consider some people whom you feel are most unlikely to be interested in knowing Christ. Ask the Lord to begin doing the impossible to draw these people to Himself; and if He so chooses, to even use you to be His witness to those people."

C5. Example five: Multiplied impact through our fruit (Matthew 13:23)

5a. Briefly summarize the parable of the sower in terms of the different responses of men (rocky, thorny, no fruit reproduced).

5b. Focus of application: "It could be very discouraging if we only focused on the poor results of the other types of soil as we set out to share our faith. But notice the dynamic impact of the life of the person represented by the good soil. He reproduced himself many times over. Our attitude when sharing our faith should be one of expectancy. We need to pray that the Lord will bring forth fruit from good soil to multiply our witness a hundred times over."

C6. Example six: Confidence in witnessing (Jeremiah 1:4-10)

6a. Summarize the call of Jeremiah.

Jeremiah saw only his youthfulness and lack of ability to speak in relation to his task.

6b. Focus of application: "But God made Jeremiah adequate for the task by creating him with the task in mind. He knew his every weakness and set him apart for a special purpose. God gives us the words to say in order to accomplish the task He created us for in sharing the good news with others. We can go in confidence, knowing that He will provide all that we need."

II. Vision Appendix

C7. Example seven: Vision for involving others in the harvest (Luke 10:1,2,7)

7a. Read the verses.

7b. Focus of application: "God has a plan to reach an area with the gospel. The plan involves many other Christians who are missing the joy of being involved in God's plan to reach our community/campus. Notice that in Luke 10:17 the laborers 'returned with joy.' Let's pray and ask God to raise up other Christians so that they can experience the joy of seeing God use them."

C8. Example eight: Other passages

8a. How God can use all men (Judges 7)

8b. Highlight on man's faith, what men of faith can do (Hebrews 11)

8c. The Great Commission as our task (Luke 24:46-49)

8d. Our goal of becoming like Christ, in seeking and saving the lost (Luke 6:40; 19:10)

8e. Our commitment to Christ in the midst of an evil society (II Timothy 3:1-5)

8f. We can expect God to use the Word of God as we share Christ (Hebrews 4:12)

III. Practical Ministry— Strategy Appendix

This Strategy Appendix contains a chart which you can use to identify your current strategy and decide which strategy and training units would be best for your group each week. See Lessons 11 and 13 for a step-by-step plan to develop the **Practical Ministry** (Vision, Strategy, and Training) section of your group meeting.

Time Frame: 3-5 minutes

OUTLINE

III. PRACTICAL MINISTRY-STRATEGY APPENDIX
A. Purpose
B. Strategy Chart for STUDENT and ADULT Ministries
C. Strategy Explanations

A. Purpose

The Strategy Appendix is meant to help the Discipleship Series leader involve his group in faith stretching, spiritually productive activities.

This section of your lesson plan gives the group its reason for existence. Teaching Bible content should never become an end in itself. This perspective, of course, has far-reaching implications for the leader. The leader must be involved as a life model of the strategy he is seeking to implement.

Choosing the correct strategy at the correct time is very important. If you are in doubt as to which strategy to employ with your group, talk to your Discipleship Group leader or a Campus Crusade for Christ staff member.

To effectively use the three to five minutes you have to discuss strategy, simply review the previous week's progress, successes, pitfalls and needs. Then talk about what will be done in the coming week to implement the strategy.

The leader is not bound to ideas presented here, but is encouraged to use them as potential ideas for an actual strategy he will implement. It is important for the development of the Discipleship Group member that he be involved in these activities in addition to the regular Bible Study time.

III. Strategy Appendix

B. Strategy Chart for STUDENT and ADULT Ministries

The following chart contains *strategies* designed to reach a campus or community. The right-hand column identifies the *training needed* to develop the skills in that strategy. The *training units* will explain steps to take and are found in the Training Appendix. The *audience* column suggests whether the training is designed for the student community, the adult community or either (general). Following the chart is a series of explanations of the particular strategies listed here.

How to Use the Strategy Chart:

1. Before you meet with your group, select the strategy in the left-hand column of the Strategy Chart that pertains to your group's present needs and your goals for the group.

2. Again, if you are unsure which strategy may be most helpful to your group at this point in their development, you may want to consult your Campus Crusade staff (Campus ministry or Here's Life—one ministry can help if the other is not in your area).

3. Once you have determined your strategy, refer to the corresponding far right-hand column, "Training Needed."

4. Look back to the number of its corresponding "Training Unit."

5. Turn to the PRACTICAL MINISTRY-TRAINING APPENDIX and read Point A. Purpose.

   The individual training units are numbered consecutively. Turn to the number of the unit you need for a guide to working out your strategy.

III. Strategy Appendix

Strategy (See following pages for explanations of Strategies a-k)	Audience	Training Unit	Training Needed
a. Basic Evangelism and Follow-up	General	1 2 3 7 8	Basic Evangelism Series (Contained in Discipleship Group Lessons 7,8,9,10) How to Use the Follow-up Booklets Establishing Relationships Using Campus Crusade Tools: Van Dusen Letter and Campus Crusade Magazines Preparing and Sharing a Personal Testimony
b. Helping Your Disciples Find Disciples	General	2 3 4 5	How to Use the Follow-up Booklets Establishing Relationships How to Challenge People to a Discovery Group How to Teach a Discovery Group
c. Sharing the Ministry of the Holy Spirit	General	6	How to Share the Ministry of the Holy Spirit
d. Following up Evangelistic Meetings and Campus Classics	General	11 3 10 4 7	Using the Four Transitional Questions Establishing Relationships Using the Phone to Make Appointments How to Challenge People to a Discovery Group How to Present the Van Dusen Letter
e. Helping Your Disciples to Disciple Others	General	13	Using the Leadership Group Leader's Guides
f. Evangelistic Meetings	Adult	16 17	Using a Home Bible Study as an Evangelistic Outreach Evangelistic Speaking and Entertaining

III. Strategy Appendix

Strategy	Audience	Training Unit	Training Needed
g. Dorm Outreach	Student	7	Using Campus Crusade for Christ Tools: Van Dusen Letter and Campus Crusade Magazines
		10	Using the Phone to Make Appointments
h. Team Meetings	Student	8	Preparing and Sharing a Personal Testimony
		9	How to Emcee a Meeting
		10	Using the Phone to Make Appointments
i. Reaching Student Leaders	Student	14	How to Identify Student Leaders
		10	Using the Phone to Make Appointments
j. Publicizing Events (Josh, College Life, LTC, etc.)	Student	12	How to Publicize Events
k. Recruiting for Conferences	Student	15	How to Recruit for Conferences

III. Strategy Appendix

C. Strategy Explanations

C1. Strategy a. Basic Evangelism and Follow-up (See Training Units 1,2,3,7,8)

This is the foundation of all ministry. It involves the day-to-day exposing, winning, building and sending of others for Christ. It involves Discipleship Group members sharing with and following up their friends, neighbors, classmates, professors, co-workers, etc.

C2. Strategy b. Helping Your Disciples Find Disciples (See Training Units 2,3,4,5)

Soon after the Discipleship Group is formed (sometimes before), the leader must start encouraging and helping the members to begin their own ministries and to find their own disciples. This is multiplication. This strategy is on-going until all the members have their own Discovery Groups.

C3. Strategy c. Sharing the Ministry of the Holy Spirit (See Training Unit 6)

On many campuses, in neighborhoods and in work situations, Discipleship Group members will encounter large numbers of carnal Christians as they share their faith. It becomes crucial, therefore, that the Discipleship Group members become proficient and zealous in communicating the truths of the Spirit-filled life to involve more believers in reaching the world.

C4. Strategy d. Following up Evangelistic Meetings and Campus Classics (See Training Units 11,3,10,4)

One of the greatest ways to win people to Christ and find new disciples is to do a good job of follow-up after mass evangelistic events (College Life, Josh, etc.). Yet sadly, sometimes the ball is dropped. Each Discipleship Group should become proficient in this area especially before such a mass event occurs.

C5. Strategy e. Helping Your Disciples to Disciple Others (See Training Unit 13)

Once your disciples have found those whom they will be training, a great part of the leader's strategy will be to help them do a good job of discipling their people. If they are not encouraged and trained to do so, they will often lose their disciples.

III. Strategy Appendix

C6. Strategy f. Evangelistic Meetings (See Training Units 16,17)

One of the greatest ways to win people and find new disciples is through evangelistic meetings. These easily organized meetings are a proven means of reaching various groups. Minor variations of these meetings make them usable in numerous situations.

C7. Strategy g. Dorm Outreach (See Training Units 7,10)

The organized outreach strategy of the Discipleship Group could be to saturate a dorm and see the maximum number of multiplying disciples raised up out of it. This strategy would take several months (if not all year) to implement.

C8. Strategy h. Team Meetings (See Training Units 8,9,10)

In order to reach various groups, students must become proficient in doing team meetings. Campuses have been turned upside down when many Discipleship Groups have learned how to do a team meeting. Using this strategy, they are able to saturate most of the dorms, clubs, Greek houses and athletic teams with the gospel each year. The team consists of an emcee, one or two people giving their testimonies, and a main speaker.

C9. Strategy i. Reaching Student Leaders (See Training Units 14,10)

Often the most neglected person on the campus in terms of being helped by Christians is the student leader. Other students often are shy around them or hold them in awe. This strategy segment will help accomplish the winning, building, and sending of this strategic segment.

C10. Strategy j. Publicizing Events (See Training Unit 12)

The Discipleship Group should learn how to publicize Classics, College Life, LTC, etc., so that more new people will come and more people can be drawn into the movement and eventually reach the world.

C11. Strategy k. Recruiting for Conferences (See Training Unit 15)

Before a conference, the group should learn how to challenge and recruit others to go to it. Conferences are among the best disciple-building activities. The excitement of spending quality time with motivated students from other campuses, listening to gifted teachers of the Word, discussion groups, singing, sharing together, can tremendously expand their vision and help them realize they are part of a worldwide movement for Jesus Christ.

IV. Practical Ministry—
Training Appendix

This Training Appendix contains 17 training units which you can use to develop the **Training** portion of the **Practical Ministry** section of your Discipleship Group meeting. See Lessons 11 and 13 for a step-by-step plan to develop the entire Practical Ministry (Vision, Strategy and Training) section of your meeting.

Time Frame: 10-15 minutes

OUTLINE

IV. PRACTICAL MINISTRY-TRAINING APPENDIX
A. Purpose
B. Training Units
C. Sample Surveys

A. Purpose

This section is designed to aid the Discipleship Series leader in equipping his group members with a strategy for reaching people for Christ. Training will make your group members more effective servants of the Lord.

A1. There are 17 training units included in this appendix. You have only 10 to 15 minutes in each lesson for training, (with the exception of lessons 7-10) so you may need to spend more than one week on some of the training units.

A2. It is best to arrange the training so that the Discipleship Group can take action on it that week. Units need not be taught consecutively. Use the unit that correlates with your present strategy.

A3. Turn in this section to the particular training unit as indicated on the chart in III. PRACTICAL MINISTRY-STRATEGY APPENDIX.

A4. Use roleplay and two-by-two practice often, particularly when training in conversations and in one-on-one dialogue. (See Lessons 7-9 for good examples.)

A5. Don't be afraid to review training as needed.

A6. Create a climate in which each person feels free to ask questions, so that you will know when information is not clear.

A7. Try to help the members practice their training each week.

IV. Training Appendix

A8.	The Training Appendix is in outline form. You will have to "put the flesh on the bones."

A9.	Your Discipleship Series leader or Campus Crusade staff can help you. Ask them to lend you appropriate resource material. (Student ministries: *Campus Ministry Manual, Sharing the Abundant Life on Campus*; Here's Life Ministries: *Way of Life Discipleship Build Class materials*; Military Ministry: *Sharing the Abundant Life in the Military Community*.)

## B.	Training Units

### B1.	Training Unit 1—Basic Evangelism Series

See Discipleship Group Leader's Guide 7,8,9 and 10 for sample training segments. This will give you the pattern for future segments.

### B2.	Training Unit 2—How to Use the Follow-Up Booklets (Beginning Your New Life Series)

2a.	Make sure each Discipleship Series member has a set of Beginning Your New Life booklets.

Point out the segments of each book, especially those common to all (something to read, Bible passages to look up, questions to answer, places to record the answer, action point, encouragement to join a group and answers to the questions).

Have them look at "Beginning Your New Life!" Explain that this is the booklet they give to people right after they have prayed and received Christ. Point out the Gospel of John within it. Explain that they should encourage the new believer to read the first three chapters of John, and answer as many of the questions in the booklet as he can. This will set the stage for making follow-up appointment 1 (See Lesson 9).

Have Discipleship Group members practice two-by-two, giving the booklet to a new believer, asking him to read it, answering the questions and making the follow-up appointment.

2b.	How to motivate a believer for further involvement

It is one thing to win someone to Christ, but it is another thing to help the new Christian want to continue following Christ.

IV. Training Appendix

After a person indicates that he has received Christ, seek to arrange an appointment within 24 hours to help him grow in Christ. Arrange a specific time and place to meet the new believer.

Give him a "Beginning Your New Life" booklet; encourage him to read the first three chapters of John and to begin answering the questions. Seek to create a desire within the new Christian to see you again by: making the person aware of his need to grow; by relating Christ to an existing need in the person's life and offering to help meet that need; and by using the relationship you establish with the new Christian as a bridge to involve him in the church.

2c. Follow-up Appointment 1

    c1) Relate to group members the following material about conducting the first follow-up appointment:

        Establish rapport when you meet him. Ask him about his week, studies, job, weekend, hobbies, family, fraternity, etc.

        Never ridicule him or laugh at his questions.

        Ask if he read the booklet and had a chance to do any of the questions.

            "Yes"—go over it with him and clarify and answer questions.
            "No"—help him answer the questions (pages 3-6) right there. Don't scold him.

        Cover page 7 verbally even if he has done the answers.

        Point out that one place to find fellowship is by meeting weekly with you to learn how to grow in Christ.

        Explain that you have some great material that has really helped you and you would like to share it with him. Then give him "Beginning Your New Life in Christ." Show him the reading material and the questions and set a time to get together next week to discuss it.

        Express your desire to get to know him better. If appropriate, invite him to College Life or some other Campus Crusade function. Seek to be his friend—he may become your disciple.

IV. Training Appendix

c2) Have two-by-two practice in establishing rapport at a first follow-up appointment. Practice using the booklet in two simulated situations: 1) the new Christian has read the booklet and done the questions and 2) he has not.

2d. Follow-up Appointment 2

d1) Each week you can proceed with training in booklets 2-5 as you did for the first booklet. However, you do not *have* to conduct training on every booklet, since the formats are similar. Be sure the members understand how to use them. You should go with them on some of their follow-up appointments.

d2) Encourage the group members to be sensitive to a new Christian and not to be locked into concentrating on content.

d3) Be sensitive about when to challenge a new Christian to a Discovery Group.

B3. Training Unit 3—Establishing Relationships

3a. This material will help your members learn how to build a relationship with a person whom they are following-up or just seeking to get to know. Much of this material lends itself to roleplay and demonstration. You could have some fun by demonstrating the "wrong" ways to do something, and then have them do it the right way.

There are many suggestions here, so it would be a good idea to have them take notes, or to duplicate this as a hand-out after you have covered it verbally.

Remember, you don't have to cover it in one lesson.

3b. How to relate to the individual with whom you are sharing Christ. (Many of these thoughts apply to any witnessing situation, but in particular they apply to sharing by appointment or in an informal get-together.)

b1) Remember that nearly everyone responds to love. Be casual, friendly and warm, yet speak with confidence. Share, do not preach. Be yourself, and others will be themselves too. Represent Jesus Christ in the power of the Spirit (I Corinthians 2:4,5).

IV. Training Appendix

b2) Dress according to the styles of the students or adults with whom you work.

b3) Use a breath freshener.

b4) Learn to use the vocabulary that is familiar to the students or adults with whom you work, but do not overdo it.

b5) Select an appointment location that is well-known and convenient to reach, yet provides some privacy, if possible.

b6) Meet over a cup of coffee or soft drink to establish a casual atmosphere.

b7) Repeat the person's name and learn to pronounce it correctly when introduced.

b8) Spend a few minutes in getting acquainted with the person to whom you are witnessing, before you share the gospel.

b9) Maintain a good sense of humor.

b10) Listen carefully to the person with whom you are sharing your faith so that you can make specific applications for him in your presentation of the Four Spiritual Laws. Take hints from the things he says.

B4. Training Unit 4—How to Challenge People to a Discovery Group

4a. It really is not difficult to challenge someone to a Discovery Group. As the leader of your Discipleship Group, you can communicate some of your own personal insights and experiences of challenging people to your Discovery Group. Allow a great deal of discussion in this training time since members are apt to have many fears and questions when they think seriously about starting their own groups.

4b. Start this training by asking what things the Discipleship Group members think are important when challenging someone to a Discovery Group. Then share some of your own insights and experiences. Finally, the following material summarizes some important points in the challenge. Have a roleplay and then a two-by-two practice of this material.

b1) Tell them that the group will provide:

—An opportunity to examine further the claims of Christ

IV. Training Appendix

—Interaction with others who are interested in Jesus Christ

—Information on how to experience the abundant life

—An opportunity for fellowship and Bible study

b2) Tell them that, in order for the group to function properly, requirements for each member would be:

—To be faithful in attendance

—To actively participate, realizing that each person is considered a real and important part of the group and that what each one has to share is important

—To be understanding toward each person in the group. They should recognize that another person's needs, reactions and comments may be very different from their own

—To prepare any lessons that are assigned

b3) Finally, tell them the time and place for the first Discovery Group. Don't give them their study guides until the first session. However, you may show it to them to give them an idea of the material you will be covering.

B5. Training Unit 5—How to Teach a Discovery Group

Refer to the Discovery Group Leader's Guide of the Discipleship Series.

B6. Training Unit 6—How to Share the Ministry of the Holy Spirit

6a. There is a great deal of material here. You should be selective in communicating it. Probably you could spend at least three training lessons on the ministry of the Holy Spirit. You might use one or more lessons on the use of the Holy Spirit Booklet and then use other lessons to cover the materials suggested in points 6e. and 6f. of this section. This will help your group members to understand their own Spirit-filled walk as well as communicate it better to others.

This truth is the foundation of victorious Christian living. Your group members *must* master it. Use appropriate demonstration and roleplay in training your group.

6b. The booklet entitled, "Have You Made the Wonderful Discovery of the Spirit-filled Life?" can be used to share the ministry of the Holy Spirit in the life of the believer. The booklet is written

IV. Training Appendix

in such a way that it can be used by anyone who has under-stood and applied this teaching in his personal life. It is com-pletely effective, even when simply read from beginning to end.

In essence, the Holy Spirit booklet contains the basic principles from three of Dr. Bill Bright's main lectures, which are: "The Cleansed Life," "The Spirit-filled Life," and "Walking in the Spirit."

6c. Have your group members follow this procedure when using the booklet:

    c1) After sharing the Four Spiritual Laws, if a person indicates that his life is represented by the circle with Christ on the throne:

        First of all, say, "That's great! Tell me about it. When did you ask Christ to come into your life?" This will give him an opportunity to share his testimony and will give you an opportunity to make sure that he understands what is involved in receiving Christ as Savior and Lord.

        If you are convinced that he does know Christ personally and does not have assurance of his salvation, you can say, "There is a third circle . . ." Basically, this brief statement is the only transition you need in order to move quickly and smoothly from the Four Spiritual Laws into the presenta-tion of the ministry of the Holy Spirit.

    c2) If you are talking to someone whom you know to be a Christian, you can introduce the Holy Spirit booklet by say-ing one of the following:

        "Have you made the wonderful discovery of the Spirit-filled Life?"

        "I have a booklet that really makes sense in telling how to live the abundant Christian life. I would like to share it with you."

        "I have finally found how it is possible to live the Christian life without being on a spiritual roller coaster."

        God will give you other ways to introduce the booklet and share it with your friends. However, keep your introduction simple and direct so that you do not waste time talking around the subject. Get down to the heart of the message.

IV. Training Appendix

If there is any area of doubt in your mind concerning the person's relationship with Christ, always be sure to share the Four Spiritual Laws before introducing the Holy Spirit booklet.

You may wish to include the Holy Spirit portion of your training testimony. Share how you learned to be filled with the Holy Spirit and the change it has made in your life.

6d. Be sure to use the Holy Spirit booklet correctly.

    d1) Each time you share the booklet, make sure you ask the question indicated in the booklet and give the person the opportunity to pray the prayer and make this commitment in his own life. As you share, you do not need to share it word-for-word. You may share it "thought-for-thought," but if so, be sure you share applications from your own life.

    d2) Each time you share the Holy Spirit booklet, make sure you also explain the section on "How to Know That You Are Filled With the Holy Spirit" and the principle of spiritual breathing.

    d3) Where time is a factor, you can share the principles of the Spirit-filled life in the booklet without reading all the scriptural references. Simply call his attention to the references with the suggestion that he look them up and read them at a later time.

    d4) When you talk about confession of sin under point 4 of the booklet, you can suggest the helpful idea of making a written list of everything in his life which he knows to be displeasing to God, writing I John 1:9 across the list, claiming its promise by faith, and then destroying the list.

6e. Show the group members how to use and master concepts 2,3 and 4 of the Transferable Concepts. Follow the plan suggested in the study guide in each booklet.

6f. Call attention to and instruct people to use the booklet, "Beginning Your New Life in the Spirit."

IV. Training Appendix

B7. Training Unit 7—Using Campus Crusade for Christ Tools: Van Dusen Letter and Campus Crusade magazines

7a. How to use Campus Crusade magazines as evangelistic tools.

Collegiate Challenge and *Athletes in Action* magazines are colorful publications designed exclusively to communicate the claims of Jesus Christ and the dynamics of knowing Him in a personal way to the non-Christian on the secular college and university campus. Because of the universal interest in collegiate life existing in the hearts of both young and old, these magazines have a wide, strong appeal to people of all ages from every walk of life.

Businessmen share them with their clients. Homemakers share them with their neighbors, and students distribute them among their fellow students.

Strategically placed in the hands of non-Christians, the magazines can be used as extremely effective evangelistic tools in sharing with them the wonderful discovery of knowing Christ personally. They can be used as evangelistic tools in the following ways:

a1) Give a magazine to someone you know. Ask him to read either the entire publication or a particular article. Using the four simple questions below, move quickly and inoffensively into a personal presentation of the Four Spiritual Laws, giving the person an opportunity to pray and receive Christ.

Ask four questions:

"What did you think of the publication (or article)?"

"Did it make sense to you?"

"Have you made the wonderful discovery of knowing Christ personally?"

"You would like to, wouldn't you?"

Continue with the Four Laws presentation, giving the person an opportunity to pray and receive Christ. Leave copies with those who are especially interested.

IV. Training Appendix

a2) Approach individuals at random. Ask them if they would take a few minutes to read an article, or part of one, and give you their opinion; or make an appointment for the next day.

a3) Use the editions which contain the Four Spiritual Laws. Ask a person to glance through the publication. Then turn specifically to the Four Spiritual Laws and ask if he has ever read through them.

a4) Use these publications in contacting individuals after evangelistic meetings and campus classics, especially when the speaker has written a feature article.

a5) Be familiar with the articles before you try to share the publication.

a6) Approach coaches, athletes, and sports-minded people with *Athletes in Action*. Give them the magazine and set up an appointment for the next day to present the Four Spiritual Laws.

a7) Use the *Collegiate Challenge* with administrators or professors as an introduction to Campus Crusade for Christ.

7b. How to Present the Van Dusen Letter

The Van Dusen letter was written by Dr. Bill Bright to a prominent businessman who had requested information on how he could become a Christian. (The name Dr. Van Dusen is fictitious.) Millions of copies of this letter have been distributed around the world in most of the major languages. It is estimated that thousands, including some who later joined our staff, have become Christians as a result of reading this letter.

In essence, the Van Dusen letter contains an amplified presentation of the Four Spiritual Laws that communicates effectively to non-Christians.

b1) Use the Van Dusen letter prior to sharing the Four Spiritual Laws.

You can leave a Van Dusen letter with a person by saying, "Here is a letter that really makes sense to me. I would like you to read it, and the next time we get together I would like to know what you think of it."

The next time you see that person, you can ask four simple and direct questions that will give you an opportunity to

IV. Training Appendix

speak specifically about the claims of Christ and give him an opportunity to respond. The four questions are:

"What did you think of the letter?"

"Did it make sense to you?"

"Have you made the wonderful discovery of knowing Jesus Christ personally?"

"You would like to, wouldn't you?"

If the person is ready to accept Christ right then, pray with him. If he is not ready, say, "You probably noticed as you read the letter that God actually set down laws, spiritual laws, governing our relationship to Him. Let me review these spiritual laws with you . . . ." (Continue with the basic presentation of the Four Spiritual Laws.)

b2) Use the Van Dusen letter for random contacts on campus, in a dorm, with clerks in a store, with people you meet during the day, while at work, studying in the library, at leisure or traveling; as time permits, ask someone to read the letter right away and then ask the same four questions as above. These transitions may be used as you give him the letter:

"I would like you to read this letter. It will take only 10 or 15 minutes." (Give the background of the letter as explained here.)

"Hello, my name is ____ and I'm working with one of the Christian groups here on campus, Campus Crusade for Christ. Have you ever heard of Campus Crusade? One of the things we are doing is trying to get the reactions of as many students as possible to the contents of this letter. (Show the Van Dusen letter.) This is an actual letter that was written to a man who was interested in knowing how to experience a vital relationship with Jesus Christ. Would you be willing to take a few minutes to read this and give me your opinion? (Most students are interested in reading the letter, and many will receive Christ as a result. If he is not interested, politely thank him and move on to someone who is ready.)

"Most people are interested in learning how they can know God personally. This letter has helped thousands of people to make this great discovery. I would like to have you read it and tell me what you think of it."

IV. Training Appendix

Ask the new Christian to share the letter with some of his friends or relatives. This sample letter can be written out by hand on personalized stationery and sent to any number of friends, relatives and acquaintances.

B8. Training Unit 8—Preparing and Sharing a Personal Testimony

8a. How to prepare a personal testimony

Any subject matter can be presented more effectively by careful organization. A carefully prepared testimony, given in the power of the Holy Spirit, can be of immediate and effective use in nearly every witnessing situation. It should be our desire to present Christ in such a clear and attractive, yet simple way that those who hear will not only want to know Him, but they will also know how to know Him personally.

A carefully and intelligently worded three-minute testimony will communicate far more effectively than a prolonged one that includes a lot of extraneous material which will distract from, rather than emphasize, the point of personal commitment to Christ and what this can mean in a person's life.

a1) Remember, the same Christ lives in you, whether you trusted Him early or later in life. Do not be concerned whether or not your testimony will be exciting--just that it be interesting.

a2) Be realistic. Do not infer that Christ eliminates all the problems of life, but rather that He enables you to live them out with peace and confidence. "I am with you always," He said.

a3) Be positive, not negative, from start to finish.

Prepare your testimony so that you can share it in a group situation as well as with an individual.

a4) Avoid the following when writing your testimony:

Including statements which reflect negatively on the church and other organizations or people.

Mentioning denominations, especially in a derogatory way.

Preaching at people. This is a testimony, not a "preachimony."

IV. Training Appendix

Using stereotypes. People who work together for a period of time on a team tend unwittingly to copy one another.

Speaking in generalities or using overworked terms such as: straight-laced, sober and sad; fantastic, exciting and great; peace, purpose and happiness; or changed (without giving specific changes).

Using words that are meaningless to non-Christians. Terms like "salvation," "saved," "born again," and "conversion," need to be defined if used. Terms like "glorious" and "hallelujah" are so ridiculed in some areas that you would do well not to use them at all.

a5) Ask the Lord to give you wisdom and guidance as you write (James 1:5,6).

a6) Follow a three-point outline:

Life *before* knowing Christ

How you came to know Christ (be specific)

Life *after* you received Christ (changes He has made, what He means to you now)

a7) Emphasize the last point above if you became a Christian as a small child.

a8) Begin with an interesting, attention-getting sentence and close with a good conclusion. Include relevant, thought-provoking, personal experiences.

a9) Write in such a way that others will feel associated with you in the past and present experiences.

a10) Give enough details to arouse interest.

a11) Use at least one, but at the most two, Scripture verses.

a12) Edit carefully and rewrite as necessary before final draft.

a13) Student Ministries: Note sample testimonies in the *Collegiate Challenge* magazine. Here's Life Ministries: Note sample testimonies in *Worldwide Challenge* magazine.

a14) Choose something characteristic of your experience that is of general interest to non-Christians. Build your own testimony around a theme. Examples: personal success (your

IV. Training Appendix

own past viewpoint), life's goals (past and present viewpoint), God's personal plan for you.

a15) Emphasize the fact that the thing that made the difference in your life was accepting Christ as Savior and allowing Him to be Lord and Master of your life. Keep in mind that your testimony should give enough details so that someone else would know how to trust the Lord after hearing it. Tell how He entered your life.

8b. How to share your testimony

b1) Memorize your testimony and practice it until it becomes natural.

b2) Share your testimony with loving enthusiasm in the power of the Holy Spirit (Ephesians 5:18).

b3) Smile often! Ask the Lord to give you a happy, radiant countenance. Use a natural speaking voice.

b4) Avoid exhibiting nervous habits (especially with your hands) and other mannerisms, such as rubbing your nose, jingling coins in your pocket, swaying, clearing your throat, and using "uh's" and "ah's." Exhibit good posture. Do not talk on the way to or from your seat.

b5) Avoid arguing and using other high pressure methods to obtain a "decision" for Christ. Remember, men are born of the Spirit, "not through persuasiveness or logic of men."

8c. Help group members prepare a testimony

c1) Discuss how to prepare a testimony with them.

c2) Testimonies should be written out, checked and returned with constructive criticism. Also, each member should give his testimony verbally to the Discipleship Group leader, exactly as he would give it in a real situation.

c3) Most people need help in writing a good testimony. The leader may find he has to devote most of two lessons, maybe three, to this task before the testimony is written well enough to begin memorizing.

c4) A good way to begin is for the Discipleship Group leader to take down on paper the key thoughts as the group member relates his experiences. Encourage him to talk until his best

IV. Training Appendix

ideas begin to come. Every man who has found Christ has elements in his story which are genuinely interesting and appealing. Your job is to locate those points and then to capture them on paper so that they will not be lost.

c5) As you are listening, when a group member uses a particularly good phrase or an expression that catches the ear, jot it down immediately. The fact that the idea is his and not yours makes it doubly valuable. Be sure he remembers it and uses it. Do the same when he tells of an unusually interesting experience. Help him to find and to recognize his best thoughts.

c6) Women are usually better than men at describing feelings in an ear-appealing manner; with caution, encourage them to do so. Men are best when they talk in terms of action experiences, so give them assistance in expressing their feelings.

c7) Every team member should understand that a testimony prepared for a non-Christian audience always remains the same and should be memorized. In giving testimonies to different groups (all Christians, etc.), a stronger emphasis in one way or another might be made. As a person matures in Christ, his "after" experience might be made more current, or he might even revise his testimony, though the basics will always remain the same.

c8) Testimonies should not be over three minutes or, if really outstanding, not over five minutes. The leader should insist on strict adherence to the time schedule.

B9. Training Unit 9—How to Emcee a Meeting (Student Ministries)

9a. Introduction by Emcee (This presentation should be memorized by your group members verbatim)

"It's good to be here tonight. As your president mentioned, we are working with a student Christian movement on campus called Campus Crusade for Christ. We have been speaking in fraternities, sororities, dorms and to athletic teams all over campus, challenging students to investigate the claims of Christ. I want to set your mind at ease. We are not here to talk about any particular church or religion. We think that if a person wants to consider himself intellectually well-rounded, he at least owes it to himself to consider the claims of Jesus of Nazareth, whether he is Protestant, Catholic or Jewish in background. Campus Crusade for Christ was begun in 1951 on the

IV. Training Appendix

UCLA campus by a young businessman by the name of Bill Bright. Since then, the movement has spread to over 200 major campuses in this country and into more than 100 foreign countries.

"I think that Arnold Toynbee made a very valid statement when he said that most people have not rejected Christianity but a caricature of it—a bad picture. Most students have had some kind of religious background, but they junked it when they came to college because of hypocrites that they had seen or for some other reason."

(At this point you may want to insert a joke but be sure that it suits the personality of the speaker. If you are not a good joke-teller, proceed to the testimony.)

9b. Introduction of Testimonies

"On the college campus today students are not interested in a hypothetical philosophy. They are looking for something that works in their everyday experience. Every time we speak we like to have a couple of students share briefly about what this personal relationship with Christ has meant in their own lives. First, I would like to introduce _____ (name, class, major, home town, etc.)."

B10. Training Unit 10—Using the Phone to Make Appointments (Student Ministries)

10a. This section is designed to help Discipleship Series members to make follow-up phone calls after evangelistic meetings (team, college life, classics, etc.) and to make appointments with specialized groups.

10b. Calling for an appointment (with little or no previous contact except possibly by letter)

(This approach can be followed in contacting presidents of fraternities, sororities, dormitories or other groups for purposes of arranging evangelistic meetings as well as contacting individuals for personal interviews.)

"Hello, Jim? My name is _____. I am a (year in school) associated with Campus Crusade for Christ here at _____ University. I am meeting with a number of student leaders here on campus to explain to them the program and purpose of Campus Crusade and how it relates to them as student leaders. I wonder if you have time tomorrow or the next day when we could get together for a few minutes."

IV. Training Appendix

(If no other time is available, ask for a luncheon date. Be sure to pay the check for both of you. Be sure to have a clear understanding of the time and place to meet.)

You may also vary this initial conversation to make Collegiate Survey or Student Leadership Survey appointments, especially if individuals have signed up for a survey at registration or have received a letter from Campus Crusade about being surveyed.

"Hello, Jim. My name is _____. I am associated with Campus Crusade for Christ here at _____ University. I am involved in taking the National Collegiate Religious Survey which we take on over 200 campuses in the U.S. I know you (received a letter about this, signed up for this at registrations, etc.) and wanted to find a time when we could get together for 30 minutes.

"The survey is designed to get your reaction to about 20 questions and to a small booklet called the Four Spiritual Laws. When would be a good time?" (You may delete the section on the Four Laws when calling student leaders.)

10c. Calling for an appointment after an evangelistic meeting (team meeting, College Life, classic, etc.)

"Hello, Sally. My name is _____. I'm a (year in school) involved in Campus Crusade for Christ here at _____. We spoke tonight in your (house, dorm, etc.). (If you spoke in the meeting, point that out.)

"We're trying to get together personally for a few minutes with those who were there to answer any questions they might have, and to give them the information we promised. Could we get together and talk tomorrow or the next day for about 20 minutes? When would be a good time?"

B11. Training Unit 11—Using the Four Transitional Questions (See Training Unit 7, "Using Campus Crusade for Christ Tools.")

B12. Training Unit 12—How to Publicize Events (Student Ministries)
12a. Even though this material is centered on recruiting for College Life (a regularly scheduled evangelistic meeting), the same strategy and training is used in publicizing other events like Classics and, with modifications, LTC.

IV. Training Appendix

12b. Publicize College Life

b1) Word-of-mouth publicity is crucial. Students will seldom come as a result of other forms of publicity without receiving a personal, verbal invitation to come.

Be enthusiastic when inviting students to College Life. (Enthusiasm is from the Greek word "*en theos*" and means "God in one.") Tell them about the movement, and also show your interest in them as persons. Tell them you will pick them up; tell them that the meeting lasts an hour. (On commuter campuses it lasts only 50 minutes. Assure them that they'll have time to make it to their next class.)

Promote College Life when talking to Christian friends.

b2) Encourage the College Life committee to brainstorm on how to promote attendance.

B13. Training Unit 13—Using the Leadership Group Leader's Guides

This training should be used as your Discipleship Series members are starting their own groups. Show them how you teach and lead, using the section in the Leader's Guide entitled "Leading your Group."

B14. Training Unit 14—How to Identify Student Leaders (Student Ministries)

This is a very simple list of suggestions that your group members can use to find out who the leaders are on your campus.

14a. Make a list of which student groups on campus influence the rest of the student body the most, (athletes, Greeks, politicians, etc.).

14b. Find the names and phone numbers of these individuals from the Student Activities Office.

14c. Develop a "Five Most Wanted List" for which you can pray and believe God to reach.

14d. Read the school newspaper and note who are the student body officers, club officers and influencers on campus.

14e. Read the yearbook to see who the leaders were last year (they are probably still around).

IV. Training Appendix

14f. Identify the leaders in your living unit.

14g. Identify those students in your honorary societies, academic and otherwise.

14h. Get a roster of "Who's Who in American Colleges and Universities" for your campus.

B15. Training Unit 15—How to Recruit for Conferences (Student Ministries)

15a. These suggestions will help your Discipleship Series members to get other students to come to conferences.

a1) Distribute the brochures at least a month before the conference.

Give supplies of these brochures to the action groups on campus so that they, in turn, can distribute them.

Give brochures to students on your campus who are interested, but not active in the program.

Obtain a mailing list of Campus Crusade student leaders on other campuses and mail brochures to them.

Send brochures to students on campuses where Campus Crusade is not active.

Distribute in collegiate groups at churches.

a2) Announce the conference at all get-togethers.

a3) Have teams of students "hustle out" Christians from surrounding campuses where there is no ministry.

a4) Publicize with skits at College Life. Advertise in campus paper.

a5) Encourage students to personally invite others.

a6) Organize a calling committee to call students at random—especially international students.

a7) Use direct mail approach to invite hundreds or thousands of students who have never come to any Campus Crusade for Christ meetings, as well as those who have previously attended meetings.

a8) Keep a file on publicity ideas.

15b. Here is a sample statement that you might use in recruiting other students:

"Jeff, I've got something exciting to tell you. In three weeks there's going to be a conference for college students who want to learn more about Christ and the Bible.

"I'm going because these things have changed my life. There will be 150 students there from all over (name of state) from schools like (name other schools). It is so exciting to be there with so many other committed students.

"I'd sure like you to come with me. I think you'd really like it. Can you come?"

(At this point, he will probably ask you about cost, length of time, speaker, location, etc. You can give him this information from the brochure. Then give him the brochure.)

"Jeff, if you need a day or two to think about it, that's great. Tell you what—I'll call you day after tomorrow to see if you can go, Okay? I think you'd love it and you'd meet some great people. I'll even drive you there if you'd like.

"Talk to you in a couple of days."

B16. Training Unit 16—Using the Home Bible Study as an Evangelistic Outreach

The use of an Evangelistic Home Bible Study outreach allows the leader to reach those who are interested in learning more about Christ, but who have not yet invited Him into their lives. Groups can be formed among neighbors, relatives and friends, co-workers, and other groups.

The Evangelistic Home Bible Study curriculum is most useful if the majority of those present are non-Christians (80% or more). If the percentage of non-Christians is lower, the first six lessons of the discipleship curriculum will serve the purpose of having people become Christians in an environment of movement and sharing.

16a. Overall format

a1) Prayer

a2) Sharing (watch the time)

IV. Training Appendix

a3) Bible study

16b. Bible study format

b1) Preview ("Here's what we're going to study.")

b2) View (Doing the study together)

It would be best not to give homework assignments—everyone should do the work together.

Leave booklets with the leader. (No one can forget the booklet or work ahead of the group.)

b3) Review ("Here's what God taught us.").

16c. Planning for the Evangelistic Home Bible Study

c1) Selecting the best schedule

The duration of the Bible study should be six to eight weeks.

The class should meet once a week for one-and-a-half to two hours.

The make-up of the group will determine the time of day it meets. For example, women may want to meet in the morning, while men may want to meet for an early-morning breakfast.

A mixed group will probably meet in the evening around 7 or 7:30 p.m.

c2) Select the best location. The non-Christian will generally be more inclined to attend the Bible study if it is held in a home rather than in a church.

c3) Host and/or hostess reponsibilities

The couple in whose home the Bible study is meeting should serve as host and hostess each week. There are certain duties for which they are solely responsible:

Prepare the facilities for the Bible study.

Greet people as they arrive, introduce them to each other.

IV. Training Appendix

Make the guests feel at home.

At the first session, give some opening remarks and introduce the leader.

Be available to prevent or eliminate distractions.

Secure, prepare and serve refreshments after the Bible study hour. Keep the refreshments simple.

c4) Curriculum

Use the Introductory Step to the "Ten Basic Steps" as the beginning study material for the Bible study. It is designed primarily for the non-Christian, since it helps him to understand the Bible, presents the claims and the person of Jesus Christ and shows him clearly how to become a Christian and how to live the Christian life.

16d. Inviting individuals to the Bible study

d1) Personal—most effective. Make home visits for friends, neighbors and relatives and appointments (lunch or office) for businessmen.

d2) Telephone call. Use this as a last resort to invite a person, or use the phone call as a reminder to those you have invited personally.

d3) Written or printed invitations. Handwritten invitations should be neat, well-written and precise. Printed invitations are generally not suitable for a beginning Bible study, but may be used as growth strategy for an established Bible study.

d4) Sample conversation

"We are beginning an informal Bible study in our home, using this booklet (show them the Introductory Step). We will be meeting from 7 to 9 p.m. on Tuesdays for eight weeks, and we would love to have you join us.

"You may feel as I used to—that I could never profit from studying the Bible, because it is such a big book and so hard to understand. However, I've learned that when a group of friends study together, it's a lot easier and a great deal of fun.

IV. Training Appendix

"The other people who will be joining us for this study are (give names). We are all beginners and will start with the basics.

"I know you will enjoy it. Will you be able to join us?"

16e. Conducting the Bible study

e1) The first session—the following is a suggested schedule:

Host and hostess greet and introduce guests, then serve refreshments. This is the only session where refreshments would be served at the beginning. Guests may continue enjoying their refreshments during the "get acquainted" time to follow.

Host gives opening remarks and introduces leader. The leader should then take charge, opening in prayer. Keep it brief and not too "religious sounding." Call on appropriate members of the group from time to time to give the opening and closing prayers. Be careful not to embarrass anyone who is shy or too spiritually immature.

Get acquainted with each other—if the group is not too large, have each person give his name and other pertinent facts about himself pertaining to family, jobs, hobbies, etc.

Get acquainted with the purpose of the class. (This is extremely important.) Share with the group that the purpose of the class is to study the Bible to find out what it has to say about Jesus Christ and Christianity. Explain that you will study the Bible as the Word of God. Explain that your purpose is not to question the Bible or argue whether or not it is true, but that the purpose is to study it for content.

Get acquainted with the study material. Preview the book and assign reading only (no workbook assignments although the book can be taken home for this). Assign reading of the article, "Uniqueness of Jesus" in the introduction booklet.

Briefly acquaint the students with the Bible—New Testament, Old Testament, book and chapters and Table of Contents.

Close in prayer. (Leader leads in a short prayer.)

IV. Training Appendix

e2) Second meeting of the Bible study group

Walk through the article on the "Uniqueness of Jesus" with the group in order to insure understanding of the content.

Do the questions and answers in the lesson workbook in the class. Proceed with the questions in sequence but do not try to adhere to a rigid schedule. The most important thing is to meet needs, not follow a schedule. Do one to three workbook questions at a time and allow time for each member in the class to read the questions and the Scripture relating to the questions and to write their answers.

Discuss the questions after the class members have written out their answers. Spread the discussion around so that individuals who need to be developed are called on. Nothing kills the potential of an informal Bible study like a few people dominating the discussion by displaying their knowledge while the rest are spectators. Have the individual give his answer to the question and then an explanation of the answer. Continue to call on others regarding the same question until an adequate answer is received. Then move on to the next question.

Be ready at the conclusion of the meeting to review the class' progress with summary comments.

e3) At the third or fourth Bible study session:

Have a trained Christian give his three-minute, prepared testimony on how he came to know Christ, and go through the Four Spiritual Laws. Give an introduction to establish rapport. Have him share his personal testimony of how he came to know Christ. Have him share two practical illustrations—ways in which God has specifically worked in his everyday life—and make a transition into the Four Spiritual Laws. He should give a Four Laws booklet to each person, using the following sample transition:

"I would like to give each of you a booklet that has been very helpful to me. I would like to go over the contents of it for two reasons: One, you may know what you believe, but do not know how to share what you believe with others; or two, perhaps some of you are wondering how you can have a personal relationship with God."

Have him read the booklet as guests follow along in their booklets, giving them an opportunity to pray by reading through the suggested prayer. He should read the question

IV. Training Appendix

and statement immediately following the prayer in the booklet. Have him invite the audience to pray silently with him as he reads the prayer aloud again, phrase-by-phrase, if they have never before invited Christ into their lives.

He may use this sample invitation to pray if they desire:

"For many of you, this prayer will express the desire of your heart. Let me suggest, if you are not sure that Christ is in your life, that we pray this silently as I pray aloud. Let's pray." (Then he should pray a sentence at a time, pausing for them to follow.)

Have him share the rest of the booklet. Have him give a blank three-by-five card to everyone and use this sample closing remark:

"I'm asking you to do one more thing for me. Please write three bits of information: Your name and address; any comments you have about this talk—was it helpful? Could it be improved?; put an "X" by your name if you prayed today for the first time and invited Jesus Christ into your life.

Repeat this information two or more times. Have them fold the cards and leave them in a convenient location which you identify. Initiate a conversational atmosphere to avoid an awkward silence.

Talk with individuals after the talk. Ask Christian friends beforehand to converse with visitors. They may open the conversation by saying:

"What did you think of the talk?"

"Did it make sense?"

"Have you made the wonderful discovery of knowing Jesus Christ personally?"

"Did you pray today?"

Make a follow-up appointment with those who respond.

IV. Training Appendix

e4) General operating principles to follow in subsequent meetings of the Bible study group

4a) At the beginning of each lesson, preview what the class will be learning in that section.

4b) At the conclusion of each Bible study meeting, review the group's progress in the current lesson.

4c) At the conclusion of each lesson, review the progress of the group.

4d) Remember, no assignments are given unless it is simply to read an article in the study.

4e) All written work in the books is to be done by the group as a whole in the meeting time. This stops people from dropping out because they have not done their homework.

4f) As a general practice, it is best that they purchase their own study booklet.

4g) As a general practice, it is not desireable that sessions last longer than an hour-and-a-half or two hours.

4h) Use good "guided discussion" techniques.

"Guided discussion" (preview-view-review) differs from "lecture" and "question-answer."

The lecture method: particularly adapted to larger audiences and involving an imparting of the speaker's conclusions to the audience.

The question/answer method: based entirely on the teacher or speaker asking questions and getting answers back from the group.

The guided discussion (preview-view-review): involves teaching people in such a way that the method of teaching is easily grasped by those being taught with the result that they will be able to teach others in the same manner.

4i) Prepare physical arrangements.

Regulate the size of the group with probably no less than three members and no more than 15.

IV. Training Appendix

Arrange the chairs or seating in such a way that the participants are facing each other, either in a circle or around a table.

Although you are the leader, be part of the group. Keep an informal and relaxed atmosphere.

4j) Keep the discussion going.

Speak as little as possible while leading the discussion.

Draw each member of the group into the discussion. Watch the expression on the participant's face, and observe the reactions to ascertain the feelings of each individual. Use this knowledge to draw them into active participation.

Avoid getting off on irrelevant tangents. Recover quickly from tangents by restating the original question.

Control the involvement of participants so that no one dominates the interaction. Ask the dominant individual privately to help get others involved in active participation. Request non-participants to state their opinions as well.

Respond in love if an individual reaches a wrong conclusion.

4k) Encourage the participants to make applications.

Ask, "How can this be applied to us?"

Ask, "Does this have any bearing on us?"

At the end of the discussion, request the participant to apply the conclusions arrived at prior to the next meeting.

Begin the next meeting with the question, "How were you able to apply what we discovered last time?"

4l) Have "loaner" Bibles, spare pencils and some study booklets available at every session.

e5) What to do when the initial six to eight week period is completed.

Encourage everyone, whether they have received Christ or not, to join a Discovery Group.

B17. Training Unit 17—Evangelistic Speaking and Entertaining (Here's Life Ministries)

If you have learned how to present your personal testimony and you know how to share the Four Spiritual Laws booklet, you are ready to speak and entertain evangelistically.

This unit will equip you to share in both informal and formal situations in such a way that people listening will clearly understand how to receive Christ and have an opportunity to do so. Let's look at each aspect of an evangelistic party:

17a. Format:

a1) Start with refreshments or meal and casual conversation.

a2) Introduction of speaker by host

a3) Speaker's opening remarks

a4) Speaker's testimony and illustration

a5) Transition to Four Spiritual Laws

a6) Four Spiritual Laws presentation, including invitation to pray and filling out comment cards

a7) Casual conversation and refreshments

17b. Invitations

b1) At an informal gathering in a home, always invite three times as many guests as you desire to have attend.

b2) People can be invited from numerous areas:

Neighbors and friends

Members of clubs

Co-workers

Business associates

IV. Training Appendix

b3) Use written invitations.

b4) Follow up the invitations with a personal phone call.

b5) Gatherings should be scheduled at times convenient to your target audience.

Example:

Mornings for housewives

Evenings for couples and professional people

Breakfasts for businessmen

17c. Introduction of the speakers by the host

c1) Give the speaker's name.

c2) Give a brief background of the speaker (provided by the speaker ahead of time.)

c3) Mention the topic.

Example: "Bill Bright will be sharing the reality of Christianity in a businessman's world."

The speaker would provide the topic title such as: "The Reality of Christianity in a Businessman's World."

The speaker would provide the topic title such as: "The Reality of Christianity in a Woman's World," "Coping with Stress in Business," etc.

17d. Developing a biographical sketch

d1) The biographical sketch is used by the host/hostess to introduce the speaker.

d2) It should be short enough to be typed on a three-by-five card and simple enough to be read by the host.

d3) It should contain just a few statements about yourself, such as: where you were born, where you went to school, your occupation, family interests, and family information.

d4) The purpose of the biographical sketch is to help your audience identify with you and to put them at ease.

IV. Training Appendix

Have the group members write out their biographical sketches by the next session. Collect them and critique them by the following session.

17e. Speaker's opening remarks

e1) Give a short introduction to establish rapport.

e2) Sample:

"I would like to thank you (name of hostess) for inviting me into your home this morning. It's fun to get together over a cup of coffee. We have so much to talk about—children, husbands, recipes, diets, etc. But today, (name of hostess) has invited me to talk about a subject that relates to all these areas of our lives. The best way for me to begin to share the reality of Christianity in a woman's world is to share with you how Jesus Christ has become a reality in my own life."

e3) Modify this introduction as necessary for the group. The introduction should be memorized. Have the group members write out their introduction to be turned in at the next session. Critique and return so it can be memorized.

17f. Practical illustrations

Have group members develop and write out their illustrations by the next session. Have them rework these illustrations, as necessary.

Along with their testimonies, include one or two practical illustrations—ways in which God has specifically worked in their everyday lives.

For example:

f1) Relationship with their spouse

f2) Relationship with their children

f3) Adjusting to changes

f4) Changing attitudes

f5) Lessons learned in love, patience, etc.

IV. Training Appendix

17g. Four Spiritual Laws presentation

g1) Transition: "And now I would like to give each of you a booklet that has been very helpful to me. I would like to go over the contents of it for two reasons: You may know what you believe, but do not know how to share what you believe with others; or perhaps some of you are wondering how you can have a personal relationship with God."

g2) Read the booklet as the guests follow along.

g3) You should give an opportunity to pray by reading through the suggested prayer. Read the question and statement immediately following the prayer in the booklet.

Invite the audience to pray silently with you as you read the prayer aloud again, phrase-by-phrase, if they have never before invited Christ into their lives.

You may use this sample invitation to pray if they desire.

"For many of you, this prayer will express the desire of your heart. Let me suggest that if you are not sure that Christ is in your life, that we pray this silently as I pray aloud. Let us pray." (Then pray a sentence at a time, pausing for them to follow you.)

g4) Share the rest of the booklet.

g5) Give all present a blank three-by-five card.

g6) Use this sample closing remark:

"I'm asking you to do one more thing for me. Please write three bits of information: your name and address, any comments you have about the talk—was it helpful? Could it be improved?; put an "X" by your name if you prayed today for the first time and invited Jesus Christ into your life.

Repeat this information two or more times. Have them fold the cards and leave them in a convenient location which you identify.

g7) Thank the host/hostess, suggest more refreshments. Initiate a conversational atmosphere to avoid an awkward silence.

g8) Talk with individuals after the talk. Ask Christian friends beforehand to converse with visitors. They may open the conversation by saying:

"What did you think of the talk?"

"Did it make sense?"

"Have you made the wonderful discovery of knowing Jesus Christ personally?"

C. Sample Surveys

National Student Religious Survey

1. SEX

::::: MALE   :::::FEMALE

2. SCHOOL _____

3. CLASS

::::: FRESHMAN   ::::: SOPHOMORE   ::::: JUNIOR   ::::: SENIOR   ::::: GRADUATE

4. ARE YOU A MEMBER OF ANY RELIGIOUS GROUP?

::::: YES   ::::: NO   ::::: USED TO BE   ::::: IN PROCESS OF JOINING

5. WOULD YOU CARE TO GIVE THE NAME OF THIS GROUP?

::::: NOT A MEMBER   ::::: ASSEMBLY OF GOD   ::::: BAPTIST   ::::: BUDDHIST   :::::CHRISTIAN   ::::: CHRISTIAN SCIENCE   ::::: CHURCH OF CHRIST

:::::CONGREGATIONAL   ::::: EPISCOPAL   :::::HINDU   :::::INDEPENDENT CHRISTIAN   ::::: ISLAM   ::::: JEWISH   ::::: LUTHERAN

:::::LDS—MORMON   ::::: METHODIST   ::::: NAZARENE   :::::PRESBYTERIAN   ::::: REFORMED   ::::: ROMAN CATHOLIC

:::::SEVENTH DAY ADVENTIST   ::::: OTHER

6. AT WHAT AGE DID YOU BECOME A MEMBER?   :::::NOT A MEMBER

:::::0-2   :::::3-5   :::::6-10   :::::11-15   :::::16-18   :::::19-21   :::::22-25   :::::26-30   :::::31-40   :::::41 AND UP   ::::: NOT SURE

7. AT PRESENT, HOW OFTEN DO YOU ATTEND SERVICES?

::::: MORE THAN ONCE A WEEK   ::::: ONCE A WEEK   :::::ONCE A MONTH   ::::: TWICE A MONTH   ::::: SELDOM   :::::NEVER

8. ARE YOU ACTIVE IN ANY STUDENT RELIGIOUS GROUP? WHICH ONE?

::::: NO   :::::BAPTIST   ::::: CHRISTIAN SCIENCE   ::::: CHURCH OF CHRIST   :::::EPISCOPAL   ::::: JEWISH   ::::: LDS—MORMON

:::::LUTHERAN   :::::METHODIST   :::::PRESBYTERIAN   ::::: ROMAN CATHOLIC

::::: CAMPUS CRUSADE (STUDENT LIFE)   ::::: YOUTH FOR CHRIST (CAMPUS LIFE)   :::::YOUNG LIFE   ::::: OTHER

9. ABOUT WHICH RELIGIOUS FOUNDER DO YOU KNOW THE MOST?

::::: MOHAMMED   ::::: BUDDHA   :::::MOSES   ::::: JESUS CHRIST   ::::: OTHER   ::::: NONE

10. WHO IS JESUS CHRIST ACCORDING TO YOUR UNDERSTANDING?

::::: SECOND PERSON OF TRINITY; SAVIOR; GOD-MAN   ::::: MAN, LEADER   :::::FOUNDER OF CHURCH   ::::: CREATOR; SUPREME BEING; RULER OF WORLD

:::::PROPHET   ::::: I DO NOT KNOW   :::::NOT SURE   ::::: OTHER

11. FROM WHAT SOURCE DID YOU GAIN THIS UNDERSTANDING?

::::: BIBLE   ::::: BOOKS   ::::: CATECHISM   ::::: CHURCH MINISTER   ::::: SUNDAY SCHOOL   ::::: CHURCH SCHOOL

::::: PROFESSORS   ::::: FRIENDS, STUDENTS   :::::OTHER

12. IN YOUR OPINION, HOW DOES ONE BECOME A CHRISTIAN?

::::: BELIEVE IN CHRIST AS PERSONAL SAVIOR   :::::LIVE A GOOD LIFE   ::::: BELIEVE THE BIBLE   ::::: UNDERSTAND AND FOLLOW TEACHINGS OF CHRIST

::::: HOLD PERSONAL CONVICTIONS   :::::BAPTISM   ::::: JOIN CHURCH OR SEE MINISTER   ::::: REARED TO BE OR BORN   :::::DON'T KNOW

13. ACCORDING TO EARLIER RESULTS OF THIS SURVEY, THE MAJORITY OF STUDENTS TODAY FEEL THE NEED FOR A MORE PERSONAL RELIGIOUS FAITH. WHY DO YOU THINK THEY HAVE THIS NEED?

::::: I DO NOT KNOW   :::::NEED TO BELIEVE IN SOMETHING   ::::: COMPLEX WORLD PROBLEMS   :::::INSECURITY

:::::NEED ADDITIONAL STRENGTH   ::::: NEED GUIDANCE   ::::: CONFLICTING MORAL STANDARDS   ::::: OTHER

14. DO YOU FEEL THE NEED FOR A MORE PERSONAL RELIGIOUS FAITH?

::::: YES   ::::: NO   ::::: I DON'T KNOW

::::: RC   ::::: N   ::::: AC   :::::WP   :::::NO   :::::HS   :::::FP   :::::FL   :::::FC   :::::FT

FOLLOWING IS A KEY TO THE CODE USED: RC-RECEIVED CHRIST, N-NO DECISION, AC-ALREADY CHRISTIAN, WP-WILL PRAY, NO-NO OPPORTUNITY, HS-APPROPRIATED FILLING OF HOLY SPIRIT, FP-FOLLOW-THROUGH PERSONALLY, FL-FOLLOW-THROUGH BY LETTER, FC-FOLLOW-THROUGH BY CHURCH, FT-FOLLOW-THROUGH BY TEN BASIC STEPS.

INTERVIEWER _____   DATE _____

Community Religious Survey

1. SEX

::::: MALE ::::: FEMALE

2. WHAT IS YOUR OCCUPATION?

::::: PROFESSIONAL, TECHNICAL ::::: MANAGER ::::: PROPRIETOR ::::: CLERICAL ::::: SALES ::::: SKILLED LABOR ::::: UNSKILLED LABOR

::::: HOUSEWIFE ::::: STUDENT ::::: MILITARY ::::: UNEMPLOYED ::::: OTHER

3. ARE YOU A MEMBER OF ANY RELIGIOUS GROUP OR CHURCH

::::: YES ::::: NO ::::: USED TO BE ::::: IN PROCESS OF JOINING

4. WOULD YOU CARE TO GIVE THE NAME OF THIS GROUP?

::::: NOT A MEMBER ::::: ASSEMBLY OF GOD ::::: BAPTIST ::::: BUDDHIST ::::: CHRISTIAN ::::: CHRISTIAN SCIENCE ::::: CHURCH OF CHRIST ::::: CONGREGATIONAL ::::: EPISC

::::: HINDU ::::: INDEPENDENT CHRISTIAN ::::: ISLAM ::::: JEWISH ::::: LUTHERAN ::::: LDS - MORMON ::::: METHODIST ::::: NAZARENE ::::: PRESBYTERIAN

::::: REFORMED ::::: ROMAN CATHOLIC ::::: SEVENTH DAY ADVENTIST ::::: OTHER

5. AT WHAT AGE DID YOU BECOME A MEMBER?

::::: NOT A MEMBER ::::: 0-2 ::::: 3-5 ::::: 6-10 ::::: 11-15 ::::: 16-18 ::::: 19-21 ::::: 22-25 ::::: 26-30 ::::: 31-40

::::: 41 AND UP ::::: NOT SURE

6. AT PRESENT, HOW OFTEN DO YOU ATTEND SERVICES?

::::: MORE THAN ONCE EACH WEEK ::::: ONCE A WEEK ::::: ONCE A MONTH ::::: TWICE A MONTH ::::: SELDOM ::::: NEVER

7. ARE YOU MARRIED?

::::: YES ::::: NO

8. HOW MANY CHILDREN DO YOU HAVE?

::::: 1 ::::: 2 ::::: 3 ::::: 4 ::::: 5 ::::: 6 ::::: 7 ::::: 8 OR MORE

9. ARE THEY ENROLLED IN SUNDAY SCHOOL?

::::: YES ::::: NO

10. ABOUT WHICH RELIGIOUS FOUNDER DO YOU KNOW THE MOST?

::::: MOHAMMED ::::: BUDDHA ::::: MOSES ::::: JESUS CHRIST ::::: OTHER

11. WHO IS JESUS CHRIST ACCORDING TO YOUR UNDERSTANDING?

::::: SECOND PERSON OF TRINITY; SAVIOUR; GOD-MAN ::::: CREATOR; SUPREME BEING; RULER OF WORLD ::::: FOUNDER OF CHURCH ::::: MAN, LEADER ::::: PROPHET

::::: NOT SURE ::::: OTHER

12. IN YOUR OPINION, HOW DOES ONE BECOME A CHRISTIAN?

::::: BELIEVE IN CHRIST AS PERSONAL SAVIOUR ::::: UNDERSTAND AND FOLLOW THE TEACHINGS OF CHRIST ::::: JOIN A CHURCH OR SEE A MINISTER ::::: BELIEVE THE BIBLE

::::: LIVE A GOOD LIFE ::::: HOLD PERSONAL CONVICTIONS ::::: REARED TO BE ONE ::::: BAPTISM ::::: BORN ONE ::::: I DO NOT KNOW

13. ACCORDING TO EARLIER RESULTS OF THIS SURVEY, THE MAJORITY OF PEOPLE TODAY FEEL THE NEED FOR A MORE PERSONAL RELIGIOUS FAITH. WHY DO YOU THINK THEY HAVE THIS NEED?

::::: I DON'T KNOW ::::: INSECURITY ::::: NEED GUIDANCE ::::: NEED TO BELIEVE IN SOMETHING ::::: AWAY FROM HOME AND FAMILY ::::: CONFLICTING MORAL STANDARDS

::::: COMPLEX WORLD PROBLEMS ::::: NEED ADDITIONAL STRENGTH ::::: OTHER

14. DO YOU FEEL THE NEED FOR A MORE PERSONAL RELIGIOUS FAITH?

::::: YES ::::: NO

END OF SURVEY

::::: RC ::::: N ::::: AC ::::: WP ::::: NO ::::: HS ::::: FP ::::: FL ::::: FC ::::: FT

FOLLOWING IS A KEY TO THE CODE USED: RC-RECEIVED CHRIST, N-NO DECISION, AC-ALREADY CHRISTIAN, WP-WILL PRAY, NO-NO OPPORTUNITY, HS-APPROPRIATED FILLING HOLY SPIRIT, FP-FOLLOW-THROUGH PERSONALLY, FL-FOLLOW-THROUGH BY LETTER, FC-FOLLOW-THROUGH BY CHURCH, FT-FOLLOW-THROUGH BY TEN BASIC STEPS.

INTERVIEWER_____ DATE_____

COMMUNITY _____

V. Prayer Appendix

Use the ideas in this Prayer Appendix to supplement the suggestions given in **Prayer** section of the actual lesson plans.

Time Frame: 5-10 minutes

OUTLINE

V. PRAYER APPENDIX
    A. Purpose
    B. Conversational Prayer
    C. Samples of Leading a Conversational Prayer
    D. Motivating Your Group to Pray
    E. Scripture References for Specific Prayer
    F. Portions of Praise
    G. Portions of Promise

A. Purpose

Group prayer was one characteristic of the early Christians. We read in Acts 12:12 that Peter "went to the house of Mary . . . where many were gathered together for prayer." Earlier in the book of Acts, we read that the disciples "went up to the upper room, where they were staying . . . These all with one mind were continually devoting themselves to prayer, along with the women . . ." (Acts 1:13,14). Old Testament characters also made use of group prayer. For example, II Chronicles 6:13-42 records Solomon praying as all Israel gathered around.

Remember that the purpose of your prayer time is to communicate with God. It should never be viewed as a ritual or as a time to "preach" to one another. Your Discipleship Group will draw together as you learn to share your hearts before God with one another. Also you will increase unity as you pray for the fulfillment of group strategy goals.

B. Conversational Prayer

During a time of conversational prayer the group members should talk to God as they would to a friend who is present in the room. Members should use modern conversational language and avoid "preaching" at others. Encourage the group (especially a group unfamiliar with group prayer) to feel free to pray sentence prayers, expressing only a brief thought in six words or so. They need not pray long, elaborate prayers. Everyone is free to pray, or not to pray, as the Spirit directs. Do not be concerned about silence. Allow God to speak to you and the other individuals in the group during times of silence.

V. Prayer Appendix

C. Samples of Leading Conversational Prayer

C1. Introduce prayer topics one at a time. Using this method, the leader introduces a topic which the group then prays about. When the group finishes praying for that topic, the leader introduces another. Both the number of topics introduced and the types of topics may vary. Below is a sample:

    1a. "Thank you" for one thing (e.g., the Lord Jesus, God's love, His forgiveness, the beautiful day, etc.)

    lb. "Thank you" for something which has happened in your life in the last 24 hours

    1c. "Please help . . ." (yourself or someone else)

    1d. Ask for one thing for yourself.

    1e. Thank God for how He will meet those desires and requests.

C2. Allow the group to share prayer requests.

    2a. As a prayer request is offered, you may wish to ask another member to be responsible to pray for that request during the prayer time. This insures that each person's request will be prayed for by at least one other person during the prayer time.

    2b. You may wish to have group members record on a sheet of paper each request as it is offered. This list would then be used during the group prayer time as well as a help for the members to pray for each other during the week.

    2c. You may allow group members to volunteer to pray for requests without assigning them or writing them down. The group would then rely on their ability to remember the requests as they went into the prayer time.

    2d. You may wish to pray for each request as soon as it is given before allowing the next request to be shared.

C3. Pray through Scripture. This method allows the group to use one or more passages of Scripture as their prayer guide. You are free to choose passages from anywhere in the Old or New Testaments that you feel will provide the group with an easy, fruitful guide for prayer. The following is a sample:

    3a. Choose a Psalm of praise or a passage of Scripture (e.g., Psalm 103, Psalms 145-150 or one of the Scripture passages listed in Portions of Praise and Portions of Promise, E and F of this outline).

    3b. Teach the group to pray using the following procedure:

V. Prayer Appendix

b1) First person reads a phrase or entire verse aloud, pausing to verbalize a simple prayer as inspired by the Scripture and led by the Lord.

b2) Other members of the group join in audibly or silently agree.

b3) The next person continues reading a different verse, pausing to pray aloud as he is impressed by the Lord.

b4) Each continues in like fashion around the group.

b5) The following is an example of how a group consisting of Jack, Doug, Bill and Paul might begin praying through Psalm 103:

Jack reads: "'Bless the Lord, O my soul; and all that is within me, bless His holy name.'"

Jack prays: "Father in Heaven, I do bless Your holy name. Thank You for sending Jesus Christ to be my Lord and Savior."

Doug prays: "I agree with that prayer. Help me, Lord, to remember to offer You praise and thanksgiving at all times for all things and to bless Your name."

Bill reads: "'Bless the Lord, O my soul, and forget none of His benefits.'"

Bill prays: "Thank You, Lord, for all the blessings You give to Your children."

Paul prays: "Yes, Lord, thank You for the privilege of coming to You in prayer with my brothers."

Jack prays: "Father, we thank You that we live in a land where we are free to worship You. We ask Your protection and provision for those of Your children who are undergoing persecution for Jesus' sake."

Doug reads: "'Who pardons all your iniquities, who heals all your diseases.'"

Doug prays: "Oh, Father, thank You that when we confess our sins You forgive them and cleanse us of all unrighteousness; and thank You that You are the Great Physician who can heal all diseases. We remember George and his illness and ask that You will restore him to perfect health."

Jack prays: "I agree, Father."

Paul reads: "'Who redeems . . . etc.'"

V. Prayer Appendix

C4. Introduce the ACTS acrostic. (This can be developed at length with one or more studies on each word.) Guide the prayer time praying silently or aloud, except always pray silently for personal confession.

4a. Adoration

a1) Definition: Worshiping and praising God, exalting Him in your heart and your mind and with your lips.
a2) Read Psalms such as 103 and 145 or choose praise portions from Exhibit 8A.
a3) Take time to adore God, praising Him for His attributes such as His lovingkindness, His holiness, His compassion, His majesty, etc.

4b. Confession

b1) Definition: Agreeing with God concerning any sins He brings to mind in order to restore fellowship with Him.
b2) Review I John 1:5-9
b3) As you spend time adoring God, He will bring to mind what you need to confess.
b4) Allow time for confession (let God speak to each person about any unconfessed sin).

4c. Thanksgiving

c1) Definition: Rendering thanksgiving to God; a prayer expressing gratitude.
c2) Look at I Thessalonians 5:18, Ephesians 5:20, Psalm 108:3, Psalm 50:23.
c3) Spend time in thanksgiving.

5d. Supplication

d1) Definition: Imploring God by means of a petition or an entreaty.
d2) Read Philippians 4:6,7; Psalm 116:1,2
d3) Lead the group in supplication, praying aloud.

C5. Introduce the PRAY acrostic (may be developed in the same way as ACTS).

5a. Praise

5b. Repent

5c. Ask for someone else

V. Prayer Appendix

    5d. Your own needs

C6. Pray for the fulfillment of the Great Commission, using Scripture.

    6a. Win men to Christ through prayer.

        a1) Pray that God would prepare their hearts to understand and respond to the gospel (John 6:44).
        a2) Pray that God would raise up believers to share the gospel with the unbelievers (Matthew 9:37,38; Colossians 4:3).
        a3) Recognize that Satan has blinded and captivated the unbeliever and acknowledge (claim) Christ's victory over him (Ephesians 6:12, II Corinthians 4:3,4; II Timothy 2:25,26; I John 3:8).
        a4) Persist in these prayers (Daniel 10:12,13a; Luke 18:1-8).

    6b. Build men in Christ through prayer.

        b1) Thank God for them (Philippians 1:3).
        b2) Pray for deliverence from evil (unprincipled) companions (II Thessalonians 3:2).
        b3) Pray that they might walk worthy of the Lord (Colossians 1:10).
        b4) Pray for wisdom and revelation in the knowledge of Christ (Ephesians 1:16).
        b5) Pray for them to be strengthened with might by His Spirit in the inner man (Ephesians 3:14).
        b6) Pray for their unity in the Spirit with other believers (John 17:23).
        b7) Pray that their love may abound and that they may approve things that are excellent (Philippians I:9).
        b8) Pray for boldness and opportunities to share the gospel (Colossians 4:3; Ephesians 6:19,20).
        b9) Pray that they may completely mature and be fully assured in all the will of God (Colossians 4:12).
      b10) Persist in these prayers (Ephesians 6:18).

    6c. Send men for Christ through prayer.

        c1) Recognize the problem of the labor shortage (Matthew 9:37,38; Romans 10:13-15).
        c2) Make a list of candidates to be sent by the Lord (Isaiah 6:8; Matthew 9:37,38) and pray persistently for them.
        c3) Pray that laborers would be thrust forth in specific communities and countries.
        c4) Claim the fulfillment of the Great Commission in your area and the world according to His command and promise (Matthew 28:18-20; I John 5:14,15).

V. Prayer Appendix

    c5) Mobilize and teach others to pray for laborers (II Timothy 2:2).

    c6) To help expand the group's world vision, pray for a specific country, overseas mission group or overseas Christian worker. (Your group may want to "adopt" a country to pray for regularly as a group.)

    c7) Sing a hymn prayerfully, and afterwards, use the words of the hymn to guide the prayer time.

    c8) Select one or more attributes of God, and spend the time meditating on those attributes and praising Him for His attributes.

    c9) Share answers to prayer and spend the time thanking God for the answers and His faithfulness.

D. Motivating Your Group to Pray

D1. How to stimulate intercessory prayer

    1a. Remind participants of historical men and women of faith who saw God answer intercessory prayer in a mighty way.

        a1) When Abraham prayed, Lot was saved (Genesis 19:29).

        a2) When Hezekiah prayed, God turned back Sennacherib (II Kings 19).

        a3) Jesus healed in response to intercession. A few examples:

            3a) Mark 2:3: Four friends brought the paralytic before Jesus.

            3b) Matthew 15:22: A Canaanite woman came to Jesus on behalf of her daughter.

            3c) Matthew 17:15: A man sought healing for his son.

        a4) An angel set Peter free in response to united prayer (Acts 12:1-17).

        a5) The early church flourished as Paul interceded for them: Romans 1:9; Ephesians 1:15-19, 3:14-19; Philippians 1:3-11; Colossians 1:9-12, etc.

        a6) The earnest prayer of a righteous man has great power and wonderful results. In James 5:17,18 we read, "Elijah was as completely human as we are, and yet when he prayed earnestly that no rain would fall, none fell for the next three and a half years! Then he prayed again, this time that it would rain, and down it poured and the grass turned green and the gardens began to grow again" (TLB).

    2b. Emphasize the priority God places on praying for those in authority (I Timothy 2:1-4).

V. Prayer Appendix

    3c. Encourage individuals to make note of the intercessory prayers of Jesus, Paul, Peter, etc. in their personal Bible study and to pattern their own prayers along similar lines.

    4d. Pray through Scripture portions to intercede for others, letting the Scripture guide your prayers and express your thoughts to God.

        Examples:

            d1) Ephesians 1:16-19—pray for a member of your family.
            d2) Ephesians 3:14-16—pray for your Sunday school teacher or superintendent.
            d3) Philippians 1:9-11—pray for a Christian friend.
            d4) Colossians 1:9-11—pray for your pastor.

D2. How to encourage praying in one accord

    2a. Instruct individuals to:

        a1) Concentrate on what the other person is praying, agreeing in your heart.
        a2) Trust the Holy Spirit to direct your thoughts and prayers when it is your turn.
        a3) Do not be thinking ahead to what you will pray—you will miss the other person's prayer and neglect to pray in accord.

    2b. Emphasize that the early church was accused of turning the world upside down when they practiced praying in one accord (Acts 4:24-31 and Acts 17:5-7).

    2c. An earthquake opened prison doors for Paul and Silas when they prayed together (Acts 16:25,26).

    2d. Remember that Jesus Christ Himself is actually present in the room. He promises in Matthew 18:19,20, "I also tell you this—if two of you agree down here on earth concerning anything you ask for, my Father in heaven will do it for you. For where two or three gather together because they are mine, I will be right there among them" (TLB).

D3. How to encourage individuals to pray continually

    3a. Remind them that God commands us to pray without ceasing (I Thessalonians 5:17).

    3b. Encourage them to recognize that God is present wherever they go and that He is always ready to answer prayer.

V. Prayer Appendix

3c. Talk about how important it is to thank God for everything He allows to come into our lives (I Thessalonians 5:18)—everything from a beautiful day to a flat tire. (Your prayers can be a good example. Keep them simple, sincere, brief and reflective of your faith.)

3d. Encourage them to talk to God when they feel a need—any time of the day or night.

3e. Suggest that they use their time twice by developing a habit of praying as they go about daily activities which do not require total concentration; for example, while showering, driving, gardening, working with their hands.

D4. Other means of motivating your group to pray

4a. Read short motivational verses or excerpts on prayer by Christian writers. Some suggested authors are Andrew Murray, E.M. Bounds, C.T. Studd, George Mueller, Hudson Taylor, Bill Bright, Charles Finney.

4b. Study some or all of the following motivational passages on prayer from the prayer life of Jesus.

  b1) He prayed while being baptized by John (Luke 3:21).
  b2) He fasted and prayed in the wilderness before being tempted (Matthew 4:2).
  b3) He prayed in a lonely place after news of John the Baptist's death (Matthew 14:13).
  b4) He prayed often in lonely places and in the wilderness (Luke 4:42; 5:16).
  b5) He prayed in the early morning before going through Galilee (Mark 1:35).
  b6) He prayed all night before calling the twelve (Luke 6:12).
  b7) He prayed alone after feeding the 5,000 (Matthew 14:23).
  b8) He prayed before He was transfigured (Luke 9:28,29).
  b9) He praised God aloud when the 70 returned (Luke 10:21).
  b10) He prayed before teaching on prayer (Luke 11:1-4).
  b11) He prayed aloud before raising Lazarus from the dead (John 11:41-42).
  b12) He prayed for Peter (Luke 22:32).
  b13) He talked aloud with God during His last public discourse (John 12:28).
  b14) He prayed for the disciples after His farewell discourse (John 17).
  b15) He prayed in Gethsemane (Matthew 26:39-44; Mark 14:35-39).
  b16) He prayed on the cross (Luke 23:34,46).
  b17) He prayed at Emmaus after the resurrection (Luke 24:30).

V. Prayer Appendix

4c. Encourage your group members to prepare and use a personal prayer diary. The Great Commission Prayer Crusade's *Personal Prayer Diary* is a popular journal because of its easy to use format. It is organized by days of the week with praise portions, specific suggestions for prayer, and plenty of blank space for personal requests. Its handy 5½ x 8½ size makes it easy to use and carry.

4d. Many additional suggestions may be found in The Great Commission Prayer Crusade's *Prayer Handbook* and *Strategy Manual*. Encourage your group to take time to read these practical guides to prayer. All of the suggestions in this appendix were adapted from the *Prayer Handbook*.

E. Scripture References for Specific Prayer

Use this section to claim scriptures for various areas of need in the lives of group members. You may wish to copy these pages and pass them out during your prayer time.

E1. Yourself: Pray for purification of your thoughts and deeds, that you may be a fit instrument and channel for God's love where you live, work, worship and play.

Colossians 1:9-12; Philippians 4:8; I Corinthians 1:26-31; II Corinthians 2:14,15; I Peter 1:13-16; 5:6

E2. Your home and family: Pray for a Christ-centered home and family. Seek God's wisdom and guidance in applying His principles.

James 1:5, 13-18; Ephesians 4:31,32; 5:22-6:4; I Peter 3:8,9; Proverbs 3:33; Psalm 127:1a.

E3. The congregation: Pray that, as individuals, we will realize God's love and draw upon His wisdom and understanding.

Ephesians 3:13-19; 5:1-4; Psalm 1:1-3; 16:11; 37:23,24

E4. The church: Pray for the church and church-related organizations—for unity within the body of Christ.

John 17:11; Acts 1:14, 2:42; Ephesians 4:1-3, 11-16; Philippians 2:1-7; I Corinthians 12:12,13

E5. The community: Pray for a Christian ministry of reconciliation in your community.

II Corinthians 5:17-20; 2:14-16; 3:5; Jeremiah 33:3-8; I Corinthians 10:24; Psalm 127:lb

V. Prayer Appendix

E6. The nation: Pray for national repentance acknowledging God's mercy and forgiveness. II Chronicles 7:14. Throughout history there seem to have been various crises which threatened the well-being of a nation and demanded specific, united prayer. In each case, united prayer brought dramatic, powerful intervention by God on their behalf.

Ezekiel 8:17,18; II Chronicles 13:12; 15:2; 20:3-6,12; 24:20; 30:12; Ezra 8:21-23

E7. The world: Pray for a spirit of revival to sweep the world, that the nations of the world will worship the Lord with reverence.

Psalm 2; 33:8,10-12

E8. Those in authority: Pray for the leaders of our country—local, state and national—that they may have wisdom, integrity, protection, guidance and an awareness of God's presence in mind and heart.

I Timothy 1:6; 2:1-6; I Corinthians 2:5; 3:18-20; Romans 13:1; I Samuel 12:14,15; Jeremiah 33:3

E9. Those who are non-believers: Pray for the evangelization of our country and of the world. Pray for the lost to be freed from the enemy, enlightened through the gospel and granted repentance and drawn by the Father.

Romans 10:1; I Timothy 2:4-6; II Timothy 2:25,26; Ephesians 2:2; II Corinthians 4:3,4; II Peter 3:9; Matthew 9:37,38; Romans 10:13-15; John 14:13,14; John 6:44; Revelation 3:20

E10. The sick, discouraged and persecuted: Pray for God's mercy, strength and lovingkindness for those in distress. Pray that they may claim His promises and be aware of His presence.

Acts 3:16; Philippians 2:27; James 5:14,15; Matthew 4:23,24; I Peter 5:7; Acts 3:19; II Corinthians 1:3,4; 4:16,17; 12:8-10; Psalm 118:5,6; 121:2; Ephesians 5:20

E11. Prisoners: Pray for those who are prisoners of: drugs, alcohol, immorality, obscenity, pornography, crime, prejudice, unbelief and despair.

Matthew 5:44,45; John 8:36; II Corinthians 3:17; Romans 6:19-23; I Corinthians 10:13

E12. Christian witness: Pray that Christians will become vital witnesses for Christ through their lives and words.

II Corinthians 2:14-17; 5:14-21

V. Prayer Appendix

E13. Mass media: Pray for a greater Christian influence in newspapers, magazines, television and movies.

Colossians 2:8; Proverbs 1:7; 2:22; 15:26,28,31

F. Portions of Praise

Use this section during times when your group wishes to concentrate on praising God in prayer. You may want to copy these passages to pass out to the group during your prayer time.

F1. I Chronicles 16:31,34,36—Let the heavens be glad, and let the earth rejoice; and let them say among the nations, "The Lord reigns." O give thanks to the Lord, for He is good; for His lovingkindness is everlasting. Blessed be the Lord, the God of Israel, from everlasting even to everlasting. Then all the people said, "Amen," and praised the Lord.

F2. Psalm 24:7-10—Lift up your heads, O gates, and be lifted up, O ancient doors, that the King of glory may come in! Who is the King of glory? The Lord strong and mighty, the Lord mighty in battle. Lift up your heads, O gates, and lift them up, O ancient doors, that the King of glory may come in! Who is this King of glory? The Lord of hosts, He is the King of glory.

F3. Psalm 28:6,7—Blessed be the Lord, because He has heard the voice of my supplication. The Lord is my strength and my shield; my heart trusts in Him, and I am helped; therefore my heart exults, and with my song I shall thank Him.

F4. Psalm 30:4—Sing praise to the Lord, you His godly ones, and give thanks to His holy name.

F5. Psalm 34:1-3—I will bless the Lord at all times; His praise shall continually be in my mouth. My soul shall make its boast in the Lord; the humble shall hear it and rejoice. O magnify the Lord with me, and let us exalt His name together.

F6. Psalm 50:23—He who offers a sacrifice of thanksgiving honors Me; and to him who orders his way aright I shall show the salvation of God.

F7. Psalm 56:10-12—In God whose word I praise, in the Lord, whose word I praise, in God I have put my trust, I shall not be afraid. What can man do to me? Thy vows are binding upon me, O God; I will render thank offerings to Thee.

V. Prayer Appendix

F8. Psalm 63:3-6—Because Thy lovingkindness is better than life, my lips will praise Thee. So I will bless Thee as long as I live; I will lift up my hands in Thy name. My soul is satisfied as with marrow and fatness. Any my mouth offers praises with joyful lips. When I remember Thee on my bed, I meditate on Thee in the night watches.

F9. Psalm 69:30,34—I will praise the name of God with song, and shall magnify Him with thanksgiving. Let heaven and earth praise Him, the seas and everything that moves in them.

F10. Psalm 75:1—We give thanks to Thee, O God, we give thanks, for Thy name is near; men declare Thy wondrous works.

F11. Psalm 86:12—I will give thanks to Thee, O Lord my God, with all my heart, and will glorify Thy name forever.

F12. Psalm 92:1,2—It is good to give thanks to the Lord, and to sing praises to Thy name, O Most High; to declare Thy lovingkindness in the morning, and Thy faithfulness by night.

F13. Isaiah 25:1—O Lord, Thou art my God; I will exalt Thee, I will give thanks to Thy name; for Thou hast worked wonders, plans formed long ago, with perfect faithfulness.

F14. Isaiah 38:18—For Sheol cannot thank Thee, death cannot praise Thee; those who go down to the pit cannot hope for Thy faithfulness.

F15. Daniel 2:20,23—Daniel answered and said, "Let the name of God be blessed forever and ever, for wisdom and power belong to Him. To Thee, O God of my fathers, I give thanks and praise, for Thou hast given me wisdom and power; even now Thou hast made known to me what we requested of Thee, for Thou has made known to us the king's matter."

F16. Acts 2:46,47—And day by day continuing with one mind in the temple, and breaking bread from house to house, they were taking their meals together with gladness and sincerity of heart, praising God, and having favor with all the people. And the Lord was adding to their number day by day those who were being saved.

F17. Romans 11:36—For from Him and through Him and to Him are all things. To Him be the glory forever. Amen.

F18. I Corinthians 14:15—What is the outcome then? I shall pray with the spirit and I shall pray with the mind also; I shall sing with the spirit and I shall sing with the mind also.

V. Prayer Appendix

F19. I Corinthians 15:57—But thanks be to God, who gives us the victory through our Lord Jesus Christ.

F20. Ephesians 1:3—Blessed be the God and Father of our Lord Jesus Christ, who has blessed us with every spiritual blessing in the heavenly places in Christ.

F21. Ephesians 5:19—Speaking to one another in psalms and hymns and spiritual songs, singing and making melody with your heart to the Lord.

F22. I Timothy 1:17—Now to the King eternal, immortal, invisible, the only God, be honor and glory forever and ever. Amen.

F23. Hebrews 13:15—Through Him then, let us continually offer up a sacrifice of praise to God, that is, the fruit of lips that give thanks to His name.

F24. I Peter 2:9—But you are a chosen race, a royal priesthood, a holy nation, a people for God's own possession, that you may proclaim the excellencies of Him who has called you out of darkness into His marvelous light.

F25. I Peter 4:11—Whoever speaks, let him speak, as it were, the utterances of God; whoever serves, let him do so as by the strength which God supplies; so that in all things God may be glorified through Jesus Christ, to whom belongs the glory and dominion forever and ever. Amen.

F26. Psalm 103:1—Bless the Lord, O my soul; and all that is within me, bless His holy name.

F27. Psalm 104:24,31,33,34—O Lord, how many are Thy works! In wisdom Thou has made them all; the earth is full of Thy possessions. Let the glory of the Lord endure forever; let the Lord be glad in His works; . . . I will sing to the Lord as long as I live; I will sing praise to my God while I have my being. Let my meditation be pleasing to Him; as for me, I shall be glad in the Lord.

F28. Psalm 105:2—Sing to Him, sing praises to Him; Speak of all His wonders.

F29. Psalm 106:1—Praise the Lord! Oh give thanks to the Lord, for He is good; for His lovingkindness is everlasting.

F30. Psalm 107:8,9—Let them give thanks to the Lord for His lovingkindness, and for His wonders to the sons of men! For He has satisfied the thirsty soul, and the hungry soul He has filled with what is good.

V. Prayer Appendix

F31. Psalm 113:3—From the rising of the sun to its setting the name of the Lord is to be praised.

F32. Psalm 116:12,17—What shall I render to the Lord for all His benefits toward me? . . . To Thee I shall offer a sacrifice of thanksgiving, and call upon the name of the Lord.

F33. Psalm 118:6—The Lord is for me; I will not fear; what can man do to me?

F34. Psalm 119:62—At midnight I shall rise to give thanks to Thee because of Thy righteous ordinances.

F35. Psalm 119:97—O how I love Thy law! It is my meditation all the day.

F36. Psalm 119:129—Thy testimonies are wonderful; therefore my soul observes them.

G. Portions of Promise

Use this section when your group desires to claim God's promises in prayer. You may wish to copy these verses and pass them out during the prayer time.

G1. God is not a man, that He should lie . . . (Numbers 23:19). Know therefore that the Lord your God, He is God, the faithful God . . . (Deuteronomy 7:9) . . .for He who promised is faithful. (Hebrews 10:23b). If we are faithless, He remains faithful; for He cannot deny Himself (II Timothy 2:13). For as many as may be the promises of God, in Him they are yes; wherefore also by Him is our Amen to the glory of God through us (II Corinthians 1:20).

G2. Romans 8:26—And in the same way the Spirit also helps our weakness; for we do not know how to pray as we should, but the Spirit Himself intercedes for us with groanings too deep for words.

G3. Hebrews 11:6—And without faith it is impossible to please Him, for he who comes to God must believe that He is, and that He is a rewarder of those who seek Him.

G4. James 1:5-7—But if any of you lacks wisdom, let him ask of God, who gives to all men generously and without reproach, and it will be given to him. But let him ask in faith without any doubting, for the one who doubts is like the surf of the sea driven and tossed by the wind.

G5. James 5:16—Therefore, confess your sins to one another, and pray for one another, so that you may be healed. The effective prayer of a righteous man can accomplish much.

V. Prayer Appendix

G18. Jeremiah 29:12,13—Then you will call upon Me and come and pray to Me, and I will listen to you. And you will seek Me and find Me, when you search for Me with all your heart.

G19. Jeremiah 33:3—Call to Me, and I will answer you, and I will tell you great and mighty things, which you do not know.

G20. Matthew 7:7,8—Ask, and it shall be given to you; seek, and you shall find; knock, and it shall be opened to you.

G21. Matthew 18:19,20—Again I say to you, that if two of you agree on earth about anything that they may ask, it shall be done for them by My Father who is in heaven. For where two or three have gathered together in My name, there I am in their midst.

G22. Matthew 21:22—And all things you ask in prayer, believing, you shall receive.

G23. Luke 11:13—If you then, being evil, know how to give good gifts to your children, how much more shall your heavenly Father give the Holy Spirit to those who ask Him?

G24. John 14:13,14—And whatever you ask in My name, that will I do, that the Father may be glorified in the Son. If you ask Me anything in My name, I will do it.

G25. Romans 8:28,32—And we know that God causes all things to work together for good to those who love God, to those who are called according to His purpose. He who did not spare His own Son, but delivered Him up for us all, how will He not also with Him freely give us all things?

G26. I Peter 5:7—Casting all your anxiety upon Him, because He cares for you.

G27. Psalm 55:22—Cast your burden upon the Lord, and He will sustain you; He will never allow the righteous to be shaken.

G28. Isaiah 41:10—Do not fear, for I am with you; do not anxiously look about you, for I am your God. I will strengthen you, surely I will help you, surely I will uphold you with My righteous right hand.

G29. Philippians 4:19—And my God shall supply all your needs according to His riches in glory in Christ Jesus.

G30. Matthew 6:33—But seek first His kingdom and His righteousness; and all these things shall be added to you.

V. Prayer Appendix

G6. I John 3:22—And whatever we ask we receive from Him, because we keep His commandments and do the things that are pleasing in His sight.

G7. I John 5:14,15—And this is the confidence which we have before Him, that, if we ask anything according to His will, He hears us. And if we know that He hears us in whatever we ask, we know that we have the requests which we have asked from Him.

G8. Psalm 108:13—Through God we shall do valiantly; and it is He who will tread down our adversaries.

G9. Psalm 55:1,16,17—Give ear to my prayer, O God; and hide not thyself from my supplication. As for me, I will call upon God: and the Lord shall save me. Evening, and morning, and at noon, will I pray, and cry aloud: and He shall hear my voice. (KJV)

G10. Psalm 84:11—For Lord God is a sun and shield; the Lord gives grace and glory; no good thing does He withhold from those who walk uprightly.

G11. Psalm 6:9—The Lord has heard my supplication, the Lord receives my prayer.

G12. II Chronicles 7:14—And My people who are called by My name humble themselves and pray, and seek My face and turn from their wicked ways, then I will hear from heaven, will forgive their sin, and will heal their land.

G13. Psalm 10:17—O Lord, thou hast heard the desire of the humble; Thou wilt strengthen their heart, Thou wilt incline Thine ear.

G14. Psalm 37:3-5—Trust in the Lord, and do good; dwell in the land and cultivate faithfulness. Delight yourself in the Lord; and He will give you the desires of your heart. Commit your way to the Lord, trust also in Him, and He will do it.

G15. Psalm 145:18—The Lord is near to all who call upon Him, to all who call upon Him in truth.

G16. Proverbs 3:5,6—Trust in the Lord with all your heart, and do not lean on your own understanding. In all your ways acknowledge Him, and He will make your paths straight.

G17. Isaiah 65:24—It will also come to pass that before they call, I will answer; and while they are still speaking, I will hear.

V. Prayer Appendix

G31. Proverbs 16:1—The plans of the heart belong to man, but the answer of the tongue is from the Lord.

G32. Zechariah 13:9b—They will call on My name, and I will answer them; I will say, "They are My people," and they will say, "The Lord is my God."

G33. Mark 11:22-24—And Jesus answered saying to them, "Have faith in God. Truly I say to you, whoever says to this mountain, 'Be taken up and cast into the sea,' and does not doubt in his heart, but believes that what he says is going to happen; it shall be granted him. Therefore I say to you, all things for which you pray and ask, believe that you have received them, and they shall be granted you."

G34. John 9:31—We know that God does not hear sinners; but if any one is God-fearing, and does His will, He hears him.

G35. John 15:7,16—If you abide in Me, and My words abide in you, ask whatever you wish, and it shall be done for you. You did not choose Me, but I chose you, and appointed you, that you should go and bear fruit, and that your fruit should remain; that whatever you ask of the Father in my name, He may give to you.

G36. John 16:23b,24—". . . I say to you, if you shall ask the Father for anything, He will give it to you in My name. Until now you have asked for nothing in My name; ask, and you will receive, that your joy may be made full."

G37. Ephesians 3:20,21—Now to Him who is able to do exceeding abundantly beyond all that we ask or think according to the power that works within us, to Him be the glory in the church and in Christ Jesus to all generations forever and ever. Amen.

G38. I Thessalonians 5:17,18—Pray without ceasing; in everything give thanks for this is God's will for you in Christ Jesus.

G39. Hebrews 10:22,23b—Let us draw near with a sincere heart in full assurance of faith, having our hearts sprinkled clean from an evil conscience and our bodies washed with pure water . . . for He who promised is faithful.

G40. Hebrews 11:6—And without faith it is impossible to please Him, for he who comes to God must believe that He is, and that He is a rewarder of those who seek Him.

V. Prayer Appendix

Additional resources on prayer:

Great Commission Prayer Crusade's *Prayer Handbook*
Great Commission Prayer Crusade's *Strategy Manual*
Transferable Concept 9 "How to Pray"
"Beginning Your New Life in Prayer"

Discipleship Series Bibliography

Anderson, Courtney. *To the Golden Shore*. Grand Rapids, Michigan: Zondervan Publishing House. 1972.

Bailey, Ney. *Faith is Not a Feeling*. San Bernardino, California: Here's Life Publishers. 1978.

Baldwin, Ethel May and David V. Benson. *Henrietta Mears and How She Did It*. Glendale, California: Gospel Light Publications. 1966.

Barabanov, Evgeny. "A Schism Between the Church and the World," in *From Under the Rubble*, ed. Alexander Solzhenitsyn. Boston, Massachusetts: Little, Brown & Company. 1975.

Barnhouse, Donald Grey. *Let Me Illustrate*. Old Tappan, New Jersey: Revell Publishers. 1967.

Bright, Bill. *How to Experience God's Love and Forgiveness*. Arrowhead Springs, California: Campus Crusade for Christ, Inc. 1971.

Bright, Bill. *How to Walk in the Spirit*. Arrowhead Springs, California: Campus Crusade for Christ, Inc. 1971.

Bright, Bill. *Teacher's Manual for the Ten Basic Steps Toward Christian Maturity*. Arrowhead Springs, California: Campus Crusade for Christ, Inc. 1965.

Bright, Bill. *The Christian and the Holy Spirit*. Arrowhead Springs, California: Campus Crusade for Christ, Inc. 1968.

Carmichael, Amy. *If*. Fort Washington, Pennsylvania: Christian Literature Crusade. 1966.

Coleman, Robert. *Master Plan of Evangelism*. Old Tappan, New Jersey: Fleming H. Revell Company. 1964.

Elliot, Elizabeth. *Shadow of the Almighty*. New York, New York: Harper and Brothers Publishers. 1959.

Fant, David J., Jr. *A.W. Tozer—A Twentieth Century Prophet*. Harrisburg, Pennsylvania: Christian Publications, Inc. 1964.

Graham, Billy. *Call to Commitment*. Minneapolis, Minnesota: Billy Graham Evangelistic Association. 1960.

Graham, Billy. *The Holy Spirit*. Waco, Texas: Word Books. 1978.

Grubb, Norman. *C.T. Studd*. Fort Washington, Pennsylvania: Christian Literature Crusade. 1972.

Hendricks, Howard. "How to Lead I," in *The Ministry of Management*. Steven B. Douglas and Bruce E. Cook. Arrowhead Springs, California: Campus Crusade for Christ, Inc. 1972.

Henrichsen, Walter A. *Disciples are Made—Not Born*. Wheaton, Illinois: Victor Books. 1974.

Hutcheson, J. Kent. A personal interview with James Kent Hutcheson at Arrowhead Springs, California, 1979.

Hyde, Douglas. *Dedication and Leadership*. Notre Dame, Indiana: University of Notre Dame Press. 1966.

McDowell, Josh. *Evidence that Demands a Verdict*. Arrowhead Springs, California: Campus Crusade for Christ, Inc. 1972.

Orr, J. Edwin. *The Flaming Tongue*. Chicago, Illinois: Moody Press. 1973.

Radmacher, Earl D. *You and Your Thoughts*. Wheaton, Illinois: Tyndale House. 1977.

Schaeffer, Francis. *Death in the City*. Downer's Grove, Illinois: Inter-Varsity Press. 1969.

Taylor, Dr. and Mrs. Howard. *J. Hudson Taylor: God's Man in China*. Chicago, Illinois: Moody Press. 1977.

Tozer, A. W. *The Pursuit of God*. Wheaton, Illinois: Tyndale Publishers. 1958.

Unknown Author. *The Kneeling Christian*. Grand Rapids, Michigan: Zondervan Publishing House. 1971.